DATE DUE

BOOKS BY MILTON LOMASK

ANDREW JOHNSON: *President on Trial*   (1960)

SEED MONEY: *The Guggenheim Story*   (1964)

AARON BURR: *The Years from Princeton
to Vice President*   (1979)

AARON BURR: *The Conspiracy and
Years of Exile*   (1982)

AARON BURR

Milton Lomask

AARON BURR

The Conspiracy and Years

of Exile

1805–1836

Farrar · Straus · Giroux

NEW YORK

Library of Congress Cataloging in Publication Data
Lomask, Milton.
Aaron Burr.
Bibliography: v. 1, p. 411–427; v. 2, p.
Includes indexes.
Contents: v. 1. The years from Princeton to Vice
President, 1756–1805—v. 2. The conspiracy and years of
exile, 1805–1836.
1. Burr, Aaron, 1756–1836.   2. United States—Politics
and government—1783–1809.   3. Vice-Presidents—United
States—Biography.   I. Title.
E302.6.B9L7   1979   973.4'6'0924   [B]   78–31142
AACR 2

FOR RAY NEVILLE

Statements made in this book (pages 118–22) about the true authorship of the most controversial of the Burr documents, the "cipher letter," rest on a study of the documents by Dr. Mary-Jo Kline, editor of the Aaron Burr Papers. An explication of this interesting discovery by Dr. Kline has been included in the Burr Papers, published by the Princeton University Press.

CONTENTS

———————

Contents

ILLUSTRATIONS

FOLLOWING PAGE 174

Aaron Burr in 1890, painted by John Vanderlyn

General James Wilkinson, known to Spain as "Agent No. 13"

Harman Blennerhasset, painted in London at age thirty-two

A 1930s drawing of the Blennerhassett mansion, based on contemporary records

Andrew Jackson, after the battle of New Orleans, painted by Samuel Waldo

The arrest of Aaron Burr in 1807, as imagined in an old engraving

The trial of Aaron Burr, from the painting by C. W. Jeffreys

Chief Justice Marshall, who presided at Burr's trial, painted by James Reid Lambdin after Henry Inman

Jeremy Bentham, Burr's host during his exile in England

Burr's law office on Reade Street, New York City

Madame Jumel, formerly Madame de la Croix, painted circa 1854

The St. James Hotel on Staten Island, where Burr died in 1836

Aaron Burr at age seventy-eight, two years before his death, painted by James Van Dyck

PREFACE

SOME OF THE DISREPUTE surrounding the name of
Aaron Burr stems from incidents treated in the preceding volume of this work: his fatal duel with Alexander Hamilton, his
baffling behavior during the Presidential election of 1800
when he and Thomas Jefferson tied, seventy-three votes apiece,
in the electoral college. Most of it, however, comes from the
episode known as the Burr Conspiracy, which dominates this
second and final volume of my work.

Willy-nilly, the chronicler of Burr's filibuster into the
American West of his day must choose sides on the treason
issue. That Burr did no treason is legally certain. The jurors'
decision in the federal court presided over by Chief Justice
Marshall in 1807 was "not guilty." But did he *intend* to do
treason? I think not. He said he didn't, once going so far as to
describe such an idea as "odious," and his actions conformed
to his words. The only significant indications to the contrary—
dispatches written by the British and Spanish ministers to the
United States—are open to variant interpretations; and a recent
documentary study by the editor of the Burr Papers, Dr. Mary-
Jo Kline, shows that the famous "cipher letter," often cited to
prove a traitorous plot, was not written by Aaron Burr.

We may never know all we would like to know about Burr's
westward expedition. There are gaps in the record. When the
court in Richmond, Virginia, acquitted him on charges of treason and misdemeanor and he fled the country rather than face
another trial in Ohio, he sent a trunkful of his "more important papers" to the South Carolina home of his daughter Theodosia Burr Alston. Four years later, having returned to New

xiii

York and resumed his law practice, he urged his daughter to come North for a visit and to bring the papers with her. Theodosia was unwell. Fearful of the effects of a long overland journey, her husband arranged for her to travel by water aboard the pilot ship *Patriot*, which disappeared at sea. Neither Theodosia nor the papers were ever seen again.

Many of the letters Burr wrote during the years of his expedition dealt with land speculation. These were extant at the time of his death, but Matthew Livingston Davis, to whom he willed all his papers, failed to understand their importance. In his useful but insensitive *Memoirs of Aaron Burr*, Davis noted that after Burr returned from the first of his two trips to the "western country," he spent a few months "principally" in Philadelphia. During this interval, the memorialist recalls, Burr's correspondence was "Voluminous, but in no manner develops any other views than such as relate to land speculation." Davis admitted that some of these writings were "interesting," but explained that "the space yet remaining in which these memoirs are to be closed renders it absolutely necessary to exclude them from the work." What Davis did with them, none can say. His care of the reputation entrusted to his hands was egregiously negligent. He scattered Burr's papers about, giving away some of them as souvenirs and destroying others. The vanished land-speculation letters might have been helpful in clarifying their author's activities in the West.

Missing documents are not the only problem. When in 1806 President Jefferson proclaimed the existence on "the western waters . . . of criminal enterprizes" and threatened "condign punishment," panic swept the country. Everywhere men hastened to disassociate themselves from Aaron Burr, even those whose connection with his expedition was marginal. For weeks thereafter, a historian has written, "newspapers reported the rumors of nearly hysterical individuals as facts." Then came Burr's arrest and the gathering of depositions in preparation for the trial at Richmond. Like the "facts" in the press, these legal statements must be read in the light of the hysteria that produced them.

For the events of Burr's long life after the "conspiracy," the record is more satisfactory. Firsthand reports of the trial at Richmond abound, and most of the journal Burr kept during his exile in Europe has survived. As for the twenty-four years remaining to him after his return to the United States: the recent resurrection of his law papers, coupled with rich additions to his personal correspondence, makes it possible to follow in considerable detail the events of a period which tells us more about Burr the man than does any other segment of his life.

When years ago I began work on the first volume of this biography, Burr's papers were scattered around the world. Many were beyond the reach, and in some cases beyond the knowledge, of even the most willing travelers. Today all that has changed for the better, thanks to the assembling of the available papers at The New-York Historical Society by Dr. Kline and her staff. The pursuer of the elusive Burr now has at his disposal a microfilmed edition of documents from almost two hundred public depositories and private collections. The twenty-seven reels of the microfilm are a strain on the eyes but a joy to the mind. The greater quantity of material now accessible affects the picture. It points to readily identifiable patterns in Burr's thought and conduct. "His . . . political correspondence is large," I wrote in the first volume of this work, "but one combs it in vain for so much as a single sentence that can be cited as pointing to a political philosophy." Today, with more correspondence to comb, I consider that statement misleading. From the reels of microfilm Burr's political Weltanschauung emerges. To him, politics was primarily a form of entertainment, a game to be played, as he himself said, for "fun and honor & profit." It was probably this blithe attitude, more than any single thing, that earned him the otherwise inexplicably profound hatred of Thomas Jefferson, whose view was that politics was a solemn duty and a service to mankind.

Clearly apparent from the microfilm, too, are the standards Burr lived by: loyalty to friends, tolerance for enemies, and a stubborn conviction that the way a thing is done is as essential as the thing, the form as important as the content; in short, the style is the man. This gentlemanly code derived largely from his reading, at an impressionable age, of *The Letters of Lord Chesterfield to His Son and Others*. "An absolute command of your temper," Chesterfield adjured his son in 1748, ". . . patience to hear frivolous, impertinent and unreasonable applications; . . . address enough to refuse without offending . . . dexterity enough to conceal a truth, without telling a lie; sagacity enough to read other people's countenances; and serenity enough not to let them discover anything by yours—a seeming frankness, with a real reserve. These are the rudiments of a politician." Burr could have sat for that portrait, written eight years before his birth. "Julius Caesar," Chesterfield wrote, "joined business with pleasure so properly that they naturally affected each other, and though he was the husband of all the wives of Rome, he found time to be one of the best scholars, almost the best orator, and absolutely the best general there . . . A surfeited glutton, an emaciated sot, and an enervated whore-master never enjoy the pleasure to which they devote themselves . . . Pleasure must not . . . be the business of a man of sense and character; [it should] be his relief, his reward . . ." For that portrait, too, Burr could have sat.

In the rhetoric of our own time, he was more "liberal" than almost any of the politicians around him. The grandson of Jonathan Edwards, the great exponent of predestination and the limitations of the will, shifted to the other end of the spectrum. Burr put his faith in something close to absolute freedom of choice. "My idea of the devil," he said, "is composed more of malice than of meanness." All actions were allowable, he believed—following Chesterfield—so long as no ill will was intended.

One of the more fascinating revelations flowing from the microfilm is the depth of Burr's devotion to the many persons he regarded as "family," whether the relationship was by blood or marriage or adoption. Wherever he went, whatever fitful dream he followed, he kept in touch with kinfolk. Repeatedly he involved himself in their problems, more than one of them finding in "Colonel Burr" a comforter when they were in trouble, an easy touch when they needed money. Inviting a friend to visit him at a temporary home in Albany, "I am a housekeeper," the sixty-seven-year-old colonel warned him, "with all my children about me." Reviewing the forty-nine novels and short stories and the thirty-three plays in which Burr figures as a character, Charles J. Nolan, Jr., finds that in imaginative literature the colonel appears under four guises: as a Catiline (traitor), a Lovelace (despoiler of women), a Warwick (kingmaker for his part in winning the Presidency for Jefferson in 1800), and a victim ("so maligned, so misunderstood," said Woodrow Wilson). To these four a fifth may be added: Burr the paterfamilias. It is the last and more believable of these several Burrs that I have tried to portray in the following pages, well aware of the mortality of judgments about a man as disinclined as the colonel to wear his heart on his sleeve and his thoughts on his brow.

Readers of the first volume of this biography may notice that a few incidents mentioned *en passant* in the closing pages of that book are here more fully developed. I have followed this procedure partly to make this volume as self-contained as possible, chiefly because in their enlarged form the incidents are integral to the beginnings of the Burr expedition.

One of the rewards awaiting an author when he finishes a book is the opportunity of expressing his gratitude to those who helped him get it together. For invaluable assistance, generously extended, I am deeply indebted to Dr. Mary-Jo Kline, editor of *The Papers of Aaron Burr*, and to Ray Swick, historian for the Blennerhassett Historical Park Commission of the state of West Virginia. My thanks are due also to Eleanor V. Shodell of Dr. Kline's staff; to Mrs. Barbara Joe of Washington, D.C., for her excellent translations of several of the letters of the Marqués de Casa Yrujo, the Spanish minister to the United States; to Joseph E. Jeffs, librarian, and Herbert H. Fockler, special assistant to the librarian, at Georgetown University Library; to many members of the staff of the Library of Congress, notably Peter Petcoff, C. F. W. Coker, Maryann Roos, Charles J. Kelly, and Gary J. Kohn; to Mrs. Clarissa Downing Moore of McLean, Virginia; to Mrs. Nan Fahy of Bethlehem, Pennsylvania, my nonpareil typist, who wrote at the end, "Amen. I'm going to miss the endearing old rascal!"; and for props both material and spiritual to my friend Ray Neville, to whom this second volume of Burr, like its predecessor, is affectionately inscribed.

MILTON LOMASK

McLean, Virginia

Tell me that you are engaged in some pursuit worthy of you.

Theodosia Burr Alston *to* Aaron Burr

31 October 1808

AARON BURR

I

The American Frontier

and Agent 13

For at least three years after March 1805, when Aaron Burr retired from the Vice Presidency of the United States, his story consisted of what came to be called the Burr Conspiracy. "The tale is a horrid one," a merchant of his day said of this prodigious undertaking. A mystery, a puzzle, a lock without a key—so many historians have treated it. Though it was all these things and more, its contours are readily discernible.

Other men had recouped their careers and their fortunes on what was then the American frontier. Burr thought that perhaps he could do the same. Toward the end of his Vice Presidency, his political base had eroded in the East. His pockets empty, Burr began looking beyond the Appalachian Mountain ranges. But no merely modest recovery appealed to him. He was determined to rebound in a single leap. He must do something big, and when in the spring of 1805 he crossed the mountains for the first time, major plans were on his mind. The son and grandson of the second and third presidents of Princeton University had never shared his thoughts with the hoi polloi. Such behavior was alien to a man of his temperament, and into the vacuum created by his haughty silence rushed the busy

American press. A fabulous tale began to circulate: Burr intended not to liberate Spanish-owned Mexico but to seize it and rule it himself; and he also planned to draw the Western states out of the American Union and combine them with Mexico into a vast empire of his own.

Before leaving on the first of his two tours of the frontier, Burr sought financial aid from Great Britain. It failed to come, and on his return East he turned for funds to Spain, to the very country whose New World possessions he was believed ready to invade. That effort, too, was unavailing, but somehow he acquired resources enough to take him back to the western country. This time he raised an expeditionary force and arranged for the construction of boats to carry it down the Ohio and Mississippi Rivers. The rumors multiplied, the law stepped in, and after three Western grand juries failed to uncover evidence of wrongdoing, the Jefferson Administration in Washington took over. Burr was tried before the United States Circuit Court in the District of Virginia at Richmond. The charges were treason and high misdemeanor. His treason, according to the government, consisted of an attempt to separate the western half of the United States from the eastern half. His misdemeanor, the prosecution said, was that, contrary to a federal statute forbidding military action against nations with whom the United States was at peace, he had raised an army for the purpose of attacking the dominions of Spain in the Western Hemisphere. The jurors selected at Richmond pronounced him innocent on both charges. They based their decision on the legal evidence presented, but since much of the press and public has continued to hold him guilty, the student in our time has no choice but to retry the case in the light of the available historical evidence. And that effort raises questions: *Where* was the conspiracy—in Burr's mind, or in the minds of the press and public of his day? Are we dealing with a villain, or with the victim of an early version of McCarthyism?

4

Long after it was all over, Burr's official biographer, Matthew L. Davis, asked him if he had tried to sever the Union, and he answered, "No, I would as soon have thought of taking possession of the moon, and informing my friends that I intended to divide it among them." He told Davis that the objectives which carried him westward were "*First*, The Revolutionizing of Mexico, and *Second*, a settlement on what was known as the Bastrop lands." Shortly after this conversation, the Texas part of recently independent Mexico revolted and won its own independence with the help of American settlers, and Burr spoke out again. This time he echoed Talleyrand's "*La trahison—c'est une question du temps.*" What Burr said was, "There! You see? I was right! I was only thirty years too soon. What was treason in me thirty years ago is patriotism now!"

2

THE TIME OF the Burr expedition was roughly 1804 to 1807. The place was the American West as it existed in the opening years of the nineteenth century—a sprinkle of rapidly growing settlements, extending from the western foothills of the Appalachian Mountain ranges to the Mississippi River. People referred to this transmontane region interchangeably as the Mississippi Valley, the western waters, or the western country. After the Louisiana Purchase in 1803, the area also took in the newly acquired city of New Orleans and the then still-unmeasured vastness of newly acquired Louisiana on the far side of the Mississippi. But the West of the Burr Conspiracy lay for the most part eastward of the big river: the states of Ohio, Kentucky, and Tennessee, all recently admitted into the Union; the Indiana Territory, washed by both the Ohio and the Mississippi Rivers; the Mississippi Territory along the Mississippi south of Tennessee; and the city of New Orleans near its mouth. These were the stages on which most of the drama of the conspiracy took place.

One of Burr's friends, Commodore Thomas Truxton, got the impression that the ideas behind it did not originate with Burr but were suggested to him in 1804 or thereabouts by Brigadier General James Wilkinson. "Wilkinson was the projector," Truxton told his and Burr's good friend, the Philadelphia Quaker merchant and trader on the high seas, Charles Biddle, "and . . . Burr would never have thought of such designs but for the importunities of Wilkinson." It is clear from Burr's subsequent movements that in 1804 he was considering a variety of "designs." It is also clear that all of them involved activity in the western country, where Wilkinson had lived for the better part of twenty years.

The gaudy and amply girthed general once boasted, not inaccurately, that he knew more about the regions bordering the Ohio and Mississippi Rivers than "any Christian in America." He could have said also that he knew more about the affairs of Spain in that area, having acted as an agent on the payroll of that nation since 1788. Few Americans were better qualified to outline an expedition whose main objective was an attack on Spanish-owned Mexico, using the Mississippi Valley as a staging ground and New Orleans as the place from which the assault would start. As the general in chief of the United States Army, no American was in a better position to propose that the project as a whole be tied to the then widely held expectation that in the near future the United States and Spain would be at war, at which point an attack on Mexico by private citizens would be welcomed, rather than discouraged, by the government. In 1804, when he and Burr began their discussions, the feasibility of an attack on Mexico had been on Burr's mind for years. "As early as . . . 1796," biographer Davis writes, "Colonel Burr had various conversations" with John Jay, governor of New York, "on the subject" of the Spanish provinces. "In these conversations Colonel Burr expressed his views in reference to South America, which, he said, he could revolutionize and take possession of. Governor Jay replied that the boldness of the project would contribute to its success; expressing his opinion that it was not impracticable."

Apparently, honest John Jay—diplomat, political leader, and first Chief Justice of the United States—saw nothing illegal in Burr's proposals. When in 1804 Burr ran unsuccessfully for the governorship of New York, Federalist Jay backed him "decidedly and openly" and voted for him. General Wilkinson's "importunities" may have helped Burr crystallize the plans for his Western odyssey, but the plans were his from the beginning.

3

STILL, ONE HESITATES to ascribe the ideas behind the Burr expedition to a single mind. They sprang from the land-hungry, claustrophobic collective mind of early-nineteenth-century America, a product of the land. In his study of discovery and expansion in the New World, *The Course of Empire*, Bernard De Voto perceived what it was that carried the Americans westward, ineluctably, to the South Sea's edge. It was the very contiguity of it—no mountains that could not be passed, no rivers that could not be crossed—which dictated the course of empire. So long as any foreign power, Spain or Britain or France, lay to their fore or flanks, so long were the settlers of the American West in turmoil. For they were determined to push on and out and to take possession. In their passion for Lebensraum, they gazed not only south and west at the property of Spain, but also north at that of Britain. During the formative years of the American Republic, its emissaries to Canada were diligent in their efforts to sow discontent with British rule among the people of that area; from the era of the

7

Revolution through the War of 1812, the American hope of adding Canada to the country died slow and hard.

Nor was this imperialism solely western. It was southern, too. Certainly it was Virginian. Thomas Jefferson, who carried the Old Dominion in his bones, said several times that perhaps the country was too large for a single national government to handle; perhaps someday the trans-Appalachian states would wish to go on their own, in which case let them depart the Union in peace, and good luck to them. But before Jefferson's head said that, his heart said something quite different: he wrote in 1786 that the United States ought to be regarded as "the nest from which all America, North and South, should be peopled." His only fear was that Spain might prove too "feeble" to hold her colonies in the New World until "our population" (the United States) could acquire them "piece by piece." The third President was unequivocal when it came to a question of his country's destiny, even in those years before the Louisiana Purchase opened the immense lands beyond the Mississippi River and prepared the way for the westering stream of settlement that by 1845 would make that destiny "manifest." However much Thomas Jefferson and Alexander Hamilton disagreed on other matters, they were brothers under the skin on this. "You know my general theory as to our Western affairs," Hamilton wrote Charles Cotesworth Pinckney of South Carolina in 1802. "I have always held that the unity of the Empire and the best interests of our Nation require that we should annex to the United States all the territory east of the Mississippi, New Orleans included."

Manifest or not, the course of empire did not run smooth. Like a seismograph, the new American Republic registered the shifting fortunes of the great powers of the Old World. The tensions flowing from these changes affected the trans-Appalachian country profoundly. So clearly did Aaron Burr's expedition come out of the early upheavals on the frontier that a survey of some of them, and of James Wilkinson's part therein, becomes a necessary prelude to the complex and horrid tale.

4

THE REMOTE ORIGINS of the conspiracy are visible in the negotiations responsible for the treaty of peace—officially, the Treaty of Paris—which in 1783 ended the war of the American Revolution. The France of Louis XVI had assisted the Americans in their struggle for independence and had procured for them, in addition, the limited assistance of Spain. But his Most Christian Majesty, Louis XVI, was a Bourbon and his Catholic Majesty, Charles III of Spain, was a Bourbon; and the "Family Compact" of 1760 linked them. The possessions of Bourbon Spain in the New World were extensive (some seven million square miles in all) and valuable. West of the Mississippi River they included the long stretches of Louisiana (a million square miles, more or less), and behind them Mexico with its prolific silver mines. East of the Mississippi they included the city of New Orleans—guardian of the mouth of the river and gateway to middle North America— and (courtesy of the Treaty of Paris) the lands bordering the Gulf of Mexico and known as East and West Florida. France's peace commissioners wished to keep the aggressive Americans as far as possible from bullion-rich Mexico, by confining them almost entirely to the space east of the Appalachians. But the American commissioners were shrewd—and future-minded. Ignoring their government's instructions to be guided by France, they made a separate treaty with England. By this action they obtained for their country all of what is now the United States east of the Mississippi River except New Orleans and the Floridas. While France respected these boundaries as confirmed by the Treaty of Paris, Spain did not. Nor did Great Britain.

Spain, citing prior military possession of the lower Southwest, insisted that the northern boundary of West Florida should not be at the thirty-first parallel as ordered by the treaty. Instead, it should be a hundred miles to the north along a line running east from where the Yazoo River meets the Mississippi River at what is now Vicksburg, Mississippi. Britain continued to occupy a string of forts on American soil in the Northwest. Spain's alliance with the Creek Indians of the Southwest threatened the American settlements in that region. Britain's hold on the Indian tribes north of the Ohio River exerted a similar pressure on the pioneers moving into what are now Ohio and Indiana. At intervals, both Spain and Britain initiated schemes aimed at separating the American West from the American East, their objectives being to attach the separated area to Europe or, failing that, to bring an independent West under their sway.

Spain's efforts were the more intense, motivated as they were by the fear that sooner or later an expanding United States would direct itself at the silver mines which made Mexico the most cherished of that nation's transatlantic dominions. Spain's dread of the advancing American settlers was all the stronger because Spain's hold on its colonies in the New World was year by year growing weaker. From Mexico southward to Cape Horn, there was widespread and growing dissatisfaction with the rule of Madrid. The dictum of the Declaration of Independence, that "all men are created equal," was not lost on the Latin American subjects of his Spanish Majesty. Coming on the heels of the successful American rebellion, the liberating slogans of the French Revolution seeded the outbreaks in the lower half of the Western Hemisphere which, by the end of 1826, would strip Spain of all but scattered remnants of its once gargantuan empire in the New World.

Spain's refusal to recognize the thirty-first parallel as the northern boundary of West Florida was not its only defiance of the Treaty of Paris. Even more devastating in its consequences was that nation's rejection of the stipulation that "The Navigation of the River Mississippi, from its source to the Ocean shall forever remain free and open to . . . the Citizens of the United States." To the settlers of the western country the big river was their lifeline, the only route over which they could send their tobacco and corn and cotton to market. Shortly after the close of the war in 1783, Spain served notice that it had no intention of opening the Mississippi to the "Citizens of the United States," and the fires of discontent blazed in every frontier community.

The Americans were still living under the central government established by the adoption in 1781 of the Articles of Confederation. According to the rumors reaching the West in 1785, the Confederation Congress had under scrutiny a trade agreement with Spain. Drafted by John Jay, as the American Secretary of Foreign Affairs, and Diego de Gardoqui, as Spain's first minister to the United States,* it offered tempting commercial advantages to the merchants and shipbuilders of the East but demanded an awful price from the farmers of the West. Spain would sign the Jay–Gardoqui treaty on one condition—for at least twenty-five years the United States would abandon all claims to the use of the Mississippi as a highway to market for its Western citizens.

News moved slowly in those days. For a year the people of the western country remained unaware that the Jay–Gardoqui treaty was doomed; a Congress dominated by the agrarian and Western-facing states of the South would never accept it. Yet by 1786 most Westerners were under the impression that the treaty was already signed. In their minds it was an intolerable situation—a stab in the back from their own

---

* Actually, the haughty court of Madrid was not yet ready to send a full-fledged minister to republican America. Gardoqui's title was Encargado de Negocios; i.e., chargé d'affaires. Max Savelle, *George Morgan: Colony Builder*, 202.

republican government! All along the frontier there was talk of secession, of separating from the Union, of setting up their own governments. The muffled and shadowy maneuvers in Kentucky and Tennessee, which future Westerners would remember as the Spanish Conspiracy, began to emerge. Historians differ as to the depth of this movement. Some argue that during the mid-1780's many Westerners, perhaps the majority, favored the transfer of their allegiance to Spain, thus insuring to themselves the right to navigate the Mississippi. Others find in the evidence only the ineffectual intrigues of a scattering of men eager to line their pockets by acting as secret agents of Spain. The backgrounds of the settlers favor the second interpretation. They were veterans of the Revolutionary War, who had come across the mountains to claim the bounty lands awarded them by a grateful country. Many were the descendants of Scotch-Irish Presbyterians, English Quakers, and Central European Moravians who had emigrated from the Old World to escape the tyranny of crowned heads hostile to their religious views. Fealty to monarchical Spain, home of the Holy Inquisition, was unlikely to lodge in such breasts.

In any event, by the end of 1787 the truth had penetrated the frontier. There was no trade agreement with Spain, and talk of a Spanish alliance persisted only among those who had signed on as foreign agents. Hard money was scarce in the western country; those who entered the employ of Spain could count on being paid in shiny pieces of eight from the mines of Mexico. Land speculation was rife. Some of the agents held extensive acreages in the Spanish dominions, properties that lip service to his Catholic Majesty could protect. "Treason" seems almost too pretentious a word for their motives; "greed" sounds more appropriate. And what can be said of most of the participants in the Spanish Conspiracy was also true of its pre-eminent figure, James Wilkinson. Settling in Kentucky at the end of the war, the general found in the unrest stirred by the

Jay–Gardoqui treaty negotiations an atmosphere precisely tailored to his peculiar talents.

5

NOT YET THIRTY when he reached Kentucky, Wilkinson had already demonstrated the nature and range of those talents. Bernard De Voto's description of him as a "smalltime confidence man" underrates his skills. Of moderate stature and rounded figure, handsome, with a broad flushed face and stunning dark eyes, he was an adventurer with whom some of the most important men of his day—Washington, Hamilton, and Jefferson among them—dealt seriously. They realized, as Washington and Hamilton admitted, that the qualities which made him reprehensible also made him useful. He was a curious composite: bright, inventive, and engaging, but superficial, touchy, humorless, and—as Burr would one day discover—envious and vindictive. Like many men who live by their wits, he sometimes outwitted himself. He drank much, and in drink he sometimes talked carelessly and got into trouble. Yet he was as adept at slithering out of difficulties as he was at getting into them.

That Burr should have chosen this "finished scoundrel" as his collaborator in intrigue is a striking example of his poor judgment of men, and of the justice of Andrew Jackson's observation that "Burr is as far from a fool as I ever saw, and yet he is as easily fooled as any man I ever knew." A respectable upbringing seems to have had little effect on Wilkinson's character. At the time of his birth in 1757 his father was "an esteemed merchant-planter" with lands along the Hunting Creek near the village of Benedict in southern Maryland. The boy was not quite seven when his father died, not quite seventeen when in 1773 his mother sent him to Philadelphia to study "physic and surgery." By the spring of 1775, Wilkinson was

13

practicing on his own, mending bones and dispensing pills in a rural section of eastern Maryland. But his mind was not on his work; it was, like that of law student Burr in Connecticut, on the preliminary skirmishes of the Revolutionary War, then taking place in New England. Like Burr, when word of the Battle of Bunker Hill arrived, he hastened to join the army forming under George Washington at Cambridge, Massachusetts, where his acquaintanceship with Burr began.

Like the rest of Wilkinson's life, his Revolutionary War career was picaresque. He was a lieutenant colonel with the post of "deputy adjutant-general to the army of the Northern Department of America" when in the fall of 1777 the forces of his superior, Major General Horatio Gates, defeated the British army under General John Burgoyne at Saratoga, New York. To Wilkinson fell the supervision of the negotiations of surrender, and as a reward for good performance, Gates selected him to carry official word of the victory to Congress, then meeting in the backwoods village of York, Pennsylvania. Though Wilkinson took eleven days for a 285-mile jaunt he could have done in seven, the delegates to the Congress were so delighted with his news that they brevetted him brigadier general.

A startling promotion—from lieutenant colonel to brigadier general at the age of twenty; but a few weeks later Wilkinson was in characteristic trouble and wriggling out of it in characteristic fashion. He got involved in the Conway Cabal, named for one of its authors, General Thomas Conway; it was a brief and foolish attempt by sundry army officers to replace Washington as commander in chief with Gates, who was being hailed as "the hero of Saratoga." Conway wrote a letter to Gates and entrusted it to Wilkinson to deliver. It read in part: "Heaven surely is determined to save the American cause, or a weak General [Washington] . . . had long since lost it." Stopping at Reading, Pennsylvania, en route to York, Wilkinson fell into bibulous company. Warmed by a roaring fire and lashings of rum, he quoted that part of Conway's letter to an officer friendly to Washington. Soon the commander in chief knew what was in Conway's message, and soon the hero of Saratoga knew that he knew. When Gates asked Wilkinson how the leakage could have occurred, Wilkinson blandly observed that the general's aide, Colonel Robert Troup, was a close friend of one of Washington's aides, Colonel Hamilton; perhaps Troup had disclosed the contents of the letter to Hamilton, who revealed them to Washington.

When Gates learned the truth, he upbraided Wilkinson in public for trying to blame his own error on a fellow officer, and Wilkinson challenged him. For some reason, no duel occurred then, but the two men quarreled again later. This time there was a duel—with pistols—from which both men emerged intact. Long before these posturings on the field of honor, Wilkinson had earned a reputation for lying, scheming, and carousing. On 29 March 1778 he resigned from the army under a cloud. But Wilkinson out was not Wilkinson down. A year and a half later he wangled himself the office of clothier general to the Continental Army. He was a hard worker and a good administrator. He introduced some needed reforms into the quartermaster service, but his resignation on 27 March 1781 followed the discovery of "gross irregularities in his accounts."

During the closing years of the war, he busied himself in and around Philadelphia. He acquired and farmed a country estate confiscated from a Pennsylvania Tory. He served as an officer in the local militia. He sat for two terms in the state legislature. He called the figures of the quadrille for the Philadelphia Assembly. He corresponded with Aaron Burr, using a code he and Burr had devised to insure privacy under a mail-delivery system notoriously open to curious eyes.

Their friendship rested on shared experiences in the encampments of the war. It took on an added dimension in 1778 when Wilkinson married attractive Ann Biddle of Philadelphia, a first cousin of Charles Biddle, one of Burr's most intimate friends. Prompted by some favor extended to Wilkinson by Burr, Biddle informed Burr that "Mrs. Wilkinson is much obliged to you," adding: "You have no friend feels a warmer attachment to you than James."

From the hour James Wilkinson arrived in Kentucky in 1784, he made his presence felt. He had a genius for being all things to all men. He was never at a loss for words, having that thin knowledge about a hundred things that passed for deep learning on the frontier. He gave generously of his medical skills. When his neighbors fell ill, he plied them with tartar, salts, laudanum, and "blistering plaisters." He stood in as a midwife when no woman with those skills was available. He built homes for his family in Louisville and Lexington. He impressed the settlers of those frontier communities by riding out in a lavish coach, drawn by four glistening horses and trailed by a retinue of blacks. No extravagance was too great if it pleased the slight and pixy-faced wife on whom he doted. A Kentucky contemporary saw him as "not quite tall enough to be perfectly elegant, compensated by symmetry and appearance of health and strength; a countenance open, mild, capacious, and beaming with intelligence; a gait firm, manly, and facile; manners bland, accommodating and popular; an address easy, polite and gracious, invited approach, gave access, assured attention, cordiality and ease. By these fair terms he conciliated; by these he captivated."

He opened a store in Lexington and went out on the road, selling his goods from sacks flopped over horse or donkey. He began accumulating the knowledge of the attitudes and customs of the Indians of the Southwest that years later would cause the American Philosophical Society of Philadelphia to honor him with a membership in that learned body. He acquired a tract of land on the Kentucky River and laid out on it the beginnings of Frankfort, future capital of the state. At the time of his arrival in the West, Ken-ta-ke (the Indians' name for it) was still Kentucky District and under the governance of Virginia. When in 1785 news of the Jay–Gardoqui Treaty negotiations stirred demands for separation, Wilkinson seized the leadership of a movement aimed at severing the district not only from Virginia but also from the Union, with the understanding that once the Kentuckians became independent they would be free to ally themselves either with the United States or with Spain, depending on which of those governments offered the better terms.

In the summer of 1787, Wilkinson loaded two flatboats with tobacco, put himself on a smaller and more comfortable vessel, and headed down the Kentucky River en route to its juncture with the Ohio River. His destination: New Orleans. His failure to obtain a passport to the Spanish dominions from either the governor of Virginia or the Spanish minister to the United States bothered him not at all. Certain that word of his advocacy of Spanish interests in the West had preceded him, he descended the Ohio and Mississippi Rivers, confident that when he reached the docks of New Orleans he could talk the authorities there into letting him and his cargo land. So he did. Arrested at the docks, he persuaded his captors to take him to the headquarters of the Spanish governor of Louisiana, the genial and easygoing Don Esteban Rodríguez Miró.

It was the beginning of an ardent partnership. Before Wilkinson returned to Kentucky, he had sold his tobacco. He had also taken an oath of allegiance to Spain and had made arrangements (completed later) to serve that country as Agent Number 13, in return for a yearly pension of two thousand dollars and the exclusive right to use the Mississippi as a route to market—facts endlessly rumored during his lifetime, though they would not be confirmed until the opening of the Spanish archives a century later.

Back in the bluegrass region of Kentucky, Agent 13 found ways of convincing Don Esteban Miró that he was earning his keep. As a delegate to the district assembly, he sponsored petitions, calling on the Spanish rulers to open the Mississippi to the Americans. In letters to Miró, written at the same time, he urged him to keep the river closed as the best means of persuading the Westerners to abandon their allegiance to the United States.

In November 1788, Dr. John Connolly, an American-born Englishman, came from Detroit to Louisville. Connolly said his objective was "to obtain an adjustment of old land claims" in the Louisville area. Wilkinson's nose for duplicity told him there was more to the doctor's visit. Insinuating himself into Connolly's confidence, he quickly learned what he had suspected. Connolly had come to Louisville as an agent of Lord Dorchester, Governor-General of Canada. His real purpose was to raise among the Westerners ten thousand men willing to join a British army in an attempt to seize Louisiana from Spain.

From this information Wilkinson spun a devious plot. He assured Connolly of his readiness to further Britain's aims. He informed Miró of what the doctor had told him. In his communication to the Spanish governor of Louisiana, he announced his intention of setting an assassin on Connolly. But when the assassin struck, an armed guard—dispatched by Wilkinson himself—saved the British agent's life and permitted his escape. By these twists Wilkinson endeared himself to both the Spanish and the British authorities in the New World, becoming a recipient of Spanish and British secrets which he sold in turn to interested parties.

The year that saw him weaving these schemes also saw the adoption of the Constitution, followed in 1789 by the establishment of the federal government under President Washington. A year later, the new national government tried to circumvent the closure of the Mississippi River by building a road from Kentucky to New Orleans. A reconnoitering party under a Major Doughty came west to perfect the plans. Its arrival in Kentucky enabled Wilkinson to perform another service for his Spanish employers. He advised Miró to alert the Creeks, Spain's Indian allies. An Indian attack on Major Doughty and his crew ended the road-building project and left the farmers of the frontier still dependent on a forbidden river, still clamoring for governmental action to relieve them of Spanish and British impediments to their progress.

At last, in 1795, the relief came: the negotiation of a treaty with Britain by John Jay and of one with Spain by Thomas Pinckney of South Carolina. Under Jay's treaty, Britain relinquished the American forts north of the Ohio River. Under Pinckney's, the Treaty of San Lorenzo, Spain abandoned all claims to American soil north of the thirty-first parallel, opened the Mississippi River to the Americans, and agreed for at least three years to permit them to deposit their corn, tobacco, and cotton at New Orleans for transshipment to the markets of the world.

In the western country, joy over the signing of the Treaty of San Lorenzo turned to dismay, following the influx of rumors that Spain was giving thought to ceding New Orleans and other parts of Louisiana to Napoleon Bonaparte, in return for a treaty of friendship with republican France. Spain had opened the river, but who could say what Napoleon would do once its lower reaches fell into his ambitious hands? "I believe it to be a fact," Andrew Jackson of Tennessee was writing one of his friends in January 1797, "that France has acquired by Barter From the Spaniards . . . part of Louisiana . . . therefore the[y] will be masters of the mouth of the Mississippi . . . I hope they will be good neighbors."

Out of these concerns arose another frontier intrigue, a successor to the Spanish Conspiracy of the preceding decade. This one would come to be known as the Blount Conspiracy after its progenitor, Senator William Blount of Tennessee. Because of the presence of foreign powers on this continent, and because some of the lands "on the western waters" were unsettled and not yet an integral part of the United States, conspiracy had become a way of life in the first American West. The Burr expedition, coming along later, can only be understood against this background.

Senator Blount did not share his friend Andrew Jackson's hope that the French would be "good neighbors." The senator was a heavy speculator in frontier land who saw in the rumored French takeover a threat to the value of his holdings. Since England was at war with Spain, surely England would be willing to finance an American military expedition aimed at seizing the lower portions of Louisiana before the colossus of France could get hold of them. Blount presented this proposition to Robert Liston, Britain's minister to the United States. At the same time he wrote an indiscreet letter to an American friend, outlining his plans. Somehow the letter came into the possession of President John Adams. Adams dispatched it to the Senate, and the expulsion of Blount from that body halted his conspiracy instantly. Considerable evidence exists that the enterprising Tennessean had interested a number of prominent Americans in his schemes. Among them were James Wilkinson and Thomas Jefferson, Vice President of the United States. So "thoroughly" were they involved, according to one twentieth-century historian, that for years to come Jefferson remained noticeably "subject to Wilkinson's influence."

By the time the Blount Conspiracy had run its course, Wilkinson had long since returned to the military life. By early 1792 he had become a brigadier general in the regular army. If he assumed that this promotion would enhance his value in Spanish eyes, he was correct. By the end of 1796, when he succeeded General Anthony Wayne as commander in chief, Spain owed him $32,000 for his services. Of this amount, about $26,000 had reached the hands of Agent 13.

He spent much of his time at Fort Adams on the Mississippi between Natchez and Baton Rouge. A lover of comfort, he saw to it that his quarters there were as elegant as the resources of a primitive military post allowed. His soldiers built for him a "swinging cot with a canopy and mosquito net," where he took "his ease after a cup of wine, a bit of venison, and a fragrant cigar." It was a vantage spot from which to keep an interested eye on the ups and downs of a vigorously growing West. The fears of a French takeover of the Mississippi vanished in the wreckage of the Blount Conspiracy, but the year 1802 brought another of those shifts of the economic ballast that Wilkinson so often in the past had turned to his advantage. Suddenly the "mischievous" Juan Ventura Morales, Intendant (chief civil officer) of New Orleans, barred the Americans from further use of the docks of that city as a depository for their commodities. Protests arose at once, only to subside swiftly when a year later control of the Mississippi River fell into American hands as a result of the Louisiana Purchase.

The sequence of events associated with that incredible transaction are well known: how in 1800 Napoleon persuaded Spain to cede to France all of Louisiana, including New Orleans; how news of this development, reaching the United States in 1801, fathered apprehensions that the replacement of weak Spain by strong France at the mouth of the Mississippi forecast grave difficulties for the farmers of the West; how President Jefferson, determined to keep the river accessible to American citizens, wrote his country's minister to France, Robert R. Livingston, that the "day France takes possession of New Orleans . . . we [the United States] must marry ourselves to the British fleet and nation"; how, in an effort to resolve the crisis short of so risky an alliance, he sent James Monroe to France with orders authorizing him and Livingston to purchase New Orleans if they could; and how, even before Monroe reached Paris, Napoleon, temporarily abandoning dreams of a colonial empire in the New World and always in need of money, offered to sell the United States not only New Orleans but also Louisiana, for less than five cents an acre!

6

ON 30 NOVEMBER 1803, in the stylish central square of New Orleans, the Place d'Armes—a brief ceremony occurred.

After Napoleon's acquisition of Louisiana, Spain had continued to administer the colony. Now, in preparation for its convey-ance to the United States, the red and yellow banner of that country came down the flagpole in front of the *cabildo*, the city hall. Up went the Tricolor of republican France.

Three weeks later, on 20 December, the "beautiful women and fashionable men of the city" crowded the eleven galleries of the *cabildo* to watch the Tricolor come down and the Stars and Stripes go up. Few smiles were seen, few cheers heard. New Orleans's ten thousand mostly Catholic inhabitants had as yet no idea how they would fare under a government starkly unlike any they had known. Not quite a century earlier, their city had begun as a French possession. Though forty years of Spanish ownership had intervened, its citizens—predominantly Creoles ("white persons born in the New World of French or Spanish blood or of both")—remained French in spirit. They would have welcomed a Napoleonic fleet in their port, and were not happy at the prospect of being ruled by a Protestant Anglo-Saxon governor appointed by a distant President.

On hand to take possession for the United States were a young civilian and a middle-aged soldier. The civilian was the twenty-eight-year-old, Virginia-born governor-designate, Wil-liam C. C. Claiborne. The soldier was of course General Wil-kinson, who had brought a 170-man detachment downriver from Fort Adams. Wilkinson's task was to see that nothing untoward happened during the ceremony. Nothing did, unless one counts a fouling of the halyards that caused the American flag temporarily to stick halfway up the pole. In a "hasty Scral" to Secretary of War Henry Dearborn in Washington, the general reported a rumored plot to fire the town and men-tioned other potential dangers by way of assuring his superior that he was on the job.

Indeed, Wilkinson found much to do in the newly Ameri-canized city. Still in town was the Marqués de Casa Calvo, whom Spain had sent as a special commissioner to supervise the earlier transfer of Louisiana to France. For the eyes of the Marqués, the general prepared a memorial in which he played on the fears of the retiring Spanish officials. Napoleon's sale of Louisiana had put the aggressive Americans closer than ever to the silver mines of Mexico. No one yet knew exactly where Louisiana ended and the North American lands still belonging to Spain—Texas on the west and the Floridas on the east—began. A boundary dispute portended and, as it developed, the dons would need all the friends they could get within American officialdom. Having dwelt on these matters with that mix of pompous language and nicely honed realities that only Wilkinson could achieve, he got to the point. For some years he had not been receiving his pension as Agent 13, and figured the arrears at $20,000. Presumably the Marqués de Casa Calvo considered himself clever when he cut that figure to $12,000; presumably the general was overjoyed to get twice what they owed him.

For 1804 the last New Orleans entry in Wilkinson's order book was the 24th of April. That day he sailed for the Atlantic coast, summoned to Washington by Dearborn to discuss defense plans for the country's newly acquired territory. A month later he was in New York City. There he tarried for five or six days before moving on; and there he arranged to spend a night with Aaron Burr—an occasion which will serve as well as any from which to date the beginnings of the Burr Conspiracy.

2

The "March to the City of Mexico" Begins

ARON BURR WAS forty-eight in the spring of 1804, still youthful in appearance, as would be true for years to come: a small, erect man, his head large on its slender frame, his chin round and slightly receding, his nose rectilinear, his luminous hazel eyes darkened almost to black by jutting brows. A touch of haughtiness in his expression repelled some observers, fascinated others; and his buoyant manner was that of a man "bold enough," as Alexander Hamilton remarked with transparent envy, "to think no enterprize too hazardous, and sanguine enough to think none too difficult." Just behind him that spring was the failure of his attempt to win the governorship of New York. Ahead lay the fatal duel at Weehawken with Hamilton, followed by Burr's flight to escape arrest under two grand-jury indictments: one, in his own state, for defying its anti-dueling laws; the other, in New Jersey, for murder. Nine months remained of his term as Vice President of the United States—nine months in which to ponder how best to mend his damaged finances and revive a stalled political career.

It is easy to suppose that Burr's Western expedition was a product of exclusively selfish considerations. "Perhaps," writes

Robert V. Remini in his splendid biography of Andrew Jackson, Burr's "fatal mistake" was that "his plans only served his own personal interest. Had he been able to formulate his goals in accordance with the ambitions of westerners and their perceived destiny of their section, like Jackson after him, he might have succeeded—and in the process achieved the status of hero. Instead he pursued a private need." It is indeed possible to question the depth of Burr's understanding of the problems of the western country, even to suspect that a major objective of his deeds in that region was to show the Jefferson Administration that he was still a political force to be reckoned with. But the seeming primacy of that motive does not rule out the existence of other motives alongside it. Surely he could have found a more conventional way of fulfilling merely personal desires. In the East the political doors had closed on him; the two grand-jury indictments curtailed his movements. But the West lay open and, as friends assured him, ready to serve his political ends. As a lawyer, his profession was portable. He had only to hang up his shingle in one of the settlements of Kentucky or Tennessee and wait for the voters to send him back to Washington. Hamilton's death was not mourned on the frontier, where men did not so much join Thomas Jefferson's Republican Party as be born into it.

In the western country the attractive Vice President was still popular and respected, as he would learn when he went there. The magnitude of the project he undertook, the high risks it entailed, intimate that his motives were not wholly at odds with the belief of a modern poet that all extraordinary "human quests are for the numinous." At the end of the long road in the dreamer's mind looms a holy grail, a possible utopia.

2

BURR WAS at Richmond Hill, his luxuriant country home on the northern fringes of New York City, when on 23 May a note arrived, announcing the presence of General James Wilkinson in the vicinity. "To save time, of which I need much and have little," the general wrote, "I propose to take a bed with you this Night, if it may be done without observation or intrusion—answer me & if in the affirmative, I will be with [you] at 30′ of the 8th hour—." Burr answered by the bearer of the message, and no doubt smiled to himself as he endorsed it, "Wilkinson . . . 'observation.' " Naturally the general would like the cover of twilight when he came calling on Colonel Burr. Commanders in chief serve at the pleasure of the President, and Jefferson's distrust of the Vice President and his friends was one of the better-known facts of American political life.

The general came, resplendent in one of the profusely frogged and braided uniforms he himself designed, and as always voluble; and the two friends talked. Of what? Of Louisiana and New Orleans, apparently, for shortly after Wilkinson returned to his quarters in the city the next morning he sent an officer cantering back to Richmond Hill with a cryptic note for Burr. "You are deceived, my friend," it read in part, "with respect to the size of the Rum Barrel of Louisiana the answer being 450 lbs—." Wilkinson had brought East, for delivery to the Secretary of War in Washington, a collection of manuscript maps of Texas, New Mexico, and other northern colonies of Spain. Most or all of them rested on firsthand observations of the areas by Philip Nolan, the famous horse trader of the American West who at the time of his death in 1800 was himself preparing a military invasion of the Spanish domains. That during the after-dark conference at Richmond Hill Burr's invasion plans received attention is supported by another note from Wilkinson inviting the colonel to "call" at the general's

New York lodging "at one o'clock to meet General Mason, M. Dawson and six other particular friends, and see my Maps."

No doubt Burr went. He was fond of Wilkinson and had reason to believe that his feelings were reciprocated. "Your affectionate and faithful friend"—so the commander in chief described himself in one of his frequent letters to the colonel. "I think of you always, mon beau et cher Diable"—thus he concluded another. Burr, on his part, found ways of being helpful to the general. He arranged for Wilkinson's sons, James and Joseph, to be accepted as students at the colonel's alma mater, the College of New Jersey, later Princeton University. When the land mass obtained by the Louisiana Purchase was divided for administrative purposes, with the section below the thirty-third parallel as the Orleans Territory and the section above as the Louisiana District, Burr took advantage of a temporary lapse in Jefferson's enmity to help obtain the governorship of the northern half for Wilkinson. Rumors that the general was in the pay of Spain had circulated since the days of President Washington. Naturally, Burr had heard them, but having been frequently maligned himself by journalists, he tended to regard such criticism of his friends as unworthy of credence. Charles Biddle, who saw a good deal of Burr, never heard him "speak ill of any man." So consistently tempered were the colonel's comments on people in his correspondence that it is puzzling to find him, on the occasion of the death of a prominent acquaintance, proposing with heavy humor that the epitaph for his gravestone be inscribed in "hog latin." When told that, on the eve of the duel at Weehawken, Hamilton wrote for posterity a statement expressing an intention to withhold his fire, Burr's only recorded comment was: "Contemptible, if true." Even on this matter, his lawyer's mind wanted proof. He enjoyed Wilkinson's company, his cheerful garrulity. In the spring of 1804 it never occurred to him that, in discussing his expeditionary plans with the general, he was putting his trust in one of the most accomplished double-dealers in America.

27

3

HIS DAYS WERE full that summer, many of them with matters remote from his Western schemes. In June he discovered in an Albany, N.Y., newspaper a letter quoting "General Hamilton" as saying something "despicable" about him. On the eighteenth he sent his lawyer friend William Peter Van Ness to Hamilton with a request for an explanation or retraction that was never given. About 7:30 A.M., on the hot bright day of 11 July, on a narrow tree-bowered ledge of Weehawken Heights on the New Jersey shores of the Hudson River, the two sometime friends and longtime political rivals faced one another, pistols in hand. If Hamilton had intended to withhold his fire, he failed to do so. His shot went wild. Burr's pierced his opponent's abdomen in a mortal wound. Twenty-eight hours later, at 2 P.M. the next day, Hamilton died, and the still echoing damnation of Aaron Burr as a "cold blooded murderer" had begun.

"Thousands of absurd falsehoods are circulated with industry," Burr wrote of the clamor against him in New York as news spread of the tragic outcome of the "interview" at Weehawken. One repeatedly bruited tale was that while Hamilton lay dying in agony in the Greenwich Village section of the city, Burr and his friends "caroused and gloated" amidst the marble statuary and rich tapestries of Richmond Hill. In fact, Burr passed most of the hours preceding Hamilton's death in a much more characteristic fashion—struggling to meet the sudden and unexpected demand from one of his many creditors for $1,750.

The outcry against him in New York sped to other cities. In Philadelphia, his friend Charles Biddle was worried about him. He had had business dealings with Nathaniel Pendleton, Hamilton's second at Weehawken, and on the day after the duel he wrote Pendleton. Why all the agitation? Had Burr behaved properly on the field of honor? Quite properly, Hamilton's friend Pendleton assured him. Relieved by this information, Biddle wrote another letter, this one to Burr. It was common knowledge that a grand-jury indictment was pending in New York. Should the colonel consider it prudent to leave that area, the Biddle house at 159 Chestnut Street, Philadelphia, stood open to him.

Burr reached the Quaker City on 24 July. He remained there for two and a half weeks, coming and going as he pleased. "Colonel Burr, the man who has covered our country with mourning," a local newspaper noted with surprise and distaste, "was seen walking with a friend in the streets of this city in open day."

4

ALSO IN PHILADELPHIA that summer, as Burr probably ascertained before leaving New York, were two Englishmen—Anthony Merry and Charles Williamson—both of whom were in a position to help him get his Western project underway.*

Anthony Merry, Britain's minister to the United States from 1803 to 1806, was a small, bland, middle-aged man with a face that one American found "impenetrable" and a disposition that struck another as so cautious that his reply to "What o'clock is it?" would be, "I will write my government for instructions." His many years in his country's diplomatic corps included a tour of duty in Paris, where Napoleon, amused at the contrast between Merry's name and his "grave and re-

---

* Several historians also place Wilkinson in Philadelphia at this time and assume that he and Burr conferred. This would seem to be incorrect. A gap in the general's order book makes it impossible to ascertain his exact movements during the summer, but circumstantial evidence indicates that he was not in the Quaker City. The local press frequently reported on Burr's movements about town but never mentioned the equally well-known general. See Thomas Robson Hay, "Charles Williamson and the Burr Conspiracy," *Journal of Southern History*, II (1936), 183n.

served" demeanor, spoke of him as Monsieur Toujours Rire, a nickname that was changed in Washington to Toujours Gai.

The only son of a London wine merchant, Merry followed a common practice in the England of those days and bought himself a place in the foreign service. His marriage at forty to the wealthy widow of the Squire of Herringfleet Hall in Suffolk placed at his side a woman whose exaggerated hauteur may have derived from a similar social climb. If the gossips of Herringfleet can be trusted, Elizabeth Merry—née Elizabeth Death—was a farmer's daughter who grew up to marry the squire. In truth, Elizabeth could be a most entertaining companion. She talked well, and was a charming hostess and a knowledgeable botanist. Aaron Burr liked her. "Much of grace and dignity . . . full of intelligence . . . amiable and interesting." So he wrote of her in one of the many letters he sent South to his daughter, Theodosia Burr Alston, at her elegant plantation home on the banks of the Waccamaw River in South Carolina. Gilbert Stuart's portrait of Mrs. Merry shows a handsome woman, slightly overweight—"no more than a desirable embonpoint," by the tolerant standards of Aaron Burr—with a hint of humor at the corners of her mouth and a knowing look in her fine dark eyes. Still, during the Merrys' stay in the United States, Elizabeth probably won her slow-thinking, hardworking husband no friends by her endless complaints about the dismal social life of rustic Washington and her description of the women of the federal city as tasteless frumps who neglected to decorate their homes with plants and spent their time reading "foolish novels."

In London, the announcement in early 1803 of Merry's appointment to the American legation brought a protest from William Cobbett, editor of the influential *Political Register*. In Cobbett's opinion, Toujours Gai was one of "the mere stopgaps and journeymen of the corps diplomatic." Only a topflight envoy, the journalist argued, should be sent to a country whose affairs were so vital to the interests of Great Britain. There was no need for Cobbett to add that whoever represented England in the United States would be coping with delicate problems. Already in evidence, as his readers knew, were some of the strains that would eventuate in the War of 1812. In Washington, Merry would find long lists of men whom the Department of State described as having been seized from American vessels and "impressed and detained" in the British naval service "for want of documents to prove their [American] citizenship."

From the moment the Merrys touched American soil in late 1803, bad luck dogged them. Nobody in London—and nobody in Washington except Aaron Burr—troubled to warn Merry that Thomas Jefferson distrusted all diplomats and treated those stationed in his capital with the informality he thought appropriate on the part of a republican government. When the Merrys arrived at the President's house for their first diplomatic dinner, they encountered what Jefferson later described as his "law of pele-mele." Instead of escorting Mrs. Merry to the table and seating her beside him, the President bestowed those honors on Dolley Madison, the wife of the Secretary of State. Merry's efforts to seat himself on the other side of the President were thwarted when that position was occupied by the American-born wife of the Marqués de Casa Yrujo, the minister from Spain. The potentialities of the situation were not lost on the Yrujos. The marchioness was heard to mutter, "This will be the cause of war," and the Marqués boasted in a letter to his superior in Madrid that the President had shown "a marked preference for him and his wife over the Merrys."

Most historians have treated this episode tongue-in-cheek, calling it a "miniature social tempest" or "a foolish circumstance of etiquette." At the time, however, its principals, Jefferson and Merry, took it seriously. Jefferson went so far as to break his self-proclaimed rule of never writing anonymously for the press. He drafted a defense of his law of pell-mell and arranged for William Duane, editor of the *Aurora*, the leading

Republican newspaper in Philadelphia, to publish his words as though Duane himself had written them. Merry, in a letter to his superior in London, pronounced Jefferson's actions a "studied" attempt to humiliate the Envoy Extraordinary and Minister Plenipotentiary of his Britannic Majesty. During the Merrys' early months in the United States, the New England secession movement, an attempt by a few Federalists in the Northeastern states to escape Jeffersonian democracy by withdrawing their section of the country from the Union, was taking shape. When the leaders of this conspiracy called on Anthony Merry, they knew that disgruntled diplomat would listen sympathetically to any scheme likely to embarrass Jefferson and weaken the country over which he presided.

Charles Williamson, the other Englishman Burr was pleased to find in Philadelphia in the summer of 1804, was as bold of spirit as Merry was cautious, as outgoing as Merry was reserved. During the American Revolution, Williamson served as colonel in the British army, afterwards traveling to Egypt and Turkey to conduct secret-service operations for his country's War Department. For ten years, beginning in 1791, the dapper and personable secret-service officer worked as a naturalized citizen in the United States, serving as the land promoter and agent for the English owners of the Genesee Country, a 1,200,000-acre tract in central western New York. Recently relieved of his agency and once more engaged in secret-service work for his native land, Williamson, after a visit home, had returned to the United States in 1804 to recruit British citizens in that country and Canada for what he called his "levy," a secret military organization desired by the British cabinet for possible use against the possessions of France and Spain in the West Indies.

A need for medical treatment for acute hemorrhoids had brought Merry from the drafty elegance of his legation on K Street, Washington, to the Quaker City. Why Williamson was there is unknown. Perhaps at Burr's request, for he and

Williamson had known each other for years. They had collaborated on land promotions, had served together in the New York Assembly, and years before had achieved the easy camaraderie of almost identical temperaments. They were in many ways strikingly alike: the same restless energy and love of display, the same craving for recognition, the same indifference to the abstract idea, the same admiration for the dashing deed. Both were aristocrats to the bone. Burr descended on both sides of his family from his country's religious and intellectual elite. Williamson's family belonged to the Scottish gentry, and Williamson numbered among his intimates, as Burr well knew, men high in the British government, including Henry Dundas, first Viscount Melville, first Lord of the Admiralty under Prime Minister William Pitt. Both were womanizers by reputation, and in fact. And both were adventurers, outwardly at home in the mainstreams of their respective societies, inwardly afloat on the fabled waters of the Spanish Main.

Williamson had spent most of 1801 and 1802 in New York City, renting a house at 87 Pearl Street, in which Burr had a financial interest. That they saw a good deal of each other can be taken for granted. Burr was probably the only prominent man in America to know about the levy. Williamson made a point of not mentioning the matter to Anthony Merry, explaining to his bosses in London that it would never do for the British minister to know anything about an illicit effort to raise a British army on American soil. As for Burr, one can imagine his eyes brightening at the thought of how useful such a force could be to his own gradually forming plans for liberating the Spanish colonies. When Williamson traveled to England in the fall of 1804, he would carry with him a letter from Burr, for his commander in chief, recommending an officer for service in the proposed levy.

In Philadelphia in the summer of 1804, the two friends discussed both Williamson's plans and Burr's. At Princeton years earlier, Burr had cautioned his fellow graduates in his commencement address against the folly of "Building Castles in the Air." Now the forty-eight-year-old man was doing what the seventeen-year-old student had preached against. But even building castles in the air required money. Burr spoke of those things to Williamson, and Williamson to Merry, and the minister dutifully reported what he had been told to Lord Harrowby, Secretary of State for Foreign Affairs in London. "My Lord," wrote Merry on 6 August 1804:

> I have just received an offer from Mr. Burr, the actual Vice President of the United States (which situation he is about to resign), to lend his assistance to his Majesty's Government in any Manner in which they may think fit to employ him, particularly in an endeavouring to effect a Separation of the Western Part of the United States from that which lies between the Atlantick and the Mountains, in its whole Extent—His proposal on this and other Subjects will be fully detailed to your Lordship by Col. Williamson who has been the Bearer of them to me and who will embark for England in a few days.—It is therefore only Necessary for me to add that if, after what is generally known of the Profligacy of Mr. Burr's Character, His Majesty's Ministers should think proper to listen to his offer, his present Situation in this Country, where he is cut off as much by the democratic as by the Federal Party, and where he still preserves Connections with some People of Influence, added to his great Ambition and Spirit of Revenge against the present Administration May probably induce him to exert the Talents and Activity which he possesses with Fidelity to his Employers—

Either this letter cries treason, or we must assume that Burr and Williamson had agreed that the only way to get Anthony Merry on their side was to tell that violently anti-American diplomat what they knew he wanted to hear. It is noteworthy, certainly, that Charles Williamson, in his ensuing communications to persons in or close to his Britannic Majesty's govern-

ment, attributed no disunionist intentions to Burr and identified his Western expedition as a "March to the City of Mexico."
Few measures connected with the conspiracy better illuminate
what seem to have been its objectives than the Scottish-born
secret-service officer's three-year struggle to persuade Great
Britain to underwrite Burr's attempted penetration of Hispanic
America.

5

WHEN IN ENGLAND in the fall of 1804 Charles Williamson began his long effort to assist his fellow conspirator in
America, he had reason to think he would succeed. Three hundred years of English history buttressed his expectations. Since
that long-ago day, 4 May 1493, when Pope Alexander VI
blithely divided the lower half of the Western Hemisphere
between Spain and Portugal, English eyes had rested covet-
ously on the subsequently discovered riches of Latin America.
The England of Elizabeth I was outraged at seeing the growing trade of the empire along the western shores of the South
Atlantic almost wholly controlled by the rulers of the Iberian
Peninsula. Her Majesty's sea dog, Sir Francis Drake, raided
the Spanish colonies, and the two and a half billion pounds of
booty he brought home to his queen whetted appetites for more
of what those distant lands in the New World had to offer. In
1654 Oliver Cromwell initiated an excursion to the West Indies
that won him the island of Jamaica and other bits of Caribbean
real estate. In more recent times two British Prime Ministers
had undertaken similar ventures in Central America, with dis-
appointingly meager results. And in 1804 William Pitt, presiding over his Majesty's government for a second time, was
again looking at Spain's transatlantic dominions in the hopes of
finding there a solution to problems so complex that they
strained the abilities of even that brilliant statesman.

The emergence of the Industrial Revolution had impaled

the British Isles on the horns of a dilemma. Its factories and mines were producing more porcelain and coal, more beer and paper, more woolen, cotton, iron, and leather goods than ever before. At the same time, the grip of Napoleon on the seaports of Western Europe was choking off the continental market on which England to a considerable extent depended. Pitt, as a result, was torn between two stringent demands. With a hundred thousand French soldiers poised at Boulogne on the far side of the narrow Straits of Dover, how much of his country's military resources must he keep at home against the threat of an invasion across the Channel? How much dare he send into the South Atlantic in search of new outlets for the wares of his worried mercantile constituents? Small wonder that in 1804 Pitt and other British leaders welcomed professional revolutionaries when these adventurers came to them—as did Francisco de Miranda of Venezuela—with plots and stratagems calculated to break the near-monopoly of Spain on the thriving Latin American trade.

"Spectacular and romantic was the career of Francisco de Miranda . . . Knight-Errant, and Promoter of Spanish-American liberty." Thus William Spence Robertson opens his richly detailed biography of the "Precursor," so named because it was Miranda who, almost single-handedly, lit the fuse of the rebellions that during the decade following his death in 1816 cleansed the whole of Central and South America of Spanish and Portuguese control. A man of overwhelming charm, with a vividly handsome face, articulate, learned, and dynamic, often reckless and sometimes unscrupulous in the pursuit of his goals, Miranda was the only personage of his heroic age to participate in all three of its most memorable events: the struggle of the American colonies for independence, the French Revolution, and the liberation of Latin America.

Born and educated in Caracas, the son of a Venezuelan merchant-farmer, Miranda was a thirty-one-year-old infantry captain in the army of Spain when in the closing years of the war of the American Revolution his regiment assisted in the seizure from the English of Pensacola, Florida. He was a forty-two-year-old lieutenant general in the army of revolutionary France when in the fall of 1792 the division under his command captured the Belgian seaport of Antwerp. He was in his fifty-sixth year when in 1806, with American assistance, he launched a series of attacks on the shores of Venezuela in an unsuccessful effort to free his native land from the yoke of Spain.

Deserting from the Spanish army after the battle of Pensacola, Miranda spent the rest of his life as a wandering revolutionary, sojourning for varying intervals in sections of continental Europe, in England, and in the United States. Wherever he tarried, he somehow contrived to win the favor of people of consequence. Among them were Catherine the Great, empress of Russia; General Charles F. Dumouriez, an important figure in the opening phases of the French revolutionary war; and an assortment of British notables, including William Pitt and Lord Melville. To these and other influential persons he revealed his plans for the liberation of Latin America. To them he presented precisely wrought memorials, listing the funds, men, and material he needed to achieve his aims. Though there were times when Miranda had no visible means of support, he nearly always managed to surround himself with beautiful women and to furnish his abodes with the objets d'art and costly luxuries of a man of amorous leanings and exquisite taste.

He was living in London, enjoying the comforts of a Grafton Street town house and an annual pension of seven hundred pounds, both provided by the British government, when Charles Williamson arrived in England in the fall of 1804. Williamson was well acquainted with Miranda. He knew that Pitt and Lord Melville were giving serious thought to the Precursor's revolutionary ideas. He understandably assumed they would give the same consideration to Aaron Burr's not unsimilar plans. Reaching Liverpool on 6 October, he began to attend to Burr's affairs before going on to London to attend to his own, which had to do with his efforts to raise a military corps in America for service in the West Indies. Even before disembarking from the ship that had brought him across the ocean, Williamson had written to his friend in the cabinet, Lord Melville, requesting the privilege of calling on his lordship to discuss "certain circumstances . . . I feel anxious to communicate to you," and expressing the hope that Melville would make it possible for him to communicate the same "circumstances" to Pitt.

Fourteen of Williamson's surviving letters enable us to follow his diligent efforts during the next three years to induce the British government to cooperate with the Burr Conspiracy. Not all these communications were directed to Lord Melville. Some went to Williamson's friend, Charles Hope, Lord Granton, the Lord Justice-Clerk of Scotland, who forwarded them to Melville. Others went to Sir Evan Nepean of the Board of Admiralty; still others to William Windham, Secretary of State for War and the Colonies in the administration formed after the untimely death of Pitt in 1806. In only one of them did Williamson discuss the possibility of a division of the United States, and this letter followed by only a few days the appearance in a London newspaper of an erroneous report that the American West either already had or was about to secede from the Union. Williamson thought he saw advantages for Great Britain in such a development, but his speculations to this effect contained no mention of Aaron Burr.

Like many other Englishmen, Burr's agent in Britain was not convinced that the sale of Louisiana to the United States meant that Napoleon had abandoned his plans to create a colonial empire in the New World. In one of his letters to the Lord Justice-Clerk of Scotland, Williamson suggested that Britain use the Burr expedition as a "counterbalance" to Bonaparte's ambitions. By supporting Burr's "Mexican plan," Williamson argued, Great Britain could solidify Anglo-American friendship. He suggested that Britain create goodwill in the United States by sharing with them the trade of the West Indies and

South America "when laid open by the joint Efforts of the two nations—after to aid them in the Conquest of Mexico" and in annexing the Spanish-owned Floridas.

"It will be natural to ask," Williamson wrote the Lord Justice-Clerk, on 6 January 1806, "what does the United States require from this Country? In the first place Spirits, persuasion and Encouragement to begin the business—Money to defray the Expense of equipping and moving a sufficient Force from Kentucky to the Natchez—and a Supply of Military Stores to be sent to New Orleans . . . And besides these a small Fleet cruizing in the Gulph of Mexico to keep the Spaniards quiet . . . With even this trifling Arrangement, which would not in Expense exceed £200,000, if that, I would expect before next August to see 50,000 North Americans, with Col. Burr at their head, far on their March to the City of Mexico—but should time be lost and a French force once get footing in that Country, what is now easy would then be extremely difficult."

Nothing came of Williamson's pleas. Not, however, because the authorities to whom he addressed them were uninterested, but because Napoleon's enlarging engrossment of the continent of Europe made it impractical for the British government to help Burr, Miranda, or any other would-be revolutionizer of the settlements of Spain in the Western Hemisphere. In the opening weeks of 1808 a British army commanded by Sir Arthur Wellesley was earmarked for an attack on Hispanic America in support of Miranda's plans. Then a French army invaded Spain and Portugal, and Charles IV of Spain relinquished the throne to his son, Ferdinand VII. The son's rule was short. France forced him to abdicate, and when Napoleon put his brother Joseph on the throne of Spain, a popular uprising swept the ancient kingdom, leading in time to a treaty of alliance between the Spanish patriots and Great Britain. Obviously, the British government could not entertain plots against an ally. Instead of sailing to South America, Sir Arthur Wellesley went to the Iberian Peninsula to begin the victorious six-year campaign that would make him Duke of Wellington in the wake of Waterloo.

6

WHILE WILLIAMSON labored for the cause in England, Burr pushed ahead with his own plans. When in mid-August 1804 the Vice President left Philadelphia, he carried with him a document, issued by the Marqués de Casa Yrujo, permitting him to travel in West Florida, the Spanish colony to the south of Georgia. In letters to his daughter in South Carolina and to her husband, Joseph Alston, he promised a visit if time permitted, pointing out, however, that he had much to do in the South and "must be in New-York the first week in November." As outlined in this correspondence, his original intent was to linger briefly at the plantation home of a friend on the island of St. Simons off Georgia and then tour "the Floridas for five or six weeks." But nature and events altered his itinerary in drastic ways.

Shortly after his arrival at the island plantation of Senator Pierce Butler of South Carolina, a terrible storm struck. It destroyed the cotton crop on the island, halted traffic on the nearby waterways, threatened to level the house where Burr was domiciled, and stranded him on St. Simons until the second week of September. He got to Florida, but the time schedule he had set himself permitted only a brief journey in the vicinity of the St. Johns River, "about thirty miles from St. Augustine."

What was the purpose of this look at one of the provinces of Spain, the only such look Burr would ever enjoy? To ascertain the lay of the land and the attitudes of the inhabitants toward their distant rulers? Very likely, though statements in Burr's correspondence indicate that it was primarily an attempt to deal with a more immediately pressing problem. He had as yet no idea of what would come of Williamson's efforts to get British financing for his Western plans. If those failed, he must develop

40

other sources of revenue and the sea-cotton islands off the Floridian cape offered a possibility. "I am fully persuaded," his merchant-navy friend, Captain Jacob Lewis, had written him a few months earlier, "that Cotton Lands [on the Floridian islands] may be had of superior Quality & great Extent for *very little money*." St. Simons was a sea-cotton island and, as Burr knew, its yearly yields of *Gossypium bardadence* had long since endowed its absentee owner, Senator Butler, with a fortune. But where the islands off West Florida were concerned, there was a catch. Enrique White, the Spanish governor, hated Americans. He would not allow them to settle in his domain and had issued orders forbidding the inhabitants to sell them real estate. Perhaps the colonel's discovery in Florida that the governor, a formidable character, would be unlikely to waive his rules even for so practiced a negotiator as Aaron Burr changed his plans.

In early October, he headed north. Horses were hard to come by in the deep South. Burr had traveled four hundred miles by canoe and was "about the colour of Peter Yates," the young slave who accompanied him, when he reached Statesburgh in the South Carolina uplands to spend a few days with his daughter, his son-in-law, and his two-year-old grandson, Aaron Burr Alston, known in the family circle as Gamp. The colonel had overseen every step of his daughter's education. He was now doing the same for her son. "As to the boy," he would be instructing Theodosia a few months later, "I beseech you not to undertake to teach him the various sounds of the letters abstractedly from the words in which those sounds are found . . . Go on with his a, b, & c; and when he shall have learned the language, and not till then, can you teach him (or ought it to be attempted) the principles of the construction of that language." As an educator, the colonel was ahead of his time.

When he left Statesburgh, New York was still his destination, but by the time he reached the Potomac River he had changed his mind. Learning en route that a grand jury in New

Jersey had indicted him for the murder of Hamilton—an action rendering him liable to arrest if he passed through that state—he ended his travels in Washington. On 4 November, opening day of the second session of the eighth Congress, he was in his chair, as president of the Senate, ready to begin his last four months as Vice President.

3

A Winter's Tale

BURR FOUND the political climate in Washington warmer
that winter than at any time since his inauguration as
Vice President in 1801. Thomas Jefferson was at least half
certain that the colonel had tried to steal the Presidency from
him during the election of 1800, which resulted in a tie. He was
fully certain that Burr had no interest in the great issues of the
day, regarded politics as nothing more than a source of jobs for
his friends and power for himself, and was "a crooked gun . . .
whose aim . . . you could never be sure of." His belief that
Burr was a mere machine politician did not prevent the President from using his own Administration to reduce Burr to the
level of odd man out in the government. Instead of giving control of the federal patronage in New York to Burr, he gave it to
Governor George Clinton, thus putting that potent weapon in
the hands of Burr's enemies in his home state. This maneuver
took place during the opening months of Jefferson's first term.
Since then, the Vice President's duties had been limited to running the Senate, a task he performed ably and with pleasure.

In December 1804, all this changed. Suddenly the President's confidential advisers, Secretary of State James Madison
and Treasury Secretary Albert Gallatin, were courting the Vice
President and doing errands for him. Official Washington took
notice, and some observers were puzzled. Senator William

43

Plumer of New Hampshire could only conclude that the colonel's removal of Alexander Hamilton from the scene had made him a hero in the eyes of Democrats in power. Others recognized more accurately what was going on: for example, Senator John Quincy Adams of Massachusetts watched the progress of the charade with grim amusement. He was aware that coming up in the Senate was the trial on articles of impeachment of Samuel Chase, an associate justice of the Supreme Court. It was important to the Administration that the ill-tempered and opinionated Maryland jurist be found guilty. His conviction would discourage the already well-advanced efforts of the head of the court, Chief Justice John Marshall, to confirm the right of the judiciary to declare acts of Congress unconstitutional—a right whose application, Jefferson believed, would frustrate the will of the people as expressed by their elected representatives.

When the impeachment trial began in February, Burr would be its presiding officer. His rulings on points of law could affect the outcome. Hence the necessity of Jefferson's change of attitude toward him, a truce in their vexed relationship that would end on 1 March 1805 when the senators acquitted Justice Chase of all eight charges against him.

Burr made the most of his improved status while it lasted. The purchase of Louisiana and its division into two governmental units created new jobs in the West, and the colonel's influence is discernible in the assignment of three of them to close associates. To his stepson, Bartow Prevost, went a judgeship in New Orleans, capital of the southern unit, officially the Territory of Orleans. To his brother-in-law, Dr. Joseph Browne, went the secretaryship of the northern unit at St. Louis, capital of the so-called District of Louisiana, and to General Wilkinson, the governorship of that unit under an arrangement which permitted the general to retain his position as commander in chief of the army. Reporting these developments to his daughter, Burr made no secret of his delight at seeing good friends elevated to high places in the West he was planning to visit when his Vice Presidency ended. "Wilkinson and Browne will suit most admirably as eaters and laughers," he wrote Theodosia, "and, I believe, in other particulars."

Wilkinson was in Washington that winter, and with Burr in the good graces of the Administration for the time being, the two friends had no need to confine their conferences to the after-dark hours. They spent considerable time together, copying maps of West Florida and other Spanish lands adjacent to Louisiana. The general arranged for Major James Bruff, commanding at St. Louis, to send them information concerning Mexico and the route to that province via the Spanish trading center of Santa Fe in adjoining New Mexico. Wilkinson sought similar information from General John Adair, bringing from that Kentucky land speculator and politician an enthusiastic endorsement of the Vice President's desire to move against the hated dons. "Be assured," Adair wrote Wilkinson on 10 December 1804, "the Kentuckians are full of enterprise and altho' not poor are as greedy after plunder as ever the old Romans were. Mexico glitters in our Eyes—the word is all we wait for."

The "word" Adair awaited—and Burr as well—was the momentarily anticipated declaration of war against Spain. James Monroe was en route to that country, charged by Secretary Madison with an attempt to settle the differences between the two nations. At stake, among other things, were the extent and boundaries of newly acquired Louisiana. If Monroe's mission failed (as it did), war could follow. If war came, a "march to the City of Mexico" would be a popular move, its leader a hero. If it didn't, Burr might have to consider alternative plans. Wilkinson urged him to settle in one of the trans-Appalachian states and run for Congress. The general had his reasons for this suggestion. Two of his friends, Senators John Brown of Kentucky and Jonathan Dayton of New Jersey, were about to retire from politics, and the commander of the army needed supporters in Congress.

At Wilkinson's request, Congressman Matthew Lyon also

urged Burr to seek a political career in the West. Lyon could cite personal experience as an example of what could be hoped for. Formerly a representative from Vermont, Lyon had moved to Kentucky in 1801 and had been sent back to Washington as a congressman from that state. Burr seems to have done little more than listen amiably to these proposals. Then and later, his goal was Mexico.

But map study in Washington would not get him there. For that he must collect money, and he continued to hope that Charles Williamson's labors in England would yield results. Ever the optimist, the colonel wrote his daughter that his friend was "hourly expected," but the months rolled by with no word from or sign of Williamson.

Meanwhile, another likely source of income emerged. On 17 January 1805 a group of businessmen headed by General Benjamin Hovey of Oswego, New York, petitioned the Congress for 25,000 acres of land for the purpose of constructing a canal along the eastern or Indiana side of the Falls of the Ohio at Louisville. Here was a project that experienced speculators might get something out of, and Burr and Wilkinson made haste to align themselves with Hovey and his associates. Congress failed to act on their petition, but the speculators did not give up. Eventually, they succeeded in creating an enterprise known as the Indiana Canal Company, a development that later proved to be of some help to Burr and his Western plans.

During the opening months of 1805 the potential liberator of Mexico was watching a development naturally interesting to a man thinking of New Orleans as the starting point for an invasion of the Spanish domains. The Creoles of that city were not happy with their new American rulers, and in January they sent three deputies to Washington to lay their grievances before the government. The deputies brought with them a memorial for presentation to the Congress. It demanded immediate statehood for Louisiana, argued that under an article of the treaty of cession the American government had promised the inhabitants of the former Spanish colony "all the rights, advantages, and immunities of citizens of the United States." Congress rejected both the request and the argument behind it, but the deputies from New Orleans would not leave the federal city empty-handed. On 2 March the lawmakers authorized the southern, or Orleans, half of Louisiana to establish a territorial legislature and to send a delegate, a nonvoting representative, to Congress. In addition, the Congress agreed to extend statehood to the Creoles whenever the population of the governmental entity to which they now belonged reached sixty thousand.

2

IT WOULD BE misleading to picture the Vice President as exclusively concerned that winter with the possibilities of the frontier. Many other matters demanded attention. January brought to his Washington lodgings a letter from Timothy Edwards, the guardian uncle under whose roof Aaron and his late sister, orphaned early, had passed their childhood. Years before, Timothy—a shopkeeper in Stockbridge, Massachusetts —had gone broke and Aaron, then a prosperous New York lawyer, had bailed him out. Timothy had not forgotten. "For all that . . . I now possess," he told his former ward, "I am indebted to you." The stolid, sixty-seven-year-old Bay State merchant reminded his nephew that it had been two years since they had seen each other. What a joy it would be, he wrote, if just "once more" they could "spend a day or two" together at "this end of the union."

Burr's money troubles, a chronic ailment, were that winter acute. Creditors were pressing him to dispose of the portion of his New York country estate that was still his, principally the Richmond Hill mansion. In November he reported to Theodosia that it was gone. "House and furniture . . . sold for about twenty-five thousand dollars," he told her. A few detached lots remained and would be sold. Meanwhile, his unpaid debts totaled about "eight thousand."

The two grand-jury indictments were much on his mind. "It has been intimated to me, through different channels," he informed Truxton, that the grand jury in Bergen County, New Jersey, "would be ready to grant a pardon in case I should be found guilty . . . If so, why put me to the vexation and trouble & the State to the expense of a Trial? Why not at once order a . . . discontinuance of the prosecution . . . ?" He wrote numerous letters to friends in that state, seeking their assistance in his attempt to have the indictment quashed. He spent a few days in Philadelphia, soliciting the help of influential persons there. In time, both the New Jersey and the New York charges would fade away and be forgotten, but in the winter of 1804–5 Aaron's efforts to eliminate them were unavailing. It was his understanding, he confided to Charles Biddle, that the judge in charge of the case in Bergen County was convinced that unless the Vice President were convicted of murder, "famine and pestilence would desolate the land."

The indictments alarmed his daughter, and when Theodosia worried, Aaron worried. "You treat with too much gravity the New Jersey affair," he scolded her. "It should be considered a farce, and you will yet see it terminated so as to leave only ridicule and contempt to its abettors." And in another letter: "Your anxieties about me evince a sort of sickly sensibility . . . I fear that you are suffering a debility, arising from climate or other cause, which affects both mind and body. When you are in health you have no sort of . . . apprehension about me; you confide that, under any circumstances, I am able to fulfill your expectations and your wishes. Resume, I pray you, this confidence, so flattering to me, so consoling to yourself, may I add, so justly founded!"

3

THE FOURTH OF MARCH arrived. At noon Jefferson began his second term, with George Clinton as Vice President. Burr attended the ceremonies. William Duane, editor of the Philadelphia *Aurora*, spotted him in the gallery. The former Vice President, Duane observed, was now sitting with the sovereign people. Nay, he added, with the peoples' sovereign—"the ladies." On the following day, "an engagement" took the colonel across the Potomac River to Alexandria, Virginia. Before leaving town, he sent a note to the British legation, apprising Elizabeth Merry of his intention on his return of dropping by to assure her "in person of the great respect" he bore her and to receive her "commands." Perhaps it was during this visit that the now retired Vice President held the first of several conferences with Elizabeth's husband, for toward the end of the month the British minister was drafting for Lord Harrowby his second report on the Western plans of Aaron Burr.

A curious report, more interesting for what it fails to say than for what it says. According to a memorandum written later by an English army officer, Burr told the British minister that he had a dual operation in prospect: "an expedition against Mexico," and, if that succeeded and the inhabitants of the frontier wished to join the new empire thus created, a separation of the western half of the Union. It is a measure of Merry's eagerness to see the American house divided that in his report to Harrowby, dated 29 March 1805, he said nothing about Mexico. "Mr. Burr," Merry wrote his lordship, ". . . has mentioned to me that the inhabitants of Louisiana seem determined to render themselves independent of the United States, and that the execution of their design is only delayed by the difficulty in obtaining previously an assurance of protection and assistance from some foreign power and of concerting and connecting their independence with that of the inhabitants of the Western parts of the United States, who must always have a command over them

by the rivers which communicate with Mississippi. It is clear
that Mr. Burr (although he has not as yet confided to me the
exact nature and extent of his plans) means to endeavor to be
the instrument of effecting such a connection. He has told me
that the inhabitants of Louisiana, notwithstanding that they are
almost all of French or Spanish origin, as well as those of the
Western part of the United States, would, for many obvious
reasons, prefer having the protection and assistance of Great
Britain to the support of France."

France! Burr knew what he was doing when he sounded
that name. In the mind of every Englishman of 1805 the very
mention of it conjured up the threatening figure of Napoleon.
"[B]ut," Merry's letter to Harrowby continued, ". . . if his
Majesty's government should not think proper to listen to his
[Burr's] overture, application will be made to that of France,
who will, he had reason to know, be eager to attend to it in the
most effectual manner, observing that peace in Europe would
accelerate the event in question by affording the French more
easy means of communication with the continent of America,
though, even while at war with England, they might always find
ways of sending the small force that would be required for the
purpose in question. He pointed out the great commercial advantage which his Majesty's dominions in general would derive
from furnishing almost exclusively (as they might through
Canada and New Orleans) the inhabitants of so extensive a
territory."

That the Creoles of New Orleans were fiercely discontented
under their new government was common knowledge. Not only
had the Congress refused them instant statehood; it had put
severe limits on the importation of slaves into Louisiana, a troubling edict to an economy dependent on its rice, indigo, and
cotton plantations. Everyone knew these facts. What was news
in Merry's letter was that the Orleanians were on the verge of
revolt, waiting only for Burr to lead them and for Great Britain
—or France—to fund the effort. Apparently, Merry realized

that Lord Harrowby would want some evidence of the authenticity of this startling revelation. By way of satisfying his lordship, Merry reminded him of the presence in Washington of the deputies from New Orleans and noted that Burr had become "intimate" with all three of them. In truth, Burr's intimacy consisted of having been introduced to the gentlemen. Wilkinson, who knew them, had done the honors, announcing as he did so that the colonel was the "first gentleman in America" and that he was planning a trip to Louisiana to carry out "certain projects." What projects? The general's statements left the deputies, as one of them later disclosed, thoroughly mystified.

What would the colonel need from Britain to effect the independence of New Orleans and the West? "Two or three frigates," wrote Merry, "and the same number of smaller vessels to be stationed at the Mouth of the Mississippi . . . would be the whole that would be wanted; and in respect to money, the loan of about one hundred thousand pounds would, he [Burr] conceived, be sufficient for the immediate purposes of the enterprise . . ." Having stated his monetary requirements, Burr suggested a method for what later Americans would call "laundering" the funds. The colonel, Merry wrote, "observed that any suspicion of his Majesty's government being concerned in the transaction, till after their [the western region's] independence should have been declared, which would arise if remittances were made in this country or if bills were drawn from hence, might be avoided by the appropriation to this object of a proportion of the two hundred thousand pounds which the United States have to pay to his Majesty next July, and part of which sum he would devise the means to get into his possession without its destination being either known or suspected." Seemingly, Merry did not so much as twitch an eyebrow at this nice touch. What indeed could be better for Burr's real plans than direct access to money for which no accounting could be demanded by its donors? Again Anthony Merry had heard what he wanted to hear, and Burr had demonstrated both his willingness to shave the truth in the interests of his goals and his ability for bringing other minds into line with his own. Senator Plumer—keeper of an enlightening "Memorandum" on the life of the federal city of his day—never ceased to find the colonel a fascinating study; and never for more than two or three weeks at a time could make up his mind exactly what to think of him. "No man," the New Hampshire solon decided around the time of Burr's interview with Merry, "is better fitted to brow beat or cajole public opinion. And considering of what materials the mass of men are formed—how easily they are gulled—and considering how little restraint laws human or divine had on his mind [it] is impossible to say what he will attempt—or what he may obtain."

4

BY EARLY MARCH, Burr had done everything that could be done in the East toward obtaining the funds he needed. The time had come to head for the frontier. Before leaving the federal city, however, he sent an emissary to the Philadelphia home of the Marqués de Casa Yrujo, the Spanish minister. Yrujo had granted him a permit to visit the Floridas. Burr now informed the minister that he was planning to move to Mexico, explaining—so Yrujo reported to Don Pedro Cevallos, the foreign minister of Spain in Madrid—"that the death of General Hamilton whom he killed in a duel, did not permit him to remain in the United States." To Burr's request for the necessary passport, Yrujo's answer "was such that it should have entirely dashed his hopes."

But Burr was not easily dashed. Learning that Yrujo was in Washington temporarily, he called on him in person. Barred from Mexico, the Spanish minister reported to Cevallos, the former Vice President had now "decided to go to New Orleans," then on to West Florida, and from there overland to St. Augustine. Many of Burr's maneuvers of this period are baffling: none more so than this visit to the Spanish minister. Taking shape in his mind was a plan for an armed assault to liberate Spain's colonies in the New World. Yet here he was chatting with the American representative of the royal owner of those colonies in the fashion of a man making a casual social call. Only a person as naturally unsuspicious as the colonel could have been so ignorant of, or so indifferent to, the gossipy nature of governmental Washington as to assume that his conferences with Anthony Merry had gone unobserved.

Certainly, Yrujo was aware of them. As his country and Great Britain were at war, he could only conclude that Burr was now "a spy for England," that his plans were in some way inimical to the welfare of "N[uestro] S[eñor] (Our Lord) the King," and that he was "up to no good (*no ha ido por ahí para bien*)"— a conviction strengthened by the knowledge that Burr was carrying westward "mathematical instruments" of the sort used in the making of maps. Yrujo transmitted his fears to Madrid. Simultaneously he dispatched a warning southward, for the eyes of the Spanish officials in Louisiana and the Floridas. "We surmise, with ample reason," he told them, that Burr "is journeying to New Orleans on behalf of a foreign Potentate, on a Secret Mission such that it would *shame* a man with any scruples . . . I recommend to you the greatest vigilance regarding his activities and if he becomes involved in West Florida *in any manner* which confirms our suspicions, the Provincial Governor should take possession of his person and his papers."

When Burr talked with the British minister, he was dealing with a man of remarkable mental density. No such criticism could be leveled at the Marqués de Casa Yrujo. The soft, boyish face with its delicate features which peers at us from Gilbert Stuart's portrait of the Spanish minister shielded a shrewd and venturesome mind. His marriage in 1797 to Sally McKean, daughter of Governor Thomas McKean of Pennsylvania, attached him to one of the country's most adroit political families. The haughty don knew his way around in American politics. Already he had angered Jefferson by an attempt to bribe a Fed-

eralist editor into opening the columns of his Philadelphia newspaper to articles critical of the Administration's warlike attitude
toward Spain, and favorable to the continuance of peace between
that nation and the United States. In the near future, the
Marqués would go to the press again. But this time the target
of his animadversions would not be Thomas Jefferson. It would
be Aaron Burr.

5

ON 10 MARCH the colonel advised his daughter of his
imminent departure from Washington, and on the twenty-first
he was in Philadelphia, occupying rented quarters in the home
of a French-born dentist at 75 Walnut Street and winding up
his personal affairs, in preparation for a tour of the western
waters. His intention was to linger in the Quaker City for only
ten days, but this decision rested on the supposition that during
that period General Wilkinson would be leaving Washington
en route to St. Louis and that the two of them could meet at
Pittsburgh and float down the Ohio River together. Hearing
that the general's departure had been delayed, Burr arranged to
remain where he was until the twenty-first of April, only to discover that no westbound stage would be available until the
twenty-third. At four o'clock that morning he and Gabriel Shaw,
a longtime acquaintance from New York, boarded the public
wagon that would carry them across Pennsylvania to Pittsburgh, gateway to the western waters.

4

On the Western Waters

I F THE HIGH-WHEELED COACH bearing the colonel and his companion began its westward trek on the Lancaster Turnpike, the first sixty-two miles were a bruising experience. Recently built at a cost of $465,000, the turnpike was the first rural road in America to have a foundation of stone under its gravel surface. The firmness permitted even the heavily burdened stage to cover as many as thirty-five miles a day, but the bodies of its occupants paid the price. No complaints from Burr. Years on the judicial circuit as a New York lawyer had prepared him for the discomforts of Western travel: for taverns so crowded that a dozen lodgers to a chamber was not uncommon, or so neglected that the beds "stunk intolerably," or so ill-furnished that there were no beds, only piles of verminous blankets on the floor; for meals eaten in the company of backwoodsmen and wagoners, in stale-smelling rooms which doubled as sleeping quarters for the innkeeper and his wife.

During the next six months, the polished little man from New York would journey thousands of miles in a primitive world, equally indifferent to the snags and sawyers lurking under the waters of the Ohio River and the mosquitoes and horse flies buzzing along the Natchez Trace. Wherever he stopped, he was the focus of attention, and this no doubt palliated all annoyances, for Aaron loved to be liked. It was much the same everywhere: a parade in his honor in at least two towns, balls and banquets in others, with the local newspapers minutely recording his comings and goings and speculating on the purposes of his *Wanderjahr.* After all, it was not every day that a former Vice President of the United States came riding through the West. At Lexington, Kentucky, a boy named Bob Kiser achieved instant fame as the first person in town to see the great man as he arrived—"on horseback, followed by his white manservant."* Knew him at once, the excited child boasted, "recognized him by a wonderfully faithful representation . . . of him in a collection of wax works" recently exhibited in Lexington.

"What strength of character it takes," the French novelist André Gide has written, "to hate the thing that flatters us." The homage lavished on Aaron Burr as he moved across the valley of the Ohio and down the Mississippi to New Orleans encouraged the most daring of his dreams: conquest of Mexico and the creation of an empire of his own. Prior to his first tour of the West, he was at least willing to consider suggestions that he settle for a more modest political comeback by establishing residence on the frontier and running for Congress. But, before the trip was over, that respectable possibility had ceased to interest him. The acclaim that greeted his appearances all along the line convinced him that he was destined for undertakings of a more spacious dimension.

2

"To wait" in Philadelphia beyond the twenty-first, Burr had notified Wilkinson in early April, "would mar my plans and disappoint my companions." As for the nature of

---

* The "white manservant" was probably Gabriel Shaw, no servant, but one of Burr's wealthier law clients, who traveled with the colonel at least as far as New Orleans and acted as his secretary.

these plans, the *Philadelphia Gazette* ran a story on the day after Burr's exit from the Quaker City, reporting "that a company had been formed in the Eastern States for the purpose of opening a canal around the Falls of Ohio [at Louisville, Kentucky] and . . . Colonel Burr, it has been said, was concerned in that company; and we presume his visit to that country is principally confined to that project." At the moment it was, for the project referred to by the *Gazette* was of course the Indiana Canal Company, with whose founders Burr had associated himself.

Other than the Act of Incorporation, dated 24 August 1805, no official records survive to show exactly how the canal company came into being. But from reports in the press, and from occasional passages in Burr's letters, the development is reconstructible. Having failed to get congressional sanction for the project, its promoters decided to seek a charter from the newly authorized Legislature of the Territory of Indiana. For this step, schedules had to be drafted and strategies concerted, and for these purposes Burr and some other promoters had arranged to confer at the home of Senator John Smith, one of their number, in the vicinity of Cincinnati, Ohio. As the Indiana Legislalature was scheduled to open its first session in June, it was important that this conference take place prior to that date. Hence Burr's refusal to wait for Wilkinson to catch up with him and the dispatch with which the colonel moved after leaving Philadelphia in late April.

At Pittsburgh, reached on the twenty-ninth, he and Shaw lingered only long enough for Burr to take delivery of a boat ordered earlier, hire a crew for it, and make inquiries about Wilkinson. Finding that the general had not yet arrived in the already heavily industrial metropolis of the West, he left behind a note for him to pick up when he came through. "Send your letters &c to Louisville," it read in part. "Yet I undertain [sic] hopes of meeting you at that place. Make haste, for I have some things to say which cannot be written." It would be more than a month before the unwritable things got said, for Burr would not find Wilkinson at Louisville either.

The boat which carried him and his party away from Pittsburgh on the thirtieth was an ark, "properly speaking," Aaron explained to his daughter, "a floating house, sixty feet by fourteen, containing diningroom, kitchen with fireplace, and two bedrooms, roofed from stem to stern; steps to go up, and a walk on the top the whole length; glass windows, etc." More often than not, newcomers to the Ohio basin traversed the river in a Kentucky Boat, an oblong craft with squared-off ends, surmounted by a rude shack with holes in its sides for the steering oars. In 1805, this simple flatboat could be had for forty dollars. Bent on traveling in style, Burr paid $133 for his water-borne palace.

Thirty-six hours downriver, it overtook another and more heavily laden ark. This one belonged to Congressman Lyon, traveling from Washington to his home in Eddyville, Kentucky. For four days the friends journeyed together, their boats lashed. Main topic of their conversation, according to Lyon's subsequent recollection: the political advantages Burr could enjoy were he willing to make his home in one of the transmontane states. To this discourse the colonel listened politely, no doubt nodding occasionally in his pleasant, noncommittal, Chesterfieldian way.

The fourth of May brought them to the "handsome little Town" of Marietta, Ohio, at the mouth of the Muskingum River. From this point Lyon pressed on alone, while Burr and Shaw went ashore to pass a day or two as the guests of Dr. Robert Wallace, a veteran of the war of the Revolution who, like Burr, had fought with distinction at the Battle of Monmouth in New Jersey. One of their host's sons, Dr. David C. Wallace, had just returned from a trip to Philadelphia, where he had purchased a microscope and slides for Harman Blennerhassett, a wealthy landowner residing in the neighborhood. This Blennerhassett, Burr learned, was a Briton by birth and a member of an aristocratic Irish family. Coming into the American West with his wife a few years before, he had bought the upper half of an island fourteen miles below Marietta, on the Virginia side of the river, and had converted its 179 acres into a showplace. On a rise of land visible from the river, the transplanted aristocrat had erected a fourteen-room, horseshoe-shaped mansion of poplar wood and oak and painted it a gleaming white. Fronting this impressive structure was a wide, sloping lawn, flanked on one side by a 150-foot-long graveled walk. A low hedge of "privysally" edged the outer rim of the walk and served as a border for a two-acre flower garden, planted to exotic blooms and native shrubs and broken by serpentine paths and little grottoes dripping with honeysuckle and eglantines. Bringing into the area a fortune, originally amounting to about $100,000, Blennerhassett had purchased a partnership in a Marietta mercantile firm, and his investments in this operation and in his insular holdings had contributed enormously to the economic growth of the frontier along the upper Ohio. Educated in good colleges, he now devoted much of his time to reading, study, and scientific experimentation in the library-laboratory of his island home. When Burr expressed an interest in meeting this bearer of culture, learning—and capital—to the backwoods, the younger Dr. Wallace countered with a proposition. If, on his trip downriver, Burr would convey the microscope and slides to Blennerhassett, Wallace would furnish him with a letter of introduction to that gentleman and his attractive wife. Thus it came about that as night was falling on the fifth or sixth of May 1805 Aaron Burr set foot for the first time on Blennerhassett Island, the Camelot in the wilderness which was to become the geographic center of his expedition and whose owner would be one of its most conspicuous casualties.

AND ITS MOST LAMENTABLE ONE. For there was something about bumbling, well-meaning Harman Blennerhassett which makes one wish he had never met Aaron Burr. The proprietor of the "enchanted isle," a witness would avow at the trial in Richmond, "had every kind of sense but common sense." True enough, but the other senses, the uncommon ones, were endearing. Blennerhassett was a decent, honest, charitable man, whose nearsightedness, a family weakness, was matched by a congenital inability to see the deficiency of those qualities in other people. Burr himself was overly trusting, his capacity for gulling others exceeded only by the ease and frequency with which he in turn was gulled. But in 1805 his ambitions were at flood and the uncanny influence he exerted over his intimates— a power of which he himself seems to have been unaware—was at its zenith. He needed money for his plans; Blennerhassett appeared to have it; and the singularly romantic elements of Blennerhassett's nature—elements that the possession of wealth had long permitted him to indulge—made him ripe for the plucking. His wife Margaret shared many of his traits, a mutuality of feeling and thought undergirding a marriage that was a lifelong love affair. The day would come when the Blennerhassetts would recognize their involvement in the so-called conspiracy for the mistake it was, and when in 1831 death released Harman from the poverty of his closing years he would leave behind an engagingly written journal, valuable for the clues it offers to the conduct and personality of Aaron Burr.

The early personal histories of the Blennerhassetts explain their vulnerability to Burr's imperial projects. Born in 1764, Harman grew up at Killorglin, County Kerry, in the southwest corner of Ireland, on a four-thousand-acre estate called Castle Conway that had been in his family since the reign of the first King James. As he was the last born of three sons, the likelihood of his inheriting under the law of primogeniture was remote. For this reason, his parents saw to it that he received the sort of education that would allow him to pursue a legal career. But before he had completed his schooling—most of it at Trinity College, Dublin—and had won admission to the Irish bar, both brothers were gone. Consequently, at the death of his father in 1792, he became the master of the Castle Conway estate.

Had he been content to walk the pathways of his forebears, he could have lived out his life in comfort, supported by the income from his father's fortune and the rent rolls of a well-tenanted manor. But Blennerhassett had immersed himself in the political writings of the *philosophes* of eighteenth-century France. He had witnessed at first hand some aspects of the French Revolution. In 1793 he joined the Dublin branch of the Society of United Irishmen. Originally a reform movement established to resist British oppression of large sections of the population of Eire, this group by the time Harman joined it had become revolutionary. Its members were pledged to promote the severance of the Emerald Isle from Great Britain. The minute Harman entered its ranks, he became subject to arrest, imprisonment, and the sequestration of his property. His decision two years later to sell Castle Conway and emigrate to the New World was a case of getting out before he lost everything.

But it was not his only motive. Having complicated his life by joining a radical and outlawed organization in 1793, he complicated it in another way in 1794. He married Margaret Agnew, a harmless enough step in itself, except for one thing: seven years his junior, a tall and stately beauty with lustrous, almond-shaped blue eyes and splendidly mandarin features, Margaret was his niece, a daughter of his sister Catherine. Such alliances were not unheard-of in eighteenth-century Europe; nor do they seem to have been frowned on in the higher echelons of Irish society. But the relationship worried its participants. That one of the Blennerhassetts' reasons for leaving Ireland was to get away from people who knew the circumstances of their marriage is shown by the lengths to which they went, after reaching the United States, to keep their close relationship a secret. As for their determination, after breaking their ties with the Old World, to settle on the far edges of the New, all "that was exotic and adventurous," Ray Swick notes in his vivid account of Harman's first thirty-two years, "struck a responsive chord deep within [the Blennerhassetts'] . . . beings, and in this respect they were greatly influenced by the prevailing themes of current French literature typified by Rousseau and his idyllic portrait of the unspoiled, primitive life . . . in the American West."

Arriving at New York in the summer of 1796, they remained in the city or nearby for a short time; but the area displeased them. It was not the new and unspoiled country for which they were looking, not the habitat of the "natural" aristocrats of the wood, the "savages of North America," of whom Rousseau had written with such irresistible ignorance. Besides, it was too hot and the atmosphere unhealthy, an important consideration to Harman, a dedicated hypochondriac. Like many revolutionaries, he liked the common people best in absentia. Judging from what he saw in New York, he complained to a kinsman back home, the "beau monde" of America was fifty years behind that of Europe. Onward the Blennerhassetts moved, to spend another short spell in Philadelphia. In their eyes, that place, too, had its drawbacks. The moral tone was low; the City of Brotherly Love was a Babylon! Taking issue with some "rhapsodies on American morals" in a guidebook to the Quaker City, Harman wrote that their author had "mistaken the love of order and character[,] to which the [Society of] friends are . . . attached . . . [,] for all the virtues. For here you find every where . . . a shameless prostitution . . . Alas it has tainted all orders in fortune. Mrs. [William] Bingham whose husband is now the wealthiest citizen . . . , openly parading with a French gallant whilst inferior fathers of families are more covertly but as generally corrupt, and a nurse who is not a prostitute if she could be hired, would be regarded as a phenomenon . . ." When Anne Bingham, the unquestioned queen of American society, asked the Blennerhassetts to her three-storied residence known as "The Mansion House," they declined the invitation.

Marietta first saw them in the autumn of 1797. Harman was then in his mid-thirties, "six feet high," with prematurely gray hair, bulging forehead, and large hooked nose, his markedly poor posture and graceless movements the more noticeable because of the tallness of his slim frame. By the end of the following year, the upper half of what was to become Blennerhassett Island was his; large portions of its dense forest were being cleared away. At least three years went into the erection of the mansion, the laying out of the grounds, and the raising of the barns and other outbuildings for a nearby farm, but these labors had been completed when Aaron Burr came calling. The scene he beheld in the failing reddish light of that balmy May evening in 1805 was Blennerhassett Island at its most appealing.

4

THE COLONEL WAS keeping a journal of his travels, a voluminous one apparently, for toward the end of the month he would be telling Theodosia, for whom it was written, that already it had become too bulky for the mail. Only a few fragments of it are now available, and these say nothing of his first stop at the island. For that we must rely on an account of the visit in the handwriting of Harman, Jr., second oldest of the three Blennerhassett boys.

"Burr," this document relates, "*first paid a visit* to the Island unsolicited, introducing himself in *the spring of 1805* at nightfall in company with a Mr. Shaw . . . He was received by Mr. and Mrs. Blennerhassett with the usual hospitality of the island—Mr. Blennerhassett being much pleased with the accomplished manners and agreeable wit and conversation of the ex-vice president of the U.S. They all spent the evening in general conversation till about eleven o'clock, when Burr was informed that an apartment and beds were prepared for him and companion in Mr. Blennerhassett's house . . . Burr and Shaw politely thanked the family, in spite of all pressing intreaties to stay on the island all night, preferring to sleep in his boat at the beach, saying 'there is no society in sleep, and we will see you again in the morning.' He always on his excursions made his bed himself in the simplicity of the soldier. Mr. and Mrs. Blennerhassett walked down to the boat from the house with their visitors . . . ; and on approaching the mooring, in their descent to the water's edge, Burr's foot slipped from the sand bank and he fell down. He immediately . . . recovered himself, observing 'That's an ill omen.' The parties very politely separated then, Burr and Shaw entering the boat and Blennerhassett and lady returning to their mansion."

That the conversation was "general" does not eliminate the likelihood that Burr proffered some explanation for his Western travels. Subsequent letters between him and Blennerhassett reveal that he dropped a few hints, not enough to expose the precise lineaments of what he had in mind, but enough to tantalize the star-struck occupants of the enchanted isle.

"On the morning following," the story of his visit concludes, he and his companions "came to breakfast at the house with Mr. Blennerhassett and . . . I think on that or the day following, Burr departed . . . down the river."*

Cincinnati was his next landing site. Here it was that the promoters of the Indiana Canal Company had agreed to meet

---

* The first printed accounts of Burr's 1805 visit to the island, appearing in the mid 1840's and early 1850's, correctly placed both Mr. and Mrs. Blennerhassett on hand when Burr called. Then in 1858 (Blennerhassett's biographer, Ray Swick, has informed me) James Parton "threw posterity off course by maintaining in his life of Burr that Mrs. Blennerhassett entertained Burr by herself and thus it has generally remained ever since." I am indebted to Swick for calling my attention to this account of Burr's visit in the Blennerhassett Papers at the Library of Congress.

at the home of Senator John Smith and perfect their plans. Burr, it will be recalled, had joined this movement in the hopes of getting money for his Western projects. He got it by rather devious means, it would seem, for his unique way with the language of the law is visible in the form which the company took when it materialized a few months later. Like the Manhattan Company bank that the colonel originated for the Republican Party under the guise of giving New York City a water system, the canal company turned out to be primarily a device for enriching its promulgators. Little is known of its operations except that it sold stock by promising to build a canal that was never dug, and that it used the funds raised in this manner to create a bank of issue—from which Aaron Burr is known to have obtained a loan of $25,000.

Senator Smith owned a mercantile firm in Cincinnati, but his recently built house, where the conferences occurred, was at Terrace Park, a few miles to the west. A Virginian by birth, a handsome and large-framed man of rather solemn demeanor, Smith had migrated to the Northwest in 1790, to become prominent in its affairs—first as a Baptist minister; later as a merchant, grain-mill operator, and supplier and contractor to the United States Army; and, since the admission of Ohio to the Union in 1803, a senator from that state.

Business and finance dominated the conversations at his Terrace Park home, but other topics intruded. Americans everywhere were discussing the country's differences with Spain, the frequently demonstrated determination of President Jefferson to acquire West Florida (and eventually East Florida as well) by any means, diplomatic or otherwise; and the growing prospect of war—a not unwelcome possibility to Westerners, eager to see the fertile savannahs of the Floridas in American hands. Burr made no secret of his desire to lead a liberating expedition against the Spanish colonies, asserting, however, that he would take such action only in the event of war.

Two of Burr's listeners at Terrace Park—his old friend,

65

General Dayton, and his host, Senator Smith—not only found his statements of interest but soon resolved to support his designs. Dayton was in his forty-fifth year that fall, chunkily built, with a hawklike face, his firm mouth wedged between heavy jowls. He and Burr had known each other since their mutual childhood in Elizabethtown, New Jersey, where Dayton still resided. During the war they had marched to Quebec together under Benedict Arnold. Although they belonged to opposing political parties, they often found themselves in agreement on issues coming before the United States Congress. A heavy speculator, Dayton in recent years had acquired title to 25,000 acres of military land, lying between the Little and Big Miami Rivers in the Northwest. He was interested in any development apt to increase the value of this investment, whether it took the form of a canal around the Falls of the Ohio or an attack on the colonies of Spain.

Senator Smith, an ardent Jeffersonian, had good reason to believe that what the former Vice President was proposing was in line with what the President wanted. While the Ohio senator was still in Washington, earlier in the year, Jefferson had solicited a confidential interview with him. Was it not a fact, the President asked, that Smith was well acquainted with the higher Spanish officials in the Floridas? When Smith replied in the affirmative, Jefferson stated "that a war with Spain seemed to be inevitable; and that it was . . . desirable to know the feelings of those men [the Spanish officials] toward the United States, and whether reliance could be placed on their friendship if a war should take place." He concluded these ruminations with a request that Smith visit the Floridas and sound out the officials there. Smith agreed and reported to the President "that the governor, the inferior officers, and the inhabitants [of the Floridas] generally, were not only friendly but were desirous of attaching themselves to the United States."

Burr's remarks at Terrace Park may or may not have been his first open revelation of his contemplated "march on the City of Mexico." They were certainly not his last, for after doing his part toward the founding of the canal company, he would devote much of the rest of his first tour of the frontier to an effort to interest influential Westerners in his invasion project. Readily understandable is the comment of historian Francis S. Philbrick on this behavior. "What a conspiracy!" Philbrick exclaims in his *Rise of the West*. "Not only the people of the West but those of the East, the government in Washington, and the ministers of foreign powers (by invitation) were watching its production." The celebrated Mr. Burr was moving through the West as though in a goldfish bowl. It was hardly the usual way to operate a "conspiracy."

5

ON 19 MAY the colonel spent a few hours in Louisville, examining the Falls of the Ohio, site of the projected ditch that the Indiana Canal Company would never dig. Learning that Wilkinson was still days behind him, he again left a letter for the general to pick up en route. Wilkinson, heading for St. Louis to assume his new duties as governor of upper Louisiana, reached Louisville on the twenty-eighth, and from there sent a note to his friend General Adair in Mercer County, Kentucky. "I was to have introduced my friend Burr to you," he told the Kentucky general, "but in this I failed by accident. He understands your merits and reckons on you. Prepare to meet me and I will tell you all. We must have a peek into the unknown world beyond us."

Burr, meanwhile, was pushing on. A few miles downriver from the falls, he moored the houseboat and went ashore, to spend the next two weeks traveling overland. He stopped first at Eddyville for a visit with Matthew Lyon; next at Frankfort, for talks with former Senator John Brown of Kentucky, prominent Jeffersonian politician, now connected with the establishment of the Indiana Canal Company; then at Lexington, for no known reason other than that old friends resided there and Burr could count on being cheered and feted, which he was. Somewhere along the line, probably at or near Lexington, he encountered General Adair, who learned from their conversation that "the intentions of Colonel Burr . . . were to prepare and lead an expedition into Mexico, predicated on a war between the United States and Spain."

The twenty-ninth brought the wandering colonel to Nashville, Tennessee. In this bustling, growing settlement on the banks of the Cumberland River, he enjoyed what amounted to a Roman triumph. Flying flags and booming cannons saluted his arrival. His host during a five-day stay was Andrew Jackson. At thirty-eight, the future President had not yet attained the worldwide fame that would fasten his name to an era, but he was well on his way. Twice he had represented his state in Congress. For six years he had sat on the superior court. Now, as major general of the Tennessee militia, he was its ranking military officer. His acquaintanceship with Burr ran back several years, and he was grateful to the New Yorker for the substantial part he had played, as a United States senator, in bringing Tennessee into the Union. To whatever Burr told him of his Mexico plans he listened with the approval of a man determined sooner or later—and preferably sooner—on seeing "the hated Spanish dons and their allies, the savage hostiles," expelled from the frontier West. In later years, taking up this chore where Burr had left off, Jackson would do more than any single American to win the Floridas for the United States. Of the not always entirely scrupulous methods whereby he achieved these ends, Remini writes in his biography of the great Tennessean, "Burr would have been proud."

Not yet in existence was the stately house later erected some ten miles from Nashville and named "The Hermitage." In 1805 Jackson and his beloved Rachel were living on the site of this mansion-to-be, but their domicile was a plain square blockhouse consisting of one large room on the first floor and two smaller ones above. In this unpretentious dwelling they made their distinguished guest comfortable. Into its ground-floor room crowded men and women from miles around, summoned by its proud owner to meet a visitor whose presence added cachet to the Jacksons' status as the social leaders of their community. When, on 3 June, Burr departed, the open boat which carried him 220 miles down the Cumberland to his waiting ark was provided by his Nashville hosts. Three days later, he at last caught up with General Wilkinson, who had broken his journey to St. Louis at Fort Massac, a lonely military outpost on the northern shores of the Ohio, near where that river spills into the Mississippi.

They conferred for four days. About what? Commercial and political matters only, according to Wilkinson: the Indiana Canal Company, other moneymaking possibilities, whether or not Burr should settle in the West and either run for Congress or seek appointment to some high administrative post such as the governorship of lower Louisiana. At Fort Massac the colonel abandoned his ark. Orders had been issued for a detachment of soldiers there to reinforce the country's military posts along the lower Mississippi. Fitted out to carry the first contingent south was "an elegant barge," the "private property" of Captain Daniel Bissell, the Fort Massac commandant. On this craft, crewed by a sergeant and ten oarsmen, with sails spread and colors fluttering, Burr descended the Mississippi River.

There were numerous stops along the way, a fairly long one at Natchez, Mississippi Territory—"a town of three or four hundred houses," Burr informed his daughter; "the inhabitants traders and mechanics, but surrounded by wealthy planters, among whom I have been entertained with great hospitality and taste. These planters are, many of them, men of education and refinement: live as well as yours, and have generally better houses. We are now going through a settled country, and during the residue of my voyage to Orleans, about three hundred miles, I shall take breakfast and dinner each day at the house of some gentleman on shore. I take no letters of introduction; but, whenever I hear of any gentleman whose acquaintance or hospitalities I should desire, I send word that I am coming to see him, and have always met the most cordial reception." While the barge was riding at anchor off Natchez, Robert Williams, the governor of Mississippi Territory, came aboard to shake the colonel's hand and wish him well with his plans, whatever they were.

Burr reached New Orleans 25 June and remained for three weeks. He was delighted with the place. Were it closer to the plantation of the Joseph Alstons in South Carolina, he wrote Theodosia, he would seriously consider making it his home. But she need not worry. His whereabouts would always be dictated by her whereabouts. "The city," he told her, 'is larger than I expected, and there are found many more than would be supposed living in handsome style. They are cheerful, gay, and easy. I have promised to return here next fall. I go on the 10th instant (July) by land to Kentucky, and thence, probably, to St. Louis. *À la santé Madame Alston*, is generally the first toast at every table I have been. Then we say some evil things of Mr. Alston . . . *Encore*, adieu . . . *Le pauvre* A.B.A. [Aaron Burr Alston, his grandson], I can find nothing here to send him." As a contribution to Theodosia's education, he provided her with demographic data: French- or Spanish-speaking natives of the Crescent City were called "Old Louisianans"; English-speaking newcomers from other parts of the Union, "Americans."

Among the "Americans" was his old friend Edward Livingston, of the well-known New York family. A congressman during the tie election of 1800–1, Livingston had supported Jefferson on all thirty-six of the ballots cast in the House of Representatives. Later—heatedly—he refuted repeated allegations that Burr had secretly urged him to change his vote. Jefferson made Livingston the district attorney in New York, and simultaneously Governor Clinton named him mayor of

New York City. In 1803, while he was holding both offices, misfortune fell. One of his financial agents defaulted, leaving Livingston owing the federal government close to $50,000. Divesting himself of his property in New York and resigning his high posts, he migrated to New Orleans to begin life anew. There he prospered, both as a lawyer and as an investor in local real estate. Eventually he repaid the government in full, and his codification of the laws of Louisiana state, though never adopted, produced a document of such clarity and distinction that Sir Henry Maine, famous English jurist and historian, pronounced its author "the first legal genius" of the modern era.

Burr reached the Crescent City just in time to congratulate Livingston on his marriage to a young widow, a refugee from troubled, French-owned Santo Domingo. "Without a single good feature," he reported to Theodosia, "she is very agreeable . . . Fair, pale, with jet black hair and eyes—little sparkling black eyes, which seem to be made for far other purposes than those of . . . vision."

During his stay in the city, the colonel spent considerable time with members of a local organization called the Mexican Society of New Orleans. Its three hundred adherents gathered data on Mexico and shared an ardent desire to see that region freed from its Spanish overlords. Burr, according to biographer Davis, found in the Crescent City a large number of individuals eager to participate in his projected expedition. Among them were some "of the principal militia officers, . . . the Catholic bishop, [and] . . . Madame Xavier Tarjcon, superior of the convent of Ursuline nuns . . ." On an invitation from the bishop, Burr visited the convent. "We conversed at first through the grate," he wrote of this experience, "but presently I was admitted within, and I passed an hour with them greatly to my satisfaction. None of that calm monotony which I had expected. All was gayety, *wit* and sprightliness."

Wilkinson had supplied the colonel with some letters of introduction. One was to the Marqués de Casa Calvo, the commissioner Spain had sent to New Orleans to oversee the transfer of Louisiana to the United States and whose continued presence there in 1805 was a source of worry to the youthful governor of lower Louisiana, William C. C. Claiborne. Another was to Daniel Clark, a wealthy Irish-born merchant and land speculator, who had acted as American consul in the Crescent City prior to the transfer and would represent the territory as its first nonvoting delegate to the United States Congress. When the "explosion" (as it has been called) came—when Jefferson declared Burr's Western exertions illegal and demanded his arrest—Clark, like many prominent Americans, went to considerable lengths to deny any connection with the colonel's projects. The wealthy New Orleans merchant was associated with the Mexican Society. On two extended journeys to Veracruz in 1805 and 1806 he admittedly gathered "important information as to the military and naval force in Mexico," but to what degree, if any, he contributed to Burr's expeditionary arrangements, it is impossible to say.

Officially, Governor Claiborne gave only passing notice to the visit of the former Vice President. On 26 June he wrote Madison that the colonel had arrived. Three weeks later, he wrote Jefferson that he had departed. Still, there is indication that the presence of the colonel in a city then rife with antigovernment intrigues stirred ripples of anxiety in faraway Washington. It was during Burr's three-week sojourn there that the Administration decided that henceforth important communications between Claiborne and the Secretary of State should be carried on in cipher.

In Philadelphia, months earlier, Burr had called on Yrujo, the Spanish minister to the United States: a brazen action, given the plans the colonel was considering, and, as time would prove, an indiscreet one. In New Orleans he is believed to have got in touch with Morales, the onetime Spanish intendant of that city, but for some reason he made no use of the letter of introduction to the Marqués de Casa Calvo.

Daniel Clark later explained that he entertained Burr "as well to do honour to the recommendation he brought, as because I was pleased with his society." Clark also noted that "I showed him the civilities usual on such occasions. In this I was not singular. He dined, I believe, with Governor Claiborne, and I know received the greatest attentions from several of the principal inhabitants, and, on his departure, I lent him my horses to go as far as Natchez, with a servant to bring them back."

Four days of travel—part of it by schooner on Lake Pontchartrain, the rest by horseback across West Florida—carried Burr to Natchez. There he lingered for "near a week." Already formed in his mind were the plans for the remaining two months of his Western tour. He would spend another few days with the Andrew Jacksons, a busy interval climaxed by a memorable ball hosted by the general in his honor at the Talbot Hotel in downtown Nashville. After that, his itinerary would include stops at Lexington, Frankfort, and Louisville, Kentucky. All these visits, he explained in a long communication to Theodosia, were "imposed on me by letters received since I last wrote you, and by my previous engagements." He did not say what the letters and engagements dealt with. Land speculation? The possibility of a political future for himself somewhere in the Mississippi Valley? His Mexican project? Probably a little of all three, for the one certain thing that can be said of Aaron Burr's first passage of the western waters is that it was essentially exploratory—the pilgrimage of a man in search of his future.

When he left Natchez in late May, it was to strike into the unsettled country stretching northward of that riverside settlement to the borders of Tennessee: "a vile country," he wrote his daughter, "destitute of springs and of running water—think of drinking the nasty puddle-water, covered with green scum and full of animalculae—bah!" He sent Theodosia a map so that she could follow him through 450 miles of wilderness. He called her attention to the presence on it of a road, running from

Natchez to Nashville and identified as "cut by order of the minister of war." It wasn't there, he advised her. There was nothing but bayou and swamp, underbrush and forest, venomous snakes and swarming insects. Harsh country to traverse on foot in any climate, especially in the steamy heat of a Mississippi August. En route from New Orleans to Natchez he had hired a scout, a woodsman familiar with the often all-but-invisible old Indian trail he trod. The former Vice President of the United States followed the Natchez Trace.

And there we must part company with him, temporarily, and attend to developments elsewhere. What makes these events startling is their timing. At this date (early August 1805), Burr's Mexican plans remained only plans, or only dreams. He had done nothing that even his cleverest enemy could construe as contrary to the laws of the land. He had spoken to heaven knows how many people of his desire to lead an expedition against the Spanish domains, but he had not as yet recruited a single soldier, or ordered the construction of a single boat to transport his warriors, or purchased a single weapon or barrel of military provender. Yet, even as he slogged northward on the Natchez Trace, a newspaper one thousand miles away was presenting to its readers an account of the tangle of plots soon labeled in the public mind as the Burr Conspiracy.

5

Spanish Minister Yrujo and the

Invention of a Conspiracy

H OW LONG WILL IT BE before we shall hear of *Col. Burr* being at the head of a *revolution* party on the western waters?"

Under the headline "Queries," this question appeared in the top left-hand corner of the front page of the 2 August 1805 issue of the *Gazette of the United States*, onetime journalistic mouthpiece for the political policies of Alexander Hamilton and the largest Federalist newspaper in Philadelphia. Seven more questions followed:

"Is it a fact that Col. Burr *has formed a plan* to engage the adventurous and enterprising *young men* from the Atlantic States to come into Louisiana?

"Is it one of the inducements that an *immediate convention* will be called from the *states* bordering on the Ohio and Mississippi, to form a separate government?

"Is it another, that all the *public lands* are to be seized and partitioned among those *states*, except what is *reserved* for the warlike friends and followers of *Burr* in the revolution?

"Is it part of the plan for the new states to grant these lands in *bounties* to entice inhabitants from the Atlantic States?

"How soon will the forts and magazines in all the military ports at New Orleans and on the Mississippi be in the hands of Col. Burr's revolution party?

"How soon will Col. Burr engage in the reduction of Mexico, by granting *liberty* to its inhabitants, and seizing on its treasures, aided by British ships and forces?

"What difficulty can there be in completing a revolution in one summer, among the western states, with the four temptations. 1st. of all the Congress land.—2d. Throwing off the public debt.—3d. Seizing on their own commercial revenues.—4th. Spanish plunder in conjunction with the British?"

Whence came these damaging questions? From the Marqués de Casa Yrujo? Burr thought so, saying later to his friend Erich Bollman that he "knew" Yrujo was the author of the "Queries"—a statement that Bollman repeated to Thomas Jefferson. The Spanish minister had long since demonstrated his ability to achieve his ends by anonymous contributions to the press. How better could he scuttle Aaron Burr's anti-Spanish plans, whatever they were, than by inventing a treasonable conspiracy and fastening it on the former Vice President before that nomadic gentleman could get around to putting his actual plans into operation?

Anthony Merry took the appearance of the "Queries" to mean that Burr had already "commenced" disunionist activities "in the Western Country." Literal to a fault, the British minister seemingly never so much as suspected that Yrujo had inspired their publication and that the schemes they envisaged existed only in the Spaniard's mind. Merry read them with a mixture of joy and alarm: joy because, as he reported to London, Burr's efforts seemed to be meeting "with Success"; alarm because the colonel "or some of His Agents have either been indiscreet in their communications, or have been betrayed by some Person, in whom they considered that they had Reason to confide, for the Object of his Journey has already began to be noticed in the public Prints."

Noticed it was, from one end of the country to the other. Burr was preparing to leave Lexington, after an eleven-day stay there, when a local newspaper, the *Kentucky Gazette*, reprinted the "Queries" in full. If the colonel found them too wild and wonderful to be true, he was not alone. So did the editor of the Philadelphia *Aurora*. Republishing them in that Jeffersonian organ, William Duane pronounced them "the ravings of a concealed traitor, or perhaps of some emissary of a foreign government." He was willing to ascribe them to the French minister, the English minister, or the Spanish minister; or to all three, since it was everywhere known that all three had reason to want to see the growing might of the new American Republic dissipated by internal squabbling. Duane mentioned none of the current ministers by name, but he did remind his readers that the redheaded gentleman from Spain could be pretty cagey, as witness Yrujo's recent attempt to embarrass President Jefferson by soliciting from five prominent American lawyers a legal opinion sternly disapproving of the Administration's conduct vis-à-vis his Catholic Majesty. As to why the convoluted cabals suggested by the "Queries" were laid to the former Vice President, "Mr. Burr," Duane stated, ". . . is exactly such a character as would be open to the *suspicion* of all parties . . . His fortune is destroyed as well as his political character, and disappointment is presumed to render him fit for any enterprize, however desperate."

As the "Queries" seeped across the land, from newspaper to newspaper, their unperturbed protagonist continued his travels. In Frankfort, Burr was a guest at Liberty Hall, the residence former Senator Brown had built on a design provided by Jefferson. From thence he rode to Louisville for another look at the Falls of the Ohio. Now that the Indiana Canal Company was a *fait accompli*, he does not seem to have been happy about the way it was being managed. The people in charge, he would shortly be writing a prospective investor, were badly in need of "more talents and information."

From the falls he again moved down the Ohio, heading for St. Louis and a second conversation with General Wilkinson.

2

FOR WILKINSON HAD reached his destination. From what Burr laughingly called his "palace" in St. Louis, he was beginning to cope with his dual chores as commander in chief of the army and governor of upper Louisiana, while his principal military aide there—New Jersey-born and Maryland-raised Major James Bruff—nursed dark thoughts concerning what he took to be the extra-military and extra-governmental interests of his superior officer. Weeks before Wilkinson's arrival at St. Louis in early July, Yrujo's warnings about Aaron Burr had come to the attention of the Spanish officials in Louisiana and the Floridas. Now unsettling rumors were blowing like pollen up and down the valley of the Mississippi. "The Spanish government," Daniel Clark learned from a friend, "were much alarmed by the rumour of a projected invasion of their provinces, under Col. Burr." What most distressed the wealthy New Orleans merchant was that his name was being linked with these schemes. So was Wilkinson's, and before leaving on the first of his extended trips to Veracruz, Clark took time to inform the general of the reports in a letter dispatched north by fast messenger. Meanwhile, two items in the Kentucky press had caught Major Bruff's eye. One said General Wilkinson was reactivating the old Spanish Conspiracy, "the old plan to form a separate Government west of the Allegany"; the other intimated that the former Vice President was working with him. A veteran of the Revolution, a longtime officer in the regular army, Bruff wanted no part in—no proximity to—any activity detrimental to his country. Then and there—so he related later—the major resolved "to watch the motions of General Wilkinson and Burr."

His opportunities to do so began in late June when he received a message from Wilkinson stating that the general was coming up the Mississippi and requesting the major to meet him "six or eight miles" downriver from St. Louis. Bruff did so. He found the general plainly nervous, seemingly turning over a difficult problem in his mind. Leaving the light barge on which he was traveling, he walked into the woods, beckoning the major to accompany him. He told Bruff that he had "something of importance to communicate"; but before he could elaborate on this statement, as Bruff would testify during the trial of Burr at Richmond, "some Frenchmen from St. Louis . . . [came] rushing through the bushes on us." Wilkinson "damned them" for intruding. "To their faces?" Bruff was asked at Richmond. "No, to me," he replied. As he and Wilkinson hurried back to the barge, the general said that as soon as he was settled in at St. Louis they would resume the conversation.

They did. On three different occasions Bruff was summoned to the parlor of the general's house. "Parlor" was the major's name for the room, possibly because on each occasion he was made to feel like a fly in a spider's web. Each time the general locked the door. Each time he addressed himself to a hodge-podge of topics, heavily pacing the room as he talked and speaking more often than not in what struck Bruff as a "vexed" and "agitated" manner. Again he announced he had "something of importance to communicate." Then, instead of saying what it was, he launched into an outpouring of bizarre questions and assertions, giving Bruff the feeling that he was being subjected to an inquisition, that the general was probing his views, testing him, looking for signs that he was talking to a man to whom he could entrust his "*great secret*."

Afterwards Bruff could not remember exactly in what order Wilkinson presented his thoughts, but he remembered the thoughts. The general, he recalled, "asked me what sort of government would suit Louisiana. Without hesitation, I replied a representative republic would meet both the wishes and expectations of the people." Wilkinson answered that "he was surprised to hear me say so, for the French [meaning the French-

and Spanish-speaking Old Louisianans of the territory] could not understand its principles, or be brought to attend elections; that the American inhabitants were a turbulent set, the mere emptyings of jails, or fugitives from justice, and did not deserve a free government; that a military government was best for these people, and no other was contemplated."

None other contemplated? What did Wilkinson mean by that? Assuming that Bruff understood him correctly, he meant what he said. The general told Bruff not to be deceived by the apparent democracy of the Jefferson Administration. In actuality, it was as despotic as the Federalist Administration it had replaced. Wilkinson said the leaders of the present Administration nurtured two fiendish objectives, both of which they meant to implement in the near future. First, they were going to "seize on the property of the Federalists, and divide it among themselves." Then they were going to "depopulate" most of Louisiana and give its lands to the Americans living on the eastern side of the river. If the Americans refused to move across river to their new property, the Administration would call out the army and push them "over at the point of the bayonet." Wilkinson, his startled listener noted, uttered these assertions "with a very serious face." The major found them ridiculous. When he accused his superior of attributing "principles and motives to the republicans, which they abhorred," a warm altercation ensued, cooling down only when it suddenly occurred to Bruff that if he continued to argue with the general he would never learn what his great secret was. From this point on, he followed the practice, when he could not agree with Wilkinson's statements, of saying nothing at all. His silence, he hoped, would induce Wilkinson to disclose what was on his mind. But Bruff had adopted this tactic too late. Only once, during the closing minutes of their last session, did the general so much as hint at the nature of his secret. "I have now a *grand scheme* in contemplation," he said, adding that it was one that would not only make his fortune, "but the fortunes of all concerned." Having said this, the general paused, seemingly waiting for a comment from Bruff, preferably the expression of a desire to share the wealth. Nothing coming from that quarter, Wilkinson unlocked the parlor door and waved his visitor off, leaving him—as Bruff lamented later—"with only this glimpse of the *secret* for which he had so long been preparing me."

3

A FEW WEEKS LATER, Bruff had his chance to watch the "motions" of both Wilkinson and Burr. The colonel reached St. Louis on 12 September for what turned out to be a visit of approximately one week. Bruff had no direct contact with him, but from time to time he saw the general and his guest conferring together. On the day after Burr arrived, Wilkinson took him out to a cantonment some twelve miles distant for a review of the troops. Bruff saw the two of them when they returned to town, and observed something whose significance he himself may have missed. "The colonel," Bruff testified at Richmond, "strictured the situation and laughed at the general's military notions." Bruff's brief statement, repeated in one of his letters to a friend in Maryland, conjures up a recognizable picture of Aaron Burr, patrician by birth, being patronizing to James Wilkinson, self-made upstart; of Burr displaying that "consciousness of superiority" so often attributed to him by contemporaries and so irritating to some of them. James Wilkinson was not a man to suffer criticism lightly; certainly, not a man to relish being laughed at. What part, one wonders, did long-harbored resentment play in his decision, a year and a half later, to betray Burr's plans to the government and thus open the way to the procedures leading up to the treason trial at Richmond?

Wilkinson's efforts at Richmond to show that he had no knowledge of Aaron Burr's plans and that the colonel's visit to St. Louis in the fall of 1805 was little more than a social call were unconvincing. "Mr. Burr," the general told the court, spoke at

St. Louis "of the imbecility of the Government [,] said it would molder to pieces, die a natural death, or words to that effect, adding that the people of the Western country were ready to revolt. To this I recollect replying that, if he had not profited more by his journey in other respects, he had better have remained at Washington or Philadelphia; for surely, said I, my friend, no person was ever more mistaken! The Western people disaffected to the Government! They are bigoted to Jefferson and democracy." Few of Wilkinson's listeners at Richmond were ready to believe that Colonel Burr had traveled hundreds of miles out of his road to exchange small talk with the busy governor general of upper Louisiana. Perhaps Burr did say that the Westerners were in a rebellious mood, if only by way of rehearsing the palaver he again would bestow on Anthony Merry when he returned to Washington. Perhaps Wilkinson did tell him that the Westerners were "bigoted to Jefferson." An accurate appraisal, certainly, for Jefferson was their hero, the man who had got their river for them, and most of them were indeed bigoted to him. But Burr knew it already. As Jefferson himself wrote later, if Burr ever entertained the notion that any real disunionist sentiment existed in the West, he knew better after his tour of that country.

For what actually happened during Burr's stay in St. Louis, we must depend on the colonel. It was during that visit in September 1805, Burr later told Andrew Jackson, that he and Wilkinson "settled the plan for an attack on Mexico." The "motions" of the two men, not only while Burr was at St. Louis but before he got there and after he left, show this to be the case. Four days prior to Burr's arrival, Wilkinson, in a letter to Secretary of War Dearborn, recommended that in the event of a war with Spain the United States seize the northern provinces of Mexico, meaning principally the regions now covered by the states of Texas and New Mexico. Wilkinson assured the secretary that it could be done, "that the distance to Santa Fe did not exceed nine hundred miles," that "only one mountain range had to be crossed," and that "enough food could be obtained along the route to maintain" the invasion forces. The general based these statements on information gathered by officers he had sent out to reconnoiter portions of what would come to be known as the Santa Fe Trail. A few months later, in a more elaborate effort to ascertain the best route to Mexico, he authorized another expedition into the Southwest under Lieutenant Zebulon Montgomery Pike, thus instigating the now famous exploration during which that intrepid subaltern discovered the mountaintop which bears his name. During his summer wanderings, Burr himself had made inquiries about the routes to Santa Fe, and it can be assumed that he and Wilkinson compared notes during their conference at the governor-general's "palace."

Shortly after Burr's arrival in St. Louis, Major Bruff was approached by Judge Rufus Easton of the territorial superior court. The judge, according to Bruff's testimony at Richmond, said that Burr had asked Easton "whether there was any officer of experience and enterprise who could be trusted with the command of an expedition to Santa Fe." Easton obviously hoped Bruff himself would volunteer for the job. He didn't, and the matter was dropped. A Timothy Kibbey, visiting St. Louis from nearby St. Charles at about the same time, was similarly propositioned by Wilkinson, who boasted that "in the course of eighteen months" he—Wilkinson—would be leading an "attack upon the spanish Dominions."

Some students of the conspiracy sense in Wilkinson's behavior in the fall of 1805 a degree of equivocation, suggesting that even then the general was weighing in his mind the possible advantages to himself of betraying Burr when the time was ripe. Substance for this suspicion is found in Wilkinson's statement under oath at Richmond that, soon after the colonel's departure from St. Louis, the general dispatched a letter to Washington, informing Robert Smith, the Secretary of the Navy, that "Burr is about something, but whether internal or external, I cannot discover. I think you should keep an eye on him." Though Wilkinson was unable to produce a copy of this letter, it doesn't follow that he didn't write it. If in the fall of 1805 he was already thinking of exposing his collaborator in intrigue, it would be useful when he did so to be able to point to this warning to Secretary Smith as "proof" of, first, his burning patriotism, and second, his ignorance of Burr's schemes.

Equivocation was Wilkinson's pattern. In 1805 he was still the Wilkinson who in the days of the Spanish Conspiracy was drafting eloquent petitions, urging the Spanish officials to open the Mississippi to the American settlers, and at the same time, as Agent 13, sending coded letters to the Spanish governor advising him to keep the river closed as the best way to induce the Kentuckians to leave the Union. Money was Wilkinson's greatest need. As a contemporary recorded, he always traveled "abroad" in splendor, "gold stirrups & spurs" on his horse, "gold leopard claws to his leopard saddle cloth," and gold buttons flashing from his uniform. The exploratory expeditions Wilkinson ordered into the Southwest and elsewhere were as much commercial as military, all of them in some way connected with the fur-trading and real-estate ventures in which he engaged with various local entrepreneurs, such as Auguste Chouteau, who in his thirteenth year had helped found St. Louis and who by Wilkinson's time there was its richest inhabitant. One is struck by the bitterness of the general's declaration to Major Bruff that, "having made fortunes for many who did not . . . thank him for it," he was now with his *grand scheme* going to make a fortune for himself. The general knew of Burr's calls on Anthony Merry; he knew that Charles Williamson was still trying to get British government money for the "march to the City of Mexico." If those funds materialized, then perhaps Wilkinson would stay with Burr; if not, then like a Roman haruspex divining the future in the entrails of a pig, he would study the run of events and jump whichever way promised the greatest profits to himself.

It has always been taken for granted that Wilkinson's betrayal came as a total surprise to Burr. No doubt, the act itself did. Burr's code, extraordinarily flexible in most respects, forbade that sort of behavior; a gentleman was loyal to his friends. Still, there exist persuasive indications that by the time the colonel disembarked at St. Louis in September 1805, he was beginning to realize that, insofar as his plans depended on the cooperation of James Wilkinson, he was leaning on an uncertain prop. One discerns in some of his letters a deep annoyance at Wilkinson's delays in leaving Washington after not only having agreed that he and Burr would descend the Ohio together but also, it would seem, having suggested that instead of buying a vessel for himself the colonel go as a passenger on the general's flatboat. During his first sojourn at the Falls of the Ohio, Burr spent time at Jeffersonville, on the Indiana side of the river, in the company of Judge Thomas T. Davis of the territorial court. Before leaving the area, Burr penned a note for Wilkinson, reading in part: *"Before you touch the Kentucky shore in this vicinity*, see and converse with . . . Davis . . . Your friends are apprehensive that something is meditated of your personal convenience. Verb. sat. sap." Wilkinson later claimed that this caution alluded "to an intention to arrest" him "on a false claim of debt." But was that the whole meaning of Burr's ominous "Verb. sat. sap."? Or was he saying in effect to the general, "You do have enemies, you do need friends, and you'd better stick with them"? A couple of months later, with Yrujo's "Queries" rattling across the country, Burr wrote Wilkinson: "I never take any sort of liberty with any man's secrets but my own." Definitely, this points to a growing concern in Burr's mind. He was on the frontier now, in that part of the country where people remembered Wilkinson's part in the Spanish Conspiracy and assumed him to be a pensioner of his Catholic Majesty. Surrounded by this gossip, Burr may well have begun to view Wilkinson as one of the sources of the rumors connecting the colonel's travels with traitorous machinations. Burr would have done well to have heeded these suspicions. They were essentially correct. "It is necessary . . . ," Vicente Folch, the governor of West Florida, would be writing the governor general of Cuba on 25 June 1807, "to inform your Excellency that during the disturbances of Burr the aforesaid general [Wilkinson] has, by means of a person in his confidence, constantly maintained a correspondence with me, in which he has laid before me not only the information which he acquired, but also his intentions for the various exigencies in which he might find himself."

A military acquaintance, hearing that Burr meant to make Wilkinson his second-in-command in the event of an invasion of Mexico, observed that "General Wilkinson would act as lieutenant to no man in existence." To which Burr replied: "But you are in error. Wilkinson will act as *lieutenant* to *me*." Burr overrated his powers. A wiser man would have recognized what was so obvious to others, that James Wilkinson was a law unto himself. But Burr was not a sage; he was a dreamer, one of those persons who, when a dazzling plan forms in his head, considers it already accomplished. All he understood about Wilkinson, as he later "declared most solemnly" to Matthew L. Davis, was that without him a conquest of the Spanish dominions would be impossible. Whatever men Burr could recruit on his own would be "at first little better than a mob," quite incapable of executing a difficult military mission unless assisted by the trained and disciplined troops at the disposal of the commander in chief of the army. His choices were clear. He must rely on Wilkinson or give up his project. It was a case of prudence versus risk, and in the end, true to his nature, he gambled. He put his trust in the general and hoped for the best.

4

BURR WAS STILL on the rivers, en route to St. Louis, when Daniel Clark of New Orleans undertook to apprise Wilkinson of the "absurd and wild reports" that were beginning to circulate in lower Louisiana. "The tale is a horrid one, if well told," Clark informed the general. "Kentucky, Tennessee, the state of Ohio, with part of Georgia and Carolina," the rumors ran, "are to be bribed, with the plunder of the Spanish countries west of us, to separate from the Union." The general, Clark revealed, was being "spoken of as his [Burr's] right hand man, and even I am now supposed to be of consequence enough to combine with Generals and Vice-Presidents. At any other time but the present, I should amuse myself vastly at the folly and fears of those who are affected with these idle tales; but being on the point of setting off for Vera Cruz, on a large mercantile speculation, I feel cursedly hurt at the rumours, and might, in consequence of Spanish jealousy, get into a hobble I could not easily get out of."

Clark was of the opinion—a mere "suspicion," he admitted —that the principal originator of the reports was Stephen Minor, a wealthy Mississippi planter. A Philadelphian by birth, Minor in the 1780's had become a subject of his Catholic Majesty and for a few months prior to the transfer of Natchez from Spanish to American hands in 1798 served as the commander of his Majesty's forces in that village. Though by 1805 Minor had resumed his American citizenship, he was still a captain in the Spanish army and was still living in the rambling country seat he called "Concord" on the outskirts of Natchez. Burr, during his second stop there, had called on him, but Clark's assumption that statements uttered by the ex-Vice President at that time prompted Minor to issue his "extravagancies" appears to have been wrong. If Minor helped spread the reports of a treasonable plot in the making, he did so on orders from the Marqués de Casa Yrujo. "But how the devil I have been lured into the conspiracy," Clark wrote Wilkinson, "of what assistance I can be of to it, is to me incomprehensible. Vous qui savez tout can best explain this riddle. Amuse Mr. Burr with an account of it . . ."

Clark's message left New Orleans on 7 September. If it

reached its destination on the seventeenth—ten days being the time ordinarily required for such a transmittal—it arrived in St. Louis while Burr was still there. For reasons known only to himself, however, Wilkinson did not "amuse" his guest with it at that time. Later he did send the colonel a written résumé of its contents, bringing from Burr the belief that Clark was incorrect in attributing the reports to Stephen Minor. "I love the society of that person," he wrote of the Natchez planter, "but surely I could never be guilty of the folly of confiding to one of his levity, anything I wished not to be repeated. Pray do not disturb yourself with such nonsense." If Wilkinson was disturbed, he took care to hide it when, in his next letter to Clark, he acknowledged the receipt from the New Orleans merchant "of the tale of a tub of Burr."

5

Burr left St. Louis on 19 September, crossing the Mississippi by ferry and then moving overland in the direction of Vincennes, the little capital of Indiana Territory on the banks of the Wabash. With him went a letter from Wilkinson, introducing the traveler to William Henry Harrison, the Indiana governor. "I will demand from your friendship," the general had written, "a boon in its influence co-extensive with the Union, a boon, perhaps, on which the Union may much depend . . . If you ask, What is this important boon which I so earnestly crave? I will say to you, return the bearer to the councils of our country, where his talents and abilities are all important at the present moment." What Wilkinson was saying in his flourishing manner was that he thought Harrison should send the former Vice President to Congress as his territory's nonvoting delegate. It is a measure of Burr's rapidly vanishing interest in a political career on the frontier that he did not so much as broach that matter in his conversation with Harrison.

From Vincennes, Burr moved eastward, traveling for the

most part by horse, as in those pre-steamship days few boats breasted the currents of the Ohio. It is not clear whether he again stopped at Blennerhassett Island, or whether he simply left a message for its owners, having learned they were away. By late November he was in Washington, living in his old quarters near the President's house.

6

Setbacks, Changed Plans, and the Cipher Letter

I F BURR RETURNED to Washington satisfied that the West was sympathetic to his plans, he rapidly discovered that things in the East were not going his way. Money remained his main difficulty. The Marqués de Casa Yrujo believed the former Vice President to be "replete with resources." In truth, the colonel's finances were so low in November 1805 that less than five months later he was asking William Peter Van Ness, his second in the duel with Hamilton, for a loan of twenty dollars. Burr's schemes, if he proceeded with them, would devour sums far in excess of the $25,000 he had gained as a result of the incorporation of the Indiana Canal Company.

One of his first errands in the federal city carried him to the sprawling K Street legation of the British minister. His friend Jonathan Dayton, now wholly committed to Burr's designs, had already called on Merry, remaining long enough to dazzle that credulous envoy with a glowing account of the progress of the revolution in the West. Burr, coming along two days later, hoped that by this time the minister had received an answer to his dispatch No. 15, the letter Merry had sent to London during the preceding March, in which he had conveyed to the Foreign

Office Burr's request for money and ships. Reporting on three confidential conversations with the colonel in late November, Toujours Gai described his visitor as "disappointed & mortified" to learn that an accident at sea had befallen dispatch No. 15. Two copies of it had disappeared. A third had arrived at the British Foreign Office only recently—too recently, Merry assumed, for his superiors to have communicated their reactions to it.

Confronted with this dismaying intelligence, Burr began again, repeating with embellishments most of the lies he had told Merry during their earlier conferences. Again he assured the British minister that his revolution was well commenced, that if Merry's government could be persuaded to supply him with a hundred thousand pounds and a naval presence at the mouth of the Mississippi, the rabidly anti-American Merry would yet live to see Thomas Jefferson's Republic stripped of its Western territories. This time he did not suggest that the money be "laundered" by a raid on American funds earmarked for Britain, but that the proceeds of American bonds purchased in London be channeled to Burr through Daniel Clark of New Orleans and John Barclay, one of Clark's business associates in Philadelphia. In New Orleans, he told Merry, he had received an "overture . . . from a person of the greatest Influence in East & West Florida." The incident left him "convinced" that those regions were as eager as New Orleans "to make themselves independent." He claimed to have heard from his agent in England, Charles Williamson, news that gave "him some Room to hope and expect that His Majesty's Government were disposed to afford him their Assistance." Another lie, perhaps. If Burr was in possession of a communication from Williamson —and no evidence to that effect has been found—it could not have been hopeful. Though the members of his Majesty's government were still listening attentively to Williamson's pleas in Burr's behalf, they were not doing anything about them. Burr's point was that the message from his English friend was not "explicit." He, therefore, implored Merry to write his superiors again, urging them to furnish the requisite moneys and ships forthwith. Merry obliged. Dispatch No. 48, addressed to Lord Mulgrave and relisting Burr's requests for the consideration of the Foreign Office, began its journey to London on 25 November. The colonel was gratified by the promptness of this action.

2

There was another concern, also crucial to his plans—the resolution of what Americans were calling "the Spanish question." Would there be war with Spain, or peace? It was important that Burr know.

By putting control of the Mississippi River into the hands of the settlers of the West, the Louisiana Purchase had solved one of the country's long-standing domestic worries, only to propagate a rash of international ones. The instrument of cession defined the Republic's newfound property as the "colony or province of Louisiana, with the same extent that it now has in the hands of Spain, and that it had when France possessed it; and such as it should be after the treaties subsequently entered into between Spain and other states." What did this mean? Were the western borders of Louisiana along the Rio Grande River, as the Americans alleged, or were they along the Sabine River, as the Spanish claimed? Was its eastern border the Perdido, the stream which today separates the states of Florida and Alabama; or did Spain still own West Florida, the expanse of land along the Mississippi River between the thirty-first parallel on the north and the web of lakes and bayous encircling New Orleans on the south? In other words, exactly how much acreage had the United States acquired?

In Paris the American negotiators of the purchase, Robert R. Livingston and James Monroe, put that question to Talleyrand, the French foreign minister. "I do not know," was that suave diplomat's answer. "Then," said the Americans, "you mean we shall construe it [the treaty ceding Louisiana to the United States] in our own way?" To which Talleyrand replied: "You have made a noble bargain for yourselves, and I suppose you will make the most of it."

President Jefferson naturally meant to make the most of it. He contended that the Louisiana his country had bought included West Florida, that that Spanish province became American soil the minute the banner of Castile descended the flagpole in the courtyard of the *cabildo* in New Orleans and the Stars and Stripes rose in its place. The government of King Charles IV in Madrid pronounced his position untenable, his arguments for it specious; and when in late 1804 his Catholic Majesty's representative in the United States took to the press with his protests, Jefferson—angered at such effrontery—requested his recall. It was a futile demand. Yrujo arranged with his superiors to enjoy what he delicately called a "leave" from his duties, closed his legation in Washington, moved to his town house in Philadelphia, and continued to reside in the United States for another two and a half years. Echoing in the *Aurora* the annoyance of the Administration, William Duane labeled the impetuous nobleman "the little diable espagnol" and "a miserable poppinjay," and declared that such was Yrujo's "insolence" that in "no other country under heaven would [he] . . . be suffered to remain one hour!" Yrujo countered by haling Duane into court for an inconclusive libel suit, and when in the spring of 1807 the Marqués finally condescended to leave the country, the editor of the *Aurora* informed his readers that "the expedition of *Burr* having been frustrated," the Spanish diplomat was now returning "to Madrid like a dog with his tail in an awkward position." In fact, Yrujo left the United States happy in the conviction that he had helped keep the Floridas under the control of Spain and had done as much as any man, if not more, to scotch the escapades of Aaron Burr.

The Jefferson Administration, meanwhile, had undergone considerable mental travail over the Spanish question. By the

end of August 1805, Jefferson knew what he had long suspected, that James Monroe's mission to Madrid to settle the
boundary dispute was a failure. By the end of October he was
mulling over strongly worded communications from Europe,
one from Monroe, and others from John Armstrong, who had
succeeded his brother-in-law R. R. Livingston as America's
ambassador in Paris. Both envoys advised the President to
abandon the attempt to acquire the Floridas by negotiation and
to invoke a war with Spain. It was sound advice at the time it
was given, Dumas Malone believes, observing in his magisterial
biography of the third President that "in the light of subsequent
events it can be argued that Jefferson would have run relatively
little risk and saved much later trouble if he had followed the
recommendations of his representatives abroad that he employ
force at this juncture. Had he been a Napoleon Bonaparte or
even an Alexander Hamilton or an Aaron Burr, conceivably he
might have taken military steps as a result of which his country
would have gained speedy possession of territories it was destined to acquire later by means which were not wholly diplomatic."

But Jefferson was uncertain—perhaps understandably so—
about the wisdom of committing the fledgling Republic to a war
with the dons, weak though Spain was; somewhat uncertain,
too, what position Napoleonic France, Spain's powerful ally,
might take in the event of such hostilities. The President found
support for his fears among his advisers, and at a meeting of the
cabinet on 12 November 1805 the important decision was
reached that, for the time being, a military solution of the Spanish problem would be avoided. As for the Floridas, an effort
would be made to obtain them as Louisiana had been obtained.
When Congress convened in December, it would be asked to
appropriate funds for their purchase. Hope was expressed that
France would assist with this endeavor, since the financial relations between that nation and Spain were such that any moneys

sent to the latter would eventually find their way into Napoleon's hands.

The details of this cabinet plan were not shared with the public, and for months to come, many Americans would continue to regard their country as on the brink of war. Mr. Burr was acquainted with the cabinet's decisions on Spain when on the last day of November he went to the President's house for a conference with Thomas Jefferson. That Aaron Burr knew what most people did not—that, within a few days after his return from the West, he was able to ascertain the policy of the Administration vis-à-vis Spain—is reflected in Anthony Merry's statement in his dispatch No. 48 that "Mr. Burr . . . still has the Means of knowing the Secrets of this Government."

As for Burr's two-hour talk with Jefferson, its agenda is unknown. It can be described as the event which divides those historians who perceive at least potential treason in Burr's Western movements from those who do not. And among the latter are some who find in it a sign that the real direction of the conspiracy emanated from the government—that Burr was not its author, but its victim.

The colonel was not given to writing memos of important conferences. Jefferson regularly did so, but he did not record this one. It is unlikely the busy executive talked about the weather, and he may have discussed what Mr. Burr was trying to do in the western country. Burr's Mexican plan should not have displeased a President who was "determined," Samuel Flagg Bemis notes in his *A Diplomatic History of the United States*, "to have West Florida immediately, East Florida eventually, and in due time even more of Spain's uncontested possessions" in the New World. Jefferson was familiar with the suspicions about the colonel's Western objectives, now surfacing regularly in the press. As he was vacationing at Monticello when the "Queries" about Burr's activities first appeared in the *Gazette of the United States*, he may not have read them in that Philadelphia newspaper. But a week later both the "Queries" and William Duane's comments thereon were conveniently available to him in the Old Dominion's leading Republican organ, the *Richmond Enquirer*. Some accounts of the conclave at the President's house have it that Jefferson told his caller that the Administration had opted for peace. If so, the information came as no news to Burr. Anthony Merry's dispatch No. 48, already crossing the Atlantic, quoted the colonel as saying that the President had "seceded from the Idea of recommending Congress at the approaching Meeting to adopt any severe & strong Measures in regard to Spain." "There will be no war with Spain unless we shall declare it, which is not expected." Thus, in a letter dated the day before the talk, had Burr written to his son-in-law Joseph Alston in South Carolina. When a year later he assured Henry Clay that "my views have been fully explained to . . . several Principal officers of the Govt . . . are well considered by the administration & seen by it with complacency," he was telling the truth.

3

BURR WAS NOT the only revolutionary on American soil that fall. On 9 November the ship *Polly* brought the "Knight-Errant and Promoter of Spanish-American liberty," Francisco de Miranda, to the docks of New York. Two considerations drove the Precursor to shift his revolutionary operations from England to the United States. One of them, to quote his biographer, was "discontent with the fluctuating policy of the English ministers in regard to the Spanish Indies," meaning in regard to Miranda's long-nurtured projections for liberating Latin America from its Castilian masters. The other was that the seeming imminence of a war with Spain "would procure sympathy and aid for his cause in America"—a prescient assumption as the headlong progress of his efforts during the next few months would prove.

In New York, Miranda sought out old acquaintances. One was William Stephen Smith, John Adams's son-in-law and the surveyor of the Port of New York, who years before had accompanied the Precursor on a pleasure tour of the Netherlands, Westphalia, and East Prussia. Another was Rufus King, then rapidly emerging as the leader of what remained of the Federalist Party. King's association with Miranda dated back to the Federalist chieftain's years as American minister to the Court of St. James's. To these and other influential Americans, the Venezuelan unraveled a carefully worked-out plan for an attack on his native land. Smith, taking fire at once, introduced him to Samuel G. Ogden, a New York merchant, who perceived in the projected filibuster a means of opening new markets to the American trade; he promptly agreed to supply Miranda with the ships and provisions his expedition would require. King, informed of this development, was encouraging but cautious. It was his suggestion that, before proceeding with his plans, Miranda make certain they were not contrary to the wishes of the federal government. At the end of the month, accordingly, the Precursor left New York for Washington via Philadelphia. By the first he was in the Quaker City, and there, "at the house of a common friend," he met Aaron Burr.

It was a meeting of rivals, marked by reticence on both sides. "Nothing unpleasant passed," Burr recollected later; "on the contrary," he remembered finding Miranda's "social talents and colloquial eloquence" pleasing, confessing, however, that he went out of his way "to avoid anything which might afford" the South American an opportunity "to disclose his views, since the bare suspicion of any connexion between him and me would have been injurious to my project and fatal to his." Miranda, on his part, would remember the colonel as "detestable" and "Mephistophelean." While in Philadelphia he consulted with another old acquaintance, Dr. Benjamin Rush, and the famous physician furnished him with a letter of introduction to Secretary of State Madison. On the sixth of December he arrived in the federal city, and on the seventh he called on the President, who permitted him to sit in on a meeting of the cabinet. Next he visited Madison. It was the first of two interviews. The second, occurring on the eleventh, was in response to a written invitation to Miranda from the secretary; and on the afternoon of the thirteenth he was a guest at a dinner in the President's house, at which he enjoyed the privilege, so cavalierly denied to Anthony Merry, of sitting next to the chief magistrate.

Back in New York on the twenty-ninth, Miranda assured his friends there that the government would put no obstacles in his path. Jefferson and Madison, his story went, had pointed out that as the United States and Spain were at peace, they could not openly support his contemplated attack on Venezuela; but that if private citizens saw fit to do so, the government would "wink" at whatever happened. A few months later, both the President and the secretary would dissent from this interpretation of what had taken place in Washington. Jefferson, in a letter to Duane, and Madison, in one to John Armstrong, admitted listening carefully to Miranda's recital of his plans, but asserted that they had made it clear to him that the government would not condone any effort to aid them. These denials, it would seem, can be taken with a grain of salt. After the return of Miranda to New York, some six weeks of labor went into fitting out the ships promised him by Ogden and into raising a company of volunteer fighters, among whom was a grandson of ex-President Adams. The preparations at the federally supervised Port of New York were common knowledge, and during these six weeks an order from Washington would have stopped them forever. But no such order came.

On 2 February 1806, Miranda and his expeditionary band sailed from New York on the ship *Leander*. Its registered destination was the island of Santo Domingo–Haiti; its real destination was the coast of Venezuela. Miranda would never land there from the decks of the *Leander*. Forewarned by the Marqués de Casa Yrujo, the captain general of that colony,

Guevara Vasconcelos, was forearmed. A forty-minute battle ended the invasion. Miranda escaped, but most of his followers were captured and executed. Returning later, Miranda would succeed in seizing and holding portions of Venezuela for a few months, only to be forced to abandon the area once again, after which he would make his way back to England.

In later years he blamed Aaron Burr for the failure of his expedition. He said Burr spoiled his plans by revealing them to Yrujo. Oddly enough, practically all historians of the episode accept this at face value. The only document of consequence connected with it is a report from Yrujo to Madrid, dated 1 January 1806, and dealing with one of the Spanish minister's recent conversations with Jonathan Dayton, acting as Burr's emissary. During this interview in late December, Yrujo informed his superior, "He [Dayton] . . . told me that Colonel Burr will not treat with Miranda, whom he considers imprudent, and wanting in many qualities necessary for an undertaking of such magnitude as he has on hand." Obviously, the "undertaking . . . on hand" was not Miranda's impending filibuster. Dayton was simply referring to Miranda's long-standing desire to revolutionize the Spanish Indies, of which interested observers in both Europe and America had been aware for twenty years. Had Dayton told Yrujo that Miranda was about to attack Venezuela, that watchdog of his Catholic Majesty's interests would have so notified Captain General Vasconcelos of that colony without delay. But it was not until more than a month later that Yrujo dispatched his warning to Vasconcelos; and he acted then only after learning what all readers of the Eastern press already knew, that Miranda had sailed from New York en route to the Spanish Main. It was not Burr who betrayed his rival in revolutionary intrigue.

Yrujo did not confine himself to warnings to his fellow Spaniards. He bombarded the Administration with protests, and the President and his aides did what they had to do under the circumstances. First they fired William S. Smith from his post as surveyor of the Port of New York. Then they saw to it that Smith and merchant Ogden were indicted on charges of misdemeanor. Their separate trials ran almost identical courses. The defense attorneys argued that their clients had assisted Miranda because they were convinced that the government fully approved of what he was trying to do. The presiding judge declared such reasoning irrelevant, but apparently the juries (both of them packed with Federalists, according to Jefferson) found it impressive. The jury in Smith's case took only two hours to arrive at a verdict of "not guilty"; in Ogden's they reached the same conclusion in a few minutes.

Thus ended the saga of the coming of Francisco de Miranda to the United States in the winter of 1805–6, and of his going hence—an episode singularly supportive of the likelihood that up to a point the Jefferson Administration looked on the not dissimilar strivings of Aaron Burr "with complacency."

4

WHILE MIRANDA WAS advancing his revolutionary objectives with American aid, Burr was not neglecting his. He had won many well-wishers for his expedition in the West. Now he was soliciting adherents in the East. Well before his return to Washington in November, Jonathan Dayton had "signed on," as it were; and sometime that fall Burr found in thirty-six-year-old Dr. Erich Bollman another enthusiastic supporter.

Little is known of this German-born physician. John Adams dismissed Bollman as "an adventurer with little judgment or solidity." Alexander Hamilton described him as "a man of education, speaks several languages, converses sensibly, [and] is of polite manners." Another contemporary found him "a good soul with a due portion of intelligence & much of those amiable qualities which will never make money." In the mid-1790's the doctor touched American hearts by an effort to free the Marquis de Lafayette from the Austrian prison in which republican

100

France had immured him. When the rescue attempt failed, Bollman was seized, jailed for eight months, and then released in return for a promise to leave Austria. Emigrating to the United States, he settled with his family first in Baltimore and then on the outskirts of New York City, embarked on a mercantile career, and began a warm and lasting friendship with Aaron Burr. Business concerns brought him to Washington in the fall of 1805, but "confidential intercourse" with the colonel on the subject of the expedition held him there and in Philadelphia for the next several months. A memorandum subsequently written by President Jefferson described these "interviews" as being held "chiefly at night" and as being "very transient owing to the constant occupation of Burr with others & with his plans and papers."

For Burr, it was a necessity to keep busy. How many times, in letters to the first Theodosia, his late wife, and to the second, his daughter, had he inveighed in the spirit of the Puritan ancestors he so unorthodoxly resembled against the vice of idleness! Fill the hours, he lectured at them; and in the fall of 1805 his were full enough. From his November conferences with Anthony Merry he came away alarmed by the failure of the British ministry to respond to his pleas for money and ships. For months he had regarded help from Britain as almost a certainty. Suddenly he realized that it was not assured. Funds must be sought elsewhere. He bethought himself of the star-struck proprietor of Blennerhassett Island and wrote that gentleman a beguiling letter. He expressed the conviction that the "talents" of the Irish-born aristocrat deserved a more "active" and "ennobling" sphere than the rude surroundings of the Ohio frontier. He mentioned a number of speculative possibilities, ventures calculated not only to engage Blennerhassett's mind and abilities but also to fatten his purse. His words could not have reached the owner of the enchanted isle at a choicer moment. Blennerhassett's once ample resources were disappearing rapidly, eroded by the large sums he had sunk into his sylvan retreat and into his only moderately profitable mercantile businesses in Marietta and vicinity. Already he was trying to sell his island through private channels and looking for investment opportunities. The minute his eyes fell on Burr's letter, he answered it. He would be "highly honored" to be "associated" with Burr in any project the colonel had in mind. This carte blanche was mailed in late December, but Burr, roaming the East as restlessly as he had the West, would not see it until two months later.

Meanwhile, he was seized with a dazzling idea: brilliant, daring—and preposterous. Why not let Spain pay for his contemplated attack on Spain's empire in the New World? And while picking Spain's pockets, why not at the same time throw a little sand into the eyes of Spain's all-too-observant minister to the United States? Burr seems to have arrived at these inspirations in consultation with both Bollman and Dayton. Bollman indicated as much later, and Dayton was acting on the colonel's orders when on 5 December he called on the Marqués de Casa Yrujo in Philadelphia.

A bizarre conversation ensued. Dayton sought to give the impression that he had penetrated the plans of Colonel Burr and stood ready to betray them on the assumption that his Catholic Majesty would be willing to pay a little money—say thirty or forty thousand dollars—for such a "secret." Assured by the Spanish minister that his country was always "generous" to those who served her, Dayton presented his revelations. During the preceding spring, he told Yrujo, "Colonel Burr had various secret conferences with the British minister, to whom he proposed a plan not only for taking the Floridas, but also for effecting the separation and independence of the Western States—a part of this plan being that the Floridas should be associated in this new federative republic; England to receive as the price of her services a decisive preference in matters of commerce and navigation . . ." According to Dayton, the British minister had recommended this plan "to his court" and Prime Minister Pitt and his cabinet were giving it serious consideration.

Did Dayton and Burr really believe that these statements were news to the Spanish minister? Of course not. They knew that Yrujo had long since alerted the authorities in the Spanish Indies to the possibility of a military expedition against them. What they believed was that Yrujo—himself no stranger to the arts of duplicity—would discern the motives behind Dayton's half-truths and assume, as indeed he did, that England had shown no intention of underwriting the expedition. If it had, the perpetrators would not now be coming to Spain, begging "for a few thousand dollars." They hoped that Yrujo would see in their very willingness to talk about a projected attack on Spanish land evidence that they had found that plan "ridiculous and fantastic" and had abandoned it. The whole idea behind Dayton's call on the minister, Burr explained to Bollman, was to lure Yrujo into a sense of false security, into the belief that the real objective of the conspiracy was not an assault on his country's colonies but a dismemberment of the Republic headed by Thomas Jefferson.

Yrujo's report of the interview to his superior in Madrid, Don Pedro Cevallos, suggests that Dayton's gambit was not unsuccessful, that the Marqués was at least partly persuaded that Burr had relinquished thoughts of a military blow at the Spanish Indies. He listened attentively to the ex-senator's remarks, and at the end of the interview he promised to give them thought and proposed that they discuss them further some other time. Burr had come to Philadelphia after his secret talk with Jefferson, and it is safe to suppose that he and his fellow conspirator had gotten together to plot their next move when, toward the end of December, Dayton returned to Yrujo's town house for a second consultation with the now thoroughly intrigued diplomat from Spain.

This time, Dayton began with a series of confessions. He

admitted that he had not come to Yrujo on his own but as an agent of Burr and that it was Burr himself who was offering to sell his services to Spain. He admitted, also, that he had lied about England. So far, that government had given the conspirators no encouragement. Having cleared the air with this show of frankness, the ex-senator proceeded to pour into the minister's ears a story of derring-do.

Burr, he disclosed, was not going to launch his separatist schemes on the western waters. He was going to strike first at the heart of the federal government itself. His plan, Dayton said, was "by degrees" to introduce into Washington "a number of men in disguise, well armed." At a signal from their chieftain, these desperadoes were to seize the President and other top officials, grab the public moneys deposited in the local banks, and take possession of the federal arsenal. If there were no resistance to this coup, Burr would "negotiate with the individual states" an arrangement under which he and his confederates would rule the country. If resistance arose, they would burn the navy yard, saving only enough ships to carry them and their plunder to New Orleans. There they would at once "proclaim the emancipation of Louisiana and the Western States."

Yrujo may have entertained some doubts concerning Dayton's earlier remarks, but he had none about this plan. "For one who does not know the country," he wrote Cevallos, "this plan would appear almost insane; but I confess, for my part, that in view of all the circumstances it seems to me easy to execute . . . There exists in this country an infinite number of adventurers, without property, full of ambition, and ready to unite at once under the standard of a revolution which promises to better their lot. Equally certain it is that Burr and his friends, without discovering their object, have succeeded in getting the good-will of these men, and inspiring the greatest confidence among them in favor of Burr." Recommending that Spain give Burr "half a million or a million dollars" to raise and provision an army, Yrujo reminded Cevallos of the "extreme satisfaction" with which Spain "would view . . . the dismemberment of the colossal power which was growing up at the very gates of her most precious and important colonies." Entranced by the prospect of an American Republic broken in twain, the Spanish minister gave Dayton $1,500 for his "secret," promised him another thousand in the near future, and took under advisement the former senator's request that, like Agent 13 Wilkinson, he be placed on the payroll of his Catholic Majesty with a monthly pension of $2,000.

But in Madrid, whence word of these transactions eventually drifted, there was little enthusiasm for them, and less credulity. Cevallos knew things that Yrujo did not. He knew of the presence in the files of certain letters from Agent 13, along with revealing reports from the "Viceroy of New Spain" (Mexico). He knew that Burr had not dropped his plans for a military expedition against the Spanish dominions. He warned Yrujo to act with caution. He advised him to give the conspirators only modest sums, and those only for the purpose of keeping them talking, and eventually he informed the minister that the king did not wish to encourage Burr's designs in any way. As for a pension for Dayton—nothing doing.

Burr and his aides received about $2,500 in all, a trifling reward for their attempt to deceive the Spanish ambassador, an attempt that, once it was put underway, they were obliged to continue at the expenditure of much labor for months to come.

5

As THE NEW YEAR BEGAN, Burr was so discouraged that he toyed with the idea of abandoning his Western project. True, word had reached Washington of a military border incident in the far Southwest, near the Sabine River, dividing line between Spanish-held Texas and American-held Louisiana. Crossing the river, 1,300 Spanish soldiers had taken up a position on American soil. Secretary of War Henry Dearborn had ordered the

American officer commanding in the area to chase them back (which he did) and to hold the line at the Sabine, and the President in two messages to Congress had "rehearsed the long catalogue of Spanish aggressions and acts of unfriendliness" with such vehemence that most Americans anticipated hostilities momentarily.

But Burr continued to think otherwise. "You will know before this can reach you," he wrote Wilkinson on 6 January, "that we are to have no Spanish war except in ink and words." The colonel, it would appear, had a source of information within the Administration. Probably Dearborn. He and the war secretary were on friendly terms, and Burr is known to have shown Judge Thomas T. Davis of Indiana and other Westerners a letter from Dearborn—forged by Burr, according to some sources—signifying governmental approval of his Western plans. To Wilkinson he stated that the efforts of the Administration to keep the peace were "for the best, for we are in a poor condition to go to war, even with Spain." But, for his plans, he wanted a war.

It was Charles Biddle's conjecture that in the opening weeks of 1806 Burr "would have given up his expedition if he could have procured an appointment that would have made him independent." It is a matter of record that he solicited such appointments. Learning that Edward Shippen had retired as chief justice of Pennsylvania, he asked Biddle to intercede on his behalf with Governor Thomas McKean, whose right it was to name Shippen's successor. Reluctant about speaking directly to McKean—aware that he would hesitate to bestow so valuable a berth on a non-Pennsylvanian—Biddle spoke instead to the governor's son, and there the matter stopped.

Baffled in Philadelphia, Burr went to the President in Washington. Jefferson's account of this conversation at the executive mansion on or about the twenty-second of March makes provocative reading, not so much for what it says about the interview as for the light it sheds on the thinking behind the Virginian's pervasive distrust of his former Vice President. The President penned no memorandum of the interview at the time it occurred. An intervening event impelled his decision to do so later. A lawsuit brought by Burr had had the effect of reviving the old charge that Jefferson's elevation to the Presidency at the close of the tie election in 1801 came as the result of a deal struck with his Federalist opponents. More than once, the Virginian had denied this charge. Now, in the closing paragraphs of his story of the March 1806 talk with Burr, he denied it again, citing chapter and verse in an effort to prove that he had entered the Presidency committed to no one and free to pursue those "measures which I should deem for the public good."

It is worth noting that these denials were not for public consumption. They went into Jefferson's private journal, his *Anas*. He was not trying to convince the world that he had done no wrong. He was trying to convince himself. The thing about Burr that made him so offensive to Jefferson was that the colonel did not seem to think of politics as a procedure carried on "for the public good." To him, it was a game. Its objectives were power for himself, jobs for his friends, and fun for all concerned. Jefferson was too old a hand at the business to think Burr the only American wedded to this view. But there was something about the flamboyant New Yorker—his cheerful readiness to compromise, his lack of interest in ideological implications, his tendency to regard the manipulation of men and votes as a form of entertainment—something that made him in the eyes of the Virginian the apotheosis of a creeping corruption which, if allowed to develop, might wreck the democratic process itself. "I had never seen Colo. Burr until he came as member of the Senate," Jefferson wrote in 1804. "His conduct very soon inspired me with distrust. I habitually cautioned Mr. Madison against trusting him too much. I saw afterwards . . . whenever a great military appointment or a diplomatic one was to be made, he came post to Philadelphia to shew himself and in fact that he was always at market . . ." For the writer of these

words to hear it said that, like Burr, he too could stoop to conquer was a harsher burden than Jefferson could endure. It af-
fronted his inner image of himself. Somehow it must be cast off.
Hence the righteous tone of his description of the March 1806
encounter at the executive mansion.

"About a month ago," he recorded on 15 April, "Colonel
Burr called on me and entered into a conversation, in which he
mentioned, that a little before my coming into office, I had written him a letter intimating that I had destined him for a high
employ, had he not been placed by the people in a different one;
that he had signified his willingness to resign as Vice-President
to give aid to the administration in any other place; that he had
never asked an office, however; he asked aid of nobody, but
could walk on his own legs . . . ; that I had always used him
with politeness, but nothing more; that he . . . had supported
the administration; and that he could do me much harm; he
wished, however, to be on different ground; he was now disen-
gaged from all particular business—willing to engage in something—should be in town some days, if I should have anything
to propose to him."

Of course, Jefferson had no intention of proposing anything.
He admitted that his visitor possessed "talents which might be
employed greatly to the advantage of the public." He described
himself, however, as under the impression that the public had
lost confidence in Burr. When Burr remarked that such an
impression could exist only among those who believed what they
read "in a few newspapers" (a reference to published charges
that he was plotting treason), the President protested that his
own impression did not rest on "that kind of evidence." It went
back to the late Presidential election, to the fact that at the nomi-
nating caucus not a "single voice" was raised in favor of giving
Burr a second term as Vice President. Of Burr's statement that
he could do the President harm, Jefferson wrote: "I knew no
cause why he should desire it, but . . . I feared no injury
which any man could do me; . . . I never had done a single

act, or been concerned in any transaction, which I feared to have fully laid open, or which could do me any hurt, if truly stated; . . . I had never done a single thing with a view to my personal interest, or that of any friend, or with any other view than that of the greatest public good . . ."

This marked the end of Burr's effort to rejoin the political mainstream. He pressed on with his Western plans. A need for military expertise led him to ask his friend Commodore Truxton to join the expedition. After serving as one of the country's top commanders in the quasi-war with France, Truxton resigned from the navy under circumstances that left him brooding over slights, real or imagined, on the part of the Jefferson Administration. Burr knew the proud commodore's history, knew of his longing to resume a career on the high seas that had persuaded a grateful Congress to issue a gold medal in his honor. Once Mexico was conquered, Burr said, he would need a navy and Truxton would be its admiral. The commodore asked one question. Had the government approved of Burr's project? Informed that it had not, Truxton said he would have nothing to do with it.

Burr turned to William Eaton, an army officer and diplomat whose colorful exploits during the war with the Barbary pirates in North Africa had enshrined him in the hearts of the American public as "the hero of Derne." In a later, widely publicized deposition, Eaton quoted at length from his conversations with the colonel in the winter of 1806. Burr, he maintained, told him the same tale Dayton had fed to the Spanish ambassador—that the conspirators were planning to raid the national capital and usurp the national government. Eaton described himself as horrified by this revelation, as determining at once to warn the authorities. But when he "took the liberty" of calling on the President in the spring of 1806, he said nothing about a contemplated attack on Washington. To Jefferson he expressed the conviction that were Burr's Western adventures permitted to continue, "we should soon have an insurrection . . . on the waters of the Mississippi." He implored the President to avert this catastrophe by naming Burr to a diplomatic post in Spain or England, thus getting that "dangerous" man out of the country. Jefferson waved the suggestion aside, asserting that he feared no rebellion. In the West, as in the East, the American people were loyal to their elected leaders. Eaton was not so sure; he himself was annoyed with the leaders. In North Africa he had spent sums on the government's interests out of his own pocket, and for three years the Congress had ignored his requests for reimbursement. A few months after his talk with Jefferson, he authorized a political associate to inform the President of Burr's alleged threat to overturn the government. Still later, he provided the President with a deposition on the matter. And a few weeks after that the government reimbursed him in the amount of $10,000. At the trial in Richmond, Burr's attorneys made the most of the timing of these developments, finding it easy to imply that the hero of Derne was a bought witness.

But was he? What we know of his temperament and habits suggests as much. Tall and rugged, with fierce blue eyes in a long, handsome slab of a face, Eaton drank heavily, gambled heavily, horsewhipped waiters and servants in public places, and was given to hurling outrageous and usually unfounded accusations at his enemies. Senator Plumer of New Hampshire avoided his company, having discovered that Eaton had a way of "misrepresenting" what other people said to him. "Hasty, imprudent, unguarded." So the senator characterized the hero of Derne. A happenstance strangely overlooked by Burr's biographers and by the students of his "conspiracy" is that in the winter of 1805–6 Eaton engaged in talks not only with Colonel Burr but also with the colonel's associate and confidant, Jonathan Dayton—a significant fact, for as we will have occasion to observe later, Dayton too was "imprudent" and "unguarded." It was Dayton who told Yrujo the fantastic tale of a projected assault on the federal city; and the suspicion arises that it was

Dayton—and not Burr—who repeated that Munchausenism to Eaton, and that Eaton either concealed the source of his information or made no distinction between Dayton and Burr in the matter.

6

Not until the end of February 1806 did Burr see the letter from Harman Blennerhassett, offering to join the colonel in "any enterprise you would permit me to participate in." Burr's answer on 15 April, saying that he was meditating "a speculation precisely of the character you have described," dates the beginning of the dealings that a few months later put the colonel in possession of parts of a huge stretch of virgin soil along the Washita River in Louisiana known as the Bastrop tract.

A decade earlier Felipe Neri, Baron de Bastrop—a Hollander turned subject of Spain—received from his Catholic Majesty 1,200,000 acres in the valley of the Washita. In 1779 Bastrop sold his claims to Abraham Morhouse, a speculator then operating in Kentucky; and about 1804 Morhouse transferred the claims to Edward Livingston of New Orleans and Colonel Charles Lynch of Shelby County, Kentucky. Lynch got 700,000 acres, and it was approximately one half of these that Burr was arranging to buy in the spring and summer of 1806. It is impossible to say how good a title he obtained. In those days, even the smartest of lawyers found it difficult to determine the validity of titles in the uncharted reaches of the trans-Mississippi West. Gratuitous, however, would seem to be the word for the contention of some historians that the title was bad, that Burr knew it was bad, and that the purchase was so much hocus-pocus to distract attention from traitorous designs. Three facts are firmly established: Burr executed a contract with Lynch; he paid for the lands—$5,000 down in the form of drafts on a New York merchant, along with an agreement to assume a debt of $30,000,

111

owed by Lynch to Livingston; and Henry Clay, having examined the papers, told Senator Plumer that in his opinion the transaction was legal in every respect.

At the end of July, Burr informed Truxton and Treasury Secretary Albert Gallatin that the land deal was "about to be concluded." And from this date on, the would-be conqueror of the Spanish Indies can be described as having a major plan and a contingency plan. "This much I will tell you," Senator Smith of Ohio quoted Burr as saying a few months later, "if there should be a war between the United States and Spain, I shall head a corps of volunteers and be the first to march into the Mexican provinces. If peace should be proffered . . . , I shall settle my Washita lands, and make society as pleasant as possible."

Easily, the most persuasive key to the goals of the expedition is to be found in three amazing maps, drawn by Burr and discovered among his papers long after his death. One of them, measuring 39 inches by 32, covers the lower region of the Mississippi River. Included are Natchez, New Orleans, the Bastrop lands, New Mexico, and Mexico down to Yucatan. Another, a 23-by-13-inch admiralty chart, surveys the Gulf Coast from New Orleans to Campeche. Soundings are given; islands, bars, and inlets recorded. The third document exhibits in precise detail that section of Mexico lying between Veracruz on the east and Mexico City on the west. These maps are silent but eloquent testimony to the scope of their author's plans. "Had Burr's project gone forward," Walter Flavius McCaleb writes in his study of the conspiracy, "the world might have been treated to a spectacle in some of its aspects recalling the story" of the conquest of Mexico in the sixteenth century by the Spanish conquistador Hernando Cortez. For "nothing less than the Empire of Spain in North America was at stake"—this was the objective of the Burr Conspiracy. That it was illegal is obvious, but it was not a betrayal of, or separation from, Burr's own country. It was not treasonable.

7

Burr's affairs kept him on the move in the spring and summer of 1806. He spent a week or so in South Carolina. It was his second visit to his family there since his return from the West. One of its purposes was to persuade his wealthy rice-planter son-in-law, Joseph Alston, to pledge what eventually came to about $50,000 to the support of the expedition. Mid-April found him in Washington, dining at the executive mansion with Jefferson on one occasion, dropping by there for a social chat with the President on another. Mid-May found him for a few days in Baltimore, in the company of his daughter and her four-year-old son, come north—as they did most summers—to escape the malarial heat of the tidewater South. Back in Washington again, he paid his last visit to the British legation. Merry had no news other than the revelation that he had been recalled and soon would be returning to England.

After the warmer months began, the colonel spent most of his time in Philadelphia or at Morrisville, a borough on the Delaware River north of the Quaker City. From time to time he called on Yrujo, unaware that the Marqués was no longer as certain as he once was that Burr's expedition was confined to a disruption of the American Republic. Already the Spanish ambassador had arranged for Madrid to send to the United States an investigator named José Vidal, whose task it would be to keep Burr under observation after the leader of the conspiracy returned to the West. Formerly a commander of a Spanish garrison on the American frontier and a friend of Wilkinson, Vidal was acquainted with the terrain of the western country.

Early in June, Yrujo was reporting to his government that Burr was no longer visiting him "with his accustomed frequency"—conveying this information in a manner which suggests that the protector of the Spanish interests rather enjoyed the cat-and-mouse game that his relationship with the would-be conqueror of his Majesty's colonies had become. Yrujo noted the frequent appearance in the city or at Morrisville of some of Burr's fellow conspirators: of Jonathan Dayton and Dr. Erich Bollman; of a strapping young blond from New York named Samuel Swartwout; of Peter V. Ogden, Dayton's nephew and one of the sons of the late Matthew Ogden, the close companion of Aaron's growing-up years in Elizabethtown, New Jersey. Yrujo noted also the presence in the vicinity of Burr's British agent, Charles Williamson, recently come across the Atlantic for what was to be his last brief sojourn in the United States. Yrujo was not the only dedicated observer of the comings and goings of Burr and his associates in the Philadelphia area.

"Respected Sir," editor Duane of the *Aurora* wrote Jefferson late in the year, "Two or three months ago, Mr. John Craig, merchant in this city, applied to Messrs Binny and Ronaldson for types to a considerable amount—destined for Mexico and calculated and cast for the Spanish language—to the value of 1000 \$. They [Duane's informants] understood that the person who ordered was Mr. *Fernandez* . . . They conclude that the types were intended for the conspirators."

8

MIDSUMMER 1806 BROUGHT news that again Spanish soldiers had crossed the Sabine River into what our government regarded as part of the land purchased from France and, therefore, American soil. This time Secretary of War Dearborn had ordered Wilkinson to leave St. Louis and take command of the forces being assembled along the southwestern frontier for use against the invading Spaniards. Burr's reading of this development was that now the issue of war or peace rested in the hands of his friend and collaborator.

Was Wilkinson still his friend and collaborator? In recent months the general had been ominously silent—a situation that was obviously troubling Burr and his assistants. In a letter written at Washington on 16 April, they informed the general that

the "execution of our project is postponed till December" because of "want of water in Ohio," and added that "Burr wrote
you a long letter last December replying to a short one deemed
very silly. Nothing has been heard from Brigadier [Wilkinson]
since October . . . Address Burr at Washington." Reproduc-
ing this message in his memoirs, Wilkinson attributes it to
Burr; but no signature is appended, and the repeated references
to Burr in the third person suggest that it was written by his
associate, Jonathan Dayton. That earnest gentleman had taken
unto himself the task of keeping the commander of the armies
true to the cause—a task, as future events demonstrate, that he
performed with the exuberance of a zealot.

Wilkinson answered the note on 13 May, but the contents of
his reply remain unknown. Pressed to convey this 13 May communication to the grand jury at Richmond, Burr was unable to
oblige, explaining that "I did voluntarily, and in the presence of
a witness, put the letter out of my hands," and implying that
Wilkinson had requested him to do so. As July of 1806 came
on, Burr and Dayton, now working together in Philadelphia,
were not quite sure of the general; and late that month the most
controversial document connected with the conspiracy—the notorious "cipher letter"—was on its way to Wilkinson.

This is the letter that for a hundred and seventy years historians have been studying with microscopic ardor, some finding
in it proof of treasonable intent, others nothing more than a
possibly unlawful effort to subjugate the dominions of his
Catholic Majesty. It was a falsified version of this letter that
Wilkinson sent to Jefferson, prompting the President to ar-
rogate to himself the functions of judge and jury by announcing
in a message to the Congress that his former Vice President
was a traitor to his country. This is the letter that the Chief
Justice of the United States, John Marshall, described as containing not one word that could be construed as pointing to
treasonable activity.

Much of the cryptographic code which underlies the cipher

letter and numerous versions of the letter itself can be read today at several American archives and in a number of public documents and secondary books. By comparing the ciphered versions of the letter stored at the Newberry Library in Chicago with the accepted decipherments of it, the editors of the Aaron Burr Papers at The New-York Historical Society—Dr. Mary-Jo Kline and her staff—have constructed what they call a "corrected version," a rendering almost identical to one preserved at the Alderman Library of the University of Virginia in the handwriting of Jonathan Dayton. The corrected version and the one in Dayton's hand read as follows:

Your letter postmarked 13th May is received. [Brackets surround this opening sentence in the Dayton letter.] I have at length obtained funds, and have actually commenced. The Eastern detachments, from different points and under different pretense, will rendezvous on Ohio on 1 November.

Every thing internal and external favour our view. Naval protection of England is secured. Truxton [spelled Truxtul in the Dayton version] is going to Jamaica to arrange with the [British] admiral there and will meet us at Mississippi. England, a navy of the United States ready to join and final orders are given to my friends and followers. It will be a host of choice spirits. Wilkinson shall be second to Burr only and Wilkinson shall dictate the rank and promotion of his officers.

Burr will proceed westward 1 August—never to return. With him go his daughter and grandson. The husband will follow in October with a corps of worthys.

Send forthwith an intelligent and confidential friend with whom Burr may confer; he shall return immediately with further interesting details. This is essential to concert and harmony of movement. Send a list of all persons known to Wilkinson westward of the mountains who could be useful, with a note delineating their character. By your messenger send me 4 or 5 of the commissions of your officers which you can borrow under any pretence you please. They shall be returned faithfully. Already an order to the contractor to forward 6 months provisions to points you may name. This shall not be used til the last moment, and then under proper instructions.

Our project my dear friend is brought to the point so long desired. I guarantee the result with my life [Dayton here inserts the phrase "say life" in parentheses] and honor, with the lives, honor and the fortune of hundreds, the best blood of our country.

Burr's plan of operation is to move down rapidly from the Falls on fifteenth November, with the first 500 or 1000 men in light boats now constructing for that purpose; to be at Natches between the 5 and 15 December, there to meet you; then to determine whether it will be expedient in the first instance to seize on or to pass by B.R. [Baton Rouge, then part of Spanish-held West Florida.] On receipt of this send me an answer. Draw on me for all expenses.

The people of the country to which we are going are prepared to receive us—their agents, now with me, say that if we will protect their religion and will not subject them to a foreign power, that in three weeks all will be settled.

The gods invite us to glory and fortune. It remains to be seen whether we deserve the boons.

The bearer of this goes express to you. He will hand a formal letter of introduction from me.

He is a Man of inviolable honor and perfect discretion; formed to execute rather than to project—yet capable of relating facts with fidelity and incapable of relating them otherwise; he is thoroughly informed of the plans and intentions of _____ [blank in both versions] and will disclose to you so far as you shall enquire and no further. He has imbibed a reverence for your Character and may be embarrassed in your presence—put him at ease, and he will satisfy you.

[The Dayton version is dated "22 July" at this point.]

Doctor Bollman equally Confidential better informed on the subject & more enlightened will hand you this duplicate.

[In the Dayton version, this postscript is dated "July 29" at this point.]

From Burr's day to our own, this communication has been a stumbling block to the students of his career. The very manner in which it is framed, the bombastic style so at odds with Burr's direct and unadorned writings, is baffling. When its essential contents became known in Washington, "Burr didn't write that letter!" exclaimed Senator Plumer of New Hampshire. "Wilkinson wrote that letter."

Plumer was at least half right. The cipher letter as we know it today was not written by Aaron Burr. It was written by Jonathan Dayton. As no historian of the conspiracy has ever questioned the authorship of the cipher letter, this reversal of more than a century and a half of Burr scholarship demands an exposition of the evidence on which it stands.

Let us begin with the circumstances surrounding the preparation of the letter in Philadelphia and its dispatch West—circumstances which show that there was ample opportunity for whatever Burr wrote to be destroyed and a different communication put in its place. The fact is that Burr did write a letter; for this we have the word of his young coadjutor, Samuel Swartwout. Swartwout tells his story in a deposition drafted for use at another federal trial of Burr and one of his associates, a trial ordered by the court at Richmond and slated to be held in Ohio —a trial that never occurred.

As some of our evidence rests on Swartwout's deposition, a few words about its author's reputation at the time the affidavit was taken cannot come amiss. Called to the witness stand in open court at Richmond, Littleton W. Tazewell of Norfolk, Virginia, a member of the grand jury impaneled for that trial, went out of his way to say that "I would not be willing to be understood that I doubted anything Mr. Swartwout said. Although he appeared before the grand jury under very unfavorable circumstances, and my impressions were very strong against him, yet the very frank and candid manner in which he gave his testimony, I must confess, raised him very high in my estimation . . ." Certainly the deposition, sworn to by Swartwout in 1807, rings true.

According to his account, Burr wrote a letter to Wilkinson about the twenty-second of July 1806. At the colonel's request, Swartwout put the message in cipher, using a code based on a miscellany of elements, including *Entick's Pocket Dictionary*, sets of hieroglyphics, Arabic numerals, and key words. As Wilkinson's exact whereabouts were unknown, Swartwout was to carry one copy of the ciphered letter overland by way of the Ohio and Mississippi Valleys. Dr. Bollman was to take a duplicate by sea to New Orleans. Swartwout left Philadelphia on 24 July, Bollman about a week later. Sometime during this interval, the switch of letters occurred. While Swartwout was at Pittsburgh, Peter V. Ogden, Dayton's nephew, arrived there from Philadelphia. Ogden brought with him what he said were orders from Burr, but it is now clear that these instructions came from his uncle. Swartwout, Ogden said, was to destroy the letter he had and to take West instead a sealed envelope for delivery to Wilkinson. Moving on in search of the general, Ogden and Swartwout traveled together for about two months. As for the sealed envelope, Swartwout never looked into it: "Know nothing of the contents of that paper" are his words in the deposition.

So much for the cipher carried away from Pittsburgh in late July and handed to General Wilkinson at Natchitoches (pronounced Na-kitosh) in Louisiana during the following October. What about the duplicate cipher transported by Bollman? How did it come about that this copy, delivered to Wilkinson during the following November, was identical to the one carried by Swartwout, save for a brief and unimportant postscript?

For the answer to that, we must resort to conjecture—conjecture that, in the absence of any public statement on the matter from Jonathan Dayton, is admittedly inconclusive, but convincing. Following Swartwout's departure from Philadelphia, Boll-

119

man lingered there or in the vicinity for several days—plenty of time for him and Dayton to get together and for the necessary exchange of ciphers to be accomplished. (Dayton, because of ill health, did not go West with Burr.)

Finally, there is the internal evidence, the accepted versions of the cipher letter and what it says. No copy of this document, in cipher or decoded, has ever been found in the handwriting of Aaron Burr. On the other hand, copies of it in Dayton's hand are available. Equally to the point, the letter as we now know it is a tissue of absurdities. Consider, for example, the sentence in it reading, "Burr will proceed westward 1 August . . . With him go his daughter and grandson," meaning Theodosia and little Gamp. But Burr's whole life was centered in those two; and in that summer of 1806, Gamp was only four years old and desperately ill. After his mother's arrival in the North in mid-May, Theodosia moved from place to place, frantically seeking professional help for him, finally finding in the mountains of Pennsylvania a solution to the problem. "For some time after your departure from Falsington [Pennsylvania]," she wrote in August to her stepbrother, Frederick Prevost, "I continued in the application of your recipe . . . I found there was a tumor formed under his [Gamp's] chin . . . We hastened to Philadelphia where I consulted everyone celebrated for medical skill." To no avail. The boy worsened, to the point where his mother "feared he might die." Then, on the advice of her father and the Philadelphia physicians, she removed herself and the boy to the healing springs at Bedford, Pennsylvania. "[R]eached this on the 21st July," she told Frederick, "and since that day my son has been gaining strength & Health. The tumor has dispersed without forming a head . . ." Under no imaginable circumstances could Burr have subjected his ailing grandson to the hardships of a Mexican military expedition.

Once that expedition was underway, the cipher letter states, Theodosia's husband, Joseph Alston, was to "follow . . . with a corps of worthys." But Swartwout swore that the letter he "copied and ciphered" for Burr contained no mention of Alston. Neither, according to this same source, did it mention Commodore Truxton, described in it as "going to Jamaica to arrange with the admiral there and will meet us at Mississippi." England "ready to join," says the cipher, but only a few months earlier Burr had seen to it that Wilkinson was informed that their project could not be put into execution until December, owing to "want of water in Ohio"—words designed to tell the general that the money and ships they had hoped to obtain from London were not coming to them. The attempts by Burr to mislead the British and Spanish ministers as to the goals of his enterprise tell us that he was no slave to the truth. When his purposes required it, he told lies; but he told them to men he had reason to assume might believe them, as both ministers did to some extent. He knew Wilkinson too well to expect him to accept the schoolboy fibs running through the cipher letter. "Naval protection of England is secured . . . a navy of the United States ready to join." If Wilkinson didn't recognize the falsity of those assertions, he was in a position, as the general of the armies, to check them out. Worthy of note, too, are the varying ways in which Burr is referred to in the letter. In some places, the simple "I" appears; in others, he is spoken of in the third person. These alternating usages indicate that when Dayton reconstituted the cipher, he picked up some sentences from the missive that Burr himself had written. Small wonder that when the letter became a matter of public knowledge, Burr's reactions to it were marked by the bewilderment of a man gazing on something he had never seen before. Small wonder, too, that he told his son-in-law the cipher letter was "a forgery," and pointed out to his daughter, after Wilkinson testified in Richmond, that "the General has not yet admitted the substitution of names." That he never gave Dayton away is unsurprising; his restraint was in keeping with the code by which he lived: a gentleman does not betray his friends. Which brings us to a consideration of the friend who wrote most, if not all, of the famous letter.

On this point, our resources are thin. Jonathan Dayton has not yet found a biographer, and the record provides only a few clues to the sort of man he was. A 1909 study of the Speakers of the House of Representatives—a position held by Dayton during most of the two-year period beginning in 1797—describes him as "of commanding mediocrity," though popular with his colleagues. An officer who served with him during the war of the Revolution found him a man "of talents with ambition to exert them," adding that "There is an impetuosity in his temper that is injurious to him, but there is an honest rectitude about him that makes him a valuable Member of Society." One senses in his switch of the cipher letters several of the traits mentioned: the mediocrity, the impetuosity, the rectitude. It was important in 1806 that Wilkinson be ready to join Burr whenever Burr was ready to move. Dayton, it is obvious, decided that whatever Burr had written would not have the effect of keeping the slippery general in the fold. Something more flamboyant and phlogistical was called for—something more on the order of the pomposities Wilkinson himself was wont to dash off. Dayton, of course, thought he was doing Burr a favor.

9

WITH THE PREPARATION and sending of the cipher letter, Burr's work in Philadelphia was done. Having dispatched his couriers in search of the general, he spent a portion of the month of August at Bedford with his daughter and grandson.

Then once again he headed for the western waters.

7

Preparing the Expedition; the Frankfort Grand Jury

TRAVELING WITH BURR when he said goodbye to his daughter and grandson at Bedford was a small cadre of recently acquired assistants headed by Colonel Julien De Pestre of New Jersey, a refugee from the French revolutionary wars who was to serve the expedition as its chief of staff. On 11 August the travelers passed through Chambersburg. On the twenty-first they reached Pittsburgh. There Burr put up at a tavern and began making arrangements for collecting some of the provisions and manpower his plans demanded.

Newspapers of the day reveal that his recruiting efforts were not without issue. Seven young men enlisted, some of them, according to the *National Intelligencer* of Washington, among "the first characters in Pittsburgh," the sort of men, the *Intelligencer* editorialized, who would never dream of engaging "in a treasonable plot against their country." One of them, Morgan Neville, encountered parental opposition. In the beginning his father, General Presley Neville of Revolutionary War fame, ordered his son to stay where he was. But the younger man persisted, and in time the older one not only relented but provided his son with a handsomely appointed boat for passage down the Ohio and Mississippi Rivers.

Taking note of Burr's five-day stay in the city, the Pittsburgh *Commonwealth* reported that he was en route to Kentucky, that he was traveling "*incog*," that he was being "perfectly *taciturn*" about the "object" of his journey; and expressed the hope that "the Western editors" would give "a good account" of his activities. The *Commonwealth* need not have worried. On Burr's second traverse of the frontier, as on his first, the press lighted every step of his progress, transforming what was publicized as a conspiracy—dark, secretive, skulking, and mysterious—into a Roman holiday for all to enjoy.

"Taciturn" the colonel may have been while in the city, but when on the twenty-second he and De Pestre rode south for a visit on a 7,000-acre country estate called Morganza, Burr appears to have indulged in an outburst of rodomontade, typical of the tongue-in-cheek extravagances with which, in letters to his daughter, he so often entertained himself and her. Awaiting him at Morganza was an old friend and fellow student at Princeton, Colonel George Morgan, Indian trader and land speculator, and the colonel's two sons. If Burr's purpose was to induce the younger Morgans to join the expedition, his thirty-mile jaunt to their father's manorial establishment and back was a waste of time. Our knowledge of what happened there comes from the Morgans, as detailed in their testimony at the Richmond trial— statements that Burr labeled a lie. According to the Morgans, Burr spoke slightingly of the great power centers of the Republic. He boasted that he could seize Washington with two hundred men, New York with five hundred. He predicted that within the next five years the agricultural West, weary of paying tribute to the industrial East, would leave the Union of its own volition.

Questioned by the defense attorneys at Richmond, one of the younger Morgans confessed that Burr's observations were delivered in a "light," even bantering tone, but whether voiced in jest or in earnest, they were directed at the wrong person. In his long-ago past, the older Morgan had taken a leaf from James Wilkinson's black book; had for a time competed with the general for the largess to be derived from commercial dealings with the then Spanish overlords of Louisiana. No substantial benefits seem to have accrued to him as a result of these transactions. No illegality can be assigned to them. But in the minds of Westerners with long memories they belonged to the shadowy maneuvers of the old Spanish Conspiracy; and in 1806, as a gentleman farmer, a pillar of society, and a devoted Jeffersonian, George Morgan wanted to hear no talk calculated to remind him of his brief brush with that unsavory episode. He lost no time in reporting Burr's conversation to the President, and he prevailed on two of his associates in Pittsburgh, General Neville and Judge Samuel Roberts, to do the same. The gist of these messages to Jefferson was that there was something in the "tone" of Burr's conversation that left in the minds of his listeners the "strange impression . . . that a plan was arranging or arranged for effecting [a] . . . Separation of the Union."

In his reply to George Morgan's account of Burr's remarks at Morganza, Jefferson was profuse in his thanks for "information which claims the more attention as it coincides with what has been learned from other quarters." Afterwards, in letters to Colonel Morgan himself and to one of his daughters-in-law, Jefferson wrote that Morgan's warning message was his first indication of the treasonable character of Burr's "mad project." Actually, by mid-September 1806, when Morgan's warning arrived, the President had in his files at least a dozen similar statements.

The earliest of these, reaching the executive mansion in December 1805, took the form of two hand-printed notes, postmarked Philadelphia and signed "Your Friend." One assured Jefferson that Burr's "abberations through the Western States" had as their object the "overthrow of your Administration." In the other, "Your Friend" urged the President to keep an eye on

Miranda, asserting that he and Burr were playing the same game. Both were pretending that their movements were directed at a foreign power. In actuality, both were struggling to bring down the federal government and injure "the Atlantic States."

During the first six months of 1806, the President received eight highly detailed letters on Burr's "abberations" from Joseph Hamilton Daveiss, the United States Attorney for the District of Kentucky. The theme sounding through most of Daveiss's dispatches was that Burr and Wilkinson were endeavoring to revive the old Spanish Conspiracy, the old effort to excise the American West from the Union and attach it to monarchical Spain. Young, energetic, and prepossessing, Daveiss did not content himself with writing letters. At his own expense, he undertook two extensive investigatory journeys, seeking out individuals he regarded as privy to Burr's intentions. The second of these trips took him to St. Louis, where General Wilkinson showed him a map of New Mexico and said that if Burr were "President, we should have all this country by now." Had Daveiss caught the import of that remark, it might have dawned on him that not a disruption of the Union but a conquest of the Spanish dominions was Burr's objective. Later he did come to believe that an invasion of the Spanish Indies was included in Burr's plans, writing Jefferson that the former Vice President's overall intention was "To cause a revolt of the Spanish provinces, and a severance of all these Western States and Territories from the union to coalesce & form one government."

Jefferson gave his reports only the most cursory attention. He answered the first of Daveiss's letters, but his only response to all of the Kentuckian's subsequent messages consisted of a one-paragraph note, icy with the Virginian's reluctance to trust an informant who not only happened to be a Federalist but was also a brother-in-law and protégé of Chief Justice John Marshall, whom Jefferson once characterized as "the Federalist serpent in the democratic Eden of our administration." In his answer to Daveiss's first letter, he asked the Kentucky district

126

attorney to tell him all he knew, only to discover that what Daveiss knew, or thought he knew, was more than Jefferson wanted to know. Repeatedly, in letter after letter, Daveiss insisted that practically all the supporters of Burr's project were members of the President's party. He listed, among others, former Senator John Breckinridge of Kentucky, then Attorney General of the United States; Senator Samuel Smith of Maryland, longtime Jefferson intimate; and Andrew Jackson of Tennessee. Later, Daveiss withdrew Breckinridge's name, calling its inclusion an error. Dumas Malone, suggesting that Jefferson may have erred in brushing off Daveiss's alarums, offers by way of explanation the possibility that Jefferson did so out of the feeling that the Kentucky Federalist was "a partisan troublemaker." This conjecture, if correct, makes understandable Jefferson's refusal to act on Daveiss's allegations. But it does not explain why, after the appearance of the "Queries" about Burr in a Philadelphia newspaper in August 1805, he let fifteen months pass before looking into the frequently published charge that the movements of the former Vice President imperiled the peace and wholeness of the nation.

2

DISEMBARKING FROM PITTSBURGH in late August, Burr stopped first at Belpre, Ohio, a village on the northern banks of the Ohio River, opposite Blennerhassett Island, and then at the island itself. The Blennerhassetts welcomed him effusively, happy to see the great man again and eager to hear the nature of the enterprise in which he had invited them to share. So Mexico was to be their El Dorado! An empire no less, with Burr as emperor and Theodosia the heir apparent! That is what they understood him to say. Something was said, too, of the likelihood that some day the Western part of the United States would break away and give its allegiance to Aaron I, *Imperator*. But if and when these glorious developments took effect, what services would the master of Blennerhassett Island be called on to perform? What title would he wear? Ambassador to his native England, of course. Harman was not displeased at that prospect.

Burr often misjudged what the persons he was trying to influence wanted to hear, but on this occasion he plucked the right chords. To the profoundly romantic Blennerhassetts, his picture of a distant, fairy-tale kingdom corresponded with the longing for the idyllic that had lured them across the ocean and into the American wilderness. Not that Burr limited himself to pleasant whimsicalities. He spoke also of the difficulties involved. Before the Mexican utopia could be erected, Mexico must be seized—and that might prove impossible if the expected war with Spain failed to materialize. In that case, he might go no farther than the Bastrop lands and there initiate a vast colonizing venture certain to enrich its participants. One gathers from the testimony at Richmond about this conversation that Burr told his hosts everything, and yet told them nothing. Now he spoke of a paradise to be theirs on the shores of Lake Texoco; now, of the more commonplace possibilities of a settlement along the Washita. "No man's language," Senator Plumer observed, "was ever more apparently explicit & at the same time so covert & indefinite." Whatever Burr said, the Blennerhassetts were entranced. Whatever way he decided to travel—to the ancient parterre of the Aztecs or to the Bastrop lands—they were ready to travel with him.

Now that they were committed to one another, practical problems had to be faced and mundane preparations begun. Money first. The adventurers would fly to the promised land, Bastrop or Mexico, on drafts on New York and Philadelphia mercantile houses endorsed by Harman Blennerhassett. Not that Harman would suffer financially as the result of these pledges. Had not Burr's son-in-law, wealthy rice-growing Joseph Alston of South Carolina, agreed to underwrite the expedition to the fullest extent of his great resources? He had. But in recent years Alston had suffered a succession of crop failures.

For the time being, where large purchases were concerned, Harman would sign the papers; and when smaller ones were necessary, he would cover them with whatever funds he now commanded or could command on the value of his properties. Later, after all of them had occupied their assigned quarters on the Bastrop lands or in the Halls of Montezuma, Alston—perhaps Prime Minister Alston by then—would reimburse him.

This matter settled, the time had come for hustle and bustle. The island must be examined with certain forthcoming requirements in mind. Burr had persuaded two New Yorkers—Comfort Tyler of Herkimer and Major Israel Smith of Cayuga—to begin assembling supplies and rounding up recruits in the Eastern states. Many of the men procured in those regions were to be brought into the Ohio Valley via Beaver, Pennsylvania. There must be a bivouac for them, an assembly point. Blennerhassett Island would do nicely for some if not all of them. Against their coming, certain facilities must be erected, including a kiln for the drying of corn to be ground into meal. Other foodstuffs must be brought to the area and stored. Henceforth, in short, Blennerhassett Island was to be the main workshop of the expedition, serving as a staging ground and commissary. To Harman and Margaret Blennerhassett would fall the supervision of these labors, for the leader of the expedition would not be around. So entwined in popular memory are Aaron Burr and the island that it is surprising to note that his physical presence there was negligible. Counting his first stop in 1805, a thirty-six-hour stay at most, he seems to have spent less than five days in all on its polished turf.

During his two-day visit in the late summer of 1806, he and Harman spent a fair amount of time at nearby Marietta. There they contracted for the construction of fifteen bateaux "ample enough to convey five hundred men," along with "a large keelboat for the transportation of provisions," etc., all to be delivered by their makers—Woodbridge and Company—on 9 December. The price for these vessels, $1,319, came out of Blennerhassett's pocket. They also purchased hundreds of barrels of pork. Back on the island, again, Burr thanked Margaret Blennerhassett for her hospitality. Then, on 1 September, he departed, wafting down the Ohio River with Colonel De Pestre at his side.

Behind him, the Blennerhassetts twittered in a euphoria of anticipation. Though the boats under construction on the Muskingum River below Marietta would not be ready until December, Margaret at once began packing in preparation for the journey West. Harman busied himself with Burr's affairs. He traveled considerably, seeking to interest able-bodied neighbors in the expedition and concentrating on Wood County, the governmental unit of Virginia (now West Virginia) to which Blennerhassett Island belonged. He wrote and had published in the *Ohio Gazette*, a Marietta newspaper, a series of essays signed Querist. In these he dilated on the benefits likely to accrue to the trans-Appalachian states and territories if and when they decided to withdraw, "peacefully and constitutionally," from the Union. Such talk was not uncommon on the western waters, but its promulgation in print in September 1806 fed the already briskly circulating rumors of a Spanish Conspiracy-type plot to that end under the aegis of Burr and Wilkinson. That Burr knew nothing of the Querist essays until after they appeared suggests that he lacked some of the qualities the leader of a revolution should possess. Surely any right-thinking generalissimo would have made certain that his partners in intrigue showed him their writings before they published them.

Blennerhassett called on the Henderson brothers, John and Alexander, prominent Wood County citizens. According to the testimony of the brothers at Richmond, their guest showed them a manuscript copy of one of the Querist essays, identified himself as the author, and told them that "under the auspices . . . of Colonel Burr, a separation of the Union was contemplated"; that New Orleans was to be seized, its "bank or banks" emptied, its military stores requisitioned, and the city itself and the country around it "revolutionized in the course of nine months."

When a government attorney asked if the President's name came up in this conversation, Alexander Henderson quoted Blennerhassett as saying that "if Mr. Jefferson was any way impertinent, . . . Burr would tie him neck and heels, and throw him into the Potomac."

If, as the brothers said, Harman's purpose in calling on them was to induce them to support the expedition, his visit was an exercise in naïveté. For the Hendersons and the Blennerhassetts had been at odds for years, immersed in a mutual antipathy, all the stronger because they were Wood County's leading families, its greatest slaveowners. Ethnicity may have been a component of the feud, for the Hendersons were Scots by birth and the Blennerhassetts English, but its sticking point was politics. The Hendersons were Federalists, and in one Wood County election they had blocked Blennerhassett, a Democrat, from voting, justifying their action on the grounds that his failure to show a deed to his island rendered him ineligible under the suffrage laws of Virginia. It is difficult to reconcile Blennerhassett's bizarre remarks to the Hendersons, as reported by them at Richmond, with the long-standing strain between the two families.

To the island that September came another Burr, Theodosia Burr Alston, with her husband following later. The Blennerhassetts had invited Theodosia months before, and for a time she had considered journeying West when her father did, only to discover in the late summer that the mountain air of Bedford, Pennsylvania, was doing wonders for her ailing boy and to decide to tarry there a little longer. The Blennerhassetts found her company delightful. Most people did. At twenty-three, Theodosia was precisely the paragon of brains, beauty, and wit that her father had long ago made up his mind she was going to be. From her toddling days up, he had insisted that she acquire proficiency in every branch of liberal study, driven, it would seem, by a determination to instill in the only surviving child of his marriage to the first Theodosia the same attributes he would have wanted in a son, had he been given one. "Perhaps almost subconsciously," historian Ray Swick observes, the son of President Aaron Burr of Princeton and the grandson of the great thinker, Jonathan Edwards, intended his daughter "to be the third Aaron, and, as such, a continuation of the Edwards–Burr intellectual dynasty," with the accident of gender "repaired by academic diligence."

Another girl might have withered into depression or rebelled at Burr's oppressive pedagogy. Not Theodosia. She throve, she bloomed, she loved the teacher with a more than ordinary love, and as he bent her, so she inclined. Over the years, theirs became almost too close a closeness, as though they breathed for one another. Her marriage in 1801 to Joseph Alston of a rice-rich South Carolina family effected no loosening of the ties that bound them; it merely drew another human being into a tight little family circle. The event won the unreserved blessing of the bride's father and the almost equally unreserved disapproval of the women of the socially elevated circles in which Theodosia moved. They could find nothing to admire in short, stocky, swarthy, fantastically bewhiskered Joseph Alston with his large brooding eyes, strong nose, and small pointed mouth. "Ugly and of unprepossessing manners." So Maria Nicholson, sister of Mrs. Albert Gallatin, described him. "Rich . . . a great dasher, dissipated, ill-tempered, vain and silly," she added. Meeting the couple at a ball in Washington soon after the wedding, Nelly Custis Lewis, granddaughter of Martha Washington, found "Mrs. Alston . . . a very sweet little woman very engaging and pretty—but her husband is the most intolerable mortal I ever beheld . . . more calculated to break a Wife's heart than any person I have ever seen." Margaret Blennerhassett was quick to join the pejorative chorus. "I never could love one of my own Sex as I do her," she said of Theodosia, but "how can she live with such a man as Alston?"

She lived very well with him, indeed. A quiet, steady devotion sustained the marriage. She found his company a pleasurable relief from her father. The two men could not have been more unlike. So plenteous were the older one's ambitions and so dogged his pursuit of them that those portions of the drive within him that he never got around to using could have powered an army to victory. In contrast, Alston lazed through life. He studied at Princeton, but there is no record of his ever receiving a degree. He read law, but there is no record of his ever hanging up a shingle. He went into politics, was elected regularly to the South Carolina legislature and eventually to the governorship, but there are no indications that he pined for more demanding posts.

Whatever the roots of Theodosia's affection for him, they rested deep in fertile soil. "How does your election advance?" she wrote him from New York on one of her frequent visits there. "I am anxious to know something of it; not from patriotism, however. It little concerns me which party succeeds. Where you are, there is my country, and in you are centered all my wishes. Were you a Brutus, I should be a Roman. But were you a Caesar, I should only wish glory to Rome that glory might be yours. As long as you love me, I am nothing on earth but your wife and your friend: contented and proud to be that . . . I am very happy you have chosen chess for your amusement. It keeps you constantly in mind how poor kings fare without their queens." That Alston's attachment to her harbored something sharper than mere devotion is shown by his response to her untimely death in 1813. He was only thirty-three at the time. Four years later he was dead, and his correspondence with the bereaved father indicates that he wished to go. He did not care to live without her. Neither for that matter did Burr, but the older man was made of more lasting stuff.

It is unclear when the Alstons reached the island or when they left, only that toward the end of September they were preparing to join Burr in Kentucky, and that Harman Blennerhassett was preparing to travel with them.

3

In the interval, Burr had again become the Gulliver of the West, covering thousands of miles with breathtaking rapidity. At Cincinnati he conferred with Senator John Smith, at Frankfort with Senator John Brown. Twice he visited Nashville. Again he stayed with the Andrew Jacksons at their blockhouse home, somewhat enlarged since his last visit and known now as The Hermitage. "Burr is with me," General Jackson wrote an acquaintance on the second of these occasions. ". . . Would it not be well for us to do something as a mark of attention to the Colonel—he has always [been] and still is a true and trusty friend of Tennessee." More than "something" was done. Again Burr was banqueted and toasted. Again he was given a ball, this one so elaborate and punctilious that the splendor of it was a topic of conversation in Nashville for years to come. If the citizens of that place knew of the growing suspicions of Burr's enterprise, they chose to ignore them.

Certainly, Andrew Jackson was determined to resist them. To the commander of the Tennessee militia, the former Vice President had become the potential scourge of the hated dons, the man who was preparing, when the time was ripe, to strike the first blow at Spanish power in the New World. On this matter, Jackson's dreams were almost as far-reaching as Burr's. "You no doubt have seen from the late paper," the Tennessean told a friend, "that the negotiations [by the federal government] for the purchase of the Floridas has failed." To Jackson this meant only one thing: a war impended. He saw in it a long-awaited opportunity to "conquer not only the Floridas, but all Spanish North America." Perhaps even more than that, he added, expressing the "hope" that with a couple of thousand volunteers under "firm officers and men of enterprise [we] . . . will look [also] into Santa Fe and Mexico, give freedom and commerce to those provinces and establish peace, and a permanent barrier against the inroads and attacks of foreign powers on our interior, which will be the case so long as Spain holds that large country on our borders."

At Clover Bottom, a resort area on a branch of the Cumberland River near Nashville, Jackson and two business associates operated a store, a racecourse, a tavern (described on the books as a "house of entertainment"), and a boatyard. When Burr sent the general $3,500 in Kentucky bank notes and an order for the building and provisioning of five large boats, Jackson saw to it that the necessary labor was initiated at once. Simultaneously, he commissioned a close friend to scour the nearby countryside in search of recruits for the expedition. Now, as his biographer puts it, he was "an accomplice" in the conspiracy. But not completely so. Even the stalwart Tennessean was vulnerable to the accumulating aspersions on its leader.

One day in the late autumn a young man appeared on the doorstep of The Hermitage with a letter of introduction signed by we know not whom. He identified himself as a Captain Fort ("Christian name John," according to a witness at the Richmond trial). Jackson quoted his visitor as stating that the intention of Burr and his fellow adventurers "was to divide the Union . . . by seizing New Orleans, and the bank [there], shutting the port, conquering Mexico, and uniting the western part of the Union to the conquered country." How were these ends to be achieved, the general wanted to know. With the help of General Wilkinson and the United States Army, was Fort's reply. Jackson hated Wilkinson. He found it hard to believe that Burr could lend himself to such schemes, but Wilkinson was another sort—a man believed to be in the pay of Spain and known to be quite capable of biting the hand that fed him. Where had Fort gotten his information? From Wilkinson or from Burr? From neither, the young captain answered; he had never met the general, and though he had seen Burr, he had never conversed with him. Where, then, did his information come from? From Samuel Swartwout, Fort said. Jackson knew that Swartwout was one of Burr's closest associates. Now, he wrote, "it rushed into my mind like lightning" that the former Vice President was perhaps a traitor.

Jackson, as his later activities demonstrate, was not averse to bending his country's laws in the interest of enlarging his country's property by diminishing that of the hated Spaniards; but he was not capable of any action detrimental to his country's welfare and unity. He rushed off a letter to Governor Claiborne in New Orleans, naming no names, but warning him of a possible insurrection in that vicinity. He rushed off a letter to Jefferson, again naming no names, offering the services of the militia he commanded in "the event of insult or aggression . . . on our government and country FROM ANY QUARTER." He rushed off a letter to Burr, relating what Fort had said and informing the colonel that, until the allegations were denied, there could be "no further intimacy" between them. Burr answered at once, filling his letter, according to Jackson, "with the most sacred pledges that he had not nor never had any views inimical or hostile to the United States," and that "whenever he was charged with the intention of seperating [sic] the union, the idea of insanity must be ascribed to him."

At this point, Jackson was uncertain what to think. Only later, after Burr came again to Nashville and the two men had an opportunity to talk face to face, did the general's doubts disappear. They never returned. Thereafter, he was Burr's supporter, convinced that the ex-Vice President's goals were what he said they were, equally convinced that when Jefferson acted against Burr it was in response to pressures beyond his control and because only by sacrificing Burr could he hide the extent to which his Administration had condoned the colonel's plans.

But these developments lay in the future when, in October, Burr established his expeditionary headquarters in Lexington. Here he was joined by Blennerhassett and the Alstons. Blennerhassett lingered for a few weeks, but the Alstons were soon en route home so that Joseph could attend the winter session of the South Carolina legislature. Colonel De Pestre, too, headed

East. With him went orders from Burr to call on the Marqués de Casa Yrujo in Philadelphia in a further effort to persuade the Spanish minister that an assault on his country's colonies was the farthest thing from the adventurers' mind, that their only objective was a division of the American Union. A futile errand, as De Pestre afterwards confessed, for in the fall and winter of 1806 Yrujo's reports to his superior were those of a man certain that Burr was still planning an invasion of Mexico or the Floridas or both. When José Vidal, the spy Yrujo had requested from Madrid, reached the Quaker City in October, he at once made ready to descend the Ohio and Mississippi Rivers under instructions from the Marqués to keep the movements of Burr and his followers under scrutiny at all times.

From Lexington, at frequent intervals, Burr rode out to check on the scattered elements of his operation. Some of these jaunts were to the Falls of the Ohio at Louisville. There Davis Floyd, a young Indiana lawyer and legislator who had joined the expedition as its quartermaster, was overseeing the stockpiling of some of the stores that would be carried downriver when boats were available. Back and forth Burr rode, tirelessly, cheerfully, back and forth.

He had a time schedule in mind, one that he hoped would put him on the lower Mississippi in mid-December. Could he make it? One discerns in his restless wanderings and in his correspondence a sense of growing impatience at the amount of time required to construct a flotilla of boats, to assemble provisions and men. Months before, Wilkinson had written from St. Louis to let the colonel know that "I will be ready before you are." But ready for what? He had no idea what the general was doing. No idea of whether the boundary dispute in the far Southwest—the "crisis on the frontier"—was still only a battle of words or whether it had burgeoned into the war that would make an invasion of the Spanish domains a practical possibility. Many such questions occupied his mind as back and forth he rode, tirelessly, cheerfully. More cheerfully than the circumstances warranted, for as the hard Western winter set in, whitening portions of the Ohio Valley, rumors and newspaper stories unfavorable to his reputation were on the increase.

Joseph Hamilton Daveiss had not given up. Angered by Jefferson's cavalier treatment of his warnings, the district attorney of Kentucky was now struggling to alert the public. In this endeavor he enjoyed the collaboration of Humphrey Marshall of Frankfort, a cantankerous old-line Federalist who had sat in both the legislature of Kentucky and the United States Senate and who today is best remembered as the author of the first history of his state. His ties to the district attorney were both political and familial, for Marshall was a first cousin of Chief Justice John Marshall and, like Daveiss, had married one of the Chief Justice's sisters. When in the summer of 1806 a newspaper called the *Western World* started publication in Frankfort, local gossip named Daveiss and Marshall as its silent backers. Daveiss denied the rumors and Marshall never acknowledged them. But both men wrote for the paper, and from its earliest issue the *Western World* bristled with charges that a new version of the old Spanish Conspiracy was abroad and that Burr and Wilkinson were involved.

In October, Daveiss went on another of his investigatory junkets. This one took him to Louisville for a talk with Davis Floyd. Evidence exists that Floyd knew of Burr's intention to strike at the Spanish colonies in the event of war. He was aware of the colonel's interest in settling the Bastrop lands. What Daveiss learned from him is unknown—probably nothing of substance—but what Daveiss saw on the docks of Louisville, the actual accumulations of goods and the building of boats for Burr's use, left him more certain than ever that, unless the expedition were broken up, the nation would be.

What he was so certain of passeth understanding. It is plain from the wild and undocumented assertions in the *Western World* that, where Burr's actions were concerned, the district attorney had no facts of any sort to justify his imaginings. Perhaps the explanation is to be found in a statement by one of the editors of the *Western World*, Scottish-born John Wood, author of the libelous book about John Adams that Burr, a few years earlier, had tried unsuccessfully to suppress. The journalist's statement, as recorded by Harman Blennerhassett, was that Daveiss's determination to stigmatize Burr as a traitor was motivated not by patriotism but by pique, that the district attorney was mortally offended at the failure of the former Vice President, during his first tour of the West in 1805, to call on Daveiss, reveal his plans, and solicit the public prosecutor's assistance with them. It was Wood's theory that the Kentucky Federalist saw in his attacks on Burr an opportunity to embarrass the President, whom Daveiss by the fall of 1806 had come to believe was not doing anything about Burr's schemes because he (Jefferson) either was directly "concerned" with them or "connived" at them.

In Wood County, the Hendersons were busy. On 6 October, at a gathering of the citizenry summoned by Alexander Henderson, Burr and Blennerhassett were pronounced enemies of the Republic. Then a resolution was adopted, calling for a muster of the county militia and an armed descent on Blennerhassett Island for the purpose of stopping the preparations for the expedition in process there.

When word of these actions reached Margaret Blennerhassett, she was alarmed at the possibility of mob violence. She ordered her gardener, Peter Taylor, to find her husband and Burr. He was to explain what was happening and urge the colonel to keep his distance from the island. Not knowing exactly where his employer and Burr were, Taylor hastened to Cincinnati, believing that Senator John Smith could give him an address. He found the senator in his dry-goods store and plainly agitated. A recent blast in the *Western World*, describing Burr's "mysterious movements" as directed at "a disunion of the states," had come down the river, was now everywhere in the valley a topic of discussion. At first Smith said he knew nothing, but the rough and outspoken gardener was not to be put off. Somehow, somewhere he had learned that "some time ago" Smith had filled an order for a greatcoat, sent to him by Burr. He reminded the senator of this fact, speaking loudly enough for Burr's name to be heard by the customers in the store. Smith rushed him out of the shop and into a private room on the floor above.

He told Taylor that Burr and Blennerhassett could be found in Lexington. Would the gardener, he asked, be good enough to carry a message to the colonel? Taylor said he would "carry anything so it was not too burdensome," and the senator penned a note. Reaching Lexington on 25 October, Taylor discovered that his master was temporarily out of town, but that Burr was around. On being informed that the citizens of Virginia and Ohio were in an uproar and would shoot the colonel if he came that way, Burr, according to Taylor, "looked surprised" and wondered "what the people had got into their heads."

Taylor handed him the letter from Smith. "I beg leave to inform you that we have in this quarter various reports prejudicial to your character," the Ohio senator had written. "It is believed by many that your design is to dismember the Union. Although I do not believe you have any such design, yet I must confess from the mystery and rapidity of your movements, that I have fears, let your project be what it may, that the tranquility of the country will be interrupted, unless it be candidly disclosed, which I solicit, and to which I presume you will have no objection."

Was Smith suggesting that Burr take to the press to answer the denunciations of him in the *Western World* and elsewhere? If so, he was pleading with the wrong man. All his life, Burr regarded newspaper attacks on him as unworthy of notice. Pride went before his fall, if indeed it were not one of the contributing factors to it. When, on the twenty-seventh, Peter Taylor left

Lexington, accompanied by Blennerhassett—alarmed for the safety of his wife and anxious to get home—he carried with him a letter by Burr to be delivered to Smith in Cincinnati, which closed with this postscript: "It may be an unnecessary caution, but I never write for publication."

It opened with these words: "I was greatly surprised and really hurt by the unusual tenor of your letter of the 23rd, and I hasten to reply to it as well for your satisfaction as my own. If there exists any design to separate the western from the eastern states, I am totally ignorant of it—I never harbored or expressed any such intention to any one, nor did any person ever intimate such design to me. Indeed I have no conception of any mode in which such a measure could be promoted, except by operating on the minds of the people, and demonstrating it to be their interest."

Long ago, historian Henry Adams deemed it significant that in this letter Burr denied only that he was trying to separate the Western states "by force." What the colonel "never denied," Adams argued, "was the plan of establishing a Western empire by consent." True; but in Burr's day few Americans ruled out the likelihood that someday the inhabitants of the trans-Appalachian region might find it to "their interest" to go it alone. As late as 1804, President Jefferson was telling Dr. Joseph Priestley: "Whether we remain in one confederacy, or form into Atlantic and Mississippi confederacies, I believe not very important to either part." No one in the early 1800's was sure whether the present states and territories would hang together or not; nor would any widespread certainty on this score take form until the signing at Appomattox Courthouse, over half a century later, of the document that terminated the Civil War. Apparently, Senator Smith perceived no secessionist plot in Burr's recognition of a prevailing attitude. The colonel's written denial of treasonable intent removed his "fears" concerning the aims of the expedition.

4

ON 4 NOVEMBER, Joseph Hamilton Daveiss shifted his
crusade against Burr from the columns of the *Western World*
to the quarters of the United States District Court on the second
floor of the three-story, gray-limestone building in Frankfort
that was then the capitol of Kentucky. Daveiss asked Judge
Henry Innes to issue a warrant for Burr's arrest, along with a
process to compel the attendance of witnesses. He accused the
former Vice President of a "high misdemeanor"; to wit, the
preparation of a "military expedition against Mexico." No mention of treason; not that the district attorney had relinquished his
belief in Burr's culpability on that count, but because of Daveiss's shocked discovery, after a "particular examination" of the
books, that there was "no law" against "an attempt to disunite
the states."

The federal prosecutor's action in court was duly trumpeted
by the editors of the *Western World*, John Wood and Joseph
M. Street. "On this extraordinary occasion," they wrote of the
charges now lodged against Burr,

> we are well aware that the field of conjecture will be traveled
> in every direction by the curious reader and inquisitive poli-
> ticians. With ourselves, we confess it has excited neither as-
> tonishment nor surprise, being, as we before mentioned, well
> informed of the subject eighteen months ago. This was the
> business which we proposed to unfold under the head of the
> Miranda Expedition. The expedition was only a very inferior
> part of the scheme, and Miranda himself an inferior agent in
> the plan. From the steps which have been taken by the public
> attorney, we now think it improper to enter into a detail of
> the conspiracy, being assured that he is in possession of all
> the information of which we are; and that he is a much more
> proper instrument than the editors of a newspaper to prevent
> its accomplishment. The project of Colonel Burr is doubtless
> of the most extensive nature, and if accomplished will not

only affect the interests of the Western country, but of the known world. A revolution in the Spanish provinces of North America will speedily, when aided by Miranda, lead to one in South America, and the whole, along with the Western States of the Union organized into one empire, headed by a man of the enterprise and talents of Colonel Burr, will present a phenomenon in the political history of the globe perhaps only equalled by the modern Empire of France.

Judge Harry Innes was not likely to join the editors of the *World* in their support of Joseph Hamilton Daveiss's efforts to "prevent the accomplishment" of Burr's Napoleonic strivings. Not only was the judge on the Democratic side of the political fence; he had more than once heard himself castigated by Daveiss as one of the movers and shakers of the old Spanish Conspiracy. After some consideration of the district attorney's motions against Burr, he rejected them on the grounds that he couldn't very well order the arrest of a citizen on nothing more than an affidavit to which the district attorney himself had sworn and the gist of which was that someone whom he trusted had told him that Burr was not only guilty of the misdemeanor as charged but was also fanning the fires of rebellion in the western country—a ruling which tells us that Daveiss managed to sneak the treason theme into the proceedings even though the law, as far as he knew, failed to recognize an attempt to split the nation as a criminal offense.

Daveiss later regretted that, when Innes overruled his motion, he didn't just let the whole matter drop, since the anti-Burr talk generated by his accusations was sufficiently ominous to serve his purpose. That, he admitted, was to strengthen the Federalist position in Kentucky at the next election and to weaken that of the opposition. But Burr was not about to permit him to attain these ends. The minute news of Daveiss's charges reached Lexington, he wrote Judge Innes, volunteering to appear in court as fast as he could ride to Frankfort.

Accordingly, on the morning of 8 November, the former

Vice President stepped into the spacious chamber on the second floor of the Kentucky statehouse just as His Honor was explaining from the bench why he could not let the public prosecutor put him in durance vile. Flanking Burr were two Lexington attorneys. One was Henry Clay, an engaging young political comer, whose skills as an advocate had drawn lawyer Burr's attention. Not that the Lexington legal lights had anything to do. Burr attended to everything. At his request, Judge Innes impaneled a grand jury and adjourned the court until Wednesday 12 November to allow for the procurement of witnesses.

That November Wednesday was festival time in Frankfort. Never before in the fledgling state of Kentucky had a "Grand Inquest . . . been assembled . . . under the General Government of the United States." Never before had a onetime holder of the second office in the land appeared before the bar of justice. The throng, pushing into the cupola-crowned statehouse, filled the second-floor courtroom and spilled into the adjacent corridors, into the offices on the floor below, and into the grassy "Public Square" outside.

Judge Innes had barely started giving the jurymen their instructions before sending them into another room to pursue their investigations in secret, when the district attorney interrupted. He announced that the witness around whom he had built his case—Burr's quartermaster, Davis Floyd—was no longer in Louisville. He was attending a session of the Indiana legislature at Vincennes, was thus beyond the jurisdiction of the Kentucky court. As his main witness was unavailable, the public prosecutor moved that the grand jury be discharged.

This ended whatever political hay Daveiss had reaped from his legal action against Burr. He had promised the people a courtroom drama, and he had neither actors nor script. When, after the discharge of the jury, Burr walked from the building, accompanied by his attorneys, he was the beneficiary of approving smiles and rousing cheers. "Colonel Burr," reported next day's *Palladium*, one of the local newspapers, "has throughout this business conducted himself with the calmness, moderation, and firmness which have characterized him through life. He evinced an earnest desire for a full and speedy investigation— free from irritation or emotion; he excited the strongest sensation of respect and friendship in the breast of every impartial person present."

But two weeks later the district attorney was at it again. *The Palladium* broke the news. "In the Federal Court on Tuesday morning last [25 November]," the newspaper revealed, "the attorney for the United States renewed his motion for a grand jury to enquire into the conduct of Col. Burr; which the court granted, and directed the marshal to have the jury ready on Tuesday next. Subpoenas have been issued for witnesses; and Colonel Burr, who it was apprehended had left the state, we understand is still in it.—There can be no doubt, therefore, of his attendance, and of the trial proceeding without further delay, if a true bill should be found." To which *The Palladium* added that "Since the above was written, we have been informed that the attorney introduced his motion by observing that Mr. Davis Floyd (the witness whom he deemed material, and who was absent when he attempted to bring on the investigation before) had returned [to Kentucky]; and that unless a decisive step was now taken, Mr. Burr would be afloat with his flotilla in a short time."

After a brief stay with Senator Smith at Cincinnati, Burr, too, had returned to Kentucky and was looking into the loading of his boats at the Falls of the Ohio when he learned of Daveiss's request for a second arraignment of him. He immediately wrote Henry Clay, only recently named to the United States Senate, expressing the hope that the young Lexington lawyer would put off his journey to Washington long enough to represent him again at Frankfort.

Notwithstanding the favorable outcome of his first legal tilt with Daveiss, Burr was beginning to smart under the still-rising tide of suspicion concerning the aims of his expedition. Before leaving the falls, he dispatched a letter to William Henry Harrison. "Considering the various and extravagant reports which circulate concerning me," he told the Indiana governor, "it may not be unsatisfactory to you to be informed . . . that I have no wish . . . to attempt a separation of the Union, that I have no connection with any foreign power or Government, that I never meditated the introduction of any foreign power or influence into the U.S. or any Part of the Country . . ." This message was dated 27 November. Four days later, from Frankfort, Burr sent a similar one to Henry Clay. "I have no design, nor have I taken any measures to promote a dissolution of the Union," he assured the new senator. "I have neither issued nor signed nor promised a commission to any person for any purpose. I do not own a Musket nor a bayonet nor any single article of Military Stores . . . My views have been fully explained to . . . the Principal officers of Government and I believe are well considered by the Administration . . . Considering the high station you now fill in our national Councils I have thought these explanations proper and such as to counteract the chimerical tales which malevolent persons have so industriously circulated and to satisfy you that you have not espoused the cause of a man in any way unfriendly to the laws of Government." Though later Clay came to believe Burr guilty as charged, he accepted these protestations of innocence at the time they reached him. When on Tuesday 2 December the second arraignment of the former Vice President opened before Judge Innes, Clay and his associate counsel, John Allen, were in the courtroom.

After the judge had charged the grand jury and its members had retired to their room, Clay addressed the bench. He purported to see nothing but trickery in Daveiss's decision, during the earlier arraignment, to call it off "on account of the non-attendance of a single witness [Davis Floyd] whose evidence he pretended was a most material link in the chain . . . of this secret and mysterious plan in which Colonel Burr is supposed to be engaged for the conquering of provinces and the erection of empires." He stated that when Daveiss applied for the assembling of another grand jury, he was under the impression that Burr "was beyond the reach of the jurisdiction of this court" and assumed that his failure to appear would convince the public of the colonel's guilt. He wondered what further trickery the prosecutor would attempt, now that Burr was present and Davis Floyd available for questioning.

He did not have to wonder long. Addressing the court next, Daveiss said that this time his case rested on different witnesses; namely, General John Adair of Mercer County and a Mr. C. F. Luckett. As neither of them had shown up, he asked the judge to command them to attend by letters. Innes counseled patience. He reminded the public prosecutor that in his summonses to Adair and Luckett he had neglected to specify a date for their appearance in court. Now that word of the convening of the grand jury was known throughout the state, he predicted that the missing witnesses would arrive. They did, though whether on the next day or the day after is not clear.

Tuesday's session started late and adjourned early. Wednesday's began with a surprise. As the grand jury was about to retire to begin its deliberations, Daveiss gave the foreman a document calling for the indictment of General Adair as a collaborator in Burr's schemes. The prosecutor followed this move with a demand that he be allowed to go into the room assigned to the jury and interrogate the witnesses brought before it.

At once Clay and Allen were on their feet, speaking for their client. They labeled Daveiss's proposal "novel," "contrary to accepted practice." What the district attorney suggested would convert the hearings of the grand jury into a trial of individuals against whom no true bills had as yet been returned. Daveiss countered with the assertion that most of the persons summoned before the grand jury would be reluctant to tell the "truth," that only a lawyer, experienced in the examination of witnesses, could prod it out of them. His remarks drew Burr into the dispute. He recalled his years as the public prosecutor for the state of New York. Never had he imposed himself on the proceedings of a grand jury. It simply was not done—not in any of the judicial systems with which he was acquainted. Judge Innes agreed. The district attorney, he directed, "could consult with the jury on matters of law, but not on matters of fact."

Thursday's session opened with another request from the stubborn prosecutor. Waving aloft a sheaf of papers, he revealed that he had prepared a series of written queries for the members of the panel to put to the witnesses. He asked permission of the court to deliver them to the jury. Protests from Clay and Allen, neither of whom could remember "any precedents" for such an action; but this time their client overruled them. Unless the judge had objections, Burr saw no reason why Daveiss's written queries should not go to the jury room. The judge nodded, and the lists went. To no avail. About one o'clock the grand jury filed in to say that it had reached a decision with regard to the indictment against General Adair. "No true bill," it announced, whereupon the district attorney handed the foreman a formal indictment of Burr and the jurymen again withdrew to their quarters, to begin questioning the eleven witnesses —Davis Floyd, John Adair, and C. P. Luckett among them— now on hand.

Friday's session brought another unexpected development. Half an hour after it began, the deputy marshal entered the courtroom to inform Judge Innes that the grand jury had two requests. They wanted to see a file of the *Western World* and they wanted to talk to its editors, John Wood and Joseph Street. Word of these demands sent a shiver of anticipation through the onlookers jammed into the courtroom and into the halls and offices of the Kentucky statehouse. Now, at last, the truth was about to come out. How many times, in the columns of their newspaper, had Wood and Street claimed that they knew the secrets of Burr's activities.

But when the two journalists took the witness stand in the

jury room, they might just as well have given their tongues to the cat. Under oath, Street had to confess that all the accusations he had leveled at the colonel rested on hearsay, that he had no information "that would amount to evidence." Wood went further. Once he had believed the accused man guilty of something, but recent talks with "characters whose veracity I have no reason to doubt" induced him to "believe that the present designs of Colonel Burr [are] . . . neither against the government or laws of the United States."

At two o'clock that afternoon, the grand jury came in with its findings. "No true bill," it said. "The grand jury," its report added, "is happy to inform the court that no violent disturbance of the public tranquility, or breach of laws has come to their knowledge. We have no hesitation in declaring, that having carefully examined and scrutinized all testimony which has come before us, as well on the charges against Burr, as those contained in the indictment preferred to us against John Adair, that there has been no testimony before us which does in the smallest degree criminate the conduct of either of those persons; nor can we, from all the inquiries and investigation of the subject, discover that anything improper or injurious to the interests of the Government of the United States . . . is designed or contemplated by either of them."

A roar of approval shook the courtroom, to be picked up by the crowds in the other parts of the building. That night the exonerated defendant was a guest of honor at a giant ball, with people coming from miles around to pay him homage. Never again would Aaron Burr know the adulation of the public. His expedition was about to crumble, brought down by events growing out of the crisis on the Sabine, of which the colonel was not yet aware.

8

The Betrayal

THE CRISIS ON THE FRONTIER erupted in the fall of 1805 when a few Spanish soldiers crossed the Sabine River from Texas and encamped at the little settlements of Bayou Pierre and Nana in the vicinity of the American military post at Natchitoches, near the Red River. To thousands of Americans, and especially to Westerners spoiling for a fight with the hated Spanish, the movement was a *casus belli*, an invasion of American territory. To the officials of Texas it was merely a transfer of military potential from one section of his Catholic Majesty's property to another.

The question of where, in this part of the trans-Mississippi West, American soil ended and Spanish soil began was one that no one could answer. So far, efforts to settle the issue by diplomatic means had come to naught. Jefferson believed that the unmeasured lands acquired by the Louisiana Purchase stretched to the Rio Grande River, which is to say to the very borders of Mexico. But the more or less official position of his government was that, pending the formulation of a written understanding with Madrid, international amity could be best served by permitting the dons to occupy all of the land lying between that river and the Sabine—the province of Texas and the so-called Interior Provinces of Mexico adjoining it—just so long as they kept themselves to the west of the Sabine.

Not correct, countered the authorities in Texas, in the Interior Provinces, and in New Spain (Mexico) itself. Their position—stiffly official—was not only that Texas belonged to their country but that the line dividing it from Louisiana ran, not along the Sabine, but along the Arroyo Hondo, a smaller stream some thirty miles to the east of that river. Their insistence on these terms reflected their realization that Texas was the last remaining barrier between the growing American Republic and the riches of Mexico. They saw the incident taking form on the "Sabine front" for what it was: another expression of a long-standing tension, characterized on their part by an abiding dread of the western-thrusting Americans and on that of the Americans by the spirit of expansionism which someday would carry them to the Pacific Ocean.

From War Secretary Dearborn in Washington to Major Moses Porter, commanding at Natchitoches, went instructions. Porter was to see to it that the invading Spanish recrossed the river immediately. He was to request from Antonio Cordero, the governor of Texas, assurances that no such inroads would occur again. The first of these instructions presented no difficulties. Confronted by sixty American soldiers under Captain Edward D. Turner, the commander of the Spanish troops at Bayou Pierre and Nana had no choice but to lead his thirty men back to the western bank of the river. But from Nacogdoches, the capital of Texas, came only refusal and defiance. Governor Cordero had no intention of abandoning what he regarded as a legitimate effort to assert the claims of his king to the disputed strip of land lying along the eastern shores of the Sabine.

Behind him stood Nimesio Salcedo, the captain general of the Interior Provinces, and José de Iturrigaray, the viceroy of Mexico. Contributing to their determination to hold back the aggressive Americans were recurrent reports of the impending emergence in the valley of the Ohio of an expeditionary force headed by a former Vice President of the United States and obviously directed at his Majesty's possessions—a development the more worrisome because in the eyes of the Spanish officials the failure of the Jefferson Administration to discourage the schemes of Aaron Burr could only mean that the government secretly supported them.

Salcedo rushed reinforcements to Cordero. Iturrigaray did the same. By the end of March, a thousand Spanish soldiers were massed along the Texas side of the Sabine; and from Natchitoches eastward to the lower Mississippi, alarums were sounding among the American settlers: rumors that the Spanish were inciting the Indians of the region against them, that they were incrementing their forces in West Florida with the idea of seizing New Orleans, and that they were encouraging slaves to flee from Louisiana into Texas and that those who did so were receiving their freedom along with allotments of land and "the services of a priest to instruct them in the Catholic religion."

Slowly but surely, news of the turmoil in the Southwest traveled to Washington, and in the late spring War Secretary Dearborn was sending more instructions westward—some of them to Major Porter at Natchitoches as before, others to the commander in chief at St. Louis.

2

IN THE FIRST of the orders to St. Louis, dated 14 March, Dearborn notified General Wilkinson that "existing circumstances in the Southwest" required "the reinforcement" of American posts on the lower Mississippi. To this end, the general was to make "the necessary arrangements . . . for the removal of the troops in your neighborhood, excepting one full company." These units were to descend the river to Fort Adams, the old post on the eastern shores of the Mississippi below Natchez, where they were to remain pending further instructions.

Amending these orders in a letter dispatched from Washington four days later, Dearborn informed Wilkinson that the movement of the Spaniards on the "Sabine front" had become a threat to the American outpost at Natchitoches. The commanding general, therefore, was to send three companies directly to that post. Two fieldpieces were to go with them, and Colonel Thomas H. Cushing, Wilkinson's adjutant and inspector, was to lead them.

In still another order, written in Washington on 6 May, Dearborn directed the general himself to descend the river. "From recent information received from New Orleans and its vicinity," the war secretary wrote, "the hostile views of the officers of His Catholic Majesty, in that quarter, have become so evident, as to require . . . on the part of the United States . . . the immediate exertion of the means we possess, for securing the rightful possession of the territory of the United States, and for protecting the citizens and their property, from the hostile encroachments of our neighbors, the Spaniards." Wilkinson, therefore, was to "take . . . command of the troops in that quarter, together with such militia or volunteers, as may turn out for the defence of the country."

In all his orders to Wilkinson, the war secretary stressed the importance of speed. He expressed the hope that the units destined for Fort Adams would be on their way "by the last of April next." But April and the first week of May had gone before the general got around to sending them downriver. In the dispatch ordering Wilkinson to take command on the Sabine front, the secretary urged the general to "repair to the territory of Orleans or its vicinity . . . with as little delay as practicable." This letter reached Wilkinson on 11 June, but not until the end of August—three months later—did he leave St. Louis. Dearborn's communications left no question as to how the general was to proceed after reaching the Southwest. In the event of "actual invasion" of American territory, he was to take the initiative. If the officers of his Catholic Majesty tried to occupy any "post, east of the Sabine," Wilkinson was to drive them out. But when in May Colonel Cushing began his journey to Natchi-

toches, he carried with him supplemental orders from his superior that countermanded the instructions of the Secretary of
War. When Cushing arrived at Natchitoches, the general informed him, he would "find in the hands of Major Porter, an
order from the Secretary . . . which might justify you in
pushing your neighbors [the dons] beyond the Sabine River
. . . But . . . you must not strain their construction to favor
the effusion of blood, and involve our country in the certain
calamities and uncertain events of war."

In short, let the government propose, he (Wilkinson)
would dispose. He wanted no war, not at any rate in the summer
of 1806. It did not suit his purposes—purposes readily understandable in the light of his future conduct. By the time Dearborn's orders began pouring into St. Louis, the general had
seen the laconic note Dayton or Burr or both had written him in
Philadelphia in April, conveying the news that their plans could
not be brought to term until December, owing to "want of water
in Ohio." Wilkinson knew the meaning of those words. The
funds he and the colonel had hoped to get from England were
not forthcoming. It was just the kind of data to put the general
to hard thought. A Burr with resources might be worth col-
laborating with; a Burr without them was another matter.
Which way should he move? Should he try to avoid a war and
denounce Burr as a traitor, thus endearing himself to both of
his employers, the President of the United States and the king of
Spain? Or should he invoke a war, join forces with Burr, and
reap his reward in the glory and booty reserved for the conquerors of Mexico? Whichever course he followed, it was of
the essence that Burr's plans be more advanced than they were
in the summer of 1806. Only after the colonel came into the
West again and completed his preparations there, only after
his expeditionary force became a physical presence on the rivers
gliding down to New Orleans—only then would Wilkinson
have something to denounce, if that's the way he chose to go;
or something to join, if that was his preference. Hence his delib-

erate delays; hence his supplemental orders to Colonel Cushing.

Hence, too, his frequent efforts during the summer of 1806 and well into the fall to give Aaron Burr the impression that the war the colonel wanted was about to start. Wilkinson realized that the possibility that no war was coming might induce the former Vice President to scuttle his project. On the other hand, the assumption that one was starting would entice him westward. The general knew better than to write Burr himself at this time. Such letters could be cited as evidence of his participation in the conspiracy. But there were ways of getting the word to where he wanted it. He knew that sooner or later communications to Burr's associates would be shown to the colonel. So, shortly after the receipt of his orders to move downriver, Wilkinson wrote Senator Smith of Ohio that "I shall obey the military mandate [to keep the dons on the west side of the Sabine], for there I look forward to fame and honor." After taking command in the Southwest, he wrote another letter to the Ohio senator and one to General Adair of Kentucky. "I shall as surely push them [the Spaniards] over the Sabine, and out of Nacogdoches as that you are alive . . . ," he boasted to Smith. "You must speedily send me a force to support our pretensions . . . 5000 mounted infantry . . . may suffice to carry us forward as far as the Grand River [the Rio Grande] . . . after which from 20 to 30,000 will be necessary to carry our conquests to California and the Isthmus of Darien." But Smith was a purveyor of army goods, not a recruiter of soldiers. What "force" did Wilkinson wish him to send? Burr and his followers? Long practice had given the general a firm grip on the tools of deceit. "The time looked for by many and wished for by more has now arrived for subverting the Spanish government in Mexico," he wrote Adair on 28 September. "Be you ready and join me; we will want little more than light troops . . . More will be done by marching than by fighting . . . Unless you fear to join a Spanish intriguer come immediately—Without your aid I can do nothing." But what could Adair do for him? It was not Adair but Burr—Burr and the expeditionary force he was assembling in the valley of the Ohio—that Wilkinson was trying to lure westward.

While the general tarried in St. Louis, the long-anticipated push of the Spaniards into the disputed land east of the Sabine took place, some seven hundred soldiers under Colonel Simón Herrera crossing the river on 5 August. Governor Claiborne of Orleans Territory (lower Louisiana), en route to Tennessee to visit his family, was near Natchez when word reached him of the Spanish intrusion. Canceling his trip home, Claiborne requested Cowles Mead, acting governor of Mississippi Territory, to meet him at Natchez; and on the evening of the seventeenth the two executives issued a proclamation, directing portions of the Louisiana militia to report to Colonel Cushing, now commanding at Natchitoches, and expressing regret at the absence in this hour of crisis of the commander in chief of the regular army.

On the twenty-second, the *Orleans Gazette* reported that elements of the corps under Colonel Herrera had advanced to within twelve miles of Natchitoches, and that an officer, sent out from the American post to demand "an explanation of this new encroachment" by the dons, had been informed that they intended "to occupy former positions" in the area. As Dearborn's orders had been published in the Western press—orders calling on the commander at Natchitoches to repel the intruders —the editor of the New Orleans newspaper assumed that the fighting was already underway. But in fact all was quiet on the Sabine front, Colonel Cushing interpreting Wilkinson's supplemental instructions as forbidding him to execute those promulgated by the general's superior in Washington. Governor Claiborne, hastening westward in late August to oversee the movement of the territorial militia to Natchitoches, was shocked to discover on his arrival there that Cushing was doing nothing. "My present impression is that 'all is not right,'" he wrote Governor Mead. "I know not whom to censure, but it seems to me that there is wrong somewhere. Either the orders [Dearborn's] . . . ought not to have been issued, or they should have been adhered to and supported."

By the time these plaintive words were written in early September, General Wilkinson had at last left St. Louis. On the evening of 7 September he landed at Natchez, and for the next two months his actions on the lower Mississippi and on the Sabine front were those of a man already convinced that he had more to gain from going against Aaron Burr than from going against the invading Spaniards he was under orders to oppose.

3

ONE OF WILKINSON's first actions in Natchez was to get in touch with Cowles Mead and to instruct the acting governor of Mississippi to begin at once preparing the volunteers being recruited in that territory for a drive against the Spanish. Then, ensconcing himself at the country home of Stephen Minor— wealthy planter and subject by choice of his Catholic Majesty— the general outlined his plans in a letter to the Secretary of War. He devoted much of this extended dispatch to the widely circulating reports of military movements in the Spanish Floridas— actions seemingly directed at New Orleans. It was his intention before he left for Natchitoches, he told Dearborn, to see to it that the officers of the army and navy in New Orleans were alerted and steps taken for the protection of the Crescent City. As for the situation on the Sabine front, he meant to take care of that problem by stages. First he was going to try to ascertain the "designs of the Spaniards"—a statement that would have startled Governors Mead and Claiborne, in whose eyes those "designs" could not have been more explicit. Having uncovered what the invaders were up to, Wilkinson was going to try to talk them back across the Sabine by making a "solemn appeal" to the "understanding . . . interests . . . and duty" of their superiors. "Let the President be assured," he told Dearborn, that "I shall drain the cup of conciliation . . . and that the sword shall not be drawn but in the last extremity, after reason and remonstrance have failed to preserve inviolate, our territory east of the Sabine . . . . If the strong precautions, embraced by my instructions to Colonel Cushing, of which I transmitted you a copy from St. Louis, have prevented the effusion of blood, I must believe I have done some good to the state . . . [But] should I be forced to appeal to arms, to drive them [Colonel Herrera and his contingent] effectually beyond the Sabine, or to cut them up . . . I will soon plant our standard on the left bank of the [Rio] Grand . . . In the meantime, the reduction of Nacogdoches and Baton Rouge, would . . . drive the enemy back on the side of Mexico . . . ; and should hostilities take place, and I find the occupancy of those posts necessary to counteract the hostile acts, or intention of the enemy, I shall, agreeably to your instructions, take possession of them." An ambitious program, certainly, portending as it did the "occupancy" of large hunks of Spanish turf. But the general was in no hurry to get on with it. When on 9 September he left Natchez to begin his journey to Natchitoches by way of Fort Adams and the Red River, he took two weeks to travel the some two hundred fifty miles that on his return to Natchez a couple of months later he traversed in three and a half days.

At the rapids of the Red River, reached on 19 September, he found Governor Claiborne waiting for him. So far as can be determined, the Louisiana executive uttered no complaints about the inactivity of the American forces on the Sabine front, and was seemingly satisfied, at the close of a conference with Wilkinson, that once sufficient firepower had been collected at Natchitoches, the repulse of the Spanish invaders would proceed without further ado. In the dispatch outlining his plans to Dearborn, Wilkinson had declared that until he could penetrate the "designs" of the enemy he was going to "discourage" the march of the Louisiana militia to the Sabine front. But at the rapids, face to face with the Louisiana governor, the general not only asked that the militia be hurried forward but that the 250 regular soldiers garrisoned at New Orleans be sent with it. At the conclusion of this council of war, Claiborne departed for New Orleans and Wilkinson indited a communication for the acting governor of Mississippi. To Mead he presented a detailed picture of the military alignment, as he understood it to be. Herrera, he asserted, had 1,500 men at his disposal—a gross exaggeration, since at its largest the detachment allotted to the Spanish commander numbered no more than 697. The main body of Herrera's corps was encamped at a onetime French village on Bayou Pierre, some fifty miles northwest of Natchitoches and sixty miles east of the Sabine. From thence, the general told Mead, "patrols are daily pushed forward, within eight miles of Natchitoches. These things will not be permitted with impunity, a single day after he [Herrera] shall refuse my requisition to withdraw . . . to the Westward of the Sabine. I therefore shall await with impatience the arrival of your Militia, as I shall not attempt to enjoin before I am able to enforce." This request dispatched, Wilkinson resumed his leisurely progress to Natchitoches.

From that American stronghold, he was presently reporting to Dearborn that, on his arrival there on the twenty-second, he was chagrined to find that not one "piece of artillery" was in condition "to take the Field, or a Hoof or vehicle provided for the transport." In short, the military components at Natchitoches were totally unprepared to move against the Spanish, a less than surprising condition in view of Wilkinson's instructions to Cushing to ignore the orders of the Secretary of War. Now that the commander in chief was on hand, the necessary preparations were begun. On 23 September, Wilkinson ordered Major Porter to put 1,500 infantrymen in readiness for a campaign. On the twenty-fourth he wrote a long letter for delivery, not to Colonel Herrera, but to the colonel's superior in Nacogdoches, Governor Cordero of Texas. The gist of his statement to Cordero was that since the "contested limits of Louisiana" were even then the subject of an "amicable negotiation by our respective sovereigns," any attempt by either government to occupy "new ground" constituted "a most ungracious and unwarrantable deed"; and that he (Wilkinson) had been "commanded by the President . . . to demand from you the withdrawal of the troops of Spain to the West of the Sabine."

At the general's request, Colonel Cushing handed this communication to Cordero in person, traveling for that purpose to Nacogdoches, where he was informed by the Texas governor that the decision required by Wilkinson's demands was one that only Salcedo, the captain general of the Interior Provinces, could make. Cordero indicated that in his opinion the Spanish position on the western boundary should remain what it had always been—namely, that the stretch of land between the Sabine and the Arroyo Hondo thirty miles to the east belonged to his Catholic Majesty. He assured Cushing, however, that he would transmit Wilkinson's communication to the captain general and that Wilkinson would be apprised of Salcedo's answer to it if and when Salcedo elected to make one. So matters stood when, even as Cushing was returning to Natchitoches, the situation on the Sabine front underwent a startling change.

Suddenly, unexpectedly, Colonel Herrera—acting on his own responsibility—abandoned his position at Bayou Pierre and retreated. To this day, the motives behind the Spanish commander's departure remain a subject of speculation. Obviously, he had his reasons. His force was considerably smaller than Wilkinson's. Neither of his superiors, Governor Cordero and Captain General Salcedo, had endeavored to reinforce him, and though Cordero had a large body of soldiers at his disposal, he had not so much as budged out of his camp at Nacogdoches. Left on his own by his masters, Herrera no doubt concluded—correctly, as it turned out—that they would condone whatever he did on his own. On 27 September, Herrera and his detachment marched out of Bayou Pierre, and on the thirtieth they crossed the Sabine and encamped on its Texas banks, opposite

the Louisiana settlement of Adais. End of the crisis? Not necessarily. Spanish forces had deserted the disputed land before,
only to return to it. That could happen again. The future remained uncertain.

But one result was plain: the voluntary withdrawal of the
enemy presented James Wilkinson with greater freedom of
movement than he had previously enjoyed. So long as a single
armed Spaniard lingered on the Louisiana side of the river, the
possibility of averting hostilities was remote to the point of
being nonexistent. Among the settlers of the American Southwest, the desire to push back the hated dons came close to being
a mania. Calls by Claiborne and Mead for volunteers drew
more men than the governors requested. In New Orleans the
members of the Mexican Society reveled in the nearing realization of their long-nurtured dream, the liberation of New Spain.

"We are happy to learn that the Government has at length
issued positive orders to repel the aggressions of our enemies by
force." So editor James M. Bradford addressed the readers of
his *Orleans Gazette* on 23 September. "We have indeed suffered
from them, almost beyond human endurance. Their intrigues to
disturb the repose of this country; their maintaining possession
of our territory [West Florida] between the Mississippi and
Perdido for upwards of two years; their outrageous conduct
towards our citizens on the banks of the Tombigbee:—these
and a thousand other injuries and insults demand instant re-
dress . . . If the enemy be forced to recross the Sabine, he
must be driven still farther; for it would be idle to suffer him to
remain there quietly until he received reinforcements from the
Southern provinces, which could easily be furnished him, inas-
much as the route from Natchitoches to Mexico is clear, plain,
and open; and the country through which it passes well stored
with cattle and forage. How it may be proper to pursue the
enemy is a question of policy for our Government to decide. On
this we may sincerely rely that our President, who had so large
a share in accomplishing the independence of the United States,

will seize with eagerness and exultation an honorable occasion that may offer for conferring on our oppressed Spanish brethren in Mexico those inestimable blessings of freedom which we ourselves enjoy . . . Gallant Louisianians! now is the time to distinguish yourselves . . . Should the generous efforts of our Government to establish a free, independent republican empire in Mexico be successful, how fortunate, how enviable would be the situation in New Orleans! The deposit at once of the countless treasures of the South, and the inexhaustible fertility of the Western States, we should soon rival and outshine the most opulent cities of the world." That these revolutionary sentiments could have been uttered by Aaron Burr came as no shock to readers familiar with the views of James Bradford, for the editor of the *Orleans Gazette*, convinced that the time had come "to give the wretched subjects of despotic Spain" the blessings of American republicanism, was an ardent supporter of the colonel's plans.

Since the takeover of New Orleans by the United States, Governor Claiborne had found its Old Louisianians (the Creoles) an endless source of discontent and trouble. Now, with a war with Spain seemingly imminent, he was delighted to see that they were as eager as the city's so-called Americans to battle his Catholic Majesty. Nor was this spirit confined to the American Southwest. Correspondence coming to light years later, with the opening of the Spanish archives, shows that a longing to cast off the yoke of Madrid existed among elements of the populations of the Spanish colonies themselves, and especially among the clergy. Aaron Burr's conviction that his expeditionary force would be welcomed and abetted by people in Mexico was no figment of his imagination. His elaborate enterprise might have succeeded had a conflict with Spain materialized—but that was not to be. Now that the Spanish had returned west of the Sabine, taking with them the most visible cause of dissension, the question of war or peace rested with General Wilkinson; and that perverse and flawed genius had long since earned his credentials as a manipulator of men and events.

On 4 October he wrote the Secretary of War informing Dearborn of the withdrawal of Herrera and his soldiers. Noting that the crisis was not yet over—that at any moment the enemy might decide to come back across the river and reoccupy "the ground from whence we had driven them"—he promised to continue his "preparations for defense and offense" in order to "assert unequivocally the pretensions of the Government" of the United States to the disputed land. With this aim in mind, it was his intention "to move forward to the east bank of the Sabine," sixty miles from Natchitoches. He told Dearborn that he would begin his march "in a few days." But in truth he was in no hurry to move; in no hurry either to provoke a war or to avoid one until he had reason to believe that Aaron Burr and his followers were coming in his direction. He was still at Natchitoches when Samuel Swartwout arrived at that place, bringing with him the sealed packet for the general that Swartwout had received from Peter Ogden in Pittsburgh two months before.

4

LEAVING PITTSBURGH in early August, Swartwout and Ogden had headed for St. Louis, only to learn en route that Wilkinson was no longer there, and to drop down the Mississippi to Fort Adams, where they were informed that the general had gone to the Sabine front. At Fort Adams the young couriers parted company. Ogden journeyed to New Orleans to deliver messages to Burr's friends there. Swartwout ascended the Red River. Testimony by Wilkinson at the Richmond trial, supplemented by depositions sworn to by Colonel Cushing and by Swartwout himself, make it possible to reconstruct with reasonable accuracy the events surrounding the arrival of the latter at Natchitoches on the evening of 8 October.

Wilkinson and Colonel Cushing were supping together in Cushing's quarters when Swartwout appeared and handed the colonel a letter of introduction from Jonathan Dayton. Wilkinson's story, as given from the witness stand, was that not until Cushing retired from the room did Swartwout slip "from his side pocket a letter and packet or envelope, which he said he was charged by Colonel Burr to deliver to me." Unsealing the packet in the solitude of his own quarters, the general found inside not only the cipher letter but also two shorter communications.

One of these was in plain English and dealt with Burr's purchase of the Bastrop lands. It was addressed to one "Johnn Peters" and signed, "A Stephens," but it was the general's belief that Colonel Burr had written it "in a disguised hand."

The other short enclosure, portions of it in cipher, was signed by Dayton and read in part: "It is now well ascertained that you are to be displaced in next session. Jefferson will affect to yield reluctantly to the public sentiment, but yield he will . . . You are not a man to despair . . . especially when such prospects offer in another quarter. Are you ready? Are your numerous associates ready? Wealth and glory, Louisiana and Mexico . . ." At the Richmond trial Wilkinson declared that "this letter materially influenced" his later measures, and it has been proposed that it was Dayton's warning which impelled the general to endeavor to present himself as the savior of his country by denouncing Burr. But Dayton's revelations were no news to Wilkinson. He was aware of the attacks on him in the *Western World*, knew that more than one newspaper editor had raised the question of why a man widely believed to be a pensioner of Spain and a collaborator in a plot to divide the Union continued to command the army of the United States. The threat implicit in Dayton's message may have firmed his resolve to destroy his associate in intrigue, but that resolve had been arrived at months before.

As for the cipher letter—Wilkinson decoded that as rapidly

as possible, producing what he himself described as "an imperfect interpretation" of it. Doctoring his "interpretation" here and there, in an effort to hide his role in the conspiracy, he removed the opening sentence, "Your letter postmarked 13th May is received," and changed the passage, "*Our* project *my dear friend* is brought to the point so long desired," to read "The project is brought to the point so long desired." Easily the most significant of his alterations was his elimination of the announcement that Burr's four-year-old grandson was to be a member of the expedition—a deletion which tells us that Wilkinson feared that the inclusion of that inanity would signal to others what it signaled to him, that the letter he was deciphering was not written by Burr but by Dayton, with whose handwriting—so the general testified at Richmond—he was "Perfectly" acquainted. When, at Richmond, Burr's attorneys asked if he had his "original translation" of the cipher, Wilkinson replied, "I have looked for it, but cannot find it." When asked if he had the duplicate cipher carried West by Bollman, he said, "I have not." We can only wonder why Burr's lawyers made no effort to fix the whereabouts of the original cipher, the one delivered by Swartwout. Neither that cipher letter nor its duplicate was ever introduced into testimony, and so far as we know, Wilkinson never showed either document to anyone.

He spent much of the night of 8–9 October decoding the letter. He realized at once its value to his plans. Now it no longer mattered whether Burr came West or not; here in his hands was strong evidence that the former Vice President was engaged in something illegal, perhaps even something subversive.

Next morning, Wilkinson took Colonel Cushing aside for a conversation which, as later paraphrased by the colonel, shows that at this point the general's scheme for betraying Burr was fully formed. He told Cushing that a letter in cipher handed to him by Swartwout revealed the existence "in the Western States" of a "treasonable" enterprise headed by Burr and supported by "a great number of individuals possessing wealth, popularity and talents"; that Burr had had the gall to invite Wilkinson to join the escapade and to bring the army with him; and that the general, scorning the movement as "inimical to the government of the United States," was determined "to adopt such measures as in his judgment were best calculated to defend the country." First, he was going to arrange an accommodation with the Spaniards. Then, free of that problem, he was going to remove "the greater part of his force" from the Sabine front to the Mississippi and defend New Orleans against the coming of Burr and his rich, numerous, and talented associates.

5

SWARTWOUT SPENT ten days at Natchitoches, and in his testimony at Richmond, Wilkinson described himself as repeatedly pumping the young man in an effort to extract more information about Burr's designs. Wilkinson quoted Swartwout as saying that Burr had an armed force of seven thousand men, that he was planning to "revolutionize" Louisiana, rob the banks at New Orleans, and move on from there to conquer Mexico. Swartwout remembered these interviews differently. "Never told Wilkinson that the banks at N.O. . . . were to be seized," he deposed; "never knew or heard there was a Bank at New Orleans till my arrival at Fort Adams [where, subsequent to his stay at Natchitoches], I accidentally saw a bill of one of those banks . . . never told Wilkinson that the N[ew] O[rleans] Territory was to be revolutionized . . . Wilkinson said that he had been told that Burr intended to seperate [sic] the Union. I never heard Burr say any such thing . . . heard Colo. Burr say that in case of a Spanish War he should attempt something against the Spanish colonies invited me to join which I liked much."

At the time Swartwout left the camp at Natchitoches, Wilkinson was swiftly maturing his plans. When on 15 October a troop of dragoons sent forward by Cowles Mead rode into camp, the general was pleased to find an old acquaintance—Walter Burling, a planter living near Natchez—among the volunteers. Summoning Burling to his quarters, he related the steps he was about to take—sharing with the Mississippi cotton grower the plan that, on the morning following receipt of the cipher letter, he had outlined so graphically to Colonel Cushing. Having taken Burling into his confidence, he took him into his official family, making him an aide-de-camp with the rank of captain.

In late October, the general prepared two communications for the eyes of Thomas Jefferson. Into a packet for the President went information that Wilkinson described as coming from a "public print"—information that rested "on such broad and explicit grounds as to exclude all doubts of its authenticity," a judgment the general was in a good position to make since he was so obviously the author of the "public print" from which it came. According to that source, a "numerous and powerful association . . . has been formed with the design to levy and rendezvous eight or ten thousand men in New Orleans . . . and from thence, with the cooperation of a naval armament, to carry an expedition against Vera Cruz . . . Agents from Mexico, who . . . are engaged in this enterprise . . . have given assurances, that the launching of the proposed expedition will be seconded by so general an insurrection, as to insure the subversion of the present government." To accompany this summary of the "public print," Wilkinson drafted a "confidential letter" of explanation. In his talks with Cushing and Burling, the general had identified the leader of the "proposed expedition" as Aaron Burr. But in this confidential message to Jefferson he wrote that "I have never in my whole life found myself under such circumstances of perplexity . . . for I am not only uninformed of the prime mover . . . of this daring enterprise, but am ignorant of the means by which it is supported . . . I am informed you connive at the combination, and that our coun-

167

try will justify it; but when I examine my orders of the 6th May, I am obliged to discredit . . . these imputations." Vintage Wilkinson, that little touch; just let Mr. Jefferson try to fire him now! "But should this association be formed in opposition to the laws, and in defiance of government," the general huffed on, "then I have no doubt that the revolt of this territory will be made an auxiliary step to the main design of attacking Mexico, to give it a new master in the place of promised liberty. Could the fact be ascertained to me, I believe I should hazard my discretion, make the best compromise I could with Salcedo . . . and throw myself with my little band into New Orleans, to be ready to defend that capital against usurpation and violence." Wilkinson entrusted the envelope containing these communications to Lieutenant Colonel Thomas A. Smith. Smith was to take it to Washington by an unusual route, so as to evade Burr's spies, who, Wilkinson assured him, were everywhere. He was to secrete the packet in the "soles of a slipper" and expose it only when he stood before the President of the United States.

Smith took off on 22 October, and on the following day Wilkinson began his march to the eastern bank of the Sabine, having previously informed the authorities in Texas that he had no "hostile intentions against the troops or realms of Spain" and was advancing only for the purpose of confirming the title of his government to the disputed land. The twenty-eighth of October brought the general and his army to a point twenty miles east of the river, and here Wilkinson handed his new aide and confidant, Walter Burling, two copies of a proposal designed to compromise the argument with Spain—a proposal known to history as the Neutral Ground Treaty. Actually no treaty at all (the terms of it were never submitted to the United States Senate), Wilkinson's informal memorandum set forth three suggestions: that Herrera withdraw his troops to Nacogdoches; that he (Wilkinson) withdraw his to Natchitoches; and that until such time as their respective governments settled the boundary dispute, both sides refrain from occupying any

part of the 120-mile spread of land between those two points.*
On instructions from Wilkinson, Burling delivered one copy of
the general's proposal to Herrera, stopping long enough at the
camp of the Spanish on the west bank of the Sabine to hand it
to the colonel himself and then hurrying on to Nacogdoches to
present the other copy to Governor Cordero. As always, the
Texas governor was cautious. He made no comment on Wilkinson's propositions, saying only that he would send them on to
Salcedo and abide by his superior's decision. But no decision
ever came from Salcedo, because none was needed. While Burling was traveling to Nacogdoches and back, Wilkinson had
reached the eastern bank of the Sabine, and on the morning of
5 November Captain Francisco Viana, Herrera's second-in-
command, rode into the American camp with the announcement
that the Spanish colonel—again acting on his own—had accepted the neutral-ground proposal.

The crisis was over, terminated in a way that Wilkinson had
reason to believe would win the sanction of his government.
Three years earlier, in the spring of 1804, Jefferson and his
cabinet had gone on record as favoring the establishment, pending official solution of the border problem, of a neutral area
along the Sabine. In truth, in the eyes of Washington, the general had wrought better than he himself yet realized. On 8
November, only three days after Herrera's acceptance of the
neutral-ground arrangement, the Jefferson cabinet sent new
orders West, urging Wilkinson, for reasons connected with current diplomatic negotiations in Europe, to avoid an armed
conflict with the Spanish if he possibly could. Herrera's action,
too, quickly won the approval of his superiors. On hearing about

---

* Informal and unofficial though it was, the Neutral Ground Treaty
remained in effect until 1821, when ratification of the Treaty of Amity,
Settlement, and Limits between the United States of America and his
Catholic Majesty recognized the Sabine as the official boundary between
Louisiana and Texas. McCaleb, *Conspiracy*, 135n; and see *American State
Papers—Foreign Relations*, IV, for the Treaty between the U.S. and his
Catholic Majesty.

the neutral-ground agreement, Captain General Salcedo pronounced himself pleased, promptly realizing that by endorsing a neutral region admittedly bounded on the west by Spanish soil, the United States had relinquished its often-asserted claim to most if not all of Texas. Jefferson had paid a high price for peace; but no doubt he preferred that to a conflict that could have permitted Aaron Burr to lead an expedition into Mexico and become a hero in the eyes of his fellow Americans.

6

BY 7 NOVEMBER, Wilkinson was back at Natchitoches, where communications dealing with the conspiracy awaited him. Among them was the duplicate cipher letter. Dr. Bollman, having arrived at New Orleans, had arranged for it to be carried West by a courier, whom the general later described as "a small Frenchman (whom I had never seen before, nor have I ever seen him since)." In the packet holding the duplicate was a note signed by Dayton, a frenzied essay patently designed, as were many of Dayton's communications to Wilkinson, to cajole the general into remaining true to the cause. "Every thing and even heaven itself," Dayton had written, "appear to have conspired to prepare the train for a grand explosion . . . Are you also ready? for I know you flinch not when a great object is in view." Flinching not, the general read with considerably more pleasure a letter from Natchez signed by one James L. Donaldson, who had learned from someone named Michael Myers, who purported to have gotten his information from someone close to Burr, that "a plan to revolutionize the Western country has been formed," and that "Kentucky, Ohio, Tennessee, Orleans, and Indiana are combined to declare themselves independent on the 15th November." On 15 November! That was little more than a week hence. If Wilkinson was to save the country, he must work fast.

He did. He remained at Natchitoches only long enough to

send to two of his officers instructions for fortifying New Orleans against the imminent arrival of Burr and his seven thousand followers. One of these dispatches went to Lieutenant Colonel Constance Freeman, commanding at the Crescent City; the other to Colonel Cushing, who was leading to that place most of the army previously on the Sabine front. "We must repair the old defences of the city," he instructed Freeman; "it is our only resort, as we shall not have time to do more . . . Let your measure be taken, as if by order from the secretary of war; but profess utter ignorance of motives. Manifest no hurry or emotion, for you are surrounded by secret agents . . . Quarters for the troops from this place, . . . those at Fort Adams, and Point Coupée, and one hundred from Fort Stoddert, must be provided and prepared . . . I shall be with you by the 20th instant; in the mean time, be you as silent as the grave." To Cushing he wrote: "By letters found here, I perceive the plot thickens . . . My God! what a situation has our country reached. Let us save it if we can . . . I think the officers, who have families at Fort Adams, should be advised to leave them there, for if I mistake not, we shall have an insurrection of blacks as well as whites, to combat." Rebellion! Rebellion everywhere; this was the cry the general now raised and continued to raise for the next two months. "No consideration, my friend, of family or personal inconvenience, must detain the troops, a moment longer than can be avoided, either by land or by water," he told Cushing. ". . . On the 15th of this month, Burr's declaration is to be made in Tennessee and Kentucky; hurry, hurry . . . and if necessary, let us be buried together, in the ruins of the place we shall defend."

These orders and forebodings on their way, the general himself left Natchitoches, accompanied by Walter Burling, who had become the friend of his bosom and the sharer of all his schemes and dreams. They reached Natchez on 11 November. There Wilkinson again lodged at the country home of Stephen Minor, and there on the day after his arrival he prepared for

Jefferson another long and portentous report. Into the packet that was to go to Washington, he dropped a copy of the letter from James L. Donaldson, predicting the eruption of the insurrection on 15 November.

"This is indeed a deep, dark and wide-spread conspiracy," Wilkinson warned the President, "embracing the young and the old, the democrat and the federalist, the native and the foreigner, the patriot of '76 and the exotic of yesterday, the opulent and the needy, the ins and the outs."

> My letter to the secretary of war [he continued] will expose to you my military movements . . . which may, I hope, meet your approbation; and I intreat that you may be pleased to order him to honour the drafts which may be made on him for materials and other disbursements essential to the fortifying the city of New Orleans, to enable me to defend it, to repulse the assailants, and command the pass of the river.
>
> You will perceive on inquiry that my means are greatly deficient, but may rest satisfied that nothing shall be omitted which can be accomplished by indefatigable industry, incessant vigilance and hardy courage; and I gasconade not when I tell you, that in such a cause, I shall glory to give my life to the service of my country; for I verily believe such an event to be probable; because should seven thousand men descend from the Ohio, and this is the calculation, they will bring with them the sympathies and good wishes of that country, and none but friends can be afterwards prevailed on to follow them: with my handful of veterans, however gallant, it is improbable I shall be able to withstand such a disparity of numbers; and it would seem we must be sacrificed unless you should be able to succour me seasonably by sea, with two thousand men and a naval armament, to command the mouth of the Mississippi.
>
> To give effect to my military arrangements, it is absolutely indispensable, New Orleans and its environs should be placed under martial law; for without this, the disaffected can neither be apprehended nor banished; private property can

neither be appropriated nor occupied for public purposes; the indiscriminate intercourse between town and country cannot be restrained, and my every disposition will of course be hourly and daily exposed to my adversaries. To effect this necessary measure, I must look up to your influence and authority. To insure the triumph of government over its enemies, I am obliged to resort to political finesse and military stratagem. I must hold out false colors, conceal my designs, and cheat my adversaries into a state of security, that when I do strike, it may be with more force and effect . . . independent of considerations of policy, my personal safety will require the most profound reserve, to the last moment of indecision; for were my intentions exposed, there are more than three desperate enthusiasts in New Orleans, who would seek my life, and although I may be able to smile at danger in open conflict, I will confess I dread the stroke of the assassin, because it cannot confer an honourable death.

There was more, all of it in the same vein, for Wilkinson was a fearless campaigner on paper. To convey to the President the letter and its attachment, he procured the services of an old acquaintance, Isaac Briggs, a federal surveyor stationed in the vicinity of Natchez. The general's message included an oblique reference to his recent receipt from Bollman of the duplicate of the cipher letter, but Wilkinson did not forward a translation of that document. Instead, he read his "imperfect interpretation" of it to Briggs so that when the surveyor reached the federal city he would be in a position to relate its contents to Jefferson.

Satisfied that he had won the goodwill of his American employer, the general now set out to see what he could get from his Spanish employer. Burling was his collaborator in this stratagem. The two men let it be known that the Mississippi planter was interested in buying donkeys within the domains of Spain and that Wilkinson had given him a passport for this purpose. But when Burling reached the city of Mexico, he expressed no interest in donkeys. Instead, he presented to Iturrigaray, the viceroy of New Spain, a letter from Wilkinson in which the general listed the great things he had done for his Catholic Majesty: how he not only had saved Spain from a costly war but had made it impossible for Aaron Burr to attack Mexico. Having thus inventoried his services, the general rendered a bill for them. He thought he should be paid $121,000. Iturrigaray thought otherwise. He saw no reason why Agent 13 should be rewarded for doing what he already had been paid to do. Politely, the viceroy showed Burling the door, having arranged for his safe conduct back to the United States.

It was on 17 November that Burling left Natchez on his futile errand to the city of Mexico. On the following day, Briggs began his 1,200-mile jaunt to Washington, half of it "through wilderness . . . in the midst of a severe winter." The year was ended when he reached the federal city, to deliver his packet to a President who, after nearly a year and a half of seeming indifference to the activities of Aaron Burr, had finally done something about them.

Aaron Burr at fifty-three,
painted by John Vanderlyn in 1809
Courtesy the New-York Historical Society

General James Wilkinson,
known to Spain as "Agent No. 13"

Harman Blennerhasset,
painted in London
at thirty-two (1796)

Drawing in 1930s of the Blennerhassett mansion,
based on contemporary records

Andrew Jackson, after the battle of New Orleans,
painted by Samuel Waldo

The arrest of Aaron Burr in 1807,
as imagined in an old engraving

The trial of Aaron Burr,
from the painting by C. W. Jeffreys

Chief Justice John Marshall, who presided at the trial,
painted by James Reid Lambdin after Henry Inman

Jeremy Bentham, Burr's friend and host
during his voluntary exile in England

Burr's law office on Reade Street, New York City

Madame Jumel, formerly de la Croix,
painted circa 1854

The St. James Hotel on Staten Island,
where Burr died in 1836

VERSO: Aaron Burr at seventy-eight,
two years before his death, painted by James Van Dyck
Courtesy the New-York Historical Society

9

Stirrings in Washington, Operatics in New Orleans

T HE PRESIDENT'S DECISION in the fall of 1806 to make Burr's movements a subject of governmental investigation remains to this day a puzzling action. For fifteen months Jefferson did nothing in the face of recurrent newspaper charges that the activities of the former Vice President were inimical to the interests of the nation. For fifteen months he ignored letters from alarmed citizens to the same effect. Then suddenly he acted. Why? To what extent was he moved by new information reaching him that fall; to what extent by diplomatic considerations—by the emergence, that is, of the "great probability" of an early settlement of the differences with Spain as a result of negotiations in Paris? It was this hope that impelled him to speed new orders to Wilkinson, urging the general to avoid an armed encounter with the Spaniards. The same development could have entered into his belief that the time had come to deal with Burr. So long as a negotiated solution of the Spanish problem seemed out of the question, the formation of a private expedition against their dominions could be overlooked, even as Miranda's ill-fated venture was overlooked until it came to the attention of the Marqués de Casa Yrujo. Once the situation changed, once the possibility of a peaceful settlement of the Spanish problem materialized, military actions against Mexico, whether conducted legally by Wilkinson or illegally by Burr, became intolerable.

Whatever the real motives behind Jefferson's decision to act against Burr when he did, his own account of it speaks only of his response to certain communications coming his way at the time. From a Kentuckian came a note stating that "gunboats or strong vessels resembling them" were being built for Burr at a navy yard on the Muskingum River, and the conjecture that Burr was planning to seize the "public lands" and "separate the States." From John Nicholson of Herkimer, New York, came word that Comfort Tyler, Burr's recruiting agent in that area, "had some time since gone on to Pittsburgh, the place of general rendezvous," accompanied by "Several Gentlemen." Asserting that "indirect overtures" to join the expedition had come his way, Nicholson repeated a widely bruited story that Burr, having learned of the failure of the government's efforts to buy East Florida, had himself purchased that Iberian colony with the aid of "a private company."

How much faith Jefferson put in this gimcrackery is unclear, but it is obvious that he was impressed by a communication from his Postmaster General, Gideon Granger of Massachusetts. Granger's letter, written at his home in Springfield, dealt with William Eaton's allegations that during the preceding winter Burr had tried to draw the hero of Derne into a cabal aimed at dismantling the Union. Eaton had not as yet mentioned his accusations to the President, but he had shared them with acquaintances in the Congress. One of them, Representative William Ely of Massachusetts, related them to Granger, who conveyed them to the President together with a postscript signed by Eaton, testifying to their validity. The Postmaster General's statements flattered Jefferson's belief that Burr was "a Catilinarian character," and an eagerness for proof of his suspicions pervades his tersely written summaries in late October of three cabinet meetings devoted to the question of what steps the Administration should take to expose and punish the former Vice President.

"During the last session of Congress," Jefferson noted in his recording of the first of these conferences, "Col. Burr . . . finding no hope of being employed in any department of the govmt. opened himself confidentially to some persons . . . on a scheme of separating the western from the Atlantic States . . . of his having made this proposition here we have information from Genl. Eaton, thro. Mr. Ely & Mr. Granger . . ." After months of newspaper speculation, imputing a gallimaufry of crimes to the colonel, none of the four department heads present at this meeting was inclined to argue. "We are of opinion unanimously," the memorandum continued, "that confidential letters be written to the Governors of Ohio, Indiana, Missisipi [sic], & Orleans, to the district attorney of Kenutcky, ——— of Tennessee, ——— of Louisiana, to have him strictly watched and on his committing any overt act unequivocally, to have him arrested and tried for treason, Misdemeanor, or whatever other offence the Act may amount to . . . Genl. Wilkinson being expressly declared by Burr to Eaton to be engaged with him in this design . . . and suspicions of infidelity in Wilkinson being now become very general, a question is proposed what is proper to be done to him on this account as well as for his disobedience of orders received by him June 11 at St. Louis to descend with all practicable despatch to N.O. to mark out the site of certain defense works there, and then repair to take command at Natchitoches, on which business he did not leave St. Louis until Sept. — Consideration adjourned."

Two days later, during another meeting of the cabinet, additional recommendations were arrived at. The ranking captains of the navy, Edward Preble and Stephen Decatur, were to be dispatched to New Orleans, "there to take command of the force on the water"; ten vessels berthed at Eastern ports, the *Argus* and nine gunboats, were also to be sent to the Crescent

City; Preble, on his arrival at that place, was to enjoy "great discretionary powers" in consultation "with Govr. Claiborne; and John Graham"—Secretary of the Orleans District, then temporarily in the federal city—was to "be sent thro' Kentucky on Burr's trail," with instructions to "consult confidentially with the Governors, & to arrest Burr if he made himself liable." As for what should be done about General Wilkinson, that matter was again "postponed" pending acquisition of "further information."

Less than twenty-four hours later, the cabinet at still another session discarded practically all these decisions. It is uncertain which of several likely motives provoked this sudden turnabout: the discovery that funds for sending the *Argus* and the gunboats to New Orleans were not available; or the President's guess, subsequently verified, that there was no federal law under which the regular troops, as distinct from the militia, could be used to suppress domestic insurrection—a deficiency that at Jefferson's request was rectified by the Congress a few months later; or the failure of the mail arriving "from the westward" on the day before to contain so much as "one word . . . of any movements" by Colonel Burr. "This total silence of the officers of the government," Jefferson observed in his memorandum of the 25 October cabinet meeting, "of the members of Congress, of the newspapers, proves he is committing no overt act against the law. We therefore rescind the determination to send Preble, Decatur, the 'Argus' or the gunboats, and instead . . . to send off the marines which are here to reinforce, or take place, the garrison at New Orleans, with a view to Spanish operations; and instead of writing the Governors, etc., we send Graham on that route, with confidential authority to inquire into Burr's movements, put the governors, etc., on their guard, [and] to provide for his arrest if necessary . . . Letters are still to be written to Claiborne, Freeman, and the Gov of Miss to be on their guard."

Thus ended four days of furious consideration of the activities of Colonel Burr. John Graham received his marching orders and moved West, and for four weeks, insofar as the official cognizance of the United States government was concerned, the behavior of the nomadic colonel and his followers was a case of out of sight, out of mind.

Then on 25 November General Wilkinson's courier, Lieutenant Colonel Thomas A. Smith, arrived in Washington, removed the messages secreted between the soles of his slipper, and handed them to the President, and what people later called the "explosion"—meaning the annihilation of the Burr expedition—was touched off in a matter of hours.

2

THE MESSAGES DELIVERED to the President that November day were those Wilkinson had written at Natchitoches on 20 and 21 October—the two communications in which he asserted that a "powerful association" was about to "rendezvous eight or ten thousand men in New Orleans . . . and from thence . . . to carry an expedition against Vera Cruz"; that this movement would be "seconded" by a general insurrection certain to subvert the American government; and that he (Wilkinson) was in a state of "perplexity and embarrassment," being totally in the dark as to the identity of the person or persons responsible for this menacing development. But on that score the President suffered no perplexity; he knew who the arch-conspirator was. He chose to believe what he read, or at any rate to believe that he now had in his possession evidence of "overt acts" on the part of Colonel Burr. He listened attentively to the oral communication that Lieutenant Colonel Smith had been authorized by his superior to relate: how "a Mr. Swartwout" had come to the camp at Natchitoches for the purpose of offering Wilkinson a high command in the contemplated assault on the dominions of the king of Spain.

A month earlier, Jefferson had called the attention of his

advisers to the spreading doubts about Wilkinson's fidelity to his country and to the general's failure to obey a direct order from the Secretary of War. Never again would such criticisms pass his lips. From this moment on, the President committed himself and his government to a long and at times embarrassing collaboration with a man whom the articulate John Randolph of Roanoke described as "the mammoth of iniquity . . . the only man I ever saw who was from the bark to the very core a villain."

Jefferson was quick to place the contents of Wilkinson's dispatches before his advisers. They in turn lost no time in crafting ways for coping with the danger. At a late-evening cabinet meeting, arrangements were made for sending messages to the civil and military officials of the West, urging them to keep an eye out for suspicious movements on the rivers and requesting the assistance of their militias. Another agreement called for the President to issue a proclamation, and on 27 November this document was released. It read in part:

> WHEREAS, information has been received that sundry persons . . . are . . . confederating together to . . . set on foot . . . a military . . . enterprize against the dominions of Spain, that for this purpose they are fitting out and arming vessels . . . collecting provisions, arms, military stores and other means, are deceiving and seducing honest . . . citizens . . . to engage in their criminal enterprizes, are organizing, officering and arming themselves for the same, contrary to the laws in such cases made and provided: I have therefore thought fit to issue this PROCLAMATION, . . . commanding all persons . . . engaged . . . in [said unlawful enterprizes] . . . to cease all further proceedings therein, as they will answer the contrary at their peril;—and incur prosecution with all the rigors of the law.—And I hereby . . . require all officers, civil and military, of the United States, or any of the states or territories . . . to be vigilant in searching out, and bringing to condign punish-

ment, all persons . . . engaged . . . in such enterprize
. . . and I require all good and faithful citizens . . . to be
aiding and assisting herein, and especially in the discovery,
apprehension and bringing to justice of all such offenders, in
preventing the execution of their unlawful designs, and in
giving information against them to the proper authorities.

Nowhere in this minatory echo of the mishmash of fact and
fiction supplied by Wilkinson, Granger, Eaton, and others was
there any mention of Aaron Burr or of treason. But the editors
of the *Western World* and other dealers in ingenious rumors
had done their work well. As the proclamation moved slowly
westward, Burr's name sprang into the minds of countless
readers, the idea of treason attached itself to the enterprise the
President had condemned, and a kind of hysteria swept the
country. Everywhere, men hastened to disassociate themselves
from Aaron Burr, even those who only yesterday were touting
his abilities and cheering a project they counted on to demolish
the power of the Spaniard in North America. In Cincinnati,
Judge Jacob Burnet found in this abrupt change of sentiment a
fascinating example of the fragility of human loyalty. When the
"storm broke" against Burr, the Ohio jurist and senator wrote,
"it was amusing to see those men, who had so recently been the
most devoted attendants on the Colonel, and the most vocal
in his praise, denouncing him as a traitor, and tendering
their services to the Governor . . . to arrest the culprit and
bring him to justice." In Nashville, where the contents of the
proclamation became known shortly after Burr's last stay in
that town,* a citizenry that once had toasted and lionized him
burned him in effigy; and it is now known that some witnesses
to this spectacle believed that his friend and champion, Andrew
Jackson, should have been up there with him. In Lexington, the

---

* Exactly when knowledge of the proclamation reached Nashville is
unknown, but as the violent reaction to it did not occur during Burr's final
stop there, it is obvious that the news arrived after his departure. More on
his last visit to Nashville in the next chapter.

editor of the *Gazette*, long a supporter of the former Vice President, reluctantly shifted ground. "Some weeks ago it was our opinion that Burr's designs were not unfavorable to the interests of the Union," William Bradford editorialized. "This opinion was predicated upon . . . a belief that he had too much sense to think of withdrawing the attachment of the citizens of the Western country from the government of their choice . . . Our opinion was that he meditated an attack on Mexico by the authority of the government, should a war take place with Spain . . . We now declare that opinion changed by the President's Proclamation . . ."

3

THE PROCLAMATION WAS NOT the only official document to leave Washington on 27 November. Off also went orders for Wilkinson. The general, Secretary Dearborn wrote, was to "use every exertion in your power to frustrate and effectually prevent any enterprise which has for its object . . . any hostile act on any part of the territories of the United States, or on any territories of the King of Spain." It would be almost a month before these instructions reached their destination. But the general needed no orders. From the moment he arrived in New Orleans on 25 November and began preparing that city for the momentarily expected onslaught by Burr and his army, Wilkinson was the law there.

He brought with him or was soon followed by additional troops, having emptied the garrisons at Fort Adams on the Mississippi and of Fort Stoddert on the Tombigbee River at the far eastern edge of Mississippi Territory. He saw to it that the crumbling fortifications of New Orleans were repaired, arranged with the consul from France to take over an artillery park belonging to that nation, and talked of sealing off the entire area by encircling it with a palisade of spiked pickets. He browbeat the local merchants into clamping an embargo on shipping, issuing an edict under which no vessel could enter the port of New Orleans or depart therefrom without his or Governor Claiborne's permission. He ordered the local naval officer, Captain John Shaw, to put his little fleet in readiness, called for sailors to man the two bomb ketches and four gunboats; and, when the volunteers for this duty refused to sign on for six months as stipulated by the general, demanded that they be forced into service by impressment—a request the startled governor stalwartly ignored. He offered a $5,000 reward for the seizure of the person of Aaron Burr, giving out that this action was authorized by the government, which it was not, and sending one Silas Dinsmoor northward with instructions to ask the Choctaw Indians to "intercept the paths in every direction," in an effort to capture the arch-conspirator.

The swiftness with which these draconian measures fell on the city spawned rumors—wild rumors, contradictory rumors. Many inhabitants were as certain as the general seemed to be that the arch-conspirator was about to descend upon them, backed by his hordes like Attila the Hun redivivus. Others were skeptical, sensing a giant hoax in the martial movements of the general and in his clamant pronouncements. On 6 December, he asked Claiborne to declare martial law. Rendered indecisive by the absence to date of directives from Washington and shaken by the uproar in the city, the governor asked for time to think. While he thought, Wilkinson scribbled, marshaling his arguments in a long and torrid memorandum for the governor's perusal. "Having put my life and character in opposition to the flagitious enterprise of one of the badest [sic] men of our country, supported by a crowd of coequals," he declared, "ceremony would be unreasonable and punctillo unprofitable. I therefore speak from my heart when I declare that I verily believe you are sincerely desirous to cooperate with me in all my measures, but pardon the honest candor . . . when I observe that . . . you suffer yourself to be unduly biased by the solicitation of the timid, the capricious, or the wicked, who . . . harass you with their criticisms on subjects which they do not understand, and with their opposition to measures which they do not comprehend, or which, understanding, they are desirous to prevent . . . What will our alertness import, without force and energy to support it? Shall our reverence for our civil institutions produce their annihilation, or shall we lose the house because we will not break the windows?" After two days of thought, the governor rendered his decision. Before martial law could be imposed, he reminded the general, the great writ of habeas corpus would have to be suspended. Only the territorial legislature could take that drastic action, and at the moment the legislature was not in session.

What the young governor refused to do by words, Wilkinson accomplished by deeds. Proclaiming his determination to bring to justice "all individuals who might be discovered as participants in Burr's lawless combination," the general inaugurated a series of arbitrary seizures and confinements that would continue for months. On 14 December, he ordered the arrest of the men responsible for bringing the cipher letter West: of Dr. Bollman, who was still in New Orleans, and of Swartwout and Ogden, who were at Fort Adams. On the fifteenth, a writ of habeas corpus was sued for on the doctor's behalf, but before this instrument, obtained in superior court on the following day, could be executed, Bollman had been put on a vessel and taken down the river. Meanwhile, Swartwout and Ogden had been brought to New Orleans on one of Captain Shaw's bomb ketches and Burr's friend Edward Livingston had interested himself in their cause. But the writ of habeas corpus, promptly issued in their favor by Superior Court Judge James Workman, suffered nearly the same fate as the one previously obtained for Bollman. Ogden was liberated, but Swartwout was hustled down the river. Before another spate of legal actions could run its course, he and Bollman were being sent eastward on separate ships, along with documents signed by Wilkinson, charging both of them with "misprision of treason against the Government of

184

the United States" and requesting that they be tried in Eastern tribunals. Appalled by these high-handed maneuvers and frustrated by the failure of the governor to intervene, James Workman resigned his judgeship—an action that confirmed Wilkinson's already well-established position as the supreme dictator of New Orleans.

The arrival on the twentieth of the President's proclamation added to the fears bestriding the city. Pressured by the merchants, hurting as a result of a near-stoppage of trade, Claiborne lifted the embargo on shipping. This relief came on the last day of the year, but the reign of terror persisted as the inhabitants of the Crescent City braced themselves against the coming of "one of the badest" men of the country and his "crowd of coequals."

4

IT IS INSTRUCTIVE, looking back over Wilkinson's machinations in the closing months of 1806, to note the dates on which some of them occurred. On 22 October, when the general sent his first warning to Jefferson, Burr was in Lexington, surrounded by a few friends, and overseeing the preparations for his expedition. In 12 November, when Wilkinson dispatched Isaac Briggs eastward to tell Jefferson that within a week a huge army under the colonel would be at the gates of the Crescent City, the arch-conspirator was sitting in a courtroom at Frankfort, come there to answer charges brought against him by the district attorney. And on 6 December, when Wilkinson began his takeover of New Orleans, Burr was still in Frankfort, still enjoying the goodwill of the populace after his exoneration by a federal grand jury—and still ignorant of the rapidity with which his filibuster was withering away, a development abetted by John Graham's conscientious discharge of his orders from the President to follow "Burr's trial" and make certain he did the country no harm.

I O

The "Burr War"

ONE OF JOHN GRAHAM's instructions from his government was "to inquire into Burr's movements." At his first stop, Pittsburgh, he garnered nothing of consequence, but at Marietta, reached in mid-November, he met Harman Blennerhassett, who told him that Burr had two operations in prospect: a settlement of the Bastrop lands and, in the event of war with Spain, an invasion of Mexico. In the beginning, according to Graham's subsequent reconstruction of these conversations, the transplanted Irish aristocrat was under the impression that the young government agent was in league with Burr and friendly to his projects. On learning that Graham had come West not to join the expedition but to suppress it, Blennerhassett was visibly taken aback. Apprised of the existence in Wood County of a citizens' committee formed to oppose "any illegal scheme" in that area, Graham crossed the river to meet with its members at what is now Parkersburg, West Virginia. Here he heard many things: that only recently 1,200 stands of arms had passed down the river, that Andrew Jackson was raising a thousand men for Burr's use, that between them a couple of Kentuckians had raised another eight hundred, and that still another two to three hundred were expected momentarily from Pittsburgh and elsewhere. Furnished with these impressive figures, Graham hurried to Chillicothe, then the capital of Ohio, where he persuaded Governor Edward Tiffin to initiate the events long remembered in the Ohio Valley as the "Burr War."

2

It was a war without an enemy. No doubt, to many inhabitants of the rumor-haunted valley that winter it seemed not only a necessary but a noble effort, an exercise in patriotism. But in retrospect it shrivels to much ado about nothing.

On 2 December, Governor Tiffin communicated to the general assembly the tall tales Graham had gathered from the Wood County citizens' committee. The Ohio lawmakers responded by authorizing him to call out the militia under the command of Major General Buel of Marietta and to transmit to the President an address expressive of their "attachment" to the Union. "We trust that public rumor has magnified the danger," they told Jefferson, "but should the designs in agitation be as destructive as represented, we have no doubt but all fear will shortly be dissipated before the indignation of our citizens."

On 6 December, three hundred militiamen took up positions along the Ohio, under orders to make sure that none of the craft for the fleet "Burr and Blanny [Blennerhassett]" were known to be assembling went down the river. The presence of the soldiers put the southern counties of the state in an uproar. Cincinnati jittered at rumors that only a short distance upstream 20,000 armed men were ready at a signal from Colonel Burr to descend upon them. A report one winter night that the arch-conspirator was approaching with three gunboats sent people scurrying home, to tremble behind barred doors when a local wag, unable to resist the opportunity offered by the situation, exploded a small bomb on the waterfront. Sheepish grins were in evidence when daybreak revealed that the "gunboats" belonged to a merchant en route to the markets of New Orleans with a load of dry goods. As for the soldiers bivouacked on the shores of the Ohio, they passed the time pleasantly enough, shooting at logs bobbing by on the waters, consuming "whisky and peach-brandy," and otherwise entertaining themselves. United States Senator James Ross of Pennsylvania found the behavior of the "Semi-Savages" stretched out along the "banks of the Ohio for four hundred miles" an inevitable outcome of the President's "silly" proclamation. "[T]hey stop all boats," he wrote his friend James McHenry, "take out provisions & live upon them, without pretending to make reparation to the owners; . . . Should this disgraceful scene continue . . . the interior commerce of the Western Waters will be utterly destroyed."

On 9 December an express from Chillicothe to Marietta authorized Judge Return J. Meigs of that town and General Buel to "take forcible possession" of the fifteen boats being constructed for the expedition on the Muskingum River—most of which were even then being brought to Marietta for delivery to Blennerhassett. Getting wind of this development, some of Burr's young followers, temporarily encamped at Belpre, marched the twelve miles to Marietta in an effort to prevent the takeover. Their mission failed, but when shortly after dusk the authorities seized the boats, along with about two hundred pounds of provisions, there was enough noise and movement to inspire General Edward W. Tupper of Marietta—military man, merchant, and poet—to delineate the "Battle of Muskingum" in these words:

> Our General brave, the order gave,
>   "To arms! to arms! in season!
> Old Blanny's boats, most careless float,
>   Brim-full of death and treason!"
>
> A few young boys, their mothers' joys,
>   And five men there were found, sirs,
> Floating at ease—each little sees
>   Or dreams of death and wound, sirs.

Out of the barn, still in alarm,
　　Came fifty men, or more, sirs,
And seized each boat and other float,
　　And tied them to the shore, sirs.

This plunder rare, they sport and share,
　　And each a portion grapples.
'Twas half a kneel* of Indian Meal,
　　And ten of Putnam's apples.†

What the state of Ohio acquired that evening were house-boats "calculated for shallow water" and constructed along the lines of the so-called Schenectady models employed on the Mohawk River in upstate New York. One of them, built for the use of Blennerhassett and his family, was finished in style, with separate rooms, glass windows, and a fireplace. All were either forty or fifty feet long, ten wide, and two and a half deep. One can only wonder how today's courts would regard the seizure by a state government of private property on the basis of a law hastily passed by legislators who, in their address to the President, admitted that they were acting on undocumented rumors. The confiscation of the fifteen boats has been described as marking "the beginning of the end of Burr's conspiracy." In truth, the conspiracy had already vanished, shattered by months of unfavorable attention in the press, by Burr's haughty refusal to defend himself in print, and by the mounting panic in the western country as knowledge of Graham's errand and Jefferson's proclamation gradually permeated the region. When on 6 December—three days before the seizure of the boats at Marietta—Comfort Tyler and Major Israel Smith, Burr's New York henchmen, reached Blennerhassett Island, they brought with them, after months of recruitment in the East, only four vessels and thirty-five men. It has been estimated

---

* Two quarts.
† Some apples belonging to A. W. Putnam of Belpre were on the boats.

that, had all the boats ordered by Burr remained available, he could have taken at least 1,200 persons down the rivers. Perhaps so; but in early December the number actually rendezvoused for that purpose at the island and elsewhere came to well under a hundred. An often-repeated assumption that all the members of the expedition were men has been advanced as evidence that Burr never seriously contemplated a settlement of the Bastrop lands. But an officer connected with the militia of Mississippi Territory, after a visit to one of the camps established by the Burrites in the course of their subsequent wanderings, reported seeing among them "a few women and children and some negro servants."

News of the seizure of the boats at Marietta reached Blennerhassett Island even as the event was taking place. Along with it came other unsettling reports: that, in Ohio, warrants were out for the arrest of Blennerhassett and Tyler, that at Parkersburg the Wood County militia was mustering, and that an armed invasion by that body could be expected at any moment. Then, if not before, the resolve was taken to push down the river in Tyler's vessels. Winter had set in, with three inches of snow on the ground and the air damp and penetrating. There was talk of ice in the Ohio, a circumstance that entered into the decision that Mrs. Blennerhassett and her small sons stay behind until transportation safer than Tyler's craft could be obtained.

By the evening of the tenth, the preparations for departure had assumed lively proportions. Destined to be a subject of much wordage and debate at Richmond, this night of "hub-bub and confusion" on Blennerhassett Island—like many aspects of the Burr Conspiracy—was open to the public. Lanterns flashed and joggled as men trotted from mansion to waterfront, loading the boats beached on a sandbar off the shoreline. A mammoth bonfire blazed at water's edge. Several of Harman Blennerhassett's Ohio acquaintances came visiting, some to settle un-

190

finished business dealings with the departing master of the island, some simply to wish the adventurers godspeed. Among the callers was the soldier-poet General Tupper. Both Blennerhassett and Burr had tried to interest the general in the Bastrop lands as a speculative venture, and the general had given the matter some thought. His visit that hectic December night was a friendly one, though at the Richmond trial the prosecution put considerable energy into an unavailing attempt to prove it otherwise. It is plain from testimony presented at the trial that the moving pageantry on the island was visible to the militia encamped along the Ohio side of the river. Apparently, it stirred no alarms in those quarters. When in the dark hours of the morning of the eleventh the little flotilla pushed off, no canoes darted out from the Ohio shore, no shots came from the patrols positioned there under orders to halt the expedition.

Daybreak brought the Wood County militia to the island. Swarming ashore and slogging up the long front slope, the invaders found the mansion deserted save for a huddle of frightened servants, Mrs. Blennerhassett having already taken a skiff to Marietta in an effort to induce the Ohio authorities to release the family houseboat so that she could follow her husband.* The commander of the attacking force, Colonel Hugh Phelps, and Blennerhassett were good friends. Had the colonel remained on the island, it might have fared better; but learning that the adventurers were fleeing downriver, Phelps hastened with a mounted detachment to Point Pleasant at the mouth of the Great Kanawha, in hopes of cutting them off there; a wasted mission, for the conspirators slithered past that place in the dark of night and were soon bearing down on the Falls of the

---

* Evidently, she took her two boys with her, as there is no mention of them in contemporary accounts of the happenings on the island during her absence. See, for example, the statement by Morgan Neville and William Robinson in Archer Butler Hulbert, *The Ohio River*, 304–5; and the recollections attributed to Blennerhassett in BH Papers (Safford), 191.

Ohio, where they were joined by Davis Floyd with additional boats and additional hands.*

Left to their own devices on the island, the warriors from Wood County raided the Blennerhassetts' larder and liquor supply and trashed the mansion. On 13 December, fourteen young men, come downriver from Pittsburgh to join the expedition, hauled in at the island, only to be overpowered by its drunken conquerors and subjected to a mock trial. "On our arrival at the house," two of their number stated later, "we found it filled with militia; another party of them were . . . making fires around the house, of rails dragged from the fences . . . At this time Mrs. Blennerhassett was from home. When she returned . . . she remonstrated against this outrage on the property, but . . . the officers declared that while they were on the island, the property absolutely belonged to them . . . There appeared to be no kind of subordination among the men; the large room they occupied on the first floor presented a continued scene of riot . . . the furniture . . . ruined by bayonets; and one of the men fired his gun against the ceiling . . . We were detained from Saturday evening until Tuesday morning . . . When we left the island a cornfield near the house, in which the corn was still remaining, was filled with cattle, the fences having been pulled down."

Mrs. Blennerhassett went with them, the Ohio authorities having failed to free any of the impounded boats. It is a picture to dwell on, this handsome and aristocratic woman beginning a journey down an icy and windy river that not until a month later would reunite her with her husband on the lower Mississippi.

And Burr? As these events unraveled, what did he know of them, and what was he doing? He knew nothing; nothing, that is, of the war being waged in his honor. At the end of his second

---

* Four boats and thirty people seem to be the most acceptable figures, judging from the varying accounts of the size of the flotilla as presented at Richmond.

arraignment in Frankfort, he lingered for a few days in the Kentucky capital. It is not known what affairs detained him. It is known that during this interval he discussed his plans at some length with a number of persons, including Charles Lynch, the man from whom he had purchased the Bastrop lands. Burr said he was anxiously awaiting word from Wilkinson. If hostilities had erupted on the Sabine front, he intended to lead all his followers to that area; if not, he would stop at the Bastrop tract. He was still looking for recruits; any individual willing to sign on for six months could count on ten dollars a month in wages and a hundred to a hundred and fifty acres of land along the Washita as a bonus.

When on the tenth Burr rode out of Frankfort, he was not alone. General Adair accompanied him. Their destination was Nashville, where Burr hoped to make his peace with Andrew Jackson and take delivery of the boats Jackson was having constructed for him at his Clover Bottom works near the Cumberland River. Sometime after reaching the Tennessee capital on 13 December, the travelers parted company. Adair headed overland for New Orleans.

Finally, Burr got in touch with Jackson. By mail he had assured the general of his loyalty to the Union, but the Tennessean wanted more than that. He wanted an oath of allegiance, delivered in person. He got it, and believed it. In a letter to an intimate friend, he described himself as satisfied that the former Vice President's intentions were legal and that his Mexican project enjoyed the approval of the Secretary of War. To what degree the statements in this letter echoed Burr's words, to what degree they simply expressed their author's passionate longing to see the might of the hated dons reduced in the New World, it is impossible to say.

Burr was disappointed to learn that, of the five boats he had ordered, only two were near completion. Now in a great hurry to be off, he canceled work on the other three, arranging a settlement with Jackson under which the general returned

$1,725.62 of the purchase price. Although at the time of Burr's arrival in Nashville, he was not invited to stay with the Jacksons and put up at a tavern, we find him a few days later writing from The Hermitage and advising his correspondent to answer him at that address. When, after a wait of eight days, he started down the Cumberland with the two finished boats and a few hands to navigate them,* seventeen-year-old Stockley Donelson Hays, one of Mrs. Jackson's nephews, was with him. Jackson himself had urged the young man to go—had, also, in a moment of caution, furnished him with a letter of introduction to Governor Claiborne of New Orleans and ordered him, should he detect anything treasonable in Burr's behavior, to put himself under the governor's care.

On 22 December, the day Burr began his journey down the Cumberland, the boats commanded by Blennerhassett and Comfort Tyler were standing off Shawneetown, a Kentucky village on the lower Ohio, where they had put in to await instructions. On the twenty-fourth the instructions arrived, an express brought upriver by Stockley Hays, informing them that Burr would be on the Ohio presently and asking them to meet him at the little island opposite the mouth of the Cumberland. Here, on the twenty-seventh, the juncture took place and Burr learned that most of his boats had been confiscated and that the western country had risen against him—jolting revelations, coming as they did on the heels of the news, reaching him at Nashville, that General Wilkinson had made an accommodation with the Spaniards. It is anybody's guess why at this moment the colonel didn't dismiss his puny force and give up. But giving up was not Aaron Burr's way. Stubbornly, hopefully, he forged on. If for the moment Mexico seemed to be out of the question, there

---

* Weeks before, Jackson had seen to it that an effort was made to recruit men for the expedition. Some seventy-five individuals are believed to have responded, but none was ever delivered to the colonel. Either Jackson's temporary distrust of Burr impelled him to call off the effort, or it simply frittered away. Henry Adams, *History of the United States*, III, 287.

was still the Bastrop tract—an area close to the dominions of Spain, a good place to stop until changing circumstances permitted him to resume the march to the city of Mexico.

Disembarking at the island opposite the mouth of the Cumberland, he gathered his little company in a semicircle around him. It was a get-acquainted session, his first meeting with the young men and women his aides—Comfort Tyler, Davis Floyd, and Israel Smith—had persuaded to join the expedition. Moving about in the cold December drizzle, he shook hands with everybody. He told them that such purposes of the journey as they did not yet know would be disclosed to them when the time was ripe. It was a typical Burr performance, friendly but reserved—and noncommittal. Throughout his political life, the colonel had exhibited a marked reluctance to expose his aims until all the relevant conditions and likely consequences were visible to him. The trait persisted. Psychologically minded Dr. Benjamin Rush of Philadelphia vouchsafed a useful key to Burr's personality when he observed that the former Vice President's Western plans were "directed like doctor's prescriptions by *pro re nata* circumstances."

On the twenty-ninth, the flotilla rested a mile below Fort Massac, last outpost of civilization on the Ohio. Captain Daniel Bissell, commanding there, came aboard to renew an old friendship and to pay his respects. What the captain saw, as he later reported to Andrew Jackson, were "about ten boats of different descriptions, navigated with about six men each, having nothing on board" other than what people going to settle a new land would carry with them. The captain could have added that most of the travelers were young men, looking forward, as several testified at the Richmond trial, to beginning new lives on their own homesteads along the Washita River. Burr declined Bissel's invitation to breakfast at the fort, but gladly accepted, if indeed he himself did not seek, an arrangement under which one of the captain's men, a Sergeant Jacob Dunbaugh, was given a twenty-day leave to join the expedition.

At Richmond the government prosecutor stated that even as "Burr's assemblage descended from the mouth of the Cumberland and . . . all along the rivers . . . their military array and warlike posture continued, and their number were increasing." But, so far as can be determined, Sergeant Dunbaugh and "some men" picked up a few days later constituted the sum total of the increasing numbers. Contemporary estimates of the size of the expedition at journey's end range from about sixty to a hundred.

On the next to last day of the year, the travelers changed rivers, pleased to put behind them the storms of the Ohio as they debouched into the wide and, for the time being, placid waters of the Mississippi. They spent New Year's Day at New Madrid, on the western shore, taking on tomahawks and other supplies. Then Burr, using a keelboat and accompanied by a few associates, hastened across river and down to Chickasaw Bluffs, where Memphis stands today, to enjoy the hospitality of Lieutenant Jacob Jackson, in charge of the little fort at that place. In a deposition sworn to for the trial at Richmond, the Virginia-born lieutenant gave the impression that this visit on 5–6 January 1807 marked his first connection with the Burr Conspiracy. But General Wilkinson thought otherwise. One month before Burr climbed to the little military post at Chickasaw Bluffs, the general sent his aide, Lieutenant Daniel Hughes, northward from New Orleans with orders to put Jackson under arrest—a circumstance which suggests that, like so many of Burr's longtime supporters, the young Virginian suffered a lapse of memory when his eyes fell on the President's proclamation. At Richmond, Jackson quoted Burr as observing "that the subjects of Spain were in a very distressed situation, and that his project would tend to relieve them from the tyranny of their" masters. The lieutenant recalled believing Burr's statement that the government was secretly in favor of his Mexican plan. Jackson, however, described himself as sternly rejecting his visitor's repeated requests that some of the soldiers at Chickasaw Bluffs be released to the expedition. Notwithstanding his scruples on this point, he accepted from Burr a sum of money, with the understanding that it was to be spent for gathering recruits against the day when the invasion of the dominions of Spain could be effected.

From the Bluffs, the rest of the fleet having arrived there, the adventurers drifted on, still blissfully unaware that the ripple they were carving in the waters of the spacious river had become the source of an uproar extending from Washington on the Potomac to the far ends of the country.

3

FOR SEVERAL WEEKS after his proclamation of 27 November, Jefferson did nothing of consequence about the Burr problem. His silence did not prevent the Philadelphia *Aurora*, the leading Democratic newspaper, from telling its readers that the Administration had "penetrated to the bottom . . . the projects of Mr. Burr." Editor Duane wrote as if he had a score of detectives at his disposal, all of them hot on the colonel's heels and privy to his thoughts. Burr, said Duane, was trying to give the impression that he had several objectives in mind. As a matter of fact, he had but one "*Grand design* . . . that of *raising himself to a powerful station* over a separate government and an independent territory—to become himself the lawgiver and the founder of a new power . . ." Duane's belief was that the design was "by no means too stupendous for the man!" and that under "particular circumstances" it might be accomplished. "If the people of the western country were tired of peace, prosperity, and civil liberty," the Quaker City editor wrote, "if the country was invaded at one extreme, and a great body of disaffected men . . . at the other ready to open their arms to any daring leader who would promise them national plunder. If he had young men from all over and money, stores, brass field pieces, ammunition, arms, etc. etc. . . . then indeed might Mr.

Burr have calculated on sometime elevating himself either to an *empire*—or a gibbet."

4

THOMAS JEFFERSON, in his annual message to the new Congress on 2 December, gave the conspiracy but passing notice. In this communication, as in the proclamation, he mentioned neither Burr nor treason. Both, however, were on his mind. The former Vice President, he told his son-in-law Thomas Mann Randolph, was "unquestionably very actively engaged" in a scheme to sever the Union. "We give him all the attention our situation admits," he added; "as yet we have no legal proof of any overt act which the law can lay hold of."

Then came events calculated to move the executive to drastic action. On New Year's Day, Isaac Briggs rode up to the executive mansion, bringing with him Wilkinson's second warning— the one in which the general cited the cipher letter and prophesied that the arch-conspirator would prove too wily for him, that the dagger of the assassin would terminate his struggle to save the nation. The student of these events wonders how Jefferson managed to peruse the general's frenzies with a straight face. He read them earnestly, as a matter of fact; and listened in the same manner to Briggs's memorized recital of the contents of the cipher. "[I]s Wilkinson sound in this business?" the President inquired. To which Briggs replied: "There is not the smallest doubt of it."

What more did the President need? Nothing but a prod from the Congress, and that materialized almost at once. Jefferson's references to the existence in the West of a criminal attempt by "sundry persons . . . to set on foot . . . a military . . . enterprize against the dominions of Spain" had stirred questions in the House of Representatives. On 16 January, John Randolph of Roanoke, fast emerging as leader of an anti-Jefferson faction within the Democratic Party and seeking ways in which to embarrass the Administration, pointed out that to date the President had presented to the lawmakers no evidence to support his charges. At Randolph's behest, the House voted resolutions calling on the executive to lay before it "any information" in his possession "touching any illegal combination of private individuals against the peace and safety of the Union . . ." On the twenty-second, the President obliged, transmitting to the House a variety of documents, including his only recently received copy of Wilkinson's translation of the cipher letter. Jefferson accompanied these papers with a lengthy message, all of it dealing with the conspiracy. For the first time, he identified the main objective of that movement as an attempt to divide the nation and named Burr as its leader; for the first time, he took notice of what he called the "pretended purchase by the archconspirator of a tract of country on the Washita, claimed by a Baron Bastrop," adding that this "was to serve as the pretext for all of his preparations, an allurement for such followers as really wished to acquire settlements in that country, and a cover under which to retreat in the event of a . . . discomfiture . . . of his real design." Jefferson admitted that the information in his hands consisted "chiefly . . . of letters, often containing such a mixture of rumors, conjectures, and suspicions, as renders it difficult to sift out the real facts." Under these circumstances, he asserted, "neither safety nor justice will permit the exposing names, except that of the principal actor, whose guilt is placed beyond question."

Poor Burr! With a President for enemy, what could his friends be expected to do for him? John Adams was quick to spot the error. If Burr's guilt were "as clear as the noonday sun," he wrote Dr. Rush, "the first magistrate ought not to have pronounced it before a jury had tried him." The former President found it difficult to believe Burr capable of all the terrible things the press was attributing to him. "Although I never thought so highly of his natural talents . . . as many of both parties have represented them," he told Rush, "I never

believed him to be a fool. But he must be an idiot . . . if he
has really planned and attempted to execute such a project as
is imputed to him . . . It is utterly incredible that any foreign
power should have instigated him. It is utterly incredible that
without foreign aid he should have thought that the trans-
Alleghenian people would revolt with him . . . Any man who
has read the circular letters to their constituents from members
of the House of Representatives in Congress from some of the
southern states, while I was President, must be convinced that
there were many among them who had no more regard to truth
than the Devil. At Present I suspect that this lying spirit has
been at work concerning Burr . . ."

Adams was not alone in his skepticism. Noting that two
thousand copies of the President's 22 January message had
been printed for distribution, a Washington correspondent to
the Federalist *Columbian Sentinel* of Boston speculated that
the cipher letter "may be a hoax" and pronounced himself "an
unbeliever in the truth of the principal charges against the
said Burr . . . The evidence of his guilt comes the wrong
way.—It has been, it seems, derived from Wilkinson; on whose
judgement or solidity I place very little reliance. It will be
found, on a careful examination of dates, that, at the moment
when . . . Wilkinson was expecting the approach of Burr,
with 6000 armed 'spirits,' to sack New-Orleans, and play the
devil with Mexico;—at that moment he (Burr) was cool as
a cucumber, attending Courts in Kentucky, which could find
nothing against him . . . When Wilkinson's ague was the
most violent, Burr, it is proved, was not within a thousand miles
of New-Orleans.—I may be deceived . . . but I think the
alarm to be grossly exaggerated;—that the mountain in labor
will produce but a very little mouse; and that mouse be the
itinerant route of Burr, in the interior, in pursuit of that very
land speculation [Bastrop] which the President mentions in his
message . . ."

What Thomas Jefferson really thought about Burr's Western venture will never be known. The President said different things to different people. In a letter to the Marquis de Lafayette in France, he repeated what he had told his son-in-law and others, that Burr's goal was a severance of the Union. But in a letter to James Bowdoin, the United States minister to Spain, he wrote in another vein. "No better proof of the good faith of the United States [toward Spain]," he told Bowdoin, "could have been given, than the vigor with which we have acted, and the expense incurred, in suppressing the enterprise meditated lately by Burr against Mexico. Although at first, he proposed a separation of the western country, and on that ground received encouragement and aid from Yrujo, according to the usual spirit of his government towards us, yet he very early saw that the fidelity of the western country was not to be shaken, and turned himself wholly towards Mexico. And so popular is an enterprise on that country in this, that we had only to lie still, and he would have had followers enough to have been in the City of Mexico in six weeks." Given Jefferson's admitted uncertainty as to what Burr was trying to do, along with his realization in early 1807 that the forces attached to the arch-conspirator were minuscule, his decision to commit himself, his government, and his country to a costly and time-consuming effort to send the former Vice President to the gallows as a traitor can only be described as a personal vendetta. The great symbol of political corruption—so Burr loomed in the third President's "teeming but abnormally suspicious mind" —must be destroyed.

The President's message to Congress disturbed even some of the individuals who had taken his proclamation in stride. Senator Plumer, though certain that the cipher letter was not Burr's work, was nonetheless impressed by stories of the colonel's evil doings as related to him by the President himself. In the end, however, the thoughtful New Hampshire politician concluded that "Burr's object was the Mexican provinces—not a seperation [sic] of the union." For a time, Burr's son-in-law

Joseph Alston broke ranks, assuring the governor of South Carolina in an anguished communication that at the time the cipher letter was written "I had never heard, directly or indirectly from Col. Burr, or any other person, of the meditated attack on New Orleans; nor Had I any more reason to *suspect* an attack on . . . any . . . part of the United States, than I have at this moment to suspect that our militia will be forthwith ordered on an expedition against *Gibraltar*." To which the troubled rice planter added that he "had long had strong grounds for believing that Col. Burr was engaged by other objects, of a very different nature . . . and which I confess the sentiments of my heart approved . . . Without adverting to that integrity of principle, which even my enemies, I trust, have allowed me, can it be supposed that a man situated as I am—descended from a family which has never known dishonor, happy in the affection and esteem of a large number of relations and friends, possessed of ample fortune, and standing high in the confidence of his fellow-citizens—would harbor, for one instant, a thought injurious to the country which was the scene of those blessings?" Later Alston repented this action of a frightened man, wrote and published a pamphlet in defense of his father-in-law, and stood by him during the trial in Richmond.

Even as Jefferson's message began its travels across country, Dr. Bollman and Sam Swartwout, the first of the five men seized by Wilkinson in New Orleans and hustled East, arrived at the national capital. A prison awaited them, along "with an officer and 15 soldiers of the Marine Corps" under orders to guard them "night and day."

No sooner were the two prisoners in town than one of them, Dr. Bollman, was on his way to the executive mansion to be questioned by the President and the Secretary of State. The German-born physician was a voluble soul. He talked at length; and later, at Jefferson's request, he drafted a fourteen-page report expanding on his verbal statements. Detailed though these were, they made but a single point—that Burr's sole goal was an attack on the Spanish dominions. Before answering any questions and again before preparing his extended paper, Bollman obtained in writing the President's promise that nothing the doctor said would be used against him and that "the paper shall never go out of his [Jefferson's] hand." This promise the President did not honor.

The presence of Swartwout and Bollman in the federal city gave rise to protests at the illegal nature of their detention and to a move by three well-known lawyers to sue out writs of habeas corpus for them. Here was a potential source of embarrassment to an Administration on record as viewing any associate of Burr as part of a treasonable endeavor. The President lost no time in obtaining from William Eaton a deposition describing Burr's alleged threats to overthrow the government and drop the chief magistrate into the Potomac. In the Senate the Administration spokesman, William Branch Giles of Virginia, did his bit. Giles proposed, and the Senate overwhelmingly endorsed, a motion to suspend the great constitutional writ of habeas corpus for three months. Fortunately for all the victims of Wilkinson's high-handed behavior, the House of Representatives refused to go along. When, after sundry legal twists and turns, the case of Bollman and Swartwout reached the Supreme Court of the United States, the accusation was no longer that they had condoned treason on Burr's part, as Wilkinson had suggested, but that they themselves had committed treason by "levying war against the United States." So exciting to governmental Washington were the hearings in the austere courtroom of the national capitol that for two days neither branch of the Congress could achieve a quorum.

Among the four lawyers for the defendants was fifty-five-year-old Luther Martin of Baltimore, a grizzled oak of a man, notably rough on the outside, notably tender within, a steady consumer of appalling quantities of brandy, and one of the most effective advocates ever produced in America. His grating voice would be heard often and memorably during the proceedings at Richmond a few months hence. From the pen and lips of another titan, Chief Justice Marshall, came the ruling of the majority of the court—an opinion destined to throw a long shadow across those proceedings.

One of Marshall's many landmark statements, his opinion in the case of Bollman–Swartwout was in essence a treatise on treason. Treason is the only crime that the framers of the United States Constitution chose to define in that document, leaving to the country's lawmakers and jurists the task of cataloguing all the others. The Founding Fathers had their reasons. Too long, in too many parts of the world, had treason been so broadly construed that in some places at some periods a man could be charged, convicted, and tortured to death for merely dreaming of a desire to kill or depose the sovereign. Even colonial America had known instances of this, Virginians in the mid-seventeenth century becoming liable to action for treason if they expressed sympathy for the enemies of the lately executed King Charles I of England. Too long in too many countries treason, too comprehensively described, had proved a convenient instrument whereby crowned heads could rid themselves of critics and political opponents. Article 3, Section 3 of the Constitution reads: "Treason against the United States shall consist *only* [emphasis added] in levying war against them, or in adhering to their Enemies, giving them Aid and Comfort. No Person shall be convicted of Treason unless on the Testimony of two witnesses to the same overt Act, or on Confession in open Court."

Even this carefully phrased exercise in limitation required at least one additional definition. What was a levying of war? What clearly visible action must the two witnesses to it be in a position to see? Manfully, the Chief Justice coped with that question, straining for the exact word and the lucid construction. "To constitute that specific crime for which the prisoners now before the court have been committed," said Marshall, "war must be actually levied against the United States. However flagitious may be the crime of conspiring to subvert by force the government of our country, such conspiracy is not treason. To conspire to levy war, and actually to levy war, are distinct offences . . . To complete the crime of levying war . . . there must be actual assemblage of men for the purpose of executing a treasonable design. In the case now before the court, a design to overturn the government of the United States in New-Orleans by force, would have been unquestionably a design which, if carried into execution, would have been treason; and the assemblage of a body of men for the purpose of carrying it into execution, would amount to levying war against the United States; but no conspiracy for this object, no enlisting of men to effect it, would be an actual levying of war." To which Marshall added his conviction that "constructive treason"—the extension of the crime by construction to "doubtful cases"—was by Article 3, Section 3 of the Constitution forever forbidden in the United States.

The testimony available to the court consisted of Eaton's deposition and an affidavit sworn to by Wilkinson, listing his reasons for sending Bollman, Swartwout, and others eastward, and setting forth his translation of the cipher letter. Eaton's statement was of little use to the judges, as its recital of Burr's alleged plans could not be equated to an "overt Act." Wilkinson's affidavit was another matter. Marshall devoted considerable wordage to the general's version of the cipher letter. Some of its sentences struck the Chief Justice as worthy of being quoted in full. "Burr's plan of operations," one of them read, "is to move down rapidly from the falls . . . with the first 500 to 1000 men in light boats . . . to be at Natchez between the 5th and 15th of December, there to meet Wilkinson; then to determine whether it will be expedient in the first instance to seize on or to pass by Baton Rouge." Nothing in that sentence, Marshall argued, pointed to an attack on American soil; Baton Rouge was Spanish property. Two other sentences, thus quoted, stated that "The people of the country to which we are going are prepared to receive us. Their agents now with Burr say that if we will protect their religion . . . in three weeks all will be settled." Those words couldn't refer to the United States, where freedom of religion prevailed. On the other hand, they were clearly "fitted" to the conditions existing in Mexico. "There certainly is not in the letter delivered to General Wilkinson," Marshall concluded, ". . . one syllable which has a necessary or natural reference to an enterprize against any territory of the United States."

Next, the judge turned to Wilkinson's recollection of the remarks made to him by Swartwout after that young man had delivered the letter to the general at Natchitoches. Swartwout, according to Wilkinson, said that Burr and seven thousand men were coming down the river and that no doubt there would be "some seizing" of money and shipping when they reached New Orleans. Perhaps Swartwout made those statements, perhaps not; but his making them and Wilkinson's listening to them did not add up to a levying of war by Burr and his followers. In short, the evidence before the court did not justify the charges against Swartwout and Bollman, and both of them, therefore, were free to go.

Had Marshall confined himself to the question facing the bench—namely whether, given the evidence on hand, "the accused shall be discharged or held to trial"—all would have been well. But into his thoughtful treatise the judge dropped an obiter dictum—an incidental comment, not binding on the court and immaterial to the issue before it. "It is not the intention of the court," Marshall said, "to say that, no individual can be guilty of [levying war] . . . who has not appeared in arms against his country. On the contrary, if war be actually levied, that is, if a body of men be actually assembled for the purpose of effecting by force a treasonable purpose, all those who perform any part, however minute, or however remote from the scene of action, and who are actually leagued in the general conspiracy, are to be considered as traitors, but there must be an actual assemblage of men to constitute a levying of war." In the months ahead, these remarks had striking consequences, providing Marshall with many unhappy moments and the federal government with a peg on which to hang a charge of treason against Aaron Burr—developments of which more will be said.

The release of Bollman and Swartwout pleased Washingtonians troubled by Wilkinson's choleric antics. It angered the President and his political supporters. Jefferson, we are told, "vented spleen by censuring sharply a marine officer for entertaining Swartwout after his release," and some congressional Democrats "muttered threats of impeachment and discussed a constitutional amendment" under which the Supreme Court would be stripped of jurisdiction over criminal matters. From the floor of the House, where he sat as the delegate from his territory, Daniel Clark of New Orleans dispatched a word of caution to his old friend Wilkinson. That gentleman, the wealthy merchant believed, should stop acting like some ancient Roman commander, hurrying his prisoners of war to the capital in anticipation of a grand triumph to himself at that place. "You are calumniated from all quarters," Clark wrote the general; "and believe me, if the sense of the people should be found hostile to your conduct, you will be abandoned by the administration." But on that score Wilkinson had no cause for alarm. The President was holding his hand. Jefferson wrote him frequently, urging him to keep up the good work in New Orleans, requesting that he send on any information against Burr he had and especially the "original" of the cipher letter (a document no one but Wilkinson ever laid eyes on), and dismissed criticisms of the general's behavior as coming from people who either did not understand the perils posed by the conspiracy or were participants in it. "You have doubtless, seen a good deal of malicious insinuation in the papers against you," the President wrote. "This of course, begat suspicion and distrust in those unacquainted with the line of your conduct. We, who know it, have not failed to strengthen the public confidence in you . . ."

5

ON THE FAR SIDE of the Appalachians, even as the federal city was rocking to these events, the Burr war flamed westward, spurred by the President's announcements and by the growing knowledge of the investigatory activities of John Graham. At Christmas time, the Kentucky legislature authorized the mobilization of the militia. That nothing came of its attempt to nab the conspirators did not prevent some of the soldiers' heirs, acting over half a century later, from petitioning the national government for bounty lands due veterans of military campaigns under an 1855 law—claims the pension office in Washington rejected on the grounds that the pursuit of Aaron Burr was not a "war" as that term was defined on the statute books.

At Natchez in Mississippi Territory, Cowles Mead, secretary of the territory and in the absence of Robert Williams its acting governor, trained his eye on the river, momentarily expecting the appearance of the arch-conspirator and his armed thousands. To Mead the situation was all the more unnerving because in his heart he knew that, if Burr was a villain, Wilkinson was an even darker one. The "Pensioned," he called the portly dictator whom many others were now hailing sarcastically as the "hero of New Orleans." A "wily" man, Mead warned Governor Claiborne: "Consider him a traitor." Still, in the absence of any other information, Mead had no choice but to act as if Wilkinson's bellowed alarums were gospel truth. Responding promptly to orders from War Secretary Dearborn, the acting governor issued a proclamation calling for the arrest of the "Burr Conspirators," ordered a general muster of the militia, prorogued the legislature for one week—

expressing the wish that during that period its members would "suspend the elegance of debate for the clangour of military array"—and posted sixty guards along the river. These chores attended to, he could only wait and wonder.

He would have waited with less trepidation had he been able to see the little flotilla as it came abreast the low, shelf-like shores of Mississippi Territory on 10 January 1807. Burr, moving ahead in a fast bateau, put in about noon at a settlement at the mouth of Bayou Pierre, a tributary of the Mississippi northward of Natchez. With him came about a dozen of his closest associates, including Robert A. New, Jr., the son of a former Virginia congressman. Arrangements were made for them to spend the night at the home of Peter Bryan Bruin, one of the judges of the territorial supreme court, a federal tribunal. It was a night the leader of the expedition would have reason to remember. Judge Bruin had saved for him the 6 January issue of the Natchez *Mississippi Messenger*, carrying the acting governor's proclamation, a copy of Wilkinson's translation of the cipher letter, and the information that the general had sent this document to the President. It was bad enough for Burr's plans that the general had made a deal with the Spanish. Now it was clear that his old friend had betrayed him. Of Wilkinson's conduct, "perfidious!" he exclaimed. Of the vacuous cipher letter now come to his attention for the first time: "vile falsifications."

The game was up, and its leader's behavior during the next few weeks tells us that he knew it. Already, however, two of his lieutenants, Davis Floyd and Alexander Ralston, had moved by bateau downriver to Natchez for a conference with Burr's friend John F. Carmichael, a physician living in the vicinity of Fort Adams. If Carmichael's subsequent description of this talk can be trusted, it was an important one. Burr's plan, the doctor's deposition indicates, had been to use his house as a rendezvous. Here General Adair was to have rejoined the expedition, after conferring with its supporters in New Orleans.

Here Wilkinson was to have come, prepared to join his forces with those the colonel had brought down the rivers. From here the expeditionary force was to have moved against Baton Rouge, West Florida, the only Spanish stronghold remaining on the Mississippi. Floyd and Ralston made a point of telling Carmichael that newspaper accounts charging their chief with disunionist ambitions were incorrect. Mexico, an invasion of the Spanish dominions, remained Burr's plan. Informed that General Wilkinson was arresting Burrites in New Orleans, the young visitors expressed surprise and perplexity. Did the general's actions mean that he had deserted the expedition, or were they his way of covering up his real design? Carmichael quoted Ralston as putting this question repeatedly, but he did not quote himself as answering it one way or the other. Ralston and Davis expressed an interest in reconnoitering Baton Rouge, but gave up the idea on being told that the Spanish commandant there was on the alert. In the end, they settled for a walk around Fort Adams, temporarily deserted, as Wilkinson had moved its garrison to New Orleans. It is hard to know how much faith to put in Dr. Carmichael's recollections. Like many Westerners, he had taken fright at the President's proclamation. Not once, during his talk with Davis and Ralston, did he so much as intimate that he was no longer sympathetic to their leader's project; and, shortly after they left, he hastened to New Orleans to repeat the conversation to Wilkinson.

He found the Crescent City still in the throes of Burr-phobia. When General Adair arrived, he announced that he expected the colonel in town "in three days." Pressed as to how many people the arch-conspirator was bringing with him, Adair replied: "A servant." This was not the kind of talk the hero of New Orleans wanted to hear making the rounds. Taking no chances, Wilkinson sent 120 soldiers to the boarding house where the Kentucky general and onetime United States senator was staying, with a warrant for his arrest. Soon Adair was a prisoner aboard a vessel heading East, where a court, anticipating Chief Justice Marshall's decision in the Bollman–Swart-wout case, promptly returned him to freedom.

On 12 January, a Monday, Bayou Pierre was a scene of confused activity. Toward noon, the other boats of the flotilla arrived. Robert New, speaking for Burr, told the travelers that the territorial militia had been called out against them and asked what they wanted to do. Did they wish to quit, or did they wish to stick? They voted to stick, whereupon, at Burr's suggestion, they dropped downriver a few miles, beached their vessels at a place called Thompson's Bayou on the Louisiana shore, and set up an encampment. At Richmond, a few months later, three witnesses gave the court to understand that at this time, or a few days later, Burr's followers found hiding places for their supply of muskets, bayonets, blunderbusses, and other munitions. One member of the expedition, Sergeant Dunbaugh, told so many lies on the witness stand that his statements on this point were disregarded. But another member of the expedition, David Fisk, recalled seeing a chest filled with weapons of war on one of the boats; a delegate to the Mississippi legislature, Lemuel Henry, testified that Robert New tried to sell him forty muskets at a fraction of their value; and Harman Blennerhassett, in his account of the flight of the adventurers down the rivers, noted that when word reached the Burrite camp that Mississippi was sending men across river to "search for concealed arms, supposed to have been secreted in the brush," a party was sent out during the night "to obviate *effectually* the success of the design." That a filibustering expedition aimed at the penetration of a foreign land would carry with it the instruments required for that action would seem unarguable. The presence of military arms as evidence of treasonable intent, however, does not follow.

At separate intervals, after the departure of Burr and the flotilla from Bayou Pierre, two groups of militia descended on Judge Bruin's house: a company under a Captain Regan, and a thirty-five-man detachment under Colonel W. H. Wooldridge. Before leaving the judge's house, Burr wrote a letter to Cowles Mead and left it lying open on a table. Captain Regan found it and delivered it to his superior, Colonel Thomas Fitzpatrick. Fitzpatrick sent it by express to Mead. "The Reports which charge me with designs unfriendly to the peace and welfare of this and the adjacent Territory [Orleans]," Burr had written, "are utterly false . . . ; my pursuits are . . . justifiable . . . tending to the happiness and benefit of my Country Men . . . It is hoped Sir that you'll not suffer yourself to be made the instrument of arming Citizen against Citizen and of involving the Country in the horrors of Civil War, without some better Foundation than the Suggestions of rumor or the vile falsifications of a man notoriously the pensioner of a foreign Government . . . I pray Sir, that you will cause this letter to be read to the Militia . . ."

From his refuge at Thompson's Bayou on the Louisiana side of the river, Burr somehow contrived to keep informed of what was going on in Mississippi. Learning of the arrival of Colonel Wooldridge and his detachment at Bruin's house, he sent a skiff to Bayou Pierre so that Wooldridge and two of his officers could cross the river, talk to the leader of the expedition and his people, and examine their camp. Wooldridge's report to Mead conjures up a plainspoken man, eager to put a disagreeable task behind him and troubled by discontent among his own "malish [sic]," many of whom were already resigning from the service. Wooldridge described Burr's followers as "in good order but Darn hungry," and as consisting of about fifty-five men, plus "a few women and children." He quoted their chief as asserting that his and their intentions were innocent. On the day after Wooldridge's visit, Colonel Fitzpatrick arrived at Thompson's Bayou with sixty dragoons. He, too, inspected the camp and sent a report to Mead. The gist of it was that Burr would resist any effort by the military to seize him, his followers, or his property. He stood ready at any time, however, to submit to the civil authorities of Mississippi Territory.

Mead saw Burr's letter to himself on the morning of Tuesday, the thirteenth. He read it with an open mind, but with Wilkinson's repeated announcements of an armed horde pouring down the river still ringing in his ears, he continued to take all necessary precautions. He directed Colonel Ferdinand L. Claiborne, brother of the young governor of Orleans District, to place himself and 275 militiamen along Cole's Creek, another little tributary of the Mississippi, halfway between Natchez and Bayou Pierre. He ordered Captain Joshua Baker to post his company at Fort Adams and make certain no suspicious craft passed that place. He sent warnings to Wilkinson in New Orleans and to Commodore Shaw, who had assembled his gunboats at Point Coupée, on the Louisiana shore, some miles north of Baton Rouge. He wrote Dearborn, informing him of the contents of the letter from Burr and telling the secretary that "We are all bustle" and that "I hope in a day or two to give you a better account of this troublesome man."

On Thursday the reports drafted by Wooldridge and Fitzpatrick, covering their tours of Burr's camp, were in Mead's hands. On Friday the acting governor dispatched two confidential aides across the river with a message suggesting that Burr attend a meeting, to be held at the home of Thomas Calvit at the mouth of Cole's Creek, for the purpose of arranging the terms of his surrender. Mississippi was experiencing a colder winter than its oldest inhabitants could remember; a piercing wind roiled the waters of Cole's Creek and four inches of snow mantled its banks, when at two on Saturday afternoon Burr appeared at Thomas Calvit's house. A lengthy conference yielded a written agreement in which Mead promised Burr and his followers the full protection of the laws and the arch-conspirator gave himself up and agreed to a search of his boats by thirty men led by four "gentlemen of unquestionable respectability." From Cole's Creek Burr, escorted by the governor's aides, traveled to Washington, the little capital of the territory some seven miles inland from Natchez. Here he was bound over in $5,000 bail to a grand jury scheduled to be convened under Judge Thomas Rodney in the Supreme Court on 2 February.

Two days after these events, Mead sent to Dearborn what was to be his last report on the crisis. He reviewed the steps he had taken to contain the expedition and the details surrounding the colonel's surrender. "Thus, sir," he concluded, "this mighty alarm with all its exaggeration has eventuated in nine boats and one hundred men, and the major part of these are boys or young men just from school. Many of their depositions have been taken before Judge Rodney, but they bespeak ignorance of the views or designs of the colonel. I believe them really ignorant and deluded. I believe they are the dupes of stratagem, if the asservations [sic] of Generals Eaton and Wilkinson are to be accredited." Mead's "if" was significant.

Technically, Burr and all his followers were now under arrest. In actuality, they came and went as they pleased. Burr was a frequent guest in the homes of the wealthy planters living in the Washington–Natchez area. Tradition says that on one of these occasions he met a young woman named Madeline Price, fell in love, and proposed. Madeline was beautiful, we are told. Sensible, too, it would seem, for no marriage ensued.

On 23 January, Burr rejoined his followers on the Louisiana side of the river. To Blennerhassett, now happily reunited with his wife and sons, he brought the good news that Judge Rodney had said that "if Wilkinson, or any other military force, should attempt to remove his [Burr's] person out of the Mississippi Territory, prior to his trial, he, the Judge, would again . . . put on 'old '76' and march out in support of Col. Burr and the Constitution."

Rodney's reference to Wilkinson was no idle chatter. Even before Burr appeared on the lower Mississippi, the general had offered $5,000 to Silas Dinsmoor, the United States agent to the Choctaw Indians in that area, for the capture of Burr, phrasing his instructions to the agent in a manner that clearly indicated a determination to get his hands on the former Vice President, dead or alive. No sooner had the news of Burr's presence in the vicinity reached New Orleans than the general was joining with Governor Claiborne in a written request to Mead to send the great malefactor to them. Now exaggerated but unsettling rumors were moving upriver to the effect that Commodore Shaw and his gunboats were heading north with "a special order from the Secretary of the Navy to take Col. Burr or the next in command under him, and to take or destroy" his vessels. Bad news came in bunches, a report reaching the Burrite camp on the twenty-seventh that none of the colonel's recent drafts on a New York mercantile firm had been honored. Henceforth, Burr would find it difficult to feed his followers. Already, drunken fights were erupting among them, with more and more imprecations being directed at the colonel as the author of their worsening woes.

On the twenty-eighth, word arrived that Robert Williams, having concluded a visit to his home state of North Carolina, had returned to his duties as governor of Mississippi Territory. As Williams was an acquaintance of long standing, Burr hurried across river to pay his respects and, once back in the little town of Washington, decided to remain there pending the opening of the Supreme Court a few days hence. There is no record of his conversation with Governor Williams, if any. There is a record of his one interview with John Graham, the President's roaming detective. Graham's story, as given at Richmond, was that on reaching the Mississippi capital he learned Burr was there and sought him out. Burr complained that the press had misrepresented his intentions, and when

Graham proposed that he "make some public declaration of his real object," the colonel replied "that he was a party concerned and . . . no declaration of his could have any effect."

On the first Monday in February, the federal court opened. Occupying the bench were Peter Bruin and Thomas Rodney. Bruin, Burr's host at Bayou Pierre, was a genial gentleman reputedly addicted to the bottle. Delaware-born Rodney, a sixty-two-year-old farmer, soldier, and jurist, was the father of Caesar Augustus Rodney, Jefferson's Attorney General. Burr was represented by two local lawyers, one of whom, Lyman Harding, had joined with the colonel's friend since Revolutionary War days, Colonel Benjamin Osmun, now a planter living near Natchez, in putting up the bail set by the court.

Young George Poindexter, the attorney general for the territory, began the proceedings by requesting a dismissal of the proposed bill of indictment on two grounds: that the territorial supreme court, an appellate tribunal, could not try a cause *de novo;* and that none of the crimes imputed to the defendant had been committed within its jurisdiction. Judge Rodney was "manifestly upset" at this unanticipated motion, "which sounded as if it had been prepared for the prosecutor by Burr himself." Well acquainted with the President's proclamation, with Wilkinson's horror tales and William Eaton's deposition, the father of the Attorney General of the United States understandably relished the approval he would enjoy in the national capital were Aaron Burr brought to book in this little courtroom on the frontier. Bruin agreed with the territorial prosecutor; Rodney did not. The bench having divided, Poindexter's motion was regarded as overruled, and Judge Rodney promptly impaneled a grand jury and treated its twenty-three members to a lengthy charge studded with historical instances and Biblical allusions. Back in Kentucky, District Attorney Daveiss had limited himself officially to high misdemeanor, to the contention that Burr had raised an army for the purpose of attacking a foreign country. Here in Mississippi, the indictment shouted treason. So did Rodney's charge to the jury.

"This once illustrious Citizen," he said of the former Vice President, ". . . has been lately accused of the Nefarious design to Separate the Western Country of the United States from the Union, and to combine it with a part of the whole of Mexico, and to erect them into a New and Independent Empire for himself Or for Some Rich Patron under whom he acts. This accusation has Traversed the United States through the medium of the Press and other channels of communication, has agitated the People, and alarmed The Government in such a Manner as to put them to a great deal of trouble and expense. It will be with you gentlemen to Enquire into the truth of this accusation."

They inquired; which is to say, they spent a day reading the depositions gathered from Burr's followers, none of whom had ever heard him express a desire to sever the Union. When on Friday 4 February the jurymen returned to the courtroom, they brought no bill against the defendant, only a stinging protest at the way the authorities had handled his case. "The grand jury of the Mississippi Territory, on due investigation of the evidence brought before them," they reported, "are of the opinion that Aaron Burr has not been guilty of any crime or misdemeanor against the laws of the United States, or of this Territory, or given any just occasion for the alarm or inquietude to the good people of this territory." Having taken care of the defendant, they gave their attention to the authorities. First, to Cowles Mead in his capacity as acting governor: "The grand jurors present as a grievance the late military expedition, unnecessarily, as they conceive, fitted out against the person and property of the said Aaron Burr, when no resistance had been made to the civil authorities." Then, to General Wilkinson: "The grand jurors also present, as a grievance, destructive of personal liberty, the late military arrest [of Adair in New Orleans], made without warrant, and, as they conceive, without other lawful authority." Finally, to President Jefferson: "They do sincerely regret that so much cause has been given to the enemies of our glorious Constitution, to rejoice at such measures being adopted in a neighboring Territory, as, if sanctioned by the Executive of our country, must sap the vitals of our political existence . . ."

Judge Rodney was horrified. No indictment against the arch-conspirator. That was disappointing. A gratuitous lecture from the grand jury. That was unbearable. At this moment His Honor divested himself of "old '76" and scrapped the Constitution. Even before the defendant's lawyers could put the customary motion—namely, that their client be released from his recognizance and bond—Rodney ruled that the colonel was still under the supervision of the court and obliged to appear before it whenever so ordered. To make certain that this decision was fully understood, the judge instructed the sheriff to find Burr, not then in the courtroom, and bring him in. Either the colonel could not be found or refused to come. The sheriff returned alone, whereupon Rodney ordered the bail of "the said Aaron Burr" forfeited and adjured his securities Lyman Harding and Benjamin Osmun to produce the "body" of the defendant—a request that under the circumstances they had no intention of honoring. Frantic efforts by Burr's lawyers to reverse these unheard-of procedures came to no avail.

Now Burr was in peril. He had surrendered to the Mississippi civil authorities under the belief that due process of law would protect him from Wilkinson. But due process had failed him. By this time he was acquainted with much of what was happening in New Orleans, though even he would have been shocked had he known the lengths to which the self-anointed ruler of that distracted city was going in his effort to get into his hands the man who could pronounce the cipher letter a fraud. Indian agent Dinsmoor had made no effort to earn the $5,000 the hero of New Orleans had offered for the capture of the arch-conspirator. In truth, Dinsmoor regarded the anti-Burr brouhaha in the Crescent City as a grim joke. "We are all in a flurry here," he wrote a military friend, "hourly expecting Colonel Burr & all Kentucky & half of Tennessee at his [back] to punish General Wilkinson, set the negroes free, Rob the banks & take Mexico. Come & help me laugh at the fun." When Dr. Carmichael came babbling down to New Orleans, Wilkinson pressed him into service, persuading him on his return to his house near Fort Adams to look for Burr and grab him if possible. The doctor galloped home full of zeal, only to be dissuaded from his mission by Governor Williams. By this time, Wilkinson had learned that he could not put his trust in any one person. He ordered a couple of his officers to find the colonel, sending them into Mississippi for this purpose, along with a group of civilians "armed with Dirks and Pistolls."

Burr went into hiding. He spent time at Colonel Osmun's country place near Natchez, another period at Bayou Pierre in the home of Dr. John Cummins, one of the financial contributors to his expedition and the individual with whom he left the remarkable maps which reveal the extensive range of his now shattered plans for the invasion of the domains of Spain. On 6 February, Governor Williams issued a proclamation describing the colonel as a fugitive from justice and offering a reward of $2,000 for his apprehension. From wherever he was, Burr protested. "I have seen your proclamation," he told the governor in one of two notes to him. "It was unworthy of you to lend the sanction of your name to a falsehood—The Recognizance in which I was bound was on condition that I should appear [before the court] *in case an indictment should be found against me* and not otherwise. This special form was agreed to by Judge Rodney after nearly half an hour's discussion between him Mr. Harding and myself, drawn up at his Request by Mr. Harding and signed by the Judge in our presence and in that of Col. Azman [Osmun] and will be found in the hand writing of Mr. Harding so signed unless for fraudulent purposes the Judge shall have destroyed it . . ." To which Williams replied that he could not interfere with the processes of the court.

Burr took the only safe course open to him. He fled. Before doing so, he paid a flying visit to his followers. His brief speech quieted the mutinous among them and brought tears to many eyes. He suggested that those who wished to go on to the Bastrop lands should do so and there stake out whatever shares they thought proper. He told them to sell the boats and provisions and to divide the proceeds among themselves. Then he bade them goodbye and disappeared into the pine barrens of central Mississippi, riding a horse given him by Colonel Osmun and accompanied by a young guide, Major Robert Ashley.

Behind them, one final shiver of anti-Burrism coursed the towns of Washington and Natchez. The *Mississippi Messenger* carried the story in its 17 February issue. "On Tuesday morning last [10 February]," the Natchez newspaper reported, "a negro boy, property of Doctor Cummins of Bayou Pierre, came to the house of Mr. William Fairbanks, who lives near the mouth of Cole's Creek, and inquired the road to this city. He was riding the same horse that Col. Burr rode from Washington, and was also wearing his surtout-coat. Mr. F. immediately stopped and examined the boy and nicely stitched in the cape of his surtout, he found the following note [addressed to Burr's henchmen Comfort Tyler and Davis Floyd]: 'If you are together, keep together and I will join you tomorrow night. In the meantime put all your arms in perfect order. Ask the bearer no questions, but tell him all you may think I wish to know. He does not know this is from me, nor where I am.' "

The note bore no signature and was dated 1 February, the day prior to the opening of Burr's arraignment before the federal court. Governor Williams thought the handwriting that of the colonel, but the letter was never examined by any official body. It was clearly a forgery. If its author thought the mention of "arms" would revive the local paranoia over Burr, he guessed correctly. The territorial authorities arrested some sixty of the colonel's followers and brought them to Natchez. After a few days, all were freed, with the exception of Blennerhassett, Floyd, Tyler, and Ralston. Later, Blennerhassett and Ralston were released. Still later, Blennerhassett was rearrested in Kentucky and sent to Richmond to stand trial. Floyd and Tyler, too, were indicted by the Richmond grand jury. As for the remaining survivors of the "Burr War"—their future was not unpleasant. None went on to the Bastrop lands, but they did take the boats and provisions down to New Orleans. There they sold what they could, stored the rest, and divided the money. Young, and for the most part the products of Eastern universities, they had already found friends in Mississippi and had taken a liking to the region. Most of them stayed right there, eventually—so an early historian tells us—dispersing "themselves through the territory and [supplying] . . . it with school masters, singing masters, dancing masters, clerks, tavern keepers, and doctors."

I I

The Trial at Richmond Begins

Burr, at the time of his disappearance into the piny woods and red-clay hills of western Mississippi, was "disguised," according to Wilkinson, "in an old blanket coat begirt with a leathern strap, to which a tin cup was suspended on the left and a scalping knife on the right." Squinched on his head was a weather-stained beaver, whose broad brim, even when deliberately pulled down, failed to extinguish the luster of his dark eyes. When on the night of 18 February, in the village of Wakefield near the Tombigbee River, he and Major Ashley paused to ask directions to the farmhouse of a Colonel Hinson, the eyes gave him away. Nicholas Perkins, who supplied the requested information, was a backwoods attorney, currently eking out a living as head of the Federal Land Office in Mississippi Territory. Perkins had read the governor's proclamation offering a reward of $2,000 for the seizure of the former Vice President. He remembered the description in it, the statement that the eyes of the wanted man "sparkled like diamonds." The minute Burr and his companion moved on, Perkins made haste to rouse Sheriff Theodore Brightwell from his bed. Soon the two of them were riding in the wake of the strangers. Reaching the Hinson place about eleven o'clock, they halted at the gate for a conference. It had occurred to Perkins

222

that Burr, recognizing him, might take alarm and escape. He proposed to post himself in the woods near the farmhouse, while Brightwell went in, confirmed the identity of the man with the unusual eyes, and then slipped out to make his report. But once inside, for reasons never revealed, the sheriff stayed where he was and Perkins, after an hour or so of shivering in the bitter cold of the night, resolved to act on his own.

Borrowing a canoe from a friend who lived nearby, he paddled down the Tombigbee River, swollen and tumbled by recent rains, to Fort Stoddert, last American military post northward of the Spanish Floridas. Reaching the fort shortly after daybreak, he conveyed his suspicions to the commandant, Lieutenant Edmund Pendleton Gaines, who at once put himself at the head of a file of mounted soldiers and rode off with Perkins at his side. About nine that morning, on the crest of a hill two miles below the Hinson farm, they came upon Burr, accompanied now by Ashley and Sheriff Brightwell. Ashley they transferred to the civilian authorities, and the sheriff they let go, but Burr they carried to Fort Stoddert, to be confined under guard.

Now Lieutenant Gaines found himself in the toils of an embarrassment. Governor Williams of Mississippi Territory wrote a letter instructing Gaines to send his distinguished captive "immediately to the City of Washington," some 1,500 miles away. But where in the bottomlands of the Tombigbee River country (now part of Alabama) was he to find men willing to go as guards on a difficult trek? More to the point, the seizure of the sometime Vice President by a body of soldiers angered the three hundred families of the region. In their eyes, Burr was a folk hero, the leader against the Spanish of an expedition whose success would relieve them from the burdensome duties slapped on the farm products they shipped through the Spanish-owned port of Mobile on the Gulf of Mexico. Sensitive to this groundswell of criticism, Gaines announced that he had not arrested Burr "militarily," that the onus for that action rested on the shoulders of Nicholas Perkins. Perkins accepted the burden with pleasure. That huge and sinewy young man knew the value of a dollar, or more exactly of the $3,331 he eventually received for his labors on behalf of the government. To Gaines's intense relief, Perkins rounded up six husky civilians, each equipped with a holstered pistol and undaunted at the prospect of a trying cross-country passage. Gaines added two soldiers armed with muskets and in late March the detachment thus assembled to take the arch-conspirator to Washington began its Eastern hegira. Gaines saw it off with delight. So enamored were the local people of Burr's project and of Burr himself, he wrote General Wilkinson, that had the prisoner remained at Fort Stoddert "a week longer the consequences would have been of the most serious nature."

For hundreds of miles, Burr and his captors traveled through Indian country, following a trail so narrow they had to ride single-file, with the prisoner in the middle. Campsites selected when darkness fell were in the clearings of dense forests or in hummocky cane fields, with the horses hobbled and belled and the one tent the party carried placed at the disposal of the colonel. To Perkins, this first lap of the journey was the easiest. In these uncultivated wastes, still the habitat of wild beasts, the likelihood of Burr's friends trying to rescue him was remote. Once the Oconee River of Georgia was crossed and civilization began, the watchful leader of the expedition made a point of using little-traveled and roundabout routes. Where the terrain permitted, he put two men on either side of Burr, two behind him and two in front. Eager to be rid of a nerve-racking responsibility, he demanded an inhuman pace of his men and their precious charge: forty miles a day, day after day, frequent foul weather notwithstanding. No complaints from the prisoner, no protests even when creeks rendered unfordable by heavy rains compelled the men to swim across.

At the town of Chester in South Carolina, the long-dreaded incident occurred. Here the path of the pilgrims bordered a tavern where music was playing, with people dancing within and milling around outside. Suddenly Burr jumped off his horse and lunged toward the merrymakers. "I am Aaron Burr," he shouted, "under military arrest, and claim the protection of the civil authorities." Giant of a man though he was, Perkins could move fast. He was on the ground immediately, pistols ready, and ordered the prisoner to remount. "I will not," said Burr, whereupon Perkins dropped his arms "and being a man of prodigious strength and the prisoner a small man, seized him round the waist and placed him in his saddle as though he were a child." Another member of the group, Thomas Malone, slipped the reins of Burr's horse over the animal's head and led him away. Behind them, puzzled spectators watched as the convoy cantered on. Burr was weeping. Malone, sensing his frustration, wept with him. At Fredericksburg, Virginia, a message from the President awaited. Burr was not to be brought to Washington; he was to be taken to the capital of the Old Dominion, arrangements having been made for him to be arraigned there. Accordingly, Nicholas Perkins put himself, his crew, and his prisoner on the stage to Richmond. There, as the candles were being lit on the evening of Thursday 26 March, the hard journey ended at a Main Street inn interchangeably known as Mr. Epps's hotel or the Eagle Tavern.

2

THE GOVERNMENT'S CHOICE of the United States Circuit Court in the District of Virginia for Burr's trial was dictated by its awareness of the difficulties inherent in showing that the former Vice President had "committed High Treason against the United States by levying war against them." The overt act demanded by the Constitution could not happen in the air. It had to be grounded somewhere. But where? Where had the little colonel, flitting like a dragonfly over the western waters, paused long enough to assemble a warlike force? Grand juries in Kentucky and Mississippi Territory pronounced him innocent of such activity in those regions. Ohio, Tennessee, and Indiana Territory had seen him, but only fleetingly. That left only Blennerhassett Island. But, prior to the Bollman–Swartwout hearings in late February 1807, even the enchanted isle offered this drawback—that on the night of 10 December 1806, when the alleged conspirators gathered there in what the government considered a most threatening manner, Burr was three hundred miles away. Then, on 21 February, the Chief Justice obligingly handed down his obiter dictum, his assertion that "if a body of men be actually assembled for the purpose of effecting by force a treasonable purpose, all those who perform any part, however . . . remote from the scene of action, and who are actually leagued in the general conspiracy, are to be considered as traitors . . ." Jefferson and his legal advisers pounced on this gloss, seeing in it the little noose into which perhaps the neck of the great malefactor could be squeezed. As Blennerhassett Island belonged to Virginia, putting it within the jurisdiction of that judicial district, it followed that the circuit court in Richmond was the proper place for the inquiry.

The decision solved one problem for the Administration, only to raise another. It placed the conduct of the trial in the hands of a man with whom the President was politically at odds. In those days, each of the then six Supreme Court justices doubled as a judge of one of the nation's circuit courts. In Virginia this task fell to John Marshall, who in the eyes of the President personified, as did no other American, the spirit of nationalism, of strong central government, so offensive to Jefferson's states' rights leanings. It was John Adams who elevated Marshall to the Chief Justiceship. His doing so thwarted Jefferson's desire to give that position to his friend Spencer Roane, a fellow Virginian who shared his insistence that the will of the majority as expressed by its representatives in the Congress should prevail. Already, Marshall had done what Jefferson had feared he would do. In 1803, in the famous case of *Marbury v. Madison*, the Chief Justice pronounced a section of a federal law null and void, thus asserting the right of the courts to invalidate legislation judged to be contrary to the dictates of the Constitution. For this declaration of the supremacy of the judiciary branch of the government over the legislative branch, Jefferson could never forgive Marshall.

Jefferson's animosity toward the Chief Justice was generously reciprocated, for both men were good haters. One morning in 1789, having reason to call on Marshall in Philadelphia, Jefferson found that his kinsman (they were "third cousins once removed") was not in and left a note. "Thomas Jefferson," it read, "presents his compliments to General Marshall. He had the honor of calling at his lodgings twice this morning but was so ^{un}lucky as to find that he was out on both occasions." The insertion of the "un" above the "lucky" was duly noted by cousin John. Years later, he spoke of that slip of the pen as probably the only time in his life that Thomas Jefferson ever "came near to telling the truth."

3

ONE OF BURR's first acts in Richmond was to discard the tattered clothing in which he had fled. Garbed in black silk, hair powdered and queue fashionably tied, he was again the Chesterfieldian gentleman when, during the noon hour of Monday 30 March 1807, he was brought to the street floor of the Eagle Tavern to be examined by the Chief Justice in his capacity as circuit judge. An "awfully silent and attentive" crowd of citizens jammed the big lobby. They were there to watch the proceedings and voiced chagrin when a door to a "retired room" at the back, having opened to admit the defendant and his entourage, closed in their faces. Aware that no room in town was large enough for all those who wished to attend, Marshall had proposed that this opening gambit be conducted in private. To this suggestion the government consented on condition that, should any discussion arise among counsel, the business would be removed to a public place. During the months ahead, both parties to the contest played to the public: the prosecution on the assumption that most Americans were already certain of the guilt of the accused; the defense in an effort to change their minds.

Within the retired room, Burr and Marshall faced one another, the prisoner small and elegant, the judge tall, "ramshackle," and indifferently dressed. With Burr was one of his lawyers. With the Chief Justice were Nicholas Perkins, as a witness for the government, and Virginia District Attorney George Hay as its spokesman. Hay laid before the judge a record of the Bollman–Swartwout case, including the affidavits of Eaton and Wilkinson. Perkins recited the circumstances surrounding Burr's arrest and described the journey from Fort Stoddert to Richmond. Then Hay moved that the defendant be committed on charges of treason and misdemeanor. As Marshall could rule on this motion only after hearing arguments, Burr was admitted to bail for $5,000 for his appearance the following day and court was adjourned, to convene then in the courtroom of the state capitol.

But at ten the next morning the throng straining to get in so far exceeded the capacity of this second-floor apartment that the court moved downstairs, into the chamber of the House of Delegates. Even this room, eighty-six feet from east to west and over forty feet wide, with deep balconies reachable by U-shaped stairways at the inner corners, was too small, forcing scores of spectators to listen from the rotunda off which it stood. Under the cove ceiling of this oblong chamber, all the remaining sessions of the trials were held. Today it is a museum. Its fluted pilasters and statuary-filled niches do honor to the beauty of the original capitol as designed by Jefferson. But in 1807 it was "bare," "dingy," and "dirty," its sand-filled floor boxes much too widely spaced to catch all the tobacco juice they were meant to absorb. An oval-shaped center aisle, leading from the central door to the speaker's dais against the northern wall, held the tables for the attorneys, the box for the jury, and the desk for the clerk. Curving benches to either side and chairs above served the onlookers.

Marshall was not the only occupant of the dais. Sitting with him at most sessions was Cyrus Griffin, judge of the District of Virginia, whose almost total inactivity during the long trial can be described as a mute tribute to the overpowering personality of the tall, black-eyed jurist at his side. In winter, a bronze wood-burning stove, formed like a wedding cake, stood before the dais, its naked pipe angling out the window behind the raised throne of the speaker. Though the summer of 1807 was uncommonly hot, this bulky object seems to have remained in place—judging from the frequency with which the lawyers complained of not being able to hear one another across the aisle and from the occasional assertions of the shorthand reporters that they could not catch witnesses' words. Simple fatigue, to be sure, could have created these difficulties, for in each of the printed versions of the two stenographic records the speeches of the lawyers cover approximately eight hundred pages. Some were interesting, some brilliant; but many were also tediously repetitive, every speaker on more than one occasion opening himself to the criticism that his words continued long after their content ended.

One day sufficed for the argumentation for and against the government's plea that Burr be tried on the two charges. Opening for the prosecution, Hay cited the cipher letter and the affidavits of Wilkinson and Eaton as adequate grounds for suspecting that the former Vice President had committed treason by "assemblying an armed force, with design to seize the city of New Orleans, . . . revolutionize the territory attached to it, . . . and separate the western from the Atlantic states"; and that he had committed "a high misdemeanor, in setting on foot within the United States, a military expedition against the dominions of the king of Spain." Two of Burr's lawyers were now present. After both had had their say, Burr himself addressed the court, signaling in what for him was a long speech the high degree to which he intended to conduct his own defense. Hay had called Burr's flight in Mississippi an admission of guilt. It was no such thing, said Burr. It was sheer physical fear that had plunged him into the wilderness. He fled because he had reasons to believe that if he stayed where he was he would be seized, confined to an "armed boat" known to be waiting in the river to receive him, and carried to New Orleans to endure the tender mercies of General Wilkinson. He reminded his listeners that he had submitted voluntarily to three Western grand juries. One had discharged him for lack of evidence. The others had declared him innocent of the charges against him. As for the affidavits of Wilkinson and Eaton—those he dismissed as "abounding in crudities and absurdities."

Caesar A. Rodney, the Attorney General of the United States, closed for the prosecution. His speech was remarkable for its inclusion of an admission, never again heard from the government side of the aisle, that the reports of the conspiracy "which have resounded thro' the newspapers so long and so strongly" had implanted in the mind of the public the "general opinion" that Burr was guilty. The Attorney General described the prisoner as a man Rodney "once considered his friend," and had treated as such "in his Delaware home." It embarrassed him to have to say that the "chain of circumstances" known to the government "showed, without doubt," that the "late Vice President" had committed a "most heinous crime." But the defendant, he promised, would enjoy a fair trial. There was "no disposition in the government or in myself to persecute Col. Burr." Certainly, the Attorney General harbored no such disposition. His speech at the 21 March hearing in the house-chamber-turned-courtroom was his first and last appearance there. After that, he vanished from Richmond, leaving the on-the-spot direction of the government's cause to District Attorney Hay.

On the following day, Marshall ruled on the motion to

commit. In this opinion, as in the one penned in the Bollman–Swartwout inquest, he lingered over the famous cipher letter, relieving himself of a statement highly suggestive in the light of our present knowledge of that weird communication. "*Exclude this letter*," he announced, "*and nothing remains in the testimony which can in the most remote degree affect Colonel Burr.*"* The Chief Justice conceded that, for the time being, all his knowledge of the cipher rested on Wilkinson's translation of it in his affidavit. He revealed that some of his fellow justices on the Supreme Court had questioned the admissibility of such evidence as secondhand. He did not share their concern. Admittedly, "the original letter, or a true copy of it accompanied by the cipher," would be "more satisfactory." Admittedly, "the general's saying that the letter came from Burr was not tantamount to saying that it was in his handwriting." Admittedly, Wilkinson was for the moment too far away to be questioned. Later, however, he could be brought into court and subjected to interrogation designed to establish the validity of the letter and of his assertions about it. Meanwhile, in the view of the Chief Justice, the fact that the letter was in a cipher previously arranged between Wilkinson and Burr sufficiently supported the claim that the colonel was its author. Since that letter, as interpreted by the Supreme Court, pointed to an attack on the dominions of Spain, Burr could be committed for trial on a charge of high misdemeanor.

Treason was another matter. "Treason," the Chief Justice stated, "may be machinated in secret, but it can be perpetrated only in open day and in the eye of the world . . . The assembling of forces to levy war is a visible transaction, and numbers must witness it . . . Several months have elapsed, since this fact did occur, if it ever occurred. More than five weeks have elapsed, since the supreme court . . . declared the necessity of proving the fact, if it exists. Why is it not proved?"

* Emphasis added.

What testimony had the government placed before the circuit court in furtherance of its request that Burr be committed for treason? Exactly the same testimony that it had submitted in the case of Bollman–Swartwout, and the Supreme Court had declared that inadequate. The Chief Justice could not bring himself to dissent from the high court's decision. If, later on, the government produced better evidence, treason could be considered; but as matters stood, Marshall concluded, "I shall not . . . insert in the commitment the charge of high treason." He then set bail for the misdemeanor at $10,000, a sum promptly pledged by five sureties, and Burr left the courtroom, a free man—at least until the opening of the summer term of the circuit court on 22 May, seven weeks hence.

Consternation among the attorneys for the government, and consternation on the part of the President, to whom the news of Marshall's ruling was transmitted by fast messenger. If he could go to heaven only in the company of a political party, Jefferson said in 1789, he would simply forgo the pleasure. During the intervening years, having become the architect of the country's second political party, the third President had become intensely, even at times paranoiacally, partisan. From the moment he resolved to do something about Burr's Western adventures, he persisted in regarding them as a Federalist plot, forgetting, it would seem, that the first detailed exposure of them came to him from a Federalist district attorney in Kentucky, and overlooking the presence among the colonel's supporters of a number of Democrats. Word that the Chief Justice had refused to commit for treason not only strengthened the President's politicized perception of the expedition but also drove him to the conviction, never abandoned, that John Marshall was conducting the trial in Richmond, not as a jurist, but as a leader of the opposition.

Within less than forty-eight hours after the Chief Justice's ruling came down, Jefferson was pouring his anger about it into a letter. "[H]itherto," he wrote James Bowdoin, "we have believed our law to be, that suspicion on probable grounds was sufficient . . . to commit a person for trial, allowing time to collect witnesses till the trial." Now came Marshall with his declaration that the testimony before the circuit court was not ample enough to make out a prima-facie case for treason. The President was forgetting his law training. The Supreme Court had declared the testimony insufficient. The Chief Justice could not render it otherwise by a wave of his hand. If Marshall continued to direct the trial in this manner, the President wrote, "Burr will be discharged, because his crimes having been sown from Maine, through the whole line of the western waters, to New Orleans, we cannot bring witnesses here under four months. The fact is, that the federalists make Burr's cause their own, and exert their whole influence to shield him from punishment . . . And it is unfortunate that federalism is still predominant in our judiciary department, which is consequently in opposition to the legislative and executive branches, and is able to baffle their measures often."

The government now intensified a search already well begun. From "Maine, through the whole line of the western waters, to New Orleans," agents fanned out, looking for witnesses. Eventually, almost 140 were summoned in a gigantic endeavor to find two persons able to say that they had seen the "overt act."

Burr put his seven weeks of freedom to multiple uses. He caught up on his correspondence. Panic seized Theodosia as the details of her father's plight reached South Carolina. Burr ordered her to return "to reason." He knew how to soothe his classically educated daughter. "Was there in Greece or Rome," he wrote her, "a man of virtue and independence, and supposed to possess great talents, who was not the object of vindictive and unrelenting persecution?" He suggested that she collect all such instances "to be found in ancient history" and collate them into "an essay, with reflections, comments and applications." The exercise would calm her, he said, and please him. He, too, hunted for witnesses and documents, chores that at intervals carried him away from Richmond, to Washington and to Philadelphia. He completed his defense team. Four nationally known attorneys, all Virginians, would be at his side when the circuit court opened: John Wickham, Edmund Randolph, Benjamin Botts, and John Baker. Two more came along soon thereafter: Charles Lee, another Virginian; and Luther Martin of Maryland. None of them, so far as is known, asked for or received a fee for his services, and their recorded speeches are those of men whose hearts were in what they were doing. Wickham was the wheelhorse of the aggregation: a man of capacious mind and impressive appearance, long recognized as the leader of the Richmond bar. Portly, squirearchal Edmund Randolph, onetime governor of Virginia, had seen service as Attorney General of the United States. So had Charles Lee, brother of the Revolutionary War hero "Light-Horse Harry" Lee. Baker, a cripple, knew local politics and was popular with many of the men most likely to be called to jury service. Botts, youngest of the defense attorneys, brought to the fray wit, brilliance, and courage. And for courtroom legerdemain and legal learning, the alcoholic genius from Maryland, Luther Martin, had few superiors among the American barristers of his day.

The government team was smaller and less impressive. Heading it was earnest, competent, thin-skinned George Hay. If at times the forty-one-year-old district attorney's performance lacked luster, it probably was because he was not his own man. Jefferson was the wheel of the prosecution, Hay merely one of the spokes. Forced to look to Washington for strategy, the public prosecutor wrote over fifty letters to the President during the trial and received almost as many in return. Assisting Hay were two experienced Virginia attorneys, Alexander MacRae and William Wirt. MacRae, then lieutenant governor of the state, was a fussy old Scot, quick and well-informed, with a disposition steeped in vinegar and a penchant for sarcasm. At thirty-four, Maryland-born Wirt was the youngest of the pleaders on both sides, handsome, dashing, extraordinarily charming, and already in possession of the oratorical skills that undergirded his notable career as counselor, author, and politician.

During the closing weeks of the trial, Wirt delivered a spate of words destined to be remembered and quoted long after the thousands of other words uttered in Richmond were forgotten. Wedged into a long and well-reasoned argument, this colorful passage dealt with the differing roles Burr and Blennerhassett were believed to have played in the alleged crimes. No statements spoken or written of Burr during his lifetime have done as much as this one to fix his reputation in the public mind. "Who is Blennerhassett?" Thus the attractive Richmond attorney prefaced his account of how that gentle and scholarly Irishman, migrating to America, "sought quiet and solitude" on the western waters. "Possessing himself of a beautiful island on the Ohio," Wirt continued, "he rears upon it a palace and decorates it with every romantic embellishment of fancy. A shrubbery, that Shenstone might have envied, blooms around him. Music, that might have charmed Calypso and her nymphs, is his. An extensive library spreads its treasures before him. A philosophical apparatus offers to him all the secrets and mysteries of nature. Peace, tranquillity and innocence shed their mingled delights around him . . . Such was the state of Eden when the serpent entered its bowers."

No one needed to be told who the "serpent" was. Wirt dilated on how, by "the seductive and fascinating power of his address," the distinguished visitor to the island infused the heart of its owner with "the poison of his own ambition," how overnight Blennerhassett became a different man. "No more he enjoys the tranquil scene," lamented Wirt. "His books are abandoned. His retort and crucible are thrown aside . . . His ear no longer drinks the rich melody of music; it longs for the trumpet's clamor and the cannon's roar. Even the prattle of his babes, once so sweet, no longer affected him and the angel smile of his wife, which hitherto touched his bosom with ecstasy . . . is now unseen and unfelt. Greater objects have taken possession of his soul. His imagination has been dazzled by visions of diadems, of stars and garters and titles of nobility . . . His enchanted island is destined soon to relapse into a wilderness, and in a few months we find the beautiful . . . partner of his bosom . . . shivering at midnight, on the winter banks of the Ohio, and mingling her tears with the torrents, that froze as they fell." A grand performance. For the next hundred years, Wirt's "Who is Blennerhassett?" speech (often headlined "Who is Aaron Burr?") was a staple of school readers the country across, a frequent entry in declamatory contests. Four or more generations of American children, if they learned nothing else about Aaron Burr, learned to know him as the latter-day incarnation of the snake in the Garden of Eden.

As the 22 May opening of the circuit court approached, the quiet little port of Richmond at the head of navigation on the James—population not quite 5,000—nearly doubled in size and trebled in sound. Thousands poured in, most of them to anticipate with huzzahs the sad but obviously well-merited fate of the "Fallen Angel" on trial. From the cities of the North they came, men in the small clothes and silk stockings of an earlier and dressier era, or in the top hats and pantaloons common to the "new French fashions." From the plantations of the South, from the backwoods, from the mountains came men in red flannel shirts, gallus-restrained trousers, and deerskin jackets, their hair carelessly fastened behind with strings or flowing long and free. When the elocution reverberating in the courtroom grew too long-winded, they entertained themselves at the Hay Market Gardens, leading pleasure resort of the city, or took in the cockfights, where one could win or lose as much as fifty dollars a round.

The local hostelries could not begin to accommodate them.

For weeks, little colonies of tents and covered wagons dotted the northern banks of the river. Among the reporters from every large newspaper in the country was twenty-four-year-old Washington Irving. The future creator of Ichabod Crane found himself in the land of "hoe-cake and bacon, mint-juleps and apple-toddy," basking in the warmth of a "society polished, sociable, and extremely hospitable." Never, it seemed to Irving, had he seen in one spot so many evidences of the "goodness" of the female heart; "not a lady, I believe, in Richmond," he wrote, "whatever may be her husband's sentiments . . . would but rejoice in seeing Col. Burr at liberty." News of the trial soon made its way to England, moving Burr's agent there, Charles Williamson, to opine that the Virginia capital had been selected for it because the greater part of its "population being Negro, it is not subject to popular commotions on subjects that might agitate White Citizens."

Today's Richmond undulates like Rome across seven hills, but in 1807 practically all of it lay in the valley of the James or on Capitol Hill. On the plateau of this promontory stood the capitol, with the then fashionable section called Shockoe Hill gently sloping away to the north of it. In the eyes of a person viewing the city from one of the nearby uplands, this classic of "cubic architecture" shed a certain grandeur over the city, but close up, the scene disintegrated into a litter of unpaved streets, impassable in wet weather to anyone not on horseback. Ravines and gullies pitted Capitol Park. Pigs and cattle belonging to the neighboring residents cropped its tangled grasses.

In those days, no steps swept up the front, or southern, end of the capitol. The people assembling for the beginning of the court entered by the side doors, surging through the rotunda to reach the chamber of the delegates. By 12:30, when Burr and his counsel appeared, the room was so crowded that a handsome young attorney had to improvise a perch for himself on the iron lock of the doors. This was Winfield Scott, who forty years later, triumphing where Burr had failed, would lead a conquering army into the city of Mexico. Young Scott quickly arrived at judgments on the leading actors on the stage beneath him. Of Burr, he wrote in his memoirs: "There he stood, in the midst of power, on the brink of danger, as composed, as immovable, as one of Canova's living marbles." Of the Chief Justice: "Marshall was the master spirit of the scene." Of the actor conspicuous by his absence: "It was President Jefferson who directed and animated the prosecution. Hence every Republican clamored for execution," and the Federalists "compacted themselves on the other side."

The people gathered that warm May morning looked forward to watching a great drama. What they saw came closer to farce. From every page of the record of the trial emerges the same stark question: Was it necessary? The government produced no hard evidence of treason or even of misdemeanor. Its representatives came into court without a case. Four months later, after expending an enormous amount of energy and considerable money (at least $100,000), they walked out in the same condition.

4

BURR HIMSELF STARTED the proceedings, manifesting at once the aggressiveness and ingenuity characteristic of his defense throughout. He objected to the presence on the sixteen-man jury of two individuals he regarded as open enemies. No sooner had the two withdrawn and been replaced than the defendant was on his feet with another suggestion. He wanted the Chief Justice to give the grand jury special instructions on the law of treason. When Hay protested that the defendant was no different from "any man charged with a crime" and should receive no "special indulgences," Burr exploded: "Would to God that I did stand on the same ground with every other man! This is the first time [since his arrest by the military in Mississippi] I have . . . been permitted to enjoy the rights of a citizen. How have I been brought hither?" Apparently, he was about to review his thirty-one-day ride under armed guard from Fort Stoddert when the Chief Justice cut him short. It was "improper," said Marshall, "to go into these digressions." Burr, regaining his composure, explained that all "he wished the court to do . . . was, instruct the jury on certain points relating to the testimony." There was, "for instance," the question of what affidavits and other papers could be laid before the inquest. Hay's promise to send no evidence to the grand jury without first giving "notice" of it to Burr and his counsel brought the first day's session to adjournment.

Nothing of consequence happened at the second session. Nothing could, for the prosecution was unwilling to begin making its case until its chief witness, General Wilkinson, was on hand. The defense pounded Hay with questions: Had the general left New Orleans, was he on his way East? Hay thought he had and was. Closing his ears to defense-table humor dealing with the necessarily limited mobility of a man of the general's "gigantic 'bulk,' " the public prosecutor forecast that Wilkinson would be in court by the end of the month —no later than 30 May, he said; probably as early as the 28th. Actually, it would be three weeks before he appeared. During this interval, speculation as to his whereabouts was a source of recurrent verbal clashes. One of them shows that Burr had told his counsel that he was not the author of the infamous cipher letter. At this point, no one could say with certainty that he was, but Hay was sure that when Wilkinson talked to the members of the grand jury, he would satisfy them on that point. Botts was equally sure he would not. The sharp-spoken young defense attorney predicted that the general, testifying under oath, would find himself in the mortifying position of having to admit that the letter "was not in Colonel Burr's handwriting."

Between the second and third meetings of the court, the

district attorney prepared the first of his reports of progress to the President. He was worried, not so much by the legal tangles confronting him as by what he took to be a change in the attitude of the public toward the arch-conspirator. Burr's serenity, his pleasant manner, was drawing friends. "I am surprised and afflicted," Hay told Jefferson, "when I see how much and by how many, this man has been patronised and supported." The public prosecutor might have felt better had he been able to get out over the country and hearken to the *vox populi*. Typical, it would seem, were a string of toasts proposed at an Independence Day gathering in Elkton, Maryland. "Aaron Burr, the man who once received the confidence of a free people . . ." one went. "May his treachery to his country exalt him to the scaffold and hemp be his escort to the republic of dust and ashes."

At the opening of the third session of the court, on Monday 25 May, John Randolph, speaking as foreman of the grand jury, complained that he and his fellow panelists had nothing to do. So far, the government had sent up no bills of indictment for them to consider. Hay explained why this was. Bills had been prepared, but the prosecution did not intend to deliver them to the grand jury until its key witnesses, including Wilkinson, were present. Almost in the same breath, Hay announced his intention of asking the court itself to commit Burr on a charge of treason. Granted that request had been advanced before and the Chief Justice had turned it down, but now better testimony was available to the government. Burr was quick to call attention to the continued presence in the room of the grand jurors and to mention the "impropriety" of broaching such a subject in their hearing. Marshall concurred. Out went the grand jury, thus opening the way to another lawyers' brawl.

Burr's counsel made much of the fact that a grand jury was now in existence. It was the business of that body to determine what accusations should be brought against their client.

No longer was there any need for the court to take such action. To which government counsel retorted that unless the arch-conspirator was held for treason posthaste, he might not be available when the grand jury got around to indicting him on that count. Freedom on bail was not allowable under a charge of treason, and a defendant in jail was a defendant certain to be there when his trial began. On the streets of Richmond, wagers were being taken on this point. The odds were that when Burr saw a commitment for treason in the offing, he would abscond. The prosecutors may or may not have known of these games, but they were betting with the odds. They made no secret of their conviction that the minute Wilkinson arrived, the defendant, realizing that his doom was near, would take off.

All day, the altercation continued. On both sides, speakers strayed from the issue. Edmund Randolph contended that the government was exciting "so much prejudice against Colonel Burr that it was sufficient to make every man in the country desirous of contributing his full quota of information against him." Picking up this theme where Randolph had dropped it, Botts observed that sometimes "men emerge from the sinks of vice and obscurity into patronage and distinction by circulating interesting tales, as all those of the marvelous kind are." Hay admitted that the public strictures on Burr were unusually severe, but insisted that they "resulted from his own character and conduct." Consequently, he had "no right to complain."

Burr had the last word, most of it complaint. His lawyers, he observed, had been accused of making "declamations" against the government. But "surely," he said, "it is an established principle . . . that no government is so high as to be beyond the reach of criticism." Repeatedly, this one had subjected him to harassments "contrary to the forms of law." He begged leave to "state a few of them." His friends had been seized by the military, dragged before "particular tribunals," and forced to testify against him. An "order had been issued to kill him, as he was descending the Mississippi." Post offices had "been broken open, and robbed of his papers." He had always been of the opinion that this was "a felony," but nothing "seemed too extravagant to be forgiven by the amiable morality of this government." Perhaps, he said, these outrages "only prove . . . my case a solitary exception from the general rule. The government may be tender, mild and humane to everyone but me." Months before, he recalled, a high authority had branded him a traitor, but at this late date the government was not yet ready to prove it. Even longer ago, the same authority had proclaimed the existence in the West of a civil war. Now it appeared that the government was unable to locate the conflict. For six months, said Burr, "have they been hunting for it, and still cannot find one spot where it existed. There was, to be sure, a most terrible war in the newspapers, but nowhere else."

On the following day, Marshall ruled on the motion to incarcerate the defendant for treason. The request was a proper one, he said; the bench would listen to whatever evidence the government could furnish in support of it. Hay did his best. He submitted two depositions, both of which the court rejected, one on the grounds that it was inadequate at this stage of the proceedings; the other, because it was improperly certified. Next, Hay put two of his witnesses on the stand. Both claimed to have firsthand knowledge of the activities on Blennerhassett Island and both would be required at a later date to repeat their tales and submit to cross-examination. By the time these men were heard, the district attorney had embarked on another maneuver, designed, like his move to commit, to discourage the great criminal from disappearing. He asked that Burr's bond, now set at $10,000, be increased at once.

Marshall found this proposal hard to handle. On the one hand, he recognized that it was the duty of the court to see to it that the accused did not get away. On the other hand, he hesitated to increase bail on nothing more than the likelihood that one of these days Burr would be put on trial for treason. He described his position as "embarrassing" and expressed the hope that he might be "exempted from giving any opinion upon the case, previously to its being acted upon by the grand jury." Hay felt no sympathy for the quandary in which Marshall found himself; but Burr did. The defendant offered to extricate the Chief Justice from the horns of his dilemma by voluntarily upping his bond. He thought he could raise an additional $10,000. Hay suggested $50,000, but Marshall accepted Burr's figure, and four sureties—Luther Martin among them —put up $2,500 each.

May passed. "Still waiting for Wilkinson," Burr wrote Theodosia, "and no certain accounts of his approach. The grand jury, the witnesses, and the country grow impatient." In the courtroom, Hay was profuse with apologies. Apparently, he had been mistaken as to the general's movements. It was his present understanding that Wilkinson would not be in Richmond until 14 or 15 June. What, then, should be done about the members of the grand jury, still twiddling their thumbs? Were they dismissed for ten days, as Hay suggested, some, on arriving at home, might find it necessary to stay there. The whole term of the court could elapse before another inquest could be formed. The jurors themselves loosened this knot. They promised the judge to return on whatever day he set. Thus assured, Marshall on Wednesday 3 June recessed the court until the following Tuesday—a move taken, Washington Irving explained to a friend, so that the members of the panel "might go home, see their wives, get their clothes washed, and flog their negroes."

The summer heat came on, with the temperatures in the nineties. On 9 June, when the hearings resumed, the hall of delegates baked behind its nine tall windows. The lawyers dozed; so did the spectators, what few there were, the word having got around that nothing was going to happen here until

Wilkinson appeared. By evening, all this had changed, for during the day Burr—speaking in his "clear and distinct voice," his manner as always "emphatic"—submitted a historic "proposition" to the bench.

Burr began by recalling that, in the message to the Congress stigmatizing him as a traitor, Jefferson had mentioned a letter dated 21 October 1806, written to the President by Wilkinson. That communication, the colonel said, might be material to his defense and should be produced in court. He had the same feeling about the various government orders to the military calling for his arrest and in at least one instance authorizing the destruction of his boats. During his recent stop in Washington, Burr had spoken of these orders to Robert Smith, the Secretary of the Navy. It was the colonel's recollection that Smith confirmed the right of the defendant to see them but disapproved of the manner in which he was seeking them. Were Burr's counsel to request the papers, the secretary said, they would be supplied; but a subsequent effort by Edmund Randolph to obtain them had failed. If the district attorney now possessed the original of Wilkinson's letter and copies of the orders and was willing to turn them over to the court, well and good. If not, Burr wanted the Chief Justice to issue a subpoena *duces tecum*, to be served on Jefferson, ordering him to come into court with the requested documents or show cause why he should not do so.

Everybody was awake now. None more so than Hay, whose pained reaction to Burr's motion was that of a man incapable of grasping that the business of a defendant is to defend himself. The district attorney all but stamped his foot. Marshall, once the babble had ceased, indicated a disposition to grant the motion immediately, provided the public prosecutor "was satisfied" that the court had a right to issue such a writ to the President of the United States. Hay was not satisfied. At first, he said flatly that it could not be done. Later he retreated to reasonings more likely to be acceptable to a nation dedicated to "equal justice under the law." One of Hay's arguments, echoed by the other government attorneys, was that the timing was wrong. Of course, a man accused of a crime could have any documents he needed to protect himself. But at the moment Burr had nothing to protect himself against. There were no indictments. Let him be indicted; then he could request the evidence he needed, but not until. Another objection—Hay's brainchild—was that Burr's affidavit demanding the issuance of the writ was "farcical" in that the colonel said only that the letter and the orders he wanted *might* be pertinent to his case. Let him prove they *were* before he wasted the time of the court and threw the nation into turmoil. Defense counsel made light of the alarums erupting on the other side of the aisle. Repeatedly, they asserted that they had no desire to see Thomas Jefferson in their midst. All they wanted was the papers. Let those be sent, and they would rest content.

Luther Martin had said little since taking his place at the defense table on 28 May. Now he delivered his first long speech. "This is a peculiar case, sir," he asserted in his clanging voice. "The President has undertaken to prejudge my client by declaring that 'Of his guilt there can be no doubt.' He has assumed to himself the knowledge of the Supreme Being . . . and pretended to search the heart of my highly respected friend . . . He has let slip the dogs of war, the hell-hounds of persecution . . . And would this President of the United States, who has raised all this absurd clamour, pretend to keep back the papers which are wanted for this trial, where life itself is at stake? It is a sacred principle, that in all such cases, the accused has a right to all the evidence which is necessary for his defense. And whoever withholds, wilfully, information that would save the life of a person, charged with a capital offence, is substantially a murderer, and so recorded in the register of heaven."

Burr himself may have winced at these words, for he regarded Martin's courtroom tactics as long on zeal and short on discretion. The opposition bristled at them. Wirt denounced defense counsel's "perpetual philippics" against the government, the unending effort of the opposition, as he saw it, to make, not Aaron Burr, but Thomas Jefferson the individual on trial. Hay seized on a statement by Martin that the military orders against the defendant were "unconstitutional" and that the colonel was "entitled" to resist them. Not if he did so with force, the district attorney cried. Violent resistance to a Presidential decree, even an unjust one, was in itself treason and had been so declared by the courts of the United States.

After listening to this outpouring of invective for two days, Marshall scolded both sides. Both, he said, were endeavoring "to excite the prejudices of the people." Both were "repeatedly" accusing each other of "doing what they forgot" they had done themselves. He begged them to confine their remarks "to the point really before the court."

His rebuke had no effect. For another two days, the attorneys exchanged insults. Then Marshall ruled on Burr's motion. He was painfully aware of the difficulties it presented. As the head of one coordinate branch of the government, he did not relish having to direct an order to the head of another such branch. But Burr had proffered the thistle, and it was the obligation of the court to grasp it. Grasp it the Chief Justice did. He recognized the right of the national executive to withhold from public gaze documents, or portions of them, containing "state secrets"—passages, for example, dealing with the relations of the United States with other countries. But that problem, Marshall believed, was one to be resolved after the President conformed to the writ and the requisite papers were before the bench. As for whether a subpoena *duces tecum* could be served on the President, the Chief Justice declared that it could be and that in this instance it should be. Under the Constitution, he noted, the American head of state was elected to office by the mass of the people, returned to the mass on the expiration of his term, and remained a citizen throughout. Any citizen could be subjected to the kind of judicial process Burr had requested. "If upon any principle, the President could be construed to stand exempt from the general provisions of the constitution," said Marshall, "it would be, because his duties, as chief magistrate, demand his whole time for national objects. But it is apparent, that this demand is not unremitting; and if it should exist at the time when his attendance on the court is required, it would be sworn on the return of the sub poena, and would rather constitute a reason for not obeying the process of the court, than a reason against its being issued."

Marshall found no force in the claims of the prosecution that Burr's demand was premature and that he must prove the materiality of the letter and the orders before seeking them. "Upon immemorial usage," the Chief Justice said, ". . . and upon what is deemed a sound construction of the constitution . . . any person, charged with a crime, in the courts of the United States, has a right, before, as well as after indictment, to the process of the court to compel the attendance of his witnesses." The materiality of the papers was not germane; all that mattered was that the defendant thought them so and that his reasons for asking for them were not of a frivolous nature. "It is not for the court," said Marshall, "to anticipate the event of the present prosecution. Should it terminate as is expected on the part of the United States, all those, who are concerned in it, should certainly regret, that a paper, which the accused believed to be essential to his defence, which may, for aught that now appears, be essential, had been withheld from him."

Marshall's saying that the Administration "expected" Burr to be convicted was not lost on its attorneys. MacRae demanded an explanation. Was the judge intimating that the government "wished" for a verdict of guilty? If so, he hoped that the statement had fallen "accidentally" from His Honor's pen. MacRae wanted the whole world to know that the government wished for nothing "but a fair and competent investigation." Marshall denied any intention of impugning the motives of the Administration. However, he added, the "Gentlemen" of the prosecution "had so often, and so uniformly asserted, that colonel Burr was guilty, and they had so often repeated it before the testimony was perceived, on which that guilt could alone be substantiated, that it appeared to him probable, that they were not indifferent on the subject."

On 13 June, the subpoena *duces tecum* left Richmond en route to the President's desk; on 17 June, Jefferson replied to it in a letter addressed to Hay; and on 20 June, the district attorney read this communication to the court. Few aspects of the trial have had as much attention as this one. None has been more variously interpreted. Eminent scholars, Henry Adams and Edward S. Corwin among them, describe the President as defying and disobeying the order. "With dignity," writes Bradley Chapin in his essays on the American law of treason, "Jefferson refused to respond." Dumas Malone, to the contrary, treats Jefferson's handling of the matter as at least a partial response in that the President met all of Burr's demands. As Burr's request for the military orders was general, rather than specific, the President instructed the war and navy secretaries to search their files and send to the court whatever papers of this sort they could find. Recalling that he had given the original of Wilkinson's letter to the attorney general, Jefferson told Rodney to do the same with that document.*

"The receipt of these papers," Jefferson wrote in the communication read to the court on 20 June, "has, I presume, so far anticipated, and others this day forwarded, will have substantially fulfilled the object of . . . [the] subpoena . . . To these communications of papers, I will add, that if the defendant suppose there are any facts within the knowledge of the heads of departments, or of myself, which can be useful for his defence, from a desire of doing anything our situation will

---

* Rodney couldn't find the original, and in the end Burr accepted a "duly authenticated" copy. Robertson, *Trial*, II, 504.

permit in furtherance of justice, we shall be ready to give him the benefit of it, by way of deposition through any persons whom the court shall authorise to take our testimony at this place [Washington] . . . As to our personal attendance at Richmond, I am persuaded the court is sensible, that paramount duties to the nation at large, control the obligation of compliance with its summons in this case, as it would, should we receive a similar one to attend the trials of Blannerhasset [sic] and others in the Mississippi Territory . . . or at any place other than the seat of government. To comply with such calls, would leave the nation without an executive branch, whose agency nevertheless is understood to be so constantly necessary, that it is the sole branch which the constitution requires to be always in function. It could not, then, intend that it should be withdrawn from its station by any co-ordinate authority."

It is difficult to find defiance or disobedience in these words, though whether the President's compliance with the "object" of the writ was or was not compliance with the writ itself would appear to be moot. True, the subpoena *duces tecum*, couched in the language common to such instruments, ordered him to come into court; but attached to it was an endorsement, written and signed by Aaron Burr, stating that "transmission to the Clerk of this Court of the original letter of General Wilkinson, and of copies . . . of the other papers . . . described in the annexed process will be admitted as sufficient observance of the process without the personal attendance of any or either of the persons therein named . . ."

Jefferson's gesture of cooperation, to be sure, was for public consumption only. Privately, he seethed. Behind Burr's demands he saw the hand of the "unprincipled & impudent federal bull-dog," Luther Martin. So he wrote to Hay. A Baltimore man named Graybell, he informed the district attorney, had told a man named Gordon who had told him (Jefferson), that some twelve months ago Martin had been heard to say that Burr was fast "concerting measures to separate the Union." To the President, this gossip meant only one thing: Martin was himself part of the conspiracy. Jefferson urged Hay to look into the matter, to find proof. Graybell, he assured the district attorney, could "fix upon" the Maryland attorney "misprision of treason at least," thus adding another indication "that the most clamorous defenders of Burr are all his accomplices." Aside from obtaining an affidavit from Graybell, Hay seems to have ignored this order, and the effort of the chief magistrate to put the "federal bull-dog" in the dock alongside his "highly respected friend" faded away.

It took time for Burr's motion to be argued and disposed of. Meanwhile, other facets of the trial were giving both lawyers and public plenty to talk about. The witnesses subpoenaed by the government were beginning to flow into the courtroom, to be sworn and sent to the grand jury to tell their stories. Sam Swartwout, Colonel De Pestre, scores of others passed through. Among them was William Eaton, wearing "a tremendous hat with a Turkish sash over colored clothes." The hero of Derne, Burr informed Theodosia, "came out of the jury-room in such rage and agitation that he shed tears, and complained bitterly that he had been questioned as if he were a villain. How else could he have been questioned with any propriety?" Andrew Jackson, also hauled to Richmond by the government, unburdened himself to the panel and then took to the streets, to be seen one hot morning, standing on the steps of a corner grocery, haranguing the crowd, praising Burr and belaboring Wilkinson and the President.

Dr. Erich Bollman appeared. Jefferson, reneging on his promise never to part with the doctor's written report of the anti-Mexican expedition, had entrusted that circumstantial document to Hay. His doing so burdened the district attorney with a predicament. Hay wanted Bollman to share his version of the conspiracy with the grand jury, but the German-born physician could not be expected to do so without first receiving

immunity from prosecution for his own self-admitted participation in the escapade. It so happened that, in his eagerness to
see Burr convicted, Jefferson had resorted to one of the greatest
prerogatives available to a President; he had sent the district
attorney a batch of blank pardons. These were to be offered
witnesses who might otherwise refuse to talk lest they incrim-
inate themselves. Twice in open court, Hay tendered the doctor
one of these parchments. Twice the doctor spurned it. "Categorically then I ask you, Mr. Bollman," intoned Hay at the
second of these confrontations, "do you accept your pardon?"
Categorically the doctor replied, "I say no." Acceptance, he
reasoned, implied guilt, and he was conscious of no wrongdoing. Hay contended that, with or without the document in
his hand, the doctor was a pardoned man. What did the judge
think? Marshall didn't know what to think, but after some
discussion he agreed to let the witness go before the inquest.
Go he did, jauntily, saying afterwards that he had answered all
the questions put to him.

The thirteenth of June, a Friday, was a big day for the onlookers, now once again filling the courtroom. Sensation followed sensation. The subpoena *duces tecum* went to Washington, Dr. Bollman defied the government—and George Hay was
at last able to make a long-awaited announcement. General
Wilkinson had arrived in Richmond. He had come around
from New Orleans by sea, had brought with him "ten or eleven
witnesses," some of whom, as came out later, had been literally
shanghaied into making the voyage. Today the general was
resting from the fatigues of his journey, but Hay assured the
court that on Monday he would "appear before them."

On Monday he did, all of him, in a splendiferous uniform
of his own conception. Washington Irving provided a friend
with this picture of the scene: "Wilkinson strutted into the
Court . . . stood for a moment swelling like a turkey cock."
Burr did not so much as glance his way until the Chief Justice
"directed the clerk to swear" him in; "at the mention of the

name Burr turned his head, looked him full in the face with one of his piercing regards, swept his eye over his whole person . . . as if to scan its dimensions, and then coolly . . . went on conversing with his counsel. The whole look was over in an instant, but it was an admirable one. There was no appearance of study or constraint in it; no affectation of disdain or defiance; a slight expression of contempt played over his countenance, such as you would show on regarding any person to whom you were indifferent, but whom you considered mean and contemptible." Wilkinson supplied the President with this version: "I saluted the Bench & in spite of myself my Eyes darted a flash of indignation at the little Traitor, on whom they continued fixed until I was called to the Book—here Sir I found my expectations verified—This Lyon hearted Eagle Eyed Hero, sinking under the weight of conscious guilt, with haggard Eye, made an Effort to meet the indignant salutation of outraged Honor, but it was in vain, his audacity failed Him, He averted his face, grew pale & affected passion to conceal his perturbation."

The embodiment of "outraged honor" was sent at once to the grand jury. With him, Washington Irving wrote, went "such a mighty mass of words" that it took him "at least two days . . . to discharge the wondrous cargo." As a matter of fact, it took four. Ordinarily, grand-jury proceedings take place *in camera*, with the understanding that they are never to be exposed. But foreman Randolph, seemingly holding himself above such rules, described in letters to his friend Judge Joseph Hopper Nicholson the highlights of Wilkinson's testimony and the manner in which it was received. These revelations tell us that when a copy of what Wilkinson identified as Burr's cipher letter was placed before the members of the panel, they saw at once that the general had doctored it in an effort to hide his own participation in the conspiracy. This discovery rendered the document, previously regarded as the very cornerstone of the government's case, of no value as evidence. Later, testifying in open court, Wilkinson laid the letter on the clerk's table, but it was never taken seriously, never considered as proving anything. The general's conduct before the grand jury saw to that. Of the sixteen men on that body, fourteen were Democrats and therefore sharply aware that the reputation of a Democratic President was at stake. Nonetheless, seven members of the panel voted to indict Wilkinson along with Burr. Political considerations alone, according to Randolph, saved the "mammoth of iniquity." Not that any member of the panel "pretended to think him innocent," the snappish foreman told Nicholson; "probably you never saw human nature in so degraded a situation as in the person of Wilkinson before the grand jury, and yet this man stands on the very summit and pinnacle of executive favor."

In the chamber of the delegates, the lawyers talked on. They were in the middle of another protracted wrangle when about two o'clock, Wednesday 24 June, the grand jury filed in to deliver the first of three reports. Indicted this day for both treason and misdemeanor were Burr and Blennerhassett. On Thursday and again on Friday, the jurymen returned to present indictments on both counts against five of Burr's associates: Jonathan Dayton, Senator John Smith, Comfort Tyler, Israel Smith, and Davis Floyd. A curious list, noteworthy for its omissions. Absent were the names of the carriers of the cipher letter, Swartwout and Bollman, presumably because the courts had already cleared them of traitorous activity. The same factor would seem to explain the exclusion of General Adair. But why no mention of Colonel De Pestre, Burr's so-called chief of staff? A possible answer is found in some statements made by that gentleman to Harman Blennerhassett. "Col de Pestre," wrote Blennerhassett, "informed me his brother-in-law, a promising young man of various merit, had been turned out of his place as Clerk in the War Office, because he could not accuse the Col. of Burr-ism; and afterward, some honorable friends of the Government had the delicacy to insinuate how handsomely the Col. might be provided for in the army, if his principles or engagements were not adverse to the administration."

Curious, too, was the phraseology of the indictment of the arch-conspirator for treason. It asserted in substance:

Aaron Burr . . . being . . . under the protection of the laws of the United States, and owing allegiance . . . [thereto], not having the fear of god before his eyes . . . but being moved and seduced by the instigation of the devil, wickedly desiring and intending the peace and tranquillity of the said United States to disturb and foster, move and excite insurrection, rebellion and war against the said United States, on the tenth day of December [1806] . . . at a certain place called and known by the name of Blennerhassett's island in the County of Wood district of Virginia . . . with force and arms unlawfully, falsely, maliciously and traitorously did compass, imagine and intend to raise and levy war, insurrection and rebellion against the said United States; and in order to fulfill and bring to effect the said traitorous compassings imaginations and intentions of him, the said Aaron Burr, he . . . afterwards to wit on the said tenth of December . . . at the said . . . Blennerhasset island with a great multitude of persons . . . to wit to the number of thirty persons and upwards, armed and arrayed in a warlike manner . . . with guns, swords, and dirks . . . being then and there traitorously assembled . . . did . . . array and dispose themselves against the said United States . . .

And the grand inquest . . . do further present, that the said Aaron Burr . . . on the eleventh day of December [and the "multitude" with him] . . . in pursuance of . . . their traitorous intentions . . . did proceed from the said island down the river Ohio [and the] . . . river Mississippi . . . to take possession of a city commonly called New Orleans in the territory of Orleans belonging to the United States . . .

So great was Burr's respect for the mentality of his daughter that his report to her of the handing down of the true bill reads like the letter of one lawyer to another. The indictment, he wrote Theodosia, was "founded on the following allegations: that Colonel Tyler, with twenty or thirty men, stopped at Blennerhassett's Island on their way down the Ohio; that though these men . . . did neither use force nor threaten it, yet, having set out with a view of taking temporary possession of New-Orleans on their way to Mexico, that such intent was treasonable, and therefore a war was levied on Blennerhassett's Island by *construction;* and that, though Colonel Burr was then at Frankfort on his way to Tennessee, yet, having advised the measure, he was, *by construction of law*, present at the island, and levied war there." Obviously, in reaching its decision the jury had looked, not at the Constitution, but at the obiter dictum in Marshall's Bollman–Swartwout opinion.

It would have interested and perhaps comforted Burr had he known that the author of that opinion was also looking at it and that he was having second thoughts about it. Troubled by the "many . . . intrinsic difficulties" of the trial at Richmond, the Chief Justice was begging his colleagues on the high bench for advice and counsel. Of his round of letters to them, the only one which seems to have survived is to Associate Justice William Cushing of Massachusetts. Marshall expected "many points of difficulty" to arise once the treason inquiry got underway. "But there are some," he told Cushing, "respecting which . . . I most anxiously desire the aid of all the Judges. One of these respects the doctrine of constructive treason. How far is this doctrine to be carried in the United States? If a body of men assemble for a treasonable purpose, does this implicate all those who are concerned in this conspiracy whether acquainted with the assemblings or not? Does it implicate those who advised directed or approve of it? Or does it implicate those only who were present & within the district? . . . The opinion of the supreme court in the case of Bollman & Swartwout certainly adopts the doctrine of constructive treason . . . Ought the expressions in that opinion to be revised?"

The day was not far off when Marshall's answer to that question would save Aaron Burr from the gallows.

5

MEANWHILE, Burr was no longer a free man. His lawyers asked for bail, but this action was *pro forma.* They could cite no precedents for granting it under so grave a charge, and the former Vice President was consigned to the vermin-infested Richmond jail, where his cell mates were a man and a woman and his neighbors cutthroats and thieves. Here he spent a couple of uncomfortable nights, and here he drafted his report to Theodosia. "I beg and expect it of you," he lectured at her, "that you will conduct yourself as becomes my daughter, and that you manifest no signs of weakness or alarm."

The court, during the next few days, was the scene of a number of necessary procedures. The clerk read out the indictment and Burr pleaded not guilty. His attorneys complained that the conditions at city jail were undermining his health and made it next to impossible for them to consult with him. Moved by these pleas, Marshall arranged for Burr to be lodged in the dining room of a house on fashionable Broad Street, near the capitol, that Luther Martin had rented for himself and his daughter Maria. Heavy shutters went up at the dining-room windows and seven men were employed to guard the place night and day. Here the defendant would have remained pending the completion of the treason trial had it not been for a stipulation in the law which the court momentarily overlooked. At this point, forty-eight men had to be summoned to serve as a venire from which the petit jury could be selected. Twelve of the veniremen, said the law, must be residents of the county wherein the alleged crime occurred. As it would take time to bring these men from Wood County, three hundred miles to the west, Marshall suspended court for several weeks. There was no need, during this intermission, for the government to spend the money required to keep the prisoner close to the capitol. On the last day of June, Burr was transferred to the recently built state penitentiary, about a mile from the center of town, with the understanding that he would come back to Luther Martin's house when his trial began on the third of August.

Of the filth and odors of city jail he said nothing to Theodosia, but of his new quarters on the third floor of the state prison he wrote her at some length. His three rooms, he revealed, were "airy and healthy," and a hundred feet in length. In these luxurious surroundings he held court. "My friends and acquaintance of both sexes," he wrote, "are permitted to visit me without interruption, without inquiring their business, and without the *presence of a spy*." Even as these words were being penned, servants were pouring into the "penthouse," as Burr called his three rooms, "bringing oranges, lemons, pineapples, raspberries, apricots, cream, butter, ice," and other gifts from adoring females. A glowing picture, nicely calculated to allay Theodosia's fears. But was it an accurate one? When Washington Irving came calling, he experienced "great difficulty in gaining admission" for a few minutes. "The keeper," he learned, "had orders to admit no one but the prisoner's counsel and witnesses." As for the penthouse with its glaringly whitewashed walls and high, grated windows, he found it dreary and damp and its occupant in low spirits. Certain it is that Burr was sufficiently uncertain about the future to want his daughter at his side. "If absent," he wrote her in late July, "you will suffer great solicitude. In my presence, you will feel none, whatever may be the *malice* or the *power* of my enemies, and in both they abound." And a few days later: "I am informed that some good-natured people here have provided you a house, and furnished it, a few steps from my *townhouse*

[Martin's place] . . . whither I shall remove on Sunday; but I will not, if I can possibly avoid it, move before your arrival, *having a great desire to receive you all in this mansion.* Pray, therefore, drive directly out here." Endorsed on this message in his daughter's hand, these words: *"Received on our approach to Richmond. How happy it made me!"*

Legends sprouted wherever Theodosia passed. Local tradition pictures her as winning all hearts in Richmond, and most notably those of Washington Irving and Luther Martin. But Irving was gone from town before she arrived, and Martin's admiration for her, however deep, was properly avuncular. Indeed, little is known of her sojourn in the Virginia capital save that Alston and little Gamp came with her, that they arrived on the eve of the trial, and that they remained until shortly after it was over.

I 2

Acquittal: "Not Proved by a Single Witness"

THE TRIAL OF the People of the United States against Aaron Burr, on a charge of treason, was slow in getting started. On opening day, 3 August, George Hay, the district attorney, revealed that again he was not prepared. So numerous were the witnesses summoned by the government that Hay needed more time to count heads, attach names to them, and supply the court with a complete and accurate list. To enable him to fulfill this obligation, the hearings had to be suspended, first for four days and then for an additional three.

Meanwhile, Burr had been brought back to Luther Martin's house; Harman Blennerhassett took Burr's place on the top floor of the state prison. Blennerhassett's arrival in Richmond on 4 August terminated a long and exhausting trek from Mississippi Territory. He was a deeply troubled man when in June he left his family at Natchez and headed East. Into Burr's enterprises he had sunk the better part of what remained of his once substantial fortune. The collapse of the expedition filled him with fears for the welfare of his wife and children. His destination when he began his trip was his island estate in the Ohio River. He wanted to assess the damage there, to

see what could be salvaged. But these intentions were not to
be realized. At Nashville, on 29 June, he heard for the first
time of the government's actions against Burr and concluded
that at any moment he might be called to Richmond. Passingly,
he considered flight: a hasty retreat to Natchez to gather his
family, and after that, a dash to "asylum" in Spanish West
Florida. But the cultured romantic, passive by nature, found
it easier to think such thoughts than to perform them. "I have
little doubt," he wrote his wife Margaret, "that Jefferson, if
he can not effect our ruin by our conviction, will seek it by
harrassing us to beggary. I think if I would be prosecuted with
the virulence that has marked the proceedings against Burr,
my acquittal, by the trouble and expense that would be incurred to obtain it, would be worth little more than a con-
demnation. One thing is certain, I shall take nothing from you
to fee the lawyers."

In Kentucky, further shocks awaited him. At Danville, he
learned of the indictments against him. At Lexington, he was
met with a sheriff's attachment for some of the $10,000 worth
of Burr's unpaid bills he had endorsed. Burr's son-in-law,
Joseph Alston, had discharged a number of the colonel's out-
standing notes, but those that remained were coming due with
a rapidity that even the rich South Carolina planter could not
meet. Henry Clay was endeavoring to free the embarrassed
traveler from the clutches of the sheriff by arranging for
Alston's guarantees to be assigned to his creditors, when a
United States marshal materialized, bearing a warrant for
Blennerhassett's arrest and orders for his conveyance to the
Virginia capital.

He reached there on a day of breathless heat, bone tired
and unwell, but determined at this first opportunity to let
Margaret know that he was safe and in reasonably good spirits.
She was not to worry, he told her, in the first of the many
letters from his penthouse keep. "I was not half an hour here,"
he wrote, "when I had a lively letter from Col. Burr, a present

of tea, sugar and cakes from Mrs. Alston, and a visit from Alston and Edmond Randolph, [who] . . . assure me the prosecutions for treason have already become ridiculous among the best informed, so that none of us will probably be hanged . . . it is now generally believed, by all parties, that two of the grand jury . . . would not have concurred in finding any bill for treason, and none, probably, would have been found, if these had not mistaken the meaning of the judge's [Marshall's] . . . opinion in [the] case of Swartwout and [Bollman] . . ." On one matter, his family's financial plight, he made no effort to gild the facts. He had spoken to Alston about the money due him from that gentleman and from Burr. The wealthy South Carolinian had acknowledged the obligation, but he had not said when payments would begin. In Blennerhassett's letters home and in the journal he now began keeping for Margaret, there would be more about this frustrating problem, much more, in the months to come.

2

ON MONDAY 10 AUGUST, George Hay was at last ready to proceed, but the next order of business, the selection of a jury from the forty-eight-man venire, turned out to be another time-consuming process. For where in the commonwealth of Virginia were twelve "impartial" men to be found, twelve individuals who had not conned the depositions of Eaton and Wilkinson, to say nothing of countless newspaper reports describing Burr's Western wanderings under often uncompromising headlines such as "Ex-Vice President Turned Traitor?" "Have you said that Colonel Burr was guilty of treason?" Botts of the defense asked Hezekiah Bucky, the first man to be interrogated. "No," replied Bucky. "I only declared that the man who acted as colonel Burr was said to have done, deserved to be hung." Miles Selden, on being examined, described himself as certain that the colonel "was guilty of something" and recollected telling a friend that the conspiracy was "a federal plot and that Burr had been set on by the federalists." Another venireman confessed to having withdrawn from a cavalry unit on learning that the commander of that body had gone bail for "the traitor." Still another jabbed a finger at the defense attorneys and accused them of being afraid of him, because, said he, "my first name is *Hamilton*." On and on it went, the litany of men already convinced that Burr had committed treason. By the end of the second day of questioning, the venire had been exhausted, only four jurors had been selected, and the proceedings had to be suspended again so that a tales, another forty-eight-man venire, could be assembled. The government's lawyers were distressed; they purported to see in the defense lawyers' careful combing of the prospective jurymen a dark plot to cheat the hangman by preventing the trial from taking place at all.

They need not have worried. When the tales appeared on 15 August, Burr took a bold step. He offered, with the consent of the court, to select the remaining eight members of the panel more or less at random and without regard to their announced prejudices. This was not a noble gesture on his part, nor was it intended to be taken as such. By this time it was clear to all concerned that if the case went to a jury, no matter what its composition, Burr would be convicted. Acquittal, if it came, would have to turn on matters of law.

On Monday 17 August, the jury filed into its box and George Hay rose to open for the government. He admitted that the indictment against Burr was a legal fiction. It placed him on Blennerhassett Island on the night of 10 December 1806 when the "overt act" occurred, the assemblage of a force for the purpose of levying war on the United States. But, of course, Burr was not there. No matter, said Hay airily, citing Marshall's opinion in the Bollman–Swartwout case in support of the government's contention that a "man may *'levy war'* against his country when not present." Burr had "procured" the assemblage; that made him a part of it. Hay described the descent of the flotilla down the rivers to Bayou Pierre, where Burr learned that his cipher letter had been sent to the President. The government would show that the defendant registered "astonishment" at this intelligence, that he was heard to cry out that he had been "betrayed." Indeed he had, said Hay, and by the noblest American of them all. From "the adoption of the federal constitution, till this time," the district attorney declared, "no man has rendered more essential service to the people and government of the United States, than General Wilkinson has done, by counteracting and defeating this project. Yet, for this service, eminent and important as it is, he has been as much censured, abused, and calumniated, as if he had joined in it." Hay called on the jury "to do justice and to decide the cause according to the evidence which will be produced before you." Then he asked the court to call William Eaton to the witness stand.

When he did this, it was as though the chair occupied by Burr had caught fire, so swiftly did he spring to his feet, energetically objecting. Everybody knew what the hero of Derne had to say. He could speak of nothing but intention. But intention to commit treason was not treason. There had to be an overt act. Let the prosecution bring on the two witnesses who could describe that; then and then only should it be allowed to exhibit evidence of intent. Quickly Burr's lawyers chimed in behind him, calling on the court to forbid the government from vouchsafing testimony of any sort until it had proved the act of treason itself. Behind the defense attorneys came the opposition, and another shouting match was underway. Both "law and reason support us," thundered Martin for the defense. The motion advanced by the other side was nonsensical, said Wirt for the prosecution. Evidence should be unraveled in an orderly manner, that is to say, in a chronological one. "Would you begin to narrate a tale at the end of it?" he demanded. "If you were to write a history of the late revolution, would you begin at the siege of York?" At adjournment time, the Chief Justice said he would ponder the question overnight.

On the following morning, he read his decision. Treason, he noted, consisted of two parts: intention and act. Testimony must cover both. As for the order in which the two elements should be offered—it was his conclusion, after examining the records of similar trials, that it didn't matter. One thing only mattered, and let there be no misunderstanding about this: all testimony must be "relevant" to the act, precisely as that act was described in the charge. According to the indictment, the treason had occurred on Blennerhassett Island. No evidence pointing to some other portion of the country—to Washington, for example—could be accepted.

The ruling was a victory for the government, provided it could produce the requisite information. With evident relief, Hay directed Eaton to the stand. There the hero of Derne repeated the now familiar tale of his conversations with Burr in the winter of 1805–6, taking care to avoid any direct mention of the arch-conspirator's reportedly baleful designs on the national capital and the life of the President. Richmond's Democratic newspapers, the *Enquirer* and the *Argus*, hailed his recital as a triumph for the prosecution, but Harman Blennerhassett was "better informed" that Eaton "strutted more in buckskin than usual . . . and [that] the effect was as diverting to the whole court as it was probably beneficial to the defence."

Definitely favorable to the defense were the revelations of the next witness, Commodore Truxton. Yes, said the commodore, he and the accused were very old friends. Yes, Burr had described his projects on more than one occasion. No, never in the commodore's presence had the former Vice President said anything indicative of an intention to dismember the

Union. If war came, he hoped to invade the Spanish dominions. If not, he would cultivate the Bastrop lands.

The next occupant of the witness box was Peter Taylor, the Blennerhassetts' gardener. An uneducated man, obviously overwhelmed at finding himself momentarily at the brightly lighted center of one of the great events of his day, the young gardener gradually loosened up as he plunged into a long description of his journey to Lexington to alert his master and Burr to the threatened invasion of his master's island by the Wood County militia. What seemed to be a total recall for lengthy conversations and complicated deeds enlivened his memoirs. He remembered accompanying his master from Lexington back to the island. He remembered Blennerhassett's saying that he and Burr had bought "eight hundred thousand acres" of land near the Red River and that after the men they were recruiting had settled those lands they were going to move on and "take Mexico." What would happen, he remembered asking Blennerhassett, if some of the settlers didn't want to go on to Mexico. "O by God," he quoted Blennerhassett as replying, "I tell you, Peter every man that will not conform to order and discipline, I will stab; you'll see how I'll fix them." Taylor also remembered going on a secret errand to the mainland. He was to deliver to a Dr. Bennett a letter from Blennerhassett offering to purchase a cache of arms. He remembered his employer's alarm on learning that the offer had been rejected, his saying that somehow, some way, the gardener must recover the letter Blennerhassett had written the doctor, as it "contained high Treason." Taylor was on the island when Comfort Tyler and his men came. He was there when they left with Blennerhassett. He was asked by the district attorney if Tyler's men had "any guns." Some, Taylor answered; "some . . . went a-shooting." "What kind of guns?" a juryman inquired; "rifles or muskets?" But on this point Peter's remarkable memory failed him. He couldn't say. "Was there any powder or lead?" he was asked. Both, he replied. "I saw some powder in a long small barrel, like a churn . . . Some of the men were . . . running bullets." Later, other witnesses testified to seeing a miscellany of arms on the island: rifles, dirks, a blunderbuss, one or more fusees, a brace or two of pistols.

Weeks earlier, Taylor had shared his recollections with the grand jury. It was largely his testimony which prompted that body to include Blennerhassett in the indictments. "Gracious God!" Margaret Blennerhassett wrote her husband on learning this, "confined in a prison in the dogdays, and by the perjury of a wretch not many degrees from a brute! I used to give him credit for the utmost honesty; but it is in vain, I am convinced more and more every day, to expect principle without some refinements, at least where interest is concerned. Ashley [the Major Ashley of Burr's flight across Mississippi] tells me they have given the wretch a tract of land somewhere."

After Taylor came the Morgans of Morganza—the colonel and his two sons—to give the court their version of Burr's visit to the older man's Pennsylvania estate, their belief, based on something in their guest's manner, that he was trying to revive the old Spanish Conspiracy.

Up to this time—19 August—most of the evidence dealt with intention. Now, said Hay, he was going to put on the stand a man whose testimony would go to prove the "overt act," the actual "assemblage on Blennerhassett Island." The witness turned out to be one Jacob Allbright, a laborer of Dutch descent whom Blennerhassett had hired to help "build a kiln for drying corn." Allbright was on the island on the night of 10 December 1806 when Tyler's four boats were hastily loaded and the adventurers began their journey downriver. Along about midnight, he recalled, several of the men were standing around a bonfire when General Tupper of Marietta stepped into the circle, laid his hands on Blennerhassett, and proclaimed him arrested "in the name of the commonwealth." Immediately, according to Allbright, "seven or eight muskets" were pointed at the interloper; one of the encircling men was heard to say he would "as *lieve*" shoot "*as not*," and the general backed off.

Here at last was a confrontation in keeping with the spirit and thrust of the conspiracy as described in newspapers the country over. There was only one thing wrong with Allbright's story. It wasn't true. General Tupper was among the many witnesses brought to Richmond by the government, and during the cross-examination of Allbright, Burr elicited some simple answers to simple questions. Did the witness, he asked, know the general? He did, was the reply. Was "that him"? Burr asked, pointing at Tupper, who was sitting in the audience. It was, said Allbright.

There was no need to labor the point. Every listener got it. Since Tupper was present, why didn't the government call him to the stand to confirm Allbright's assertions? The answer is preserved in a deposition later sworn to by the general. Tupper's story was that he "neither had or pretended to have any authority . . . to arrest anyone," that he made no such effort while on the island that winter night, and that he "passed about half an hour" there, chatting in a friendly fashion with Blennerhassett and "the people belonging to the boats." No guns "were leveled at him," he deposed, "nor any incivility offered him."

When Allbright stepped down, Peter Taylor was recalled. The previous witness had never seen Burr on Blennerhassett Island. Had Taylor ever seen him there? He had not. When Taylor stepped down, Burr got to his feet. If the "gentlemen" of the opposition were "now done with the overt act," he said, "or when they have done, I will thank them to inform me, for then we shall have some considerations to offer to the court." His words were a warning, a forecast of the strategy the accused and his lawyers intended to pursue. They were tired of wordy tales that proved nothing. Sooner or later they were going to ask the court to see to it that the government either put up—or shut up.

George Hay sensed their impatience (possibly because he shared it, realizing that his witnesses were saying much and establishing little). Hastily, he assured the judge that he was prepared to adduce further evidence pointing to the overt act. Then he summoned three more men to the stand. Two of them added nothing of consequence to what had been said. The third, William Love, had gone down the rivers with the expedition as Blennerhassett's groom. During cross-examination, Burr asked him if the men gathered on the island on the night of their departure had presented "any thing like" a military appearance. His answer was yes, that

the men were in a state of preparation to defend themselves, because they expected people [the Wood County militia] to attack Blannerhassett [sic] and the island. And to the best of my opinion, they did not mean to be killed, without some return of the shot . . .

Question. Was there no disturbance among the party on the island?

Answer. None . . . I do not recollect to have seen General Tupper there.

MR. PARKER (of the jury). Did you ever see all the men with arms?

Answer. I cannot say. When I got to the mouth of Cumberland, I saw a chest of arms opened.

MR. MAC RAE. Were any chests of arms put into the boats when you left the island?

Answer. Not that I know. They might or might not have been put on board without my seeing them. Many things were put into the boats before I got in.

MR. PARKER. . . . Had you no conversation with Blannerhassett about the expedition?

Answer. Only that if I did not choose to go with him, he would recommend me to some travelling gentlemen as a servant; or, if I went to the Washita, he would make me a present of a piece of land.

MR. BURR.—Did you see any arms but those belonging to Blannerhassett?

Answer. I did not.

Question. Were they mostly young gentlemen who came in the boats?

Answer. [Yes] . . .

MR. HAY. What kind of looking men were they?

Answer. They looked like gentlemen, such as lived upon their own property.

Question. Did they look like men used to work?

Answer. They did not . . .

MR. PARKER. . . . Did you see any bullets run?

Answer. Yes: but I do not know how many. I was a servant in the house, but could not mind my own business and other people's too.

When on 20 August the last of the three government witnesses withdrew, the court was astir. Suddenly, like swarming bees, all the attorneys were at the bar, conferring with the Chief Justice. Wickham did most of the talking for the defense. The judge, he recalled, had said that the prosecution could offer merely collateral evidence so long as it was relevant; but obviously the government could not be permitted to go on producing such material forever, in view of its now demonstrated inability to establish an overt act for the collateral evidence to be relevant to. The time had come, Wickham asserted, for the court to suspend the taking of all further testimony. Would the bench entertain a motion to that effect? Marshall's response was that of a man painfully aware that his political future was on the line, that if he granted Wickham's request the Jefferson Administration would accuse him of suppressing evidence. There was "no doubt" in his mind "that the court must hear the objections to the admissibility of the evidence; that it was a right, and [Burr's attorneys]

. . . might insist on it; but he suggested the propriety of postponing their motion." What had the district attorney to say about that? The district attorney said he had three or four more witnesses acquainted with the activities on or near Blennerhassett Island on the night of 10 December. Unfortunately, some of them were absent at the moment, but two were on hand. Let them be heard, said the judge. They were, but their statements left the picture unchanged. The defense then put into formal language its motion to arrest the testimony, and the court agreed to listen to whatever the lawyers on both sides had to say about it.

3

WICKHAM LED OFF for the defense with a brilliant speech. Littleton W. Tazewell, member of the grand jury responsible for the indictment against Burr, and a respected lawyer on his own, called it "the greatest forensic effort of the American bar." Wickham's points were numerous and cogently reasoned, his review of pertinent cases in both England and America exhaustive, his language lean, his delivery compelling. His major contention was that "no person can be convicted of treason in levying war, who was not personally present at the commission of the act, which is charged in the indictment as constituting the offense." The government admitted that Burr was not on the island when the purportedly traitorous assemblage took form there. To get around this universally acknowledged fact, the prosecutors were saying that Burr "advised" and "procured" the assemblage and was therefore "legally present" on the island when it came into being. And from whence did they derive the authority for this position? From the common law as developed in England over the centuries, wherein it was stated, in the words of a great commentator, that in treason "there are no accessories . . . but that all are principals." But if the American Founding Fathers had intended the common law to apply to treason, they would not have gone to the trouble of defining that crime so specifically in the Constitution. Nor would the Congress, in the statute prescribing the chastisement for treason and other offenses, have stipulated that the "principals" were to be punished in one way and the "accessories" in another, thus recognizing a distinction between the two. Where treason was concerned, said the well-spoken Richmond attorney, there was "no common law of the United States as such." There was only constitutional and statute law. It followed that "no person can be punished for treason, or for any other offence under an act of congress, creating such offence, unless they come within the description of the act; that no person can be said to have levied war against the United States, where it had not been levied by himself, but by others; *and that no overt act of others* can, under the statute, *be made his overt act.*"

It was around this point that the Chief Justice saw fit to interrupt. Was Wickham aware, he asked, of "any adjudged case . . . where the court was called upon to decide, and did decide, that the evidence submitted to the jury did or did not amount to proof of the *overt* act?" Wickham answered that it was not only the right but the "duty" of the court to instruct the jury on all matters of law, and this duty was especially imperative in this case because the government counsel and the defense counsel disagreed as to what the phrase "levying of war" meant. The government insisted that the mere assemblage of men for a treasonable purpose constituted such an act, whereas the defense contended that no levying of war existed until the assemblage exerted force, until it actually struck a blow, as it were. Since the legal experts disagreed as to the meaning of the term, it was obviously the obligation of the court to tell the jury which was the correct definition.

Carefully, Wickham analyzed the indictment against Burr. In his view, it was such a jangle of fact and fiction that the court should have thrown it out long since. The indictment

said that the former Vice President was present at, and a part
of, the assembly on the island. But everybody knew he was
not, and the prosecution were now trying to show that he was
guilty of "procuring" the assembly from a distance. If that's
the way they saw the situation, why didn't they say so? Instead
of asking the court to pretend that Burr was where he was not,
why didn't they charge him in the indictment with procure-
ment-at-a-distance and then supply evidence to prove it? Assuming, of course, that such evidence existed. Speaking of evidence,
twelve government witnesses had testified. And what dreadful
scenes had they painted? One and one only: General Tupper's
attempted arrest of Harman Blennerhassett and the latter's
resistance. But Allbright's recital of the guns pointed at the
general did not ring true. Why hadn't General Tupper been
called to the stand to convey his version of the confrontation?
Was his story different from Allbright's? Suppose, for the
sake of argument, Wickham said, that muskets *were* leveled
at Tupper and that this was done by men gathered to commit
treason? Since none of the other witnesses remembered such
an incident, the Constitution could not be satisfied by the
testimony of Allbright alone. There had to be two witnesses
to the overt act. Allbright's tale was suspect on still another
ground: by what authority could General Tupper, coming as
a civilian from Ohio, arrest Blennerhassett on an island belonging to Virginia? Again, Wickham was willing to do a
little supposing. Suppose, he said, Tupper did have the requisite authority and suppose he had tried to arrest Blennerhassett
and Blennerhassett had resisted. Resistance to process was a
serious offense, but it was not treason. Wickham took cognizance of the repeated attempts by the government to bring out
that the men on the island were armed. Of course they were.
They were headed for the frontier. Nobody in his right mind
went unarmed to the frontier.

The minute Wickham's argument was completed, Hay was
on his feet. Two of the previously absent government witnesses

he had mentioned were now in the courtroom. Both were privy to the happenings on the island that fatal night, and he asked leave to put them on the stand. This was granted, but the two witnesses had nothing of substance to relate. After they were dismissed, Edmund Randolph delivered another argument in support of the defense motion, an impressive speech, replete with precedents from the law books.

The distraught district attorney realized that the trial had reached a critical juncture. If the defense motion prevailed, none of the remaining government witnesses, well over a hundred, would ever be heard; none of the forty witnesses Burr had collected would take the stand; the jury, with no facts to go on, would have to acquit; and the great malefactor would go free. Hay said the defense motion had taken him and his colleagues by surprise. They needed time to ponder the elaborate reasonings advanced by Wickham and Randolph, time to examine the many authorities they had quoted, the numerous trials they had described. It was now Friday 21 August. Hay asked the court to postpone argument until Monday. The defense lawyers objected. The government had been preparing its case for months, and by this time should be ready for every contingency. But Marshall welcomed the opportunity for showing impartiality. He granted Hay's plea.

On Monday, MacRae opened for the government. If the hard-shelled old Scot said next to nothing, it was probably because he was convinced that nothing remained to be said. In his purview, the treachery of Aaron Burr was already fixed by the testimony of William Eaton, the three Morgans, Peter Taylor, and Jacob Allbright. "I wish, sincerely wish," he said, "that no motion had been made, which would impose on me, as this does, the necessity of exposing freely my opinion . . . of the prisoner . . . for expressing my belief that he has committed the offence for which he is indicted." MacRae called the attention of his listeners to the kind of men Burr had tried to lure into his web, men who, like the defendant himself, had reason to hate the Jefferson Administration: Eaton, for example, who at the time of his conversations with the arch-conspirator had for years been waiting for the government to honor his monetary claims upon it; and Truxton, who would still be a ranking naval commander had Jefferson not tricked him into resigning. The old gentleman included the Morgans in this ring of malcontents, though it was common knowledge that the members of that family were devoted to the President.

It was not the most lawyerly of presentations, and no doubt George Hay was relieved when MacRae sat down and William Wirt arose.

Deftly, systematically, Wirt isolated the main points proffered by the opposition, lined them up like so many targets and fired at them skillfully. The other side was saying that Burr could not be held responsible for the gathering on Blennerhassett Island because he wasn't there at the time. But why, in their consideration of this aspect of things, had they devoted so much wordage to the laws of England? Because, said Wirt, they wanted to distract attention from the laws of America. One needn't go farther than the Supreme Court of the United States, and Wirt then quoted Marshall's assertion, in the case of Bollman and Swartwout, that "if a body of men be assembled, for the purpose of effecting by force a treasonable purpose, all those who perform any part . . . *however remote from the scene of action*, and who are actually leagued in the general conspiracy are to be considered as traitors." Both Wickham and Randolph had described this passage from the Chief Justice's decision as having no bearing on the present case because it had none on the Bollman–Swartwout case. They dismissed it as "extrajudicial, a mere *obiter dictum*"; but give "me leave," said Wirt, "to shew that they are mistaken . . . that *it is not extrajudicial;* that it is a direct adjudication of a point immediately before the court." The arrest of "Bollman and Swartwout at New Orleans, and the fact that they had not been present at any assemblage of traitors in arms, were notorious and admitted." Consequently, their case

presented to the court three distinct questions. 1. Had Aaron Burr committed treason . . . ? 2. Were Bollman and Swartwout connected with him? 3. Could they be guilty of treason, without being actually present? Now, if the court had been satisfied, that there had been an overt act, and that the men were leagued in the conspiracy which produced it, still it would have rendered a distinct and substantive question, whether their absence from the overt act . . . did not discharge them from the constitutional guilt of levying war; for though leagued in the conspiracy, and although there might have been an overt act, these men would have been innocent, if presence at the overt act were necessary to make them guilty. The question then of presence or absence was a question really presented by the case of Bollman and Swartwout. It was one important to the decision of the case, and the court thinking it so did consider and decide it in direct opposition to the principle contended for on the other side.

It seemed to Wirt that both Wickham and Randolph were implying that if there were an overt act on the island, Blennerhassett was a principal because he was there, whereas Burr was merely an accessory because he wasn't. Could anyone tolerate such nonsense? Could anyone think of retiring, inoffensive Harman Blennerhassett as the star of this dark drama, and of daring, dashing, aggressive Aaron Burr as one of the bit players? It was in connection with this thought that Wirt dazzled his audience—and posterity—with his picture of the former Vice President qua serpent crawling into the sylvan bower of Paradise to extend the apple of ambition to Harman and Margaret Blennerhassett qua Adam and Eve.

Benjamin Botts then arose to refute Wirt's contentions, paying tribute to this colorful delineation of unsuspecting innocence seduced by cunning evil. "I cannot promise you, sir, a speech manufactured out of tropes and figures," he said. "Instead . . . I am compelled to plod . . . through the dull doctrines of Hale and Foster." If Marshall tried to discourage the loudest and longest laugh of the trial, the record fails to show it. Botts accused the government of building its case on "the pernicious doctrine" of constructive treason, the very doctrine the framers of the Constitution had sought to erase from the legal blackboard of the United States. To a greater extent than any of his predecessors, he lingered over the happenings on Blennerhassett Island during the winter of 1806. The government claimed that "a great war" was fought there at that time. Indeed it was, said Botts—by the Wood County militia. It was largely the knowledge that the militia was coming, he said, that drove Blennerhassett, General Tyler, and Tyler's men to flee downriver. And now the prosecution was saying that this flight by the adventurers, this effort to avoid an encounter and keep the peace, constituted a levying of war against the United States. In Botts's mind, the invasion of the island by the Virginia soldiers and their despoiling of the mansion and its environs raised interesting questions. Who had authorized them to wreak such havoc? Only a governor or the President could call out the militia. There was no record of any instructions from the governor of Virginia. As for the President —who could bring himself to believe that Thomas Jefferson had ordered the militia of Wood County to attack the island and destroy Blennerhassett's property?

When Botts desisted, on 26 August, George Hay rose to offer the final brief for the prosecution. The district attorney was not well. An epidemic of influenza was coursing through the city, but Hay's ailment was more of the spirit. Nothing less than desperation can account for the crassness of his next statement. Marshall's acceptance of the defense plea to arrest the evidence, he pointed out, would remove the decision of this trial from the jury to the bench; and it was precisely that kind of ruling in another case which had prompted the Congress to impeach Associate Justice Samuel Chase. On that day, Harman Blennerhassett noted in his journal, "Hay had the insolence to insinuate . . . to the Chief Justice, an impeachment, if he did not overrule all the points now before the Court." When one of the defense attorneys later accused the public prosecutor of doing just that, Hay vehemently denied it. He was merely making a point of law, he said, adding that he was sure Marshall understood. Marshall of course understood very well.

After Hay was done, the counsel for Aaron Burr returned to the battle. Charles Lee contributed a brief exordium, but Luther Martin, the Maryland attorney, summing up for the defense, spoke for fourteen hours. Warmed by periodic libations and profoundly versed in the quodlibets of his profession, the "rear-guard of Burr's forensic army" (Blennerhassett's inspired term for him) alternately enthralled and exhausted his auditors. For hours, he explored the law of treason on both sides of the Atlantic, once reading aloud practically all the evidence produced by a famous English trial. He gave a new name to the Burr conspiracy. He called it the

Will o' the wisp treason. For though it is said to be here and there and everywhere, *yet it is nowhere.* It exists only in the newspapers and in the mouths of the enemies of the gentleman for whom I appear; who get it put into the newspapers . . . I have . . . heard it said that such are the public prejudices against colonel Burr, that a jury, even should they be satisfied of his innocence, must have considerable firmness of mind to pronounce him *not guilty* . . . God in heaven! have we already under our form of government (which we have so often been told is best calculated of all governments to secure our rights) arrived at a period when a trial in a court of justice, where life is at stake, shall be but a solemn mockery, a mere . . . ceremony to transfer innocence from gaol to the gibbet, to gratify popular indignation excited by bloodthirsty enemies! But if it require in such a situation firmness in a jury, so does it equally require fortitude in judges to perform their duty. And here permit me . . . to observe that in the case of life and death, where there remains one single doubt in the minds of the jury as to facts, or of the court as to law, it is their duty to decide in favour of life.

The government's case, Martin contended, rested on a complete misunderstanding of what the Supreme Court had ruled in the case of Bollman and Swartwout. The court in that instance had said "there was no proof that treason had been committed by colonel Burr or any other person; . . . that if there were any proof, it was no more than of an expedition intended against the Spanish provinces; an expedition which, as it depended on a war with Spain (of which there was then the greatest probability) would have been honourable if the war took place, and no treason if the war did not take place: a war in which if he succeeded, he would have acquired honour and glory; and which in any event would have been but a misdemeanor, by which neither his honour nor reputation could have been sullied." (Was it wise of the learned Baltimore attorney, Blennerhassett wondered, to make what came close to being "a confession of the misdemeanor"?) As for the Chief Justice's saying that to commit treason a person need not be present when the overt act occurred—that statement, Martin declared, was a *"gratis dictum"* and should be given "no more weight than the ballad or song of Chevy Chase."

Nor, said Martin, should any weight be given to the argument tendered by Wirt that the mere gathering of the men at Blennerhassett Island amounted to a "levying of war"—a position Wirt attempted to maintain by observing that the word "levy" came from the French verb *lever*, meaning "to raise": ergo, the mere raising of an army for subversive purposes could be equated to a waging of war against the United States. Not so, said Martin. Had the Founding Fathers intended the word "treason" to mean nothing more than the raising of an army, they would have said so. What they actually demanded was not only that the army be raised but also that it do something. It was not enough that the "assemblage" look warlike, it must take a warlike step. "I should rather suppose," said Martin, "that the framers of our constitution, who proceeded with so much caution and endeavoured in every part of that instrument to secure the rights and liberties of their fellow citizens, and especially a speedy trial by an impartial jury of the district, did not intend, by the terms 'levying war,' an unnatural and dangerous construction, unknown in common parlance and unusual in history or judicial proceedings. They could have not contemplated an extension of the doctrine of constructive treason which has been always held so peculiarly hostile to civil liberty. They never could have intended that acts peaceable or innocent in themselves should constitute treason."

Such was the nub of Martin's long speech. When he completed it on Saturday 29 August, Randolph took advantage of the few minutes left until the scheduled four-o'clock adjournment to add a few remarks to those he had already made—and thus, on that insufferably hot afternoon, one of the great legal debates in American history was concluded.

On Monday, Marshall delivered his decision on the motion to forbid the taking of all further testimony. Manfully he addressed himself to the vexing problems presented by his obiter dictum in the Bollman–Swartwout case. Again the words of that much-discussed passage rolled across the Virginia Hall of Delegates:

> If war be actually levied, that is, if a body of men be actually assembled for the purpose of effecting by force a treasonable purpose, all those who perform any part, however minute, or however remote from the scene of action, and who are actually leagued in the general conspiracy, are to be considered as traitors . . .

What was wrong with that statement? One thing only, said its author. It was unfinished. Helpful in understanding Marshall's reasoning is the commentary of a twentieth-century scholar. The Bollman–Swartwout opinion, Bradley Chapin writes in his *The American Law of Treason*, "was incomplete. Had the justice extended his opinion to include a statement of the correct method of proceeding against a person performing 'any part, however minute, or however remote' from treasonable action, he would have saved himself the embarrassment of the charge that he reversed this opinion in the Burr trial." In fact, Marshall did not reverse the opinion. He simply completed it. "The guilt of the accused, if there be any guilt," he said, "does not consist in the assemblage; for he was not a member of it . . . [It] consists in procuring the assemblage . . . If then the procurement be substituted in place of presence, does it not . . . constitute an essential part of the overt act? Must it not also be proved?" It did and it must, said Marshall. The government, he added, should have stated the "true facts of the case" in the indictment. In obedience to the assertion of the sixth amendment* to the Constitution that in "all criminal prosecutions the accused shall . . . be informed of the nature and cause of the accusation," the government should have charged Burr with procurement and then brought to the stand four witnesses, two to prove the overt act and two to prove the defendant's part therein; namely, his procurement of the overt act. If it be objected, the Chief Justice said, "that the advising or procurement of treason is a secret transaction, which can scarcely ever be proved in the manner required by this opinion, the answer which will readily suggest itself is, that the difficulty of proving a fact will not justify conviction without proof."

The reading of the decision took three hours. It is the longest

---

* Inadvertently, Marshall said the "eighth amendment," but he correctly quoted from the sixth.

of Marshall's reported opinions. It also is one of the most important, decreeing as it does that the deadly and illiberal doctrine of constructive treason has no place in the legal system of the United States. Marshall took note of the threats uttered by the government attorneys, their statements that impeachment faced him if he ruled for Burr. "That this court dares not usurp power is most true," he observed. "That this court dares not shrink from its duty is not less true . . . No man is desirous of becoming the peculiar subject of calumny. No man, might he let the bitter cup pass from him without self reproach, would drain it to the bottom. But if he have no choice . . . if there be no alternative presented to him but a dereliction of duty or the opprobrium of those who are denominated the world, he merits the contempt as well as the indignation of his country who can hesitate which to embrace."

The many facets of the opinion, its shadings and subtleties, need not detain us. Its essentials are found in these words:

> The present indictment charges the prisoner with levying war against the United States, and alleges an overt act of levying war. The overt act must be proved . . . by two witnesses. *It is not proved by a single witness . . .** The arguments on both sides have been . . . deliberately considered . . . The result of the whole is a conviction, as complete as the mind of the court is capable of receiving on a complex subject, that the motion must prevail. No testimony relative to the conduct or declarations of the prisoner elsewhere and subsequent to the transaction on Blennerhassett's island can be admitted, because such testimony, being in its nature merely corroborative and incompetent to prove the overt act itself, is irrelevant until there be proof of the overt act by two witnesses . . . The jury have now heard the opinion of the court on the law of the case. They will apply that law to the facts, and will find a verdict . . . as their consciences may direct.

* Emphasis added.

The law was clear. On Monday 1 September, the jurors, after a brief absence from the courtroom, returned to their box. Foreman Edward Carrington, a brother-in-law of the Chief Justice, delivered the report. "We of the jury," it read, "say that Aaron Burr is not proved to be guilty under this indictment by any evidence submitted to us. We therefore find him not guilty." Immediately, Burr and his lawyers were on their feet, protesting. The language used by the foreman, they charged, was "unusual, informal and irregular." Burr said it was understood in all courts that in a criminal case the verdict must be a simple "guilty" or "not guilty." Hay said he'd never heard of any such requirement, and as the substance of the verdict was clear, what difference did the form make? Foreman Carrington somehow managed to get the attention of the bench long enough to say that if the phrasing of the report was improper the jurors would be happy to change it, only to be contradicted by fellow juryman Richard E. Parker, "a violent Jeffersonian partisan." Parker said he would not permit one syllable to be altered. Marshall heard the noisy contenders out. He had done all he could. He had expounded the law as he saw it. He knew what to expect now—an outburst of anger in the Democratic press, the complaint that his rulings in the case had been politically motivated. Already, indeed, such accusations were being aired, and he had no desire to pour further oil on partisan flames. The verdict, he ruled, "should remain as found by the jury; and . . . an entry should be made on the record of 'not guilty.' "

4

Now THE SHADOW of the gallows was withdrawn from Aaron Burr. Withdrawn, too, from most of the men indicted with him, including Harman Blennerhassett, Jonathan Dayton, Senator John Smith, Comfort Tyler, and Major Israel Smith. With Burr declared innocent, the district attorney saw fit to ask—and the court to grant—that the treason indictments against those of his associates who had been brought to Richmond be quashed.* To be sure, the misdemeanor indictments remained in force. But as the subsequent trial of Burr on that count shows, nobody was much exercised about it. Many Virginians saw the interests of the West as identical with their own, and in that part of the country, efforts to smash the power of the hated Spanish, legal or otherwise, were regarded with complacency.

On the hopes of the government, Marshall's opinion fell with crushing effect. Hay, in his report to Jefferson, revealed that even William Wirt, previously convinced of the "*integrity*" of the Chief Justice, was now speaking of him "with the strongest terms of reprobation." Jefferson's terms were stronger yet. "The event," the President wrote Hay, "has been (what was evidently intended from the beginning of the trial) . . . not only to clear Burr, but to prevent the evidence from going before the world. But this latter case must not take place. It is now more than ever indispensable, that not a single person be paid or permitted to depart until his testimony has been committed to writing . . . The whole proceedings will be laid before Congress, that they may decide whether the defect has been in the evidence of guilt, or in the law, or in the application of the law; and that they may provide the proper remedy for the past and future." Nor could the President extract much comfort from the imminence of the misdemeanor trial. That procedure, he feared, would not cleanse the arch-conspirator from the body politic. "The criminal," he wrote Hay, "is preserved to become the rallying point of all the disaffected and the worthless of the United States, and to be a pivot on which all the intrigues . . . which foreign governments may wish

* Davis Floyd, also among those indicted, was never brought to Richmond, arrangements having been made for him to be tried in Indiana Territory. He was the only member of the expedition to be convicted (see page 381).

to disturb us with, are to turn. If he is convicted of the misdemeanor, the Judge must in decency give us a respite by
some short confinement of him; but we must expect it to be
very short."

Even before the President's commands could reach the
district attorney, that discouraged but still enterprising gentleman had hit upon a maneuver designed to bring Burr to book
as a traitor, the verdict at Richmond and the legal proscription
on double jeopardy notwithstanding. The minute the jury for
the treason trial was discharged, Hay laid his proposition
before the court. Admittedly, an overt act on Blennerhassett
Island had not been proved, but the West was large and Burr
had roamed it hugely. It was common knowledge that he had
joined the expedition at the mouth of the Cumberland. There,
or while he and his followers were floating down the rivers
from thence, the overt act had taken place. Therefore, said
Hay, let the defendant be committed to some Western court
where he could be indicted for treason properly, as a result of
having levied war against the United States all the way from
the mouth of the Cumberland to Bayou Pierre in Mississippi
Territory.

The Chief Justice needed no prompting from defense counsel to recognize the strategy behind this motion, the longing
on Hay's part to move control of the case from a Federalist
judge to Western judges, all of whom, of course, were Jefferson appointees. Gently, Marshall reminded the public prosecutor that Burr was still in the custody of the Richmond court,
still under an indictment for misdemeanor. The trial on that
count must be disposed of first. After it was over, Hay could
renew his motion to commit if he were so inclined. Accordingly, arrangements were made for impaneling a new jury,
and Burr was admitted to bail in the sum of $5,000, put up by
one William Langbourne and Jonathan Dayton.

5

AGAIN, BURR COULD GO and come on the streets of Richmond, and his first act in celebration of his freedom was to take a long walk with his daughter. The colonel, Harman Blennerhassett sneered in his journal, "exhibited himself through the greater part of town." At this point, Blennerhassett's comments on his onetime idol tended to the snappish. It was easy for him to forget that he had begged for a role in Burr's projects, equally easy to hold the leader of the aborted expedition responsible for the now sorry situation of the Irish aristocrat and his family. Little indeed was left to Blennerhassett. His cash reserves were gone. So was his island paradise, seized and sold by the Wood County authorities for a fraction of its value, to satisfy encumbrances upon it. One thing only remained, the tenuous hope that Alston or Burr or both would repay the many and generous advances he had made to the older man. When Alston pleaded poverty, he didn't believe it. The South Carolinian was reputedly one of the richest men in the Union. Nor did Blennerhassett believe Burr when he, too, pleaded poverty. It was "quite unaccountable," he wrote, that the colonel could have spent all the cash he had raised in the West. Blennerhassett's information was that Burr had obtained not less than $40,000 while at Lexington and that he had paid not more than $15,000 "to all his agents and associates." Distress seized the anxious creditor when, after Burr was declared innocent of treason, numerous individuals, previously averse to seeing their names linked to that of a traitor, began clamoring for the sums they had lent him or for payment on the goods they had sold him. Within a few weeks, the civil suits filed in Richmond courts against the colonel had mounted to $36,000 in all.

When a few days after the conclusion of the treason trial the Alstons left for South Carolina, Burr took over the house they had occupied during their Richmond stay. Blennerhassett, also free on bail, found lodgings nearby, "at a Mr. Walton's." He lost no time in getting in touch with Burr, and from one of their conferences he came away astounded by what he had seen and heard. The former Vice President, he discovered, was "as gay as usual, and as busy in speculating on reorganizing his projects for action as if he had never suffered the least interruption." Blennerhassett was appalled. Why couldn't Burr see what was so clear to everyone else, that his designs on Mexico were destroyed beyond redemption? The Irishman knew what he would do were he in the colonel's shoes. If "Burr possessed sensibilities of the right sort," he wrote in his journal, "with one-hundredth part of the energies for which, with many, he has obtained such ill-grounded credit, his first and last determination, with the morning and the night, should be a destruction of those enemies, who have so long and so cruelly wreaked their malicious vengeance upon him. But time will prove him as incapable in all his future efforts as he has been in the past."

The worried Irishman's strictures on Burr may have been colored, but they were not inaccurate. It takes a romantic to know a romantic, and Blennerhassett's Richmond journal abounds with indications that he understood the former Vice President better than most. Still, there were sides to Aaron Burr that the watchful diary-keeper never grasped. For one thing, the colonel was not disposed to hold a grudge. Only when an enemy did something grossly offensive to the gentlemanly code by which he lived could he bring himself to retaliate. He believed as fervently in free will as his famous grandfather, Jonathan Edwards, had believed in its nonexistence. He could be angry at Jefferson for interfering with his plans and at the same time be aware that he himself was to blame for the collapse. Somehow, somewhere along the line, he had done something wrong, and what had been done wrong could also be done right. The very terms in which he spoke of reviving the expedition confirms that such was his attitude.

"In six months," he told Blennerhassett and Major Smith, their "schemes could be all remounted; . . . we could now new-model them in a better mould than formerly, having a clearer view of the ground, and a more perfect knowledge of our men." One other aspect of Burr escaped the searching gaze of the Irishman. In that summer of 1807 the colonel dared not abandon his project. It was the greatest effort of his life, his largest bid for glory. To drop it now would be to admit that he was a failure; and Aaron Burr, his unique inner strengths notwithstanding, was not yet ready to confront that terrifying truth. He had to go on. He had to have a sense of mission, the feeling that he was testing himself, that he was doing something of weight with his time, something, anything, to keep at bay the ever-threatening horrors of aimlessness and boredom.

6

ON 9 SEPTEMBER the trial for misdemeanor began. Hay sent more than fifty witnesses to the stand, but before a week had passed he realized that such statements as Marshall allowed them to make were proving nothing. On 15 September the district attorney asked that the indictment be nolle prossed, but Burr insisted on having a verdict, and after a short consultation in camera, the jurors returned to proclaim the defendant "not guilty."

The ordeal was not yet over for Burr. No sooner was the jury discharged than Hay was on his feet, moving that Burr and two of his associates, Blennerhassett and Major Smith, be committed to the federal court in Chillicothe, Ohio, there to be tried again on a charge of treason. Marshall agreed to listen to testimony for and against the motion. For five weeks, witness after witness trooped to the stand, with the Chief Justice sitting, sans jury, as an examining magistrate.

Many of the men summoned to the box were members of the expedition. To most of them went the same questions:

Why had they signed up, and what did they understand Burr's goals to be? Some said they joined the project "to see the country," others out of a desire to obtain a share of the Bastrop lands. A few recalled being told that Burr also intended to strike a blow at the Spanish, though it was the recollection of most of them that he meant to do this only in the event of a war with Spain.

The Hendersons of Wood County, Blennerhassett's inveterate enemies, put on the record the story of their unbelievable conversations in 1806 with the then master of the enchanted isle. John Graham recited his adventures as the Administration's traveling sleuth. William Eaton, testifying in open court for the fourth time, was allowed at last to describe Burr's plot to overturn the national government in Washington and either "assassinate" the President or "send him to Carter's mountain." (The latter was a snide reference to Governor Jefferson's flight over the mountain in 1781, when a British raiding force invaded the Monticello section of Virginia.) The high point in the testimony came when Sergeant Jacob Dunbaugh took the stand. This was the soldier who joined the expedition at Fort Massac, having been given a twenty-day furlough by his commanding officer to do so. Dunbaugh said that while the flotilla was standing off the western shore of the Mississippi downriver from Bayou Pierre, Burr and some of his aides opened a hole in the gunwales of the colonel's boat and secreted two large bundles of arms by lowering them by cords under the surface of the water. Cross-examination brought out that Dunbaugh had overstayed his leave and had been posted as a deserter and then pardoned by General Wilkinson. The question, naturally, was whether there had been a *quid pro quo.* "Did you promise [Wilkinson] to give any information against me?" Burr asked. Despite his denial, his veracity as a witness was irretrievably damaged.

General Wilkinson occupied the witness box five days in all. Repeatedly he contradicted himself, often asking permission to retract or amend statements previously uttered. Sharply interrogated by Botts, he confessed that he had doctored the cipher letter to hide his own part in the expedition. His vocal divagations convinced nobody, least of all George Hay. By 8 October, when the portly general left the stand for the last time, the still-sick and disheartened district attorney had "washed his hands" of his star witness. "My confidence in him is shaken if not destroyed," he wrote Jefferson. "I am sorry for it, on his own account, on the public account, and because you have expressed opinions in his favor; but you did not know then what you soon will know." But precisely what Jefferson knew or came to know would never be revealed. He had no intention of deserting Wilkinson, the man on whose say-so he had branded Burr a traitor before the world. It is interesting to speculate what the effect on the image of Burr in the perspective of history would have been had the third President, at this point, admitted to George Hay, if not to the world, that Wilkinson had deceived him.

On Tuesday 20 October, Marshall ruled on the motion. He saw no justification for holding Major Smith on any charge. As for Burr and Blennerhassett, his opinion was that the testimony did not link them to treason. It did link them to misdemeanor. The two men, therefore, were to be admitted to bail ($3,000 each) for their appearance in Ohio for trial on a charge of having prepared and provided "the means for a military expedition against the territories of a foreign Prince, with whom the United States was at peace."

This trial was never to occur. Burr assumed from the beginning that it wouldn't. "Mr. Hay," he wrote Theodosia on 23 October, "immediately said that he should advise the government to *desist from further prosecution*. That he has actually so advised there is no doubt." Several factors entered into the failure of the government to go through with the trial in Ohio. One was the growing preoccupation of the authorities with the troubles with Great Britain, troubles that provoked Jefferson's embargo and eventuated in the War of 1812. Another was that the depositions gathered for use in Ohio yielded no clear-cut evidence of either treason or misdemeanor.

Now Burr and Blennerhassett were free to try to arrange between themselves the complicated matter of the Irishman's pecuniary claims against the colonel. They had discussed this problem more than once, when, in late September, Blennerhassett received jolting news. Burr was reported as saying that "after his liberation from the present motion before the Court," he was going to leave "immediately for England . . . to collect money for reorganizing his projects." The receipt of this information triggered some of the liveliest passages in the angry aristocrat's journal. Others might believe Burr's assertions. Not "Blany," as the press was wont to designate the onetime master of the fabled isle. To him, it was becoming increasingly clear that the colonel was "as careless of his facts as of his religion, where neither is exposed to scrutiny; and any liberty with them may advance his purpose for the moment." It was obvious to Blany that if Burr went to England it would be to stay there, to put himself beyond the reach of his creditors. Once there, the colonel could be counted on to accumulate guineas from England in return for furthering its interests in the New World; and if Burr "had not already exposed his duplicity and incapacity in his favorite art of intrigue to Yrujo," the diarist observed, "he would *again* as readily promise to advance, with Spanish dollars and Spanish arms, the fortunes of the Spanish minister and his master." Nor was Blennerhassett through with that subject. "This evening," he noted on 20 September, "De Pestre spent an hour with me, which was passed in a more dilated view of his past concerns with Burr. He gave me a description of the manners and character of Yrujo . . . This minister is, according to De Pestre's portrait of him, a shrewd politician, who . . . assured De Pestre . . . that had Burr opened his designs with frankness, and really projected a severance of the Union, and nothing hostile to the Spanish provinces, he, Burr, might have had an easy resort to the Spanish treasury and its arsenals . . . But Yrujo laughed at the awkwardness with which Burr endeavored to mask his designs on Mexico . . ."

If Blennerhassett was profoundly annoyed with the colonel he was also still profoundly intrigued with him. That Burr had spoken to Major Smith and De Pestre of his plan to go to England before telling him piqued him no end. After all, he noted, "I have had more of his confidence than either" of them. Eventually, Burr not only told Blennerhassett of his intention to go to England but also voiced the hope that the Irishman, well connected in that country, could furnish him with letters of introduction—a plea that came as no surprise to Blennerhassett, well aware that a desire to hobnob with the important and the wealthy was one of the colonel's more pronounced passions. At first he waved Burr's request aside, only to realize later that there might be an advantage in it for him. His efforts to extract a monetary settlement from Burr had as yet come to nothing. Perhaps if he were to dangle a favor before the great debtor's eyes! "I will hint to him," Blany wrote in his journal on 10 October, "my ability to introduce him into the first circles of England . . . This plan I shall put in execution to-morrow, of which I will note the effect upon him." Accordingly, on the morrow, he informed Burr that he had "thought of three noblemen" to whom he could "properly address" letters of introduction. "The effect of this communication" on the colonel, Blany recorded, "was rapture. The whole man changed. With all his studied reserve, he could not restrain his transports."

The letters remained unwritten when, in late October, Blennerhassett and Burr agreed to travel to Philadelphia, where perhaps their lawyers and bankers could devise a solution to their monetary disagreements. On the twenty-fourth, Blennerhassett left Richmond, accompanied by Luther Martin. Affairs connected with the civil suits against Burr in Richmond held him there for a few days, but when Blennerhassett and Martin arrived in Baltimore on the first of November, they learned that the colonel had reached that city and that he and Sam Swartwout were staying at a hotel in Gay Street. In Baltimore the travelers experienced for the first time the attentions of some of the many Americans who regarded the acquittals at Richmond as a miscarriage of justice. Blennerhassett was dining at Martin's house in Charles Street when "one of the city regiments," led by a "desperate Democratic printer," paraded by with a fife and drum corps playing the "Rogue's March."

On the following morning, handbills, threatening dire reprisals against "his Quid Majesty" (Burr) and others, plastered the buildings of Baltimore. By early afternoon, fifteen hundred angry citizens had poured into Charles Street, were bricking windows, and making "as much noise as if they were about to destroy the city." Martin, alarmed, got in touch with the mayor. The mayor, alarmed, provided a police guard and a carriage, in which Burr and Swartwout were spirited to the office of the stage, where they boarded the mail coach to Philadelphia. Blennerhassett refused to flee. Instead, he took to the garret of his lodgings near Martin's house. From there he watched the passage through the milling mob below of two carts carrying effigies of Burr, Marshall, Martin, and himself, all of them "habited" as for execution; he watched till the rioters shouted themselves out and gradually dispersed.

Next day, he left for the Quaker City. There, on 20 November, he and Burr conferred for the last time. Blennerhassett delivered what he thought of as an "ultimatum." He demanded from Burr at the very least a written promise to pay the money due him, some sort of security against the possibility that the colonel "might never return from Europe." Burr refused and talked in evasions—or so his remarks struck Blennerhassett, who had long since put in writing his amazement at the former Vice President's ability "to disguise his very hints." Now nothing remained to the desperate creditor but a recourse to the courts. Eight days later, he terminated his long association with Burr in a note in which he informed the colonel that "I feel myself released from the . . . offer I made you of introductory letters to the Lords Elgin, Courtenay and Sackville. I feel that I could not solicit their attentions to you as my friend; and I should wish to decline doing so on any other grounds." To wife Margaret he wrote: "I have broken with Aaron Burr on a writ." There would be more letters from Blennerhassett to both Burr and Alston; and once Blennerhassett even hinted at blackmail, threatening to publish a book, an exposé, which could have done little harm to the already disgraced Burr, but might have been detrimental to the political career of his son-in-law in South Carolina. An empty threat, as it turned out, from an impoverished man. In the end, Blennerhassett did receive $12,500 from Alston, a sum he regarded as $37,500 short of what was coming to him.

7

NOT A GREAT DEAL is known of Burr's activities or even of his precise whereabouts during the winter and spring of 1807–8. The murder indictment against him in New Jersey had been quashed. This gave him more freedom of movement, but the day-by-day drudgery of working with the lawyers who were struggling to satisfy a plague of creditors sufficiently to keep the colonel out of debtors' prison chained him for the most part to Philadelphia. He took refuge for a time in the home of George Pollock, a wealthy friend who, along with Luther Martin, was one of the more generous of his bondsmen. Later Charles Biddle tracked him to "a French boarding-house," and was shocked to find his old friend "pale and dejected . . . generally alone" and speaking of suicide. "How different from what he had been a short time before," Biddle wrote in his autobiography, "when few persons in the city were not gratified at seeing him at their tables, where he was always one of the most lively and entertaining of the company."

By the end of 1807, rumors of Burr's impending journey to England had reached the ears of Phineas Bond, the British consul at Philadelphia. Bond was not a man to shirk his duty. He lost no time in dispatching a letter to George Canning, the foreign minister in London, so that Canning and British officialdom generally could brace themselves against the coming of the former Vice President. "I should not, Sir," Bond wrote,

be surprised at his [Burr's] . . . making some Proposals to HM's Government; he has certainly hinted as much and has been solemnly enjoined not to think of such a scheme as there was no chance of his being listened to at such a Time as this when any Protection afforded to him would be construed into a Violation of all our assurances of a Disposition to cultivate good will with the United States.

His enterprizing spirit can not easily be curbed; driven as He may be said to be from his native Country He will be constantly exerting his great Abilities in contriving schemes to vex and harrass those whom he considers as the Authors of his Misfortunes, who have much to apprehend from the extraordinary Faculties he possesses.

He has said frequently of late that He required but a Station Point and that with a moderate supply of Money He could soon collect such a Force as would be competent to subdue the Floridas conquer Cuba and very probably revolutionize South America that He could suggest such plans to Great Britain in the conduct of the Present War [with France] as would combine Economy with Efficiency, save Millions to the Nation and eventually secure Acquisitions of incalculable Importance to the Revenue Commerce and Manufactures of Great Britain.

His Fortunes are desperate and whatever He suggests should be received with great caution, let the Event of Things be what it may—with a due Allowance for the situation in which He is placed and a fit consideration of the Motives by which he is activated.

Mr. Bond, it would appear, was a diligent reader of the Jeffersonian press in America.

8

By EARLY APRIL, Burr's pecuniary affairs were sufficiently in order to permit him to spend a few days in New York City. There he came and went under an assumed name, a precaution dictated in part by a desire to distance himself from creditors, in part by the uncertainty of his legal status. In Ohio, a grand jury had indicted him and Blennerhassett for misdemeanor. This was a meaningless action, for neither of the defendants was present to answer the accusation, and the government, after declaring forfeit the sureties pledged for them, took no further action. Still, the indictment lay on the books, a threat over the colonel's head; and in New York the old charge against him for violating the local dueling laws remained at least technically in effect.

So he went about his business incognito. From New York he sent a letter to England, addressed to Charles Williamson. Its purpose was to inform that gentleman of the colonel's impending arrival in London. Not until Burr reached England weeks later did he learn that Williamson, his closest and most useful friend there, was out of the country, cruising the West Indies on a governmental mission. This voyage was to carry Williamson to his death on 4 September, a victim of yellow fever at the age of fifty-one.

As always, Burr's most pressing problem was money. Apparently, it was during this brief stay in Manhattan that he borrowed an undisclosed sum from Mr. and Mrs. Anthony Bowrowson, onetime servants at his Richmond Hill mansion. It is a measure of his monetary predicament that he had to hock the family portraits—some twenty in all—to secure the loan.*

Blennerhassett's journal hints of another possible source of funds. Burr had gathered around him a group of friends eager to share to some extent his adventures abroad—most of them young, and some of them, according to the suspicious journal-keeper, men of fortune. In the late spring, Sam Swartwout was already in England, his appearance in London prompting the American minister, William Pinkney of Maryland, to send a cautionary note to Madison. Pinkney considered Swartwout a "bearer of dispatches" from the arch-conspirator to English cohorts. "Had him followed," the minister advised, "but learned nothing." Among the other Burrites either en route to the Old World or about to embark there were David M. Randolph of Virginia, a distant cousin of the President; William A. Hosack, a younger brother of Dr. David H. Hosack of New York, the physician on call at the Weehawken interview; and Thomas Robinson, also of New York.

Burr's Mexican project was not the only motive behind their wanderings, for some of them hoped to uncover in Europe commercial opportunities suitable for investment. Months before Burr was ready to leave the United States, he was writing friends both at home and abroad, seeking letters of introduction for Randolph and explaining that the Virginian was going to Europe "on his own business which is mercantile." And only weeks after the colonel's arrival in England, we find him perusing a letter from Swartwout containing the information that "the article of *cotton bagging* . . . prohibited by the late law of the United States, is, in the southern States and in

---

* He never repaid it, and eleven years after his death his cousin Judge Ogden Edwards of Staten Island, New York, recovered "many, though apparently not all" of the paintings. Ogden found them in the attic of a home in Short Hills, New Jersey, occupied by Mrs. Theodosia Shelburg, one of the Bowrowsons' two daughters, and her artist husband. John Edwin Stillwell, *The History of the Burr Portraits*, 3.

the Territories of Orleans and Mississippi, a dollar a yard. Here [England] it may be bought for 6*d*. sterling. Pray, could not a quantity, say 200,000 yards, be sent from this country to Mobile or St. Mary's; and thence got into the islands and Territories by smuggling? If your knowledge of the ground enables you to manage such a speculation, perhaps it might be accomplished." A "wild scheme," Swartwout admitted, but "let me know by return of the mail what you think of [it]." What the colonel thought of it is not a matter of record, though to Burr no moneymaking scheme was without interest.

Toward the middle of April, he left Manhattan, crossing the Hudson to stay at the country home of a friend near Belleville, New Jersey. By early May, he was again in New York, completing the preparations for what he was now speaking of as his "grand Hegira." Theodosia came North to see him off, and the letters passing between them at this period testify to the colonel's wish to keep his plans a secret. One of his parting orders to Theodosia was to have published in the newspapers a notice saying that her father had been seen "on his way to Canada." On the evening of 9 June, in the narrows of New York Harbor, he embarked for England on the packet *Clarissa Ann*. At Halifax, the first port of call, he introduced himself to Sir George Prevost, the Nova Scotian commander in chief and a relative on his late wife's side of the family.

When the *Clarissa Ann* sailed on, he had in his luggage introductions to members of the Prevost family and their friends in England, along with a letter to the British authorities at the port of Falmouth, instructing them to allow "G. H. Edwards" (one of the aliases under which the colonel was traveling) to proceed "without delay," as he was the carrier of dispatches for the British Secretary for War, Lord Castlereagh, at whose office he was "immediately to present himself on his arrival in London." On 13 July the *Clarissa Ann* docked at Falmouth and on the morning of the sixteenth "G. H. Edwards" stepped off the mail coach in front of the Gloucester

Coffee-house in Piccadilly. His presence in the British capital was promptly noted by the American minister and duly reported to Madison. It was Pinkney's understanding that the "object" of the former Vice President's visit "was to engage in some Enterprize against Spanish America under British auspices." Like a little stone, the impalpable Mr. Burr had plumped into the great pond of Europe. The ripples were to be less than overwhelming.

13

Exile: Wanderings in Europe

M UCH THAT WE KNOW of Burr's four years in Europe,
easily the most eclectic and implausible years of a
long and dramatic life, comes directly from the man himself. On the very evening he set foot on the *Clarissa Ann* in
1808, he began a diary of his experiences abroad, portions of
it penned in execrable French or in a jumble of French and
other languages and checkered with abbreviations not always
easy to decipher. Known now as the *Private Journal of Aaron
Burr*, it is a literary tour de force, heavy reading where his
whimsy borders on cuteness, deeply moving at times, especially in the Paris scenes. In these we see Burr lonely and
wretched and almost penniless, but courageous and even cheerful in the grip of a destitution that brought him to the brink
of starvation. A German lady, encountered along the way,
described herself as intrigued, if not amused, by the "*gauche*"
and the "*halbwilde*" in his behavior. The *gauche* and the *halbwilde* run through the diary. The story it presents is an
extended whistling-past-the-graveyard of a man nursing a
dying dream, a tragicomedy straight out of the theater of the
absurd. The journal was not meant for publication. It was
written for his daughter, and on one level it is precisely that:
an extended (over 300,000 words) and relaxed conversation
with Theodosia. But on another and to us perhaps more inter-

esting level, it is also as graphic a self-portrait as we have of Aaron Burr.

Not a particularly flattering one, but if Burr had no other virtues, he had at least the virtue of claiming none. The reader who comes to the journal hoping for insights into the times and the people and the mores finds none. There are no depths here, only bright and rippling shallows. Burr was not a thinker. He was a doer, and it is his doings he delineates in the diary, without reserve, and with no gloss applied. Plainly, he regarded Theodosia as quite capable of sharing even the most private of his hours. After all, he had raised her to see the world as it was, not as it ought to be.

He recognized perfectly the character of his life in Europe. It was "a sort of non-existence," he told her; and as the weeks became months and the months years, as he drifted from country to country, he was hard put to satisfy the most exigent of his inner urges, the terrible desire to keep himself entertained. There was a limit to how many parties he could attend, how many ceremonies he could watch, how many books he could read, how many bright and articulate people he could draw within the radiant circle of his charm. Increasingly, he turned to women—to prostitutes often, to ladies of the *haut monde* when available. To these escapades of the flesh he brought, as to all his doings, what he himself once described as "a singularity of taste."

On his third night in Paris, for example: wandering into a theater, he discovered in the adjoining box a most "pleasant" lady. "We talked ½ hour," he noted in the journal. "You appear to be full of genius," he said to her. "Upon which of all your talents do you rely most?" To which she replied, "I have cultivated only that of pleasing." Then, according to the journal, "She gave me her address and invited me to sup, which I declined. How wonderfully discreet! But then I engaged to call on her tomorrow. How wonderfully silly!" On the morrow, apparently curious to see her in her setting, he did call. He located her residence and found himself in an "elegant room" and was there accosted by a boy, who said that "Madame was expecting him—" whereupon Burr turned on his heel and made off, "congratulating myself on my escape from a dangerous siren."

For his amatory encounters he coined the name *muse*, a French hunting term meaning "the beginning of the rutting-time" in animals. "After strolling" the streets of Copenhagen for an "hour, during which," he wrote, "*mus. mauv* [bad *muse*]," he returned to his hotel, where "the chambermaid, fat, not bad; *muse* again." He was not always so indefatigable. After breakfast one morning, he wrote while in Stockholm, "*ma bel[le] Marie*" came to his lodgings, at nine the "Hanoverian woman" arrived, and at two in the afternoon Carolin appeared. The fifty-three-year-old diarist would have been happier, he confessed, had Carolin "deferred her visit until tomorrow. Mais el[le] est si jolie; 1 r.d. [one rix-dollar]." And at three the same afternoon: "Ordered a bath," he noted, adding in his curious French that there "is nothing that restores me after too much *muse* like the hot bath."

Within the tireless Casanova resided an equally tireless bookkeeper. Monotonously, he recorded the money expended on his pleasures: shillings in the British Isles, rix-dollars in the Scandinavian countries, marks in the Germanic principalities, and francs in Paris. If these routinely noted statistics do not in themselves show the depth of his determination to avoid emotional involvement, a vividly described incident at Weimar, capital of the Duchy of Saxe-Weimar in central Germany, can be cited as proof positive of it. There he was entertained by royalty, for on two occasions his host was the reigning duke, Charles Augustus, friend and patron of Goethe and creator of what was then the liveliest and most cultivated court in Europe. The American visitor was invited everywhere, introduced to everyone. He met Goethe and Madame Goethe. He met the mother of Arthur Schopenhauer. He met one

Tinette von Reizenstein, young, fetching, and unmarried. There were several rendezvous. Once he brought her a map of America and together, the journal recounts, "we went over the United States. Her remarks charmed and astonished me." Nothing delighted Burr so much as a woman with brains. Five days after his arrival in Weimar, he still had on hand so many invitations he could have pleasured himself there for another five days. But suddenly he was gone—in flight, traveling not on the public diligence, which was all he could really afford, but in a chaise drawn by hired post-horses. An entry in his journal, written at Erfurt, "fifteen English miles" away, explains. The delectably brainy "de Reizenstein" had aroused in him feelings he had "long since thought dead." This would never do. One more interview with that "sorceress," he told Theodosia, "and I might have been lost, my hopes and projects blasted and abandoned." He had not come to Europe to take a wife and pass the rest of his days paddling in the tepid waters of domestic felicity; he had come there to get funds for "X."

This was the symbol he used in both the journal and the letters to his daughter for his Mexican plan. The circumvention would seem to have been superfluous. The American authorities in Europe knew, or thought they knew, all about X, and the press there and in America thought it knew all about the colonel. The section of his journal kept in Paris visibilizes Burr, sitting alone in a cramped and cheerless rented room, reading a newly received batch of newspapers from home and from England and chuckling to himself. According to these sources, he was in France to renew his plot to dismember the United States and to that end had obtained a generous pension from a man whom he never so much as met, the Emperor Napoleon. One is struck by the eagerness of the public of his day to endow the colonel with those nonpareil powers of persuasion he liked to think of himself as owning. So clearly is the Aaron Burr of history a product of the imagination of his contemporaries as to suggest that in the eyes of many of them he was a Nietzschean superman, a being above law and above morality who dared to *do* what the generality of mankind barely dared to dream of. His fellow Americans, lovers of the tall tale and the gargantuan deed, invented the Burr that some historians have accepted.

2

GIVEN BURR'S DESIRE to put the coffers of England behind X, he could not have descended upon that kingdom at a less propitious hour. The day had gone—at least for the time being—when his Majesty's ministers could dream of coopting the riches of Spanish America. Napoleon had seen to that. In May 1806 the dictator of continental Europe ordered his brother Joseph Bonaparte to ascend the throne of Spain, simultaneously forcing the abdication therefrom of the regnant Bourbon Ferdinand VII. Burr was still in New York, completing his travel plans, when the liberal and nationalist elements among the people of Spain formed at Seville a governmental body known thereafter as the Junta General or the Central Junta, to distinguish it from a variety of provincial juntas established at the same time, and sent to London envoys empowered to seek the aid of England against the French usurper. The colonel was on the high seas when the British government proclaimed its support of the Spain of the juntas against Napoleon, and abandoned any thoughts it might otherwise have entertained of promoting the anti-Spanish schemes of the likes of Burr and Miranda.

Reaching London on 16 July, Burr was quick to sense the change in the situation. His disappointment was compounded by the absence of the friend on whom he most counted, Charles Williamson. Before setting out for the Caribbean, Williamson dropped him a note of explanation. This apparently came into the hands of Burr's companion, David M. Randolph, already in London. At any rate, on 18 July we find Randolph forwarding to Burr a number of communications, including "Col. Williamson's letters"; and on 19 July we find Burr writing to Williamson, deploring his absence as "a contingency against which I had made no provision" and adding that though "the new state of things defeats, for the present, the speculations we had proposed, yet it opens new views, not less important." What new views? Burr did not specify, but Randolph, in his message to the colonel of the day before, mentioned "letters for Paris" and observed that "we have a wide field before us," a statement which raises the likelihood that even at this early date Burr was considering an appeal for assistance to France if nothing came of his efforts in England.

Nothing did. On his first day in London, he called on Lord Castlereagh. The war secretary was "out of town." Later, however, he was "in" to the visiting American and evinced no interest in X. Three other members of the cabinet consented to receive him, but they too wanted nothing to do with the Mexican project. Nor could Anthony Merry be of help. "Although I could not see Mr. Canning [the Foreign Minister] yesterday, from his being gone into the country . . . ," *Toujours Gai* was writing the colonel in November, "I Counselled with another person, of nearly equal authority, who told me he was sure what you proposed to me yesterday would never be consented to . . ." Momentarily disheartened, Burr considered a retreat to the United States. He wrote as much to two of his friends in New York, Dr. Hosack and Timothy Green. To both he put the same question: when, in their opinion, would conditions at home be such as to let him return safely to his old haunts? "It may be expected," he wrote Green, "that after the 3rd March next [the end of Jefferson's second and last term], the persecutions against me will be less vindictive, and it is probable that there may then be no objection to my return." Burr expressed the hope that in the meantime Green would get in touch with the colonel's two largest creditors in New York and negotiate "for time, say two years, on assurances of payment which you may confidently give. They are the only cases which could cause me any trouble."

If there were answers from the doctor and Green, they have not been found. Certain it is that they did not reach Burr in England, where he continued to stay and where for a time he toyed with the idea of becoming a citizen, a thought inspired no doubt by the suggestion of one of his admirers in London that he run for Parliament. Indeed, in his communications to the Office of Home Affairs, he contended that he already was a citizen. His reasoning was, he had been born a subject of his Majesty, and once an Englishman, always an Englishman. Lord Hawkesbury (soon to become the second Earl of Liverpool), to whose department this torturous argument was addressed, did not agree. A "monstrous" notion, said Liverpool, thus ending the effort of a man *persona non grata* in his own country to take refuge in another.

By early fall, Burr had put into a letter to his daughter the unhappy news that the rulers of Great Britain were cold to his designs on Spanish America. Theodosia was still in the New York area and planning to spend the winter there—a plan dictated, very likely, by her father, convinced as he was that the damp heat of her South Carolina home was the main cause of her chronic ill health. The first of her letters to him after his embarkation for England was penned at the farm home of her stepbrother Frederick Prevost in Westchester County. The "world," she told her father, "begins to cool terribly around me. You would be surprised how many I supposed attached to me have abandoned the sorry, losing game of disinterested friendship." This was not her only worry. Except for a "few lines" written by Burr at the time of his departure, she had not as yet received so much as a single letter from him. When a short time later, a letter did arrive, she was appalled at its contents. "X . . . abandoned!" she wrote. "This certainly was inevitable, but I cannot part with what has so long lain near my heart, and not feel some regret, some sorrow. No doubt there are many other roads to happiness, but this appeared so perfectly suitable to you, so complete a remuneration for all the past . . ." How well she knew him, his need to be doing something extraordinary, as well as his need for money. "Tell me," she implored, "that you are engaged in some pursuit worthy of you."

She was lamenting before the fact. In London, Burr was still struggling to interest influential people in X, still making it known to anyone willing to listen that he had come to England "for the purpose of laying before the ministry a plan for opening Spanish America" to Britain's merchants, still arguing that the goal could be achieved "only by the liberation of those provinces from Spain."

His months in the British Isles were not idle ones. On 10 August he reported to the Alien Office to fill out the declaration required of visiting noncitizens and to receive in return a license to move freely on British soil. This was not his first stop at the Alien Office; he had found in one of its officials, John Reeves, a friend who in the years ahead would prove useful. In his declaration, Burr gave his local address as "*Craven-street No. 30.*" Miranda, after the failure of his operations in Venezuela, had returned to London. He was still there when Burr arrived, but the colonel made no effort to see him. He did strike up an acquaintanceship with Mariano Castilla of Argentina and a number of other Spanish-American revolutionaries then residing in the British capital, forging at this time those close links with the leaders of the emerging independence movements in Latin America that for the rest of his life the colonel made it a point to cultivate. This he did partly out of a genuine interest in the liberation of Spain's transatlantic lands, and partly because such alliances could be profitable to a man with legal expertise to sell. Burr was never one to scant his own financial interests. While cooperating with the Ibero-American insurgents in England, he is known to have made at least one effort to ingratiate himself with the mainland Spaniards loyal to the deposed monarchy. When in the late summer of 1808 the Marqués de Casa Yrujo passed through London, en route home to cast his lot with those forces, Burr tried through an intermediary to enlist his services in what appears to have been an effort on the colonel's part to exert some sort of influence on the newly created juntas in Seville and elsewhere. Nor was this his only contact with the patriots of Spain. Working through a member of the Cortes (the representative assembly) subsequently convened at Cadiz, he tried to persuade that body to sponsor and distribute a translation into Spanish of Jeremy Bentham's treatise *The Tactics of Legislation*. Either because the learned Englishman's ideas on government were too liberal for Iberian parliamentarians or because the name of Aaron Burr was anathema to most of them, or for both reasons, this endeavor came to naught.

Even as the doors of official England closed to the progenitor of X, those of social England opened wide to the former Vice President of the United States. His late wife's kin were numerous and well connected, and from the beginning Gamp, as Burr styled both himself and his grandson, found many ways in which to while away the hours. He was invited to evening teas and late dinners, to lavish gatherings in country homes, where the handsome middle-aged visitor from America could sparkle and be lionized. He was soon on friendly terms with a substantial cross section of the British social and literary elite: with Charles Lamb of the essays; with William Godwin, the political writer, in whose home he was made to feel like a family member and from whom he obtained a portrait of Godwin's first wife, one of his favorite writers, the late Mary Wollstonecraft; with William Cobbett, the well-known journalist—it was he who urged the colonel to run for Parliament; with General Alexander Hope, friend of Charles Williamson and of Charles's brother, David Baron Balgray, and a first cousin once removed of *their* influential friend Charles Hope

Lord Granton, the Lord Justice-Clerk of Scotland. And when there was no dinner party or "fête champêtre" to enjoy, he could always shop for presents for Theodosia and grandson Gampy: cambric handkerchiefs for her, rare coins for the boy, and books and maps for both of them. Or he could sit for Turnevelli, the mask-maker—coming away from the first fitting of the mask with "a great purple mark" on his nose, a discovery which prompted the vain and fastidious colonel to cancel an appointment with a certain "Signora B."

These distractions pleased him, but the high moment of his first stay in England occurred on 11 August when the mail brought from Jeremy Bentham a note asking the colonel "to pass some days *chez lui.*" To the visiting American, the receipt of this message was a social and intellectual milestone in his life. He had long admired the philosopher many spoke of as "the Newton of the Moral World." He was fond of asserting that in America only he and one other person—Albert Gallatin, "the best head in the United States"—truly appreciated the exponent of the doctrine that the "greatest happiness of the greatest number" should be the animating principle of all social and legal institutions and of all laws. The invitation reaching Burr that August was not altogether unexpected. At a recent dinner party he had met Pierre Etienne Louis Dumont, Bentham's disciple and editor, and it was Dumont who suggested that the former Vice President be asked to visit Barrow Green, a country place near Godstone in Surrey, twenty miles south of London, where the sixty-year-old sage was spending the summer. On the morning of the eighteenth, Burr took the stage to Godstone, arriving at Barrow Green at four in the afternoon. There he was received "with something more than hospitality." Bentham, he wrote one of his English acquaintances, "led me immediately in what he calls his 'workshop' . . . showed me his papers, and gave me an unqualified privilege of reading anything and at any time."

It was the beginning of a warm and comfortable intimacy,

marked on Burr's part by unflagging adoration. When his troubles came in Europe (an arrest and recurrent financial crises among them), he saw to it that none of these difficulties reached the ears of the friend whom he regarded as "second to no one, ancient or modern, in profound thinking." On Bentham's side, the association was one of respect, not untouched with awe. Burr, he recalled later, "was pregnant with interesting facts. He gave me hundreds of particulars respecting Washington . . . He really meant to make himself emperor of Mexico. He told me I should be the legislator, and he would send a ship of war for me. He gave me an account of his duel with Hamilton. He was sure of being able to kill him; so I thought it little better than murder. He seemed to be a man of prodigious intrepidity; and if his project had failed in Mexico, he meant to set up for a monarch in the United States. He said the Mexicans would all follow like a flock of geese." So went the sage's memories of the colonel, and Sir John Bowring, Bentham's executor and the editor of his *Works*, has written that for a while the great man seemed "seriously resolved on taking up his abode . . . on the table-lands of Mexico, and was only dissuaded by the extreme difficulty of getting there, and the representations of his friends." The *Dictionary of National Biography* reports that to the end of his days Bentham was "indefatigable" in his literary "labours and parsimonious of his time, suffering few persons to visit him." It is interesting that Burr was one of the few. On several occasions, Bentham lent the colonel the use of the Bird Cage, his house at Queen's Square Place in Westminster; and whenever the two of them were there, he was always happy to sit down with his American guest for leisurely philosophic conversations, ranging in subject from "crimes against nature" to "tattooing" and how that curious art might be "made useful" to mankind. Burr sent a bust of the philosopher to his daughter. With it went some presents from Bentham himself, a set of fire irons and a packet of what he called his "combustibles," his books.

Finding the most important one printed in French, Theodosia offered to translate it into English, a task at which she worked off and on until the uncertain state of her health compelled her to abandon it.

Was that seemingly intractable malady of hers cancer, like her mother's before her? Probably so. Burr called it "female complaints," and by the late fall he had taken alarm at her increasingly discouraging bulletins. Nothing she did, and nothing her doctors did for her, relieved the symptoms. Burr consulted eminent physicians in England and put one of them in touch with her doctors in the United States. Suddenly he was seized with an idea. She must join him in London. The sea voyage would be good for her. So would the mild English climate. For weeks he busied himself with this plan. He arranged for a house where she and her son could live. He told her that the funds she was either holding or trying to raise to cover his travels should be used instead to defray the expenses of the crossing. At first Theodosia went along with these plans; then she changed her mind. It is not clear whether she came to this decision because of an improvement in her health, as she wrote her father, or because her husband objected to what could have been a dangerous winter voyage. All that can be said with confidence is that, instead of sailing for Europe, she went home. When Burr learned this, he was furious. Her return to the "burning sun" of South Carolina struck him as "the most unaccountable . . . folly that ever was practiced by one out of Bedlam . . . I claim from Mr. Alston a promise under hand, that, upon the first appearance of disease or debility, he will . . . transport you north of the Hudson. He gave me his word before marriage, and I claim now, the renewal of that promise." He blamed both of them for the situation, but chiefly her. "You," he railed at her, "may be made to do anything; to say anything; to write anything." What he meant, of course, was that she had followed her husband's wishes, not his. Poor

Theodosia was being caught in the crossfire of two possessive males.

As the year 1808 ended, the colonel treated himself to a tour of the British Isles. En route to Oxford by stage, he related in the journal, "we took in a very pretty, graceful, arch-looking girl, about 18 . . . But M'lle was reserved and distant. At the first change of horses she agreed to take breakfast, which we did, *tête-à-tête*. I was charmed to find her all animation, gayety, ease, badinage. By the aid of drink to the coachman, our companions were kept three-quarters of an hour cooling in the coach . . . When we joined them the reserve of my little siren returned . . . finding it impossible to provoke anything beyond a cold monosyllable, I composed myself to sleep, and slept soundly for eight hours . . ." At Oxford he was wined and dined by the Provost, who spoke of "Bentham with reverence," he noted, "and probably prays for him [but] I presume he thinks that he will be eternally damned, and . . . expects to be lolling in Abraham's bosom with great complacency, hearing Bentham sing out for a drop of water. Such is the mild genius of our holy religion."

Christmas Eve he spent in Birmingham, mingling with the throngs celebrating in the streets. At "length," he recorded, "I got so well suited with a couple that we agreed to talk and see the town. I have always had a passion for certain branches of natural history." This lesson proved expensive. In the course of it, he lost a pair of gloves and twenty-eight shillings. He was also relieved of his passage ticket. On the following morning, consequently, he traveled to Liverpool riding on the outside of the coach at half price.

Edinburgh, reached on New Year's Day, was his last and longest stop. General Hope had provided him with letters of introduction, and soon he was basking in the hospitality of the local notables. Among the individuals met in the Scottish metropolis were Francis Jeffrey, founder and for many years editor of the *Edinburgh Review;* Sir Walter Scott, then at the zenith of his popularity; Sir Alexander McKenzie, the novelist and Lord Mayor. "Driving out every day," Burr informed Bentham, "and at some party almost every night. Wasting time and doing many silly things"—things he endeavored to neutralize on the mornings after by taking cream-of-tartar punch, his preferred remedy whenever he found himself "out of order" from a hangover or indigestion or both. There were frequent conferences with Baron Balgray and the Lord Justice-Clerk. These dealt with X, and it was during this period that the arrangements were made for Burr, after his return to England, to confer with Lord Melville, first in London and later at Wimbledon. These talks, too, dealt with X; but though Melville, Jeremy Bentham and his brother General Samuel Bentham, Baron Balgray, and a fair number of other private citizens continued staunchly favorable to Burr's Mexican project, his Majesty's ministers continued just as staunchly opposed.

By 7 February 1809 the colonel was again in London, and a few days later his troubles began. On the tenth, word reached him that a bookseller had filed suit for a four-year-old debt. It was "a trifling affair," Burr wrote Alston, but "by no means convenient to pay . . . out of my slender resources . . . The sum is 117 £." Hearing that a civil warrant for him was out, Burr abandoned what had become his two homes in London, Bentham's Bird Cage and 30 Craven Street, to take lodgings under an assumed name at 35 St. James Street. "The benevolent heart of J[eremy] B[entham] shall never be saddened by the spectacle of Gamp's arrest," he swore in the journal.

His new landlady turned out to be a Madame Prevost—seemingly unconnected, however, with his late wife's kin of that name. In his awful French he described her as young, "perhaps 28," as having "an air of elegance with dejection," and as being "extremely attentive." Obviously, he concluded, she had been "Sent by the Devil to scd. [seduce] Gamp." Seduced he was—not unwillingly, one gathers—within two days, after which, save for occasional outbursts of sighs and tears on Madame's part, life rocked along nicely at 35 St. James Street for several weeks.

Then a new alarm arose. Inquiries about him, Burr learned, were being made in the neighborhood. Again he fled, this time to the home of friends. Two weeks later, he was back with Madame, but his mind was not at ease. On the morning of 4 April, his journal narrates, he awakened with "a confused presentiment that something was wrong." He dressed at once and began packing, "with intent to . . . seek other lodgings." But it was too late. "At 1 o'clock," the diary continues, "came in, without knocking, four coarse-looking gentlemen," who said they had a state warrant "for him and his belongings." At first they refused to show it, but Burr was "peremptory" and the document was produced. He was not given time to read it all; just enough to know that it was signed by Liverpool, that it stated in substance that the former American Vice President was under grave suspicion, and that the ministry wished him to leave the country. Who was behind this demand —the colonel's government, or the juntas? Burr suspected both, but there is reason to believe that the request for his seizure and deportation originated with Admiral Juan de Apodaca, the Spanish envoy in London.

With Burr standing by, the invaders took possession of his trunks, "searched every part of the room for papers, threw all the loose articles into a sack, called a coach and away" they went to the Alien Office. On their arrival at that place, Burr refused to leave the vehicle. He had prepared a note for his friend Reeves. He insisted that it be delivered. It was, but an hour passed and he had handed in a second note before Reeves appeared, looking glum and saying that the colonel must be "patient," that "explanations" would be forthcoming later. Burr consented to go in then, but within half an hour there were further orders from Liverpool and the prisoner was being driven to 31 Stafford Place, to be held incommunicado in the home of a Mr. Hughes, a messenger employed by the Alien Office. He found himself in the bosom of a little family—the messenger, his wife, and a small child who had the "hooping cough." He was pleased to find the wife "pretty and quite bearable"; not so pleased to discover, after dinner, that every book on the shelves was in German except for two, both of which he had read. He was wondering what to do "for amusement" when, "happening" to learn "that Hughes played chess, we took to that and . . . played till the poor fellow [was] . . . almost crazed." On the following morning he wrote a letter to be taken to Reeves at the Alien Office. "London (Limbo), April 5, 1809," he datelined it. No reasons had been assigned for his "arrest and detention," he observed, "nor is it in my power to conjecture what they may be. It is not permitted to me to take a copy of the warrant . . . I could contend with reason or with law; but a stranger and moneyless, not with power . . . Being under engagements to supper this evening and to dinner tomorrow and Friday, pray inform me whether I may hope to comply with those engagements; or I must apologize, by reason of a subsequent and very pressing invitation from Lord Liverpool." His lordship's "invitation" prevailed. Burr spent the afternoon playing chess with Hughes, but his mind was not on it. It was on his confiscated papers. "They have got everything," he noted with apprehension. "No plots or treasons to be sure but what is worse, all my ridiculous journal." While still at the Alien Office, he had drafted a letter for J. Herbert Koe, Bentham's secretary, and had arranged for its delivery to Queen's Square Place. Koe would see to it that the colonel's friends were alerted. Perhaps they could do something. Perhaps they did, for on the following morning the prisoner was brought back to the Alien Office. Reeves was not there, but the officials on duty were courteous. "Apology and message from Lord Liverpool," the diary states under date of 6 April. "Discharged, and papers and effects restored." Great was the colonel's relief to see that the "papers had not been opened."

He asked that everything be sent to Bentham's place, only to be told that he could not stay there long. The deportation order remained in force. The authorities were planning to send him to Heligoland, a small British-controlled island in the North Sea. More specific instructions concerning this and related matters would be in his hands shortly. Now he learned for the first time that he was not the only visiting American to have been placed under lock and key for disturbing the peace of the empire. One of his young traveling companions, William Hosack, who had also been arrested, was at the moment confined at 10 Charles Street. On 7 April, Burr hastened to that address. Entry was denied, but while he was pacing the sidewalk, weighing possible courses of action, Hosack opened one of the windows and the two of them enjoyed a brief talk. Burr then went back to the Alien Office to leave with Reeves a memorandum for Lord Liverpool. Again, as in his letter to Reeves, he complained at the failure of the government to provide him with an explanation. "Having in my late letters engaged to my friends in America to wait here till June," he told his lordship, "I ought to have something to testify why I *now* leave the country." This errand attended to, Burr took passage to an outlying borough of London to consult with Dr. John Coakley Lettsome and to obtain from that highly respected physician a letter that was to have the effect of procuring the release of Hosack.

The thirteenth of the month brought by messenger another order from Liverpool. His lordship, the colonel reported in a letter of that date to a friend, "expressed his expectation that I should leave town this evening and the kingdom tomorrow . . ." To which Burr added, with admirable simplicity, "I refused." Instead, he renewed his old plea for British citizenship, an exercise in futility, as Lord Liverpool in his capacity as Secretary of State for Home Affairs had long since spoken the last word on that. On the twentieth, in a letter to the secretary, Burr outlined the conditions under which he stood ready to relieve the kingdom of his presence. "Mr. Burr's respectful compliments," he began.

> He lately received from Lord Liverpool an intimation that his [Mr. Burr's] presence in Great Britain was embarrassing to his majesty's government, and that it was the wish . . . of the government that he would remove.
>
> Without insisting on those rights which, as a natural-born subject, he might legally assert; without permitting himself to inquire whether the motives to the order were personal or political; . . . Mr. Burr at once expressed his determination to gratify the wishes of the government by withdrawing. It being understood that he could not, consistently with his personal safety, visit any country under the control or influence of France, Sweden was thought the most proper asylum; and the gentleman who spoke in his lordship's name having represented Heligoland as a place whence passages to Sweden could readily be found, Mr. Burr, relying on this assurance, assented to that voyage, and passports were made out accordingly.
>
> But it is now ascertained that this assurance was predicated in error; that there is, in fact, no direct communication between Heligoland and any part of Sweden, and that no such passage could probably be found within many months. Under such circumstances, Mr. Burr presumes that Lord Liverpool will permit the destination to be changed to Gottenburg,* and will have the goodness to direct passports to be made for that port. He has reason to believe that the minister of his Swedish majesty to this court will not object.

The colonel presumed correctly both as regards the secretary, who no doubt reflected that Sweden's gain would be England's too, and as regards Baron Karl Gustav Brinkman,

---

* Burr spelled the name of this Swedish port in a variety of ways. *The Hammond World Atlas: Superior Edition* (1973) spells it Göteborg.

Sweden's minister to the Court of St. James's. Accordingly, on the evening of 24 April 1809, at the British port of Harwich, Mr. Burr boarded "His Britannic Majesty's packet, the *Diana* ——, a sloop of sixty tons," bound for the "asylum" of Sweden.

3

AN ASYLUM IT PROVED to be, a resting place for a man at sixes and sevens as to what he should do next. Dare he return to the United States? Could such arrangements be made with his creditors there as to permit him to earn a living? The New York dueling charge against him was a dead letter —reduced to that status by the political maneuverings of his old supporters, the little band of Burrites, still functioning under the leadership of Matthew L. Davis; but the Ohio misdemeanor charge remained viable. As late as 10 March 1808, the President was speaking of it in a note to Albert Gallatin. Exercised by a false rumor that the arch-conspirator was planning to settle in New Orleans, Jefferson asked Gallatin to alert the civil and military authorities in the Crescent City. "I presume," he added, "that a writ may be obtained from Ohio grounded on the indictment by which Burr may be arrested any where and brought back to trial."

In a letter written by the colonel on his last day in England, he informed a woman friend in America that he "wished very much to pass a few weeks in Sweden." In fact, he spent more than five months there, and when he left, it was with the feeling that he was putting behind him one of the pleasantest interludes of his life. In that scenic land on the Baltic Sea, he was everywhere made to feel at home by a genial and cultured people. He was welcomed into their family circles. He was entertained at the House of Nobles, the most exclusive club in the country. He was regularly invited to balls and concerts. He was presented at court, borrowing or renting the requisite regalia and writing Theodosia that she would "have laughed

to see Gamp with his sword and immense three-cornered hat."
A list of the people mentioned in the Swedish section of the
journal includes Anders Eric Aizelius, high-ranking jurist;
Baron Gustaf d'Albedÿhill, author of respected works on international relations; Count Lars Von Engeström, minister of
foreign affairs; Carl Gottfried Helvig, artillery general; and
Dr. Henrick Gahn, founder of the Swedish Medical Association. Like the rest of Europe, the Sweden of 1809 was noticeably affected by the tremors spreading from the Napoleonic
earthquake, but it seemed to Burr that its citizens had a genius
for enjoying themselves. He loved them for it. "It is a luxury
to see people happy," he once exclaimed. "Les Swedoises"
returned his feelings. "I offer you . . . the homage of the
most sincere esteem and attachment," Baron d'Albedÿhill wrote
him, "which will accompany you whithersoever you go, even
into the other world." Accompanying these words was a gift
to Burr of a copy in Latin of the laws of Sweden, a difficult
book to come by.

Repeatedly, the visitor from America sang the praises of
Sweden. "Honesty," he wrote Theodosia, "is not a virtue here;
it is a mere habit. Coming from England, where no vigilance
can secure you against fraud and theft, it is like passing to
another planet to travel in this, where you sleep in security
without a latch to your door; where you may send your trunk,
without a lock, to any distance, without hazard, though driven
by a child, often a little girl, at all hours of night, in their
little open chairs. This circumstance, the beauty of their
roads, being everywhere like that from New-York to Harlem,
and the kindness and cheerful good-humour with which you
are everywhere received, render travelling very pleasant in
this country." He was impressed, during his attendance at
concerts in Stockholm, by "the perfect attention, and the uncommon degree of feeling exhibited by the audience. I have
nowhere witnessed the like. Every countenance was affected
by those emotions to which the music was adapted. In England

you see no expression . . . on the visage at a concert. All is sombre and grim. They cry bravo! . . . with the same countenance that they 'G—d damn' their servants and their government."

He was not unaware of the prevailing turmoil in Europe, but his occasional references to it were prudently oblique. "I have never spoken to you of politics," he advised Theodosia in the journal, "because I have personally no hand in them, which will be reason enough for you, and for twenty other good reasons." And to a Swedish woman friend: "Be careful what you write," he warned. "Every letter is liable to inspection. One indiscreet expression might expose your letters to be burned, and perhaps me with them. Avoid everything having reference to politics . . ." After all, his papers had been seized by one government; it could happen again. It has been argued convincingly that the innumerable passages in the journal dealing with fun and games were part of a deliberate effort to convince potential Peeping Toms that their author was a harmless playboy.

What the journal most definitely reveals is that its author was as determined to feed the mind as the body—following in this regard the preachments of his mentor Lord Chesterfield, who in the letters to his son repeatedly emphasized the importance of satisfying the clamors of both. Burr took lessons in the Swedish language and with the assistance of a young law student delved deeply into the principles and history of Swedish jurisprudence, accumulating a vast quantity of notes on the subject and seriously contemplating the production of a tract on it. He read endlessly. He always had; but in Sweden, with all efforts to further his Mexican project in abeyance, he had more time to do so. Like many travelers to far places, he suffered from insomnia. Often we find him reading the night through because, even after taking excessive amounts of laudanum, sleep eluded him. Again, we find him behind a book, because he could not afford to be anywhere else. "Read till eleven [at night] in Cox's volume on Sweden," a diary jotting reads. "My first business this morning was to examine into the state of finance, to determine whether or not Gamp might déjeuné. Found that he could not. Continued reading Cox, and finished the volume."

His tastes in literature were catholic. He read treatises on matters as diverse as the historical development of morality and the significance of the signs of the zodiac. He devoured any books he could find on the subject of women, and especially those supportive of his conviction that in every field of human endeavor the female was as capable as the male. If anyone wished to argue the issue, he had only to point to Theodosia. And point to her he did. She was never for any great length of time out of his thoughts. He carried with him her portrait, holding it on his lap during long stagecoach journeys lest it meet with damage if left with his luggage. He hung it on the walls of his various lodgings, so that he might look at her as he wrote to her. In Stockholm he took it to the leading painter Karl Fredrick von Breda to be varnished and framed. "Good God!" said the artist, "pardon the freedom; but can any man on earth be worthy of that woman? . . . Such a union of delicacy, dignity, sweetness, and genius I never saw." Papa's sentiments precisely. As to the pantheon of his vices: on that structure the journal leaves nothing to the imagination. *Muse* was the goddess there, closely attended by tobacco ("segars" and his pipe), good wines, and strong coffee.

Entering Sweden through the port of Göteborg on 2 May, he journeyed a few days later to Stockholm. There or in the vicinity he remained for about three months, devoting the other two months of his stay to a tour of the countryside, covering, by his own estimate, "more than twelve hundred English miles." In Stockholm he went repeatedly to the royal palace, to linger among the great art collections there. Statuary was a passion with him. In his earlier days he had spent on it enough money to have reduced appreciably the ever-enlarging

pile of his chronic indebtedness. His exploration of the countryside took him to Haga, Drottingholm, Skloster, Gripsholm,
Sigtuna, and Old and New Uppsala; to the Dannemora iron
mines and to the Botanical Garden of Linnaeus and the room
where the great Swedish botanist died. Somewhere, during
his travels, he encountered Sir Augustus John Foster, secretary
of the British legation in Washington back in Anthony Merry's
day and now the British chargé d'affaires at Stockholm. Foster's subsequent recollection of this meeting is a risible example of the widespread view of Burr as a corporealization
of Satan. Burr's "love of intrigues," Foster recalled, "led him,
under the pretext of curiosity, to view the castle of Gripsholm,
in which the deposed King Gustavus [IV] and his family were
then confined and closely guarded. Burr asked to see the young
Prince, and being suspected from his manner, of a design to
communicate some plan of the Royalists for his escape, was
rudely marched away and soon afterward ordered out of the
kingdom. Having known him . . . in Washington . . . and
wishing to be civil . . . I went up to him . . . and offered
him my services, when I must do him the justice to say, that
he showed some delicacy, for seeing that I was a young diplomat he told me he thought it right to put me on my guard, that
I might not commit myself . . . by being seen with him,
. . . I mentioned this long afterward to Lord Holland who
observed that it was the only good trait he had ever heard of
Burr . . ." The former Vice President was not alone on his
Swedish rambles. Sam Swartwout had returned to the United
States, but William A. Hosack and Thomas Robinson were
still with him. In letters to an official, Burr described them
as "two American savages." Hosack, he noted, was "the elder,
the blackest, the tallest"; Robinson, "younger and less black."
Both, he asserted, "were so far tamed as not to bite, unless
greatly excited by some strong passion, such as anger or love."

Largely responsible for the hospitality lavished on him
in Sweden was one of his old friends, Henry Gahn, the Swedish

consul in New York. Gahn is believed to have suggested the Scandinavian tour to Burr and is known to have provided him with letters of introduction. Also well acquainted with Theodosia, the consul acted as a go-between, sometimes seeing to it that correspondence between father and daughter which otherwise might have been stopped or delayed by the British got to its destination with reasonable speed. Even so, Burr had been in Sweden four months before any mail reached him from South Carolina, and when at last a letter from Theodosia was handed to him he "could have kissed the fellow" who brought it across the sea. It was in this communication, written at Rocky River Springs in South Carolina on 1 August 1809, that Theodosia paid him the most quoted of her many tributes to him, a classic of its kind. Her first knowledge that he had been banished from Albion reached her in the public prints, to be confirmed shortly thereafter by a letter in his hand. She was "stupefied . . . by the blow" and amazed at the lightheartedness with which he described it. "I witness your extraordinary fortitude with new wonder at every new misfortune," she wrote him. "Often, after reflecting on this subject, you appear to me so superior, so elevated above all other men; I contemplate you with such a strange mixture of humility, admiration, reverence, love, and pride, that very little superstition would be necessary to make me worship you as a superior being; such enthusiasm does your character excite in me. When I afterward revert to myself, how insignificant do my best qualities appear. My vanity would be greater if I had not been placed so near you; and yet my pride is our relationship. I had rather not live than not be the daughter of such a man."

Cheerful though his letters were, she found his plight a source of unending concern. She knew that his funds were dwindling dangerously. "I sometimes, often indeed, pass the night without closing my eyes," she confessed, "occupied in fruitless endeavours to suggest some mode of indemnifying you." She spoke of having written twice "to the gentleman who promised us the supply of funds," a statement which suggests that Burr, who owed so much money to so many, had money coming to him from at least one person. But there was "little to be hoped" from that quarter, Theodosia told him. "On inquiry I find that his character does not stand very high as a man of punctilious honour in money dealings . . . His conduct is a serious addition to all the accumulated difficulties which already pour in upon us, and which would absolutely overwhelm any other being than yourself."

Questions about him tortured her. When was she to see the journal? Never, as it turned out; but the tragedy of that was not yet upon them. What steps must be taken to get him safely home again? Theodosia did what she could. Madison had succeeded Jefferson in the Presidency, so she wrote to Dolley Madison. Her father had claims on the goodwill of the first lady. It was his legal guidance, proffered without fee following the death of Mrs. Madison's previous husband, that had enabled her to obtain a contested inheritance. Dolley had acknowledged the debt in a 1794 will, naming Aaron Burr as the guardian of her son. "Why," Theodosia asked her, ". . . is my father banished from a country for which he has encountered wounds & dangers & fatigue for years? Why is he driven from his friends, from an only child, to pass an unlimited time in exile, and that too at an age when others are reaping the harvest of past toils?" That the record shows no reply to these words does not mean that they were without effect. Most likely, Dolley showed them to her husband. Most likely, they were helpful in paving the way for the eventual return of the exile.

Theodosia wrote another letter in a similar vein. This one, to Gallatin, reflected her chagrin at the practice of the American press of propagating calumnies against her father, of using "expressions calculated to enliven every spark of animosity which exists in the country." Her questions to the

Secretary of the Treasury (Gallatin holding that position under Madison, as he had under Jefferson) were these: "Whether you suppose that my father's return to this country would be productive of ill consequences to him, or draw on him further prosecution from any branch of the government[?] . . . Must he ever remain . . . excommunicated from the participation of domestic enjoyments and the privileges of a citizen . . . ?" Surely, she argued, "it must be evident to the worst enemies of my father, that no man, situated as he will be, could obtain any undue influence, even supposing him desirous of it." No encouragement was forthcoming from Gallatin; no answer at all, so far as is known.

4

THERE CAME AN HOUR when the halcyon days that were Sweden to Aaron Burr had to end. His journal for 2 September 1809 finds him considering his situation and peering into the future. No mention of X, but obviously it was on his mind, together with the realization that in the whole of Europe only one man was in a position to breathe life into his moribund project. He had already made up his mind to have a look at the Germanic principalities, and those lands were the pathway to the France of Napoleon. "It is no easy matter, *ma Min.* [my Minerva]," he told his diary, "to determine how to dispose of myself. Why stay here [Sweden]? To be sure I am unmolested and live at no great expense, but *tem. fug.* [*tempus fugit*] and nothing done. When I came here it was with intent to stay till answers should be received to my letters to the United States." But so far (this was before the letter from Theodosia) no mail from there, and Burr could only assume that Great Britain as the mistress of the waves was not allowing his letters to come through. "The summary is," he noted, "that I am resolved to go without knowing exactly why or where . . . The facility of getting to a particular place may of itself determine my course. To be sure the *embarras* of travelling on the Continent is very great, but I am in utter despair of receiving letters through England." Dual and somewhat confusing motives are visible here: the possibility of reviving X, the possibility of getting home. Events would dictate and the colonel would improvise accordingly.

Leaving Sweden on 21 October 1809, he lingered long enough in Denmark to visit the tomb of Hamlet at Elsinore; to make the acquaintance of the critic Friedrich von Schlegel, whose *Treatise on Neutral Rights* Burr had studied and admired; and to meet a variety of important functionaries in Copenhagen. On the night of 25 October, as he was preparing to retire, the maid entered his hotel room with a "splendid tea-service of silver and two cups. I asked why she brought two cups, I being alone. She said, with perfect simplicity, and without any smile or queer looks, that she supposed madame would have stayed to tea." Next morning, the keeper of the journal was "a little out of humour with Gamp" and made "some pious resolutions." In Denmark, he again took stock of his finances. He found them almost depleted. Then suddenly there was manna from heaven, an unsolicited loan of a thousand marks from Diedrich Lüning, one of the many new friends acquired in Sweden. "I can not tell you," Lüning wrote, "how much I am thankful to providence for haven [sic] given me the pleasure to get acquainted with a man who I admired long ago. I esteemed you before now I love you too."

On 8 November he moved on from Copenhagen, and those sections of the journal covering his passage of the duchies and kingdoms composing the Germany of those days make fascinating reading. We see him traveling in wickerwork wagons, most of them "sans springs" and with no roofs to protect one from rain and snow. We see him on these jaunts inevitably occupying the worst place, this being the "lot of a stranger," he tells us, in all parts of Europe "except . . . *Scotland and Sweden.*" Sustained briefly by the windfall from Lüning, at other periods by small loans from his American companions, or from persons met along the way, we see him served by a succession of *valets de chambre*, some elderly and conscientious, others young and chronically inebriated. Wherever he stopped, he was invited into the homes and into the private clubs of people of social and intellectual distinction. His destination? Paris, he hoped. He couldn't be sure of getting there because of passports. Indeed, for the next two years, much of Aaron Burr's life was to be a matter of passports.

He observed some of the more unusual customs encountered on his wanderings: the presence in certain European theaters of special sections for "les courtisannes"; the use by the watchmen in the German towns of rattles while making their rounds; the practice among "les servantes and bourgeoisie" on their evenings out of wearing "strange headdress, and false hips; even girls of five years old. At the tavern I caught one to examine those hips. She screamed as if I was going to eat her, to the great amusement of twenty spectators."

For more than a month, beginning 20 November 1809, his home away from home was a rooming house in Altona, a little town on the Elbe, half a mile south of the walled city of Hamburg. Numerous Americans were living in the area, and for the first time since his departure from London he was aware of a chill in the atmosphere. All the Americans, he noted, were "hostile to A.B." They must have been exceedingly vocal about it, for ordinarily he ignored such things. "What a lot of rascals . . ." he decided, "to make war on one whom they do not know; on one who never did harm or wished harm to a human being. Yet they, perhaps, ought not to be blamed, for they are influenced by what they hear." He himself heard a disturbing rumor, that "A.B. is announced in the Paris papers in a manner no way auspicious." Nonetheless, to Paris he was determined to go.

For the requisite passport he called on the French minister in Hamburg. Twice the minister, Louis Antoine Favelet de

Bourrienne, refused to admit him, but when finally he did, his manner was "courteous . . . with a mixture of surprise and curiosity." Bourrienne is best-known as the author of memoirs of Napoleon, whose private secretary he was for a time, and his reminiscences in that work of his relations with Aaron Burr are of interest. "At the height of his glory and power," the memoirs tell us, "Bonaparte was so suspicious that the veriest trifle sufficed to alarm him." Consequently, immediately after the former Vice President arrived in Altona, Bourrienne "received orders to watch him very closely, and to arrest him on the slightest ground of suspicion if he should come to Hamburgh [sic]." But, adds the minister, Burr "was one of those in favour of whom I ventured to disobey the orders . . . from the restless police of Paris." In answer to their instructions, he stated that the American conducted himself at Altona "with much prudence and propriety; that he kept but little company, and that he was scarcely spoken of." Instead of adopting toward the visitor measures the minister regarded as "equivalent to persecution," he offered him "a passport to any frontier town," but explained that he had "no authority to do more." Passports to travel in France, he said, must come from the minister of police in Paris. He advised Burr, in his application to that official, to suggest that the document be sent to Mainz, expressing the belief that it would be at that ancient city on the Rhine before Burr could get there. The interview concluded, Bourrienne invited the colonel to dine at his country home on the morrow, which the colonel did. But probably not in comfort, for a "hollow" tooth was beginning to torment him. He tried packing it "with camphor and opium," but to no avail. The pain persisted, eventually driving him to the office of a woman dentist, who, to the delight of the great feminist, extracted with skill. Not that his dental troubles were at an end, for once the offending tooth was drawn, all the others, "neighbors of the departed," combined to torture him "in vengeance."

On 11 December he left Altona. "Robinson goes to Leipsic," he informed Theodosia at this point in the journal. "Hosack stays at Hamburgh, so that I shall make this journey alone, without a servant and without a companion, totally ignorant of the language, and in the very worst season of the year. Yet do not be alarmed, we shall get along and find amusement." At Göttingen, on Christmas Day, he found news— exciting news. The bearer of it was Professor Arnold Hermann Louis Heeren, a historian who lectured at the university there and with whom Burr had corresponded from the United States. The news was that the Emperor Napoleon had expressed his "assent to the independence of Mexico and the other Spanish colonies!" Burr's recorded comment: "Why the devil didn't he tell me this two years ago?" Now he was more than ever eager to get to Paris, more than ever convinced that the effort to obtain the sponsorship of the emperor for X was worth all of the energy he could put into it.

By 18 January 1810 he was in Frankfort-on-Main. Technically, this was as far as he could go on the frontier passport Bourrienne had given him, for at this time nearby Mainz, where he assumed his French passport was waiting for him, was on the soil of France proper. As always, he was well supplied with letters of introduction. By the end of his second day in cosmopolitan Frankfort, his circle of patrons included Monsieur de Bethmann, the Russian consul there; Jean Saracin of Chiron, Saracin and Company, a local banking firm; and young Mr. Bansa of Bansa and Sons, another banking firm. On the twentieth, he dispatched a message to the commandant of the division at Mainz, which stands on the southern banks of the Rhine where the Main flows into that river twenty-four miles southwest of Frankfort. Addressed to General Meynier, it was a polite request that the commandant "enquire whether my passport had been sent from Paris." Three days passed before there was a trustworthy answer. Meanwhile, the colonel amused himself at "the Cassino . . . the musée, and . . . the Cabinet Literaire," tickets of admission to all of which were furnished him by Monsieur de Bethmann. At a ball at the Casino ("about one hundred ladies; a great many very handsome"—it was a rare woman in Burr's eyes who was anything less than handsome) he was unable to take his eyes off a "M'lle. ——— le Lunet, elegant and striking," with a "resemblance stronger than I have ever seen to a person once dear to you and me." The first Theodosia? Very likely.

"Certainly, madame," he was telling the second Theodosia on the morning of the twenty-third, "you owe me great obligations for writing you at all at this moment. Lo! the catastrophe of my hopes. Mr. ——— called at ten . . . and with an air of mystery, with hesitation and unaffected embarrassment, said that he had a letter from his friend at Mayence [Mainz], advising not only that no passport for me had been received, but there were advices from Paris . . . requesting I might be advised by no means to hazard my person within the territories of France." Burr thanked the gentleman who brought him these tidings, announced his intention of going to Mainz on the morrow, and asked his informant for "a line of introduction to his friend" there. The gentleman evinced alarm. "He seemed to consider my resolution as madness," Burr recorded, and "declined giving a letter from the danger which must ensue from any apparent connexion with me."

But the colonel was not to be deterred. Seizure and detention were the worst things that could happen to him in Mainz, and to a man who had known the interior of an American penitentiary and a British house arrest in London, these prospects were without terror. Only in Mainz, he reasoned, could he discover "the state of things." Not that there was any doubt in his mind as to what the state of things was. The refusal of a passport, he concluded, was the work of the American minister in Paris—General John Armstrong of New York, brother-in-law of Chancellor Robert R. Livingston and member of the political faction headed by De Witt Clinton, the colonel's longtime enemy back home.

From his interview with the conveyer of the bad news, Burr hastened to the home of his friend Saracin. Saracin not only agreed with the colonel's belief that no harm could come to him in Mainz but also provided him with a letter of introduction to one of his friends there—and on the morning of the twenty-fifth a "traineau," a sledge "drawn by two," carried the colonel across the frozen Rhine to Mainz. There he took lodgings and sent his card to General Meynier and to the prefect, the Baron Jean Bon St. André. On the following day, he was received by both of them. From both came much the same story. If Bourrienne had indeed recommended him for a passport, the French authorities had no record of it. Again, he was to apply to the minister of police in Paris. Again, he arranged to do so. Meanwhile, he was told, he could either wait in Mainz or return to Frankfort; but if he stayed in Mainz he would be under the surveillance of the police. Before the day was gone, there were two incidents of harassment by the constabulary, and on the twenty-seventh he was back in Frankfort.

For another round of dinners, card parties, and masked balls. Then, on the evening of 7 February, just as he stepped into the gaming room of the Casino, the "secretary of Mr. ———" (no names given in the journal) informed him that the passport had been granted, that he could pick it up at any time after eleven the following morning. Joyous moment! Now the dream of X, killed only a few days before by the mysterious denial of the passport, was miraculously revived by its equally inexplicable issuance. On the ninth, in Mainz, he had the coveted document viséd by the prefect, and in the bitter cold of the dark hours of the morning of the tenth he boarded the diligence that would carry him to the capital of France. His coach companions included "two dames." Both were traveling sans husband and both were "very pretty," but for at least once in his life Aaron Burr was invulnerable to the well-turned ankle and the alluring eye. "I am very bad company and unsocial," the journal tells us as the diligence rolls across the French countryside a hundred and ten English miles from Mainz, "my head being so full of X matters."

5

BY THE EVENING OF Friday 16 February he was in Paris, living at the Hotel de Lyon at 7, rue Grenelle in the St.-Honoré district and girding himself for what was to be a last effort to obtain backing for X. His first job was to establish contact with the government of Napoleon. To this end, he dispatched a note to the minister of foreign affairs, Jean-Baptiste de Nonpère de Champagny, duc de Cadore, and on Monday he was granted an audience with that official. The journal provides no details on this one-hour interview, but it is perhaps noteworthy that Burr spent the greater part of Tuesday scouring the city in search of American maps.

While awaiting further word from Cadore, he got in touch with prominent Parisians—some because he had letters of introduction from friends in Germany, others because he had known them in the United States and had entertained them in that cornucopian manner of his in Philadelphia or at his Richmond Hill mansion in New York. Among those on whom he called or to whom he submitted cards were Charles Maurice Talleyrand, Prince de Bénévent; Emerich Joseph, baron de Dalberg; Constantine François de Chasseboeuf, comte de Volney; and Pierre-August Adet. Talleyrand refused to see him. To that statesman, Burr was forever *persona non grata* as the "*assassiné*" of Hamilton, whom Talleyrand regarded as the greatest man "*de notre époque.*" It was Talleyrand's understanding that the arch-conspirator had come to Europe "to induce the French government to be concerned in a project for dismembering the United States," a view the wily old manipulator of men and measures may have picked up from the local American community, whose members had agreed among themselves that anyone who spoke to Burr was to be "shunned as unworthy of society" and that "no master of vessel, or any other person, shall take any letter or parcel for him." Fortunately for the colonel, most of the other men he called on were courteous. Some were helpful. German-born Baron de Dalberg took the wandering adventurer under his wing, drawing on his long experience as a diplomat and a councilor of state to tutor the colonel in the bewildering ways of the French bureaucracy. Adet, onetime French minister to the United States, gave the visiting lawyer a guided tour of the Corps Législatif, and Volney, author of popular books of history and travel, was uniformly friendly, although as the colonel's business grew increasingly tangled and as the word spread that some of his activities were displeasing to the emperor, the kindly scholar made a point of disassociating himself from the American's affairs.

At the time Burr arrived in the French capital, he was under the impression that John Vanderlyn—the American-born artist whose career the colonel had made possible—was in Rome. Great was Burr's delight to learn during his second week in town that Vanderlyn had returned to Paris. There was a reunion, with Burr reporting to his daughter that "VDL" remained the "same as *ci-dev*.," the same as always. On 27 February the old friends enjoyed the first of what were to be many meals together, and Vanderlyn accompanied the colonel to the office of Monsieur Fonzi, the genial and talented dentist, who brightened the Paris interlude for Burr by furbishing him with a set of badly needed new teeth. Back in the 1790's, Burr had helped finance an art education for Vanderlyn in his own country and had then sent him to France to complete his training. In the intervening years, the younger man had justified the older one's faith, producing several critically acclaimed works, including portraits of Burr and his daughter and a canvas entitled "Marius Amid the Ruins of Carthage," for which its creator was awarded a gold medal in Paris. Now the protégé was to have the opportunity of helping the patron, an obligation the artist fulfilled to the extent that his own always limited resources permitted.

The business that had brought Burr to the city moved slowly. "Words cost nothing here," he reflected, "and there is an immensity of time and space between the promise of a courtier and the performance." Not until the last day of February did the eagerly anticipated word from the foreign minister arrive—a message in which Cadore stated that he had appointed a young official in the archives of the ministry of police, one Louis Roux, to listen to whatever propositions the colonel wished to lay before the Napoleonic court.

At once, Burr was all action, all drive. Again he toured the local bookstores and geographers, this time procuring maps of Mexico as well as of America. At his first meeting with Roux, on 1 March, he found the young archivist "sensible" and "amiable." They talked for half an hour, and on the following day Burr delivered to him a "supplementary communication." Three days subsequent found him preparing another communication, a letter intended for Napoleon. "When it was nearly done," the journal relates, "something occurred which altered my mind." Even so, the letter must have been sent, for on 9 March Burr called on Roux "to know if any answer" and to learn that there was none and that Cadore had expressed the hope that "I would not be impatient to leave Paris."

During those anxious March days, Burr neglected his journal. There are several gaps, and in an isolated entry late in the month he offered Theodosia an explanation. He had met a Madame Paschaud, proprietor, with her husband, of a bookstore at 3, rue des Petites Augustine. Since their first meeting, he wrote, "Have passed every evening with her save one. Have walked with her; been to the opera; dined there two or three times en famille . . . Madame is about the size and form of Mrs. Madison, though some ten years younger, still larger. Very black hair and eyes. A fine, clear, fair brunette, with the complexion of full health. Her husband is at Genève. I rather think that she must be the cause that I have not written you." His encounter with Madame was the beginning of an enduring friendship, for later we find the Paschauds' family firm publishing the 1816 edition of Jeremy Bentham's *Political Tactics*. Not that his interest in Madame was the sole burden of Burr's late-March entry. From this source we also learn that during the opening weeks of the month he dined once with Louis Roux and engaged in a series of conferences with him. From another source we learn that, by 13 March, Roux had sent to Cadore a number of documents describing his conversations with Burr to date; that on 19 March he sent the foreign minister another report, covering an additional conversation with the colonel; and that, on 14 and 19 March, Cadore transmitted all this material to Napoleon.

As preserved in the Archives Nationales in Paris, this dossier of Burr's proposals to the emperor consists of twelve documents in all. Included are four undated memoirs, evidently prepared in the archives of the ministry of police by Roux (or under his direction) and based on the oral and written communications that Burr had made to him. Accompanying each of these memoirs is a précis, a brief abstract of its contents, prepared by a clerk in Cadore's department, the ministry of foreign affairs. The writer of these précis lists the undated memoirs as "No. 1—Notes on the United States," "No. 2—Notes on Louisiana," "No. 3—Memoirs on the Spanish Colonies in America, and on the United States," and "No. 4—Memoir [sic] on the means of rescuing the Spanish Colonies from the Influence of England."

As these titles indicate, many of Burr's proposals were in line with his longing to revolutionize Spain's transatlantic possessions and were presented so as to emphasize the advantages to France and the disadvantages to England likely to ensue from the liberation of those lands under the aegis of Napoleon. In addition, the American adventurer, never a man to do things by halves, outlined schemes for depriving Great Britain of the island of Jamaica and for effecting the independence of British-owned Canada; and described the inhabitants of American-owned Louisiana as eager to return to the custody of France. Four dated communications completed the dossier. Roux's 13 March report to Cadore summarized the points made in the undated memoirs, and his 19 March account for the minister of the additional conversation with Burr had the colonel elaborating on his Canadian ideas. Cadore, in the letters covering his transmittal of the material to the emperor, offered a few comments on the colonel's suggestions. "Mr. Burr," the foreign minister told Napoleon on 14 March, "would be able to bring about changes only in Florida and Louisiana, and he could not be employed without giving a great deal of offense to the United States. His views on Jamaica are wishful thinking that he brings up only to give himself a bit of credit here." And in the 19 March letter of transmittal, Cadore characterized Burr's proposal to make Canada independent as "a project more difficult to carry out than the others."

Since the presence of these documents in the French archives came to light fifty-some years ago,* some students of

---

* In the late 1920's, Dr. Waldo G. Leland found in the Archives Nationales several manuscripts relating to Burr, and later deposited with the Carnegie Institution in Washington, D.C., some penciled notes on them. In the 1960's, Dr. Samuel Engle Burr, Jr., a collateral descendant of Aaron Burr and a longtime student of his life, arranged for an English translation of many of these documents and made this translation conveniently available in his 1969 book, *Napoleon's Dossier on Aaron Burr*. More recently, Dr. Mary-Jo Kline, editor of the Aaron Burr Papers, arranged for a translation of all the documents (much of it based on the Burr translation) for use in her edition of the papers for the Princeton University Press. Unless otherwise indicated, statements concerning the dossier in this book rest on this latest translation and on the manuscript of an "Editorial Note" by Dr. Kline entitled "Aaron Burr and Napoleon's Court."

Burr's career have detected in four of them—memoir 1 "on the United States," memoir 2 "on Louisiana," and the précis for both—indications that whatever Burr may have had in mind at the time of his filibuster into the American Southwest, he was meditating treason against his native land at the time of his coming to Paris.

By way of dealing as fairly as possible with these suspicions, it is worth pointing out that none of the documents in the dossier is in Burr's hand and that none "was signed or initialed by him to indicate his approval of its contents . . ." It is also worthy of mention that portions of the undated memoirs come close to being what today is called gobbledygook. What Burr actually said or wrote for Napoleon's eyes comes to us secondhand, even thirdhand, after having been sifted through the mind of French officialdom. Consequently, its value as a guide to Burr's thinking at the time must be regarded as minimal.

In the second of the undated memoirs, the one on Louisiana, Burr offers some demographic information about his country's recently acquired territory and describes the manner in which it has been divided for administrative purposes. Then he is quoted as asserting that "By the Cession Treaty of Louisiana, it is stipulated that all the inhabitants will enjoy the privileges of the citizens of the United States. They enjoy none whatsoever. The laws are made, and the civil and military officers are named by the United States Government in Washington . . . These officers who are sent to govern are men without education, polish, or politeness, and foreigners to the language and customs of the French. The procedures of the Tribunals are in English, of which the inhabitants do not understand a word. In all, their former customs and habits are . . . treated with disdain, so that the United States Government has become relatively unpopular in that section of the country. When I was in the District of Orleans about 3 years ago, I saw a Memoir already signed by several respectable inhabitants, addressed to the Emperor of the French, and in which were exposed the real griefs about which they were complaining; and they were begging his protection. I advised them to suppress this Memoir and promised them to come to their aid in another manner. They are still waiting for me to keep my promise."

All this would appear to be innocent enough. Burr's paraphrase of the frequently heard gripes of the Creoles of the Orleans and Louisiana Districts was a reasonably accurate one. But in the précis for this note on Louisiana some hurried and harried departmental clerk carried its thinking one step further. "Louisiana," the précis writer says, "has about one hundred thousand free inhabitants, and all French; the United States Government is unpopular with them; they turn their thoughts to the Emperor Napoleon for their deliverance." But is this the gist of what Burr was saying? In his notoriously roundabout manner of speaking, was he suggesting that the emperor put him at the head of a movement designed to detach the territory from its rightful owners; or was he simply describing a reality?

To turn next to the memoir on the United States. This note quotes Burr as claiming that "all classes of people" in his homeland "are today discontented with the actions of the government . . . The discontent is general, but it has not any fixed objective. The malcontents of the administration party, embittered, restless, feeling the need for a change and having in sight no party other than the Federalists, are quite ready to fall in under their banner solely through the love of a change. But in this Federalist party there is not a single man of marked superiority . . ." However, Burr continues, there "is a third party that is superior to the two others in talents and energy. Those making up this party . . . want something strong and stable, something which, in putting active minds to work, will assure the peace of mind of rational men. This party has a recognized leader; they ask only to follow him

and obey him. Three-fourths (and even more) of the people
of the United States have an inveterate hatred of England.
They lean towards France . . . If these feelings had been
carried on by France, they would have become compelling and
predominant. It would be straying from the immediate purpose
of this note to indicate the probable result of the lack of action
on the part of France or Mr. A. B. . . . Let it suffice to observe that the moment is favorable for giving the public mind
a direction (in conformance with the plans set forth) and for
announcing a daring crusade for carrying them out." Asserting that a couple of "Observations will throw light on this
latter point," Burr adds that "at this moment around forty
thousand American sailors [are] unemployed by reason of the
Embargo Act and suspension of trade [with Great Britain]
. . . In the United States Navy there are more than 500 young
officers or students who can be considered as the choice of the
nation, all of whom breathe forth nothing but vengeance on
the British Navy and nation. Among these young men can be
found officers ready to assume command of the 90 ships of
the line. They are all disgusted with the government because
it offers no outlook at all for promotion or glory . . . [and
all of them] long only for war, but war against Great Britain."

Strange and strained is the departmental clerk's abstract
of these statements. "This note," the précis writer asserts, "is
not at all clear: the author appears rather to have guessed at
this than to have explained it openly. It seems that he is the
head of this third party that holds to monarchy and that his
project would be to use these 40 thousand unemployed sailors
to overthrow the Republican government and that the declaration of war on the English would follow this change. It should
be noted that since the preparation of this note, the Embargo
has been lifted." If any weight should be given this admittedly
uncertain interpretation of the memoir, then surely equal
weight should be given to a statement in the note itself where
Burr is quoted as addressing himself directly to the subject of

treason. "The division of the United States into two or more governments," this section of the memoir reads, "entered into the consideration [view] of Great Britain and Spain. Mr. A. B. does not see these powers as having any object other than the odious one of putting the country in disarray. He does not see what interest a power which is not at war with the United States could have in disuniting it [the United States]. *He has none himself, nor has he any desire to see one carried out.*"*

Case closed—a moot one, obviously. It would appear that only one tenable conclusion can be drawn from the colonel's suggestions to Napoleon; namely, that they show Burr up to his old tricks, trying to get something big to do, trying to get lots of money to do it with, and willing, like many political hotspurs both before and after him, to say almost anything to attain his ends.

His proposals elicited no sign of interest from the emperor. "Have no reason to believe that my business advances, or that I shall do anything here," he was writing in the journal less than two weeks after his dossier moved from Cadore to Napoleon. But the congenitally sanguine adventurer was not yet ready to give up. As it became clear that he was unlikely to gain access to the throne of France through the foreign minister, he turned to other men in one last desperate struggle to do so.

Napoleon's brother, Jerome Bonaparte, once a guest at Richmond Hill, was now king of Westphalia. On 17 March the colonel sent him a note requesting an audience. Seemingly, there was no answer, for on 4 April Burr wrote again, this time obtaining permission to call at the Paris quarters of the Westphalian ruler that afternoon. Received "graciously," the journal relates. "Passed half an hour in private with him," at the conclusion of which Jerome instructed his chamberlain, Comte de Furstenstein (Camus), to assist Burr in translating

---

* Emphasis added.

another letter to Napoleon. The colonel delivered the English draft of this missive on the following day, receiving Furstenstein's assurance that it would be sent on, but more than two weeks passed with no reply, and when Burr learned that Jerome and his chamberlain had gone to Compiègne to be with the emperor there, he applied for a passport to that town. But this was refused and he had no choice but to wait until Furstenstein returned to Paris in late April, when Burr was told that his letter had been forwarded as promised. Thus ended his second attempt to reach the dictator of continental Europe. Meanwhile, he had put underway still another. On 21 March he wrote Joseph Fouché, duc d'Otrante, Napoleon's minister of police. To that then powerful dignitary the colonel explained that, having learned "of his majesty's assent to the independence of the Spanish American colonies," he had come "to Paris to offer his services to accomplish that object and others connected therewith." He added that he wanted "neither men nor money . . . only the authorization of his majesty," and that, being convinced that some of his (Burr's) communications to the emperor either had not reached him or had been misunderstood, their author "should, with very great regret, leave the country without having had a few minutes' conversation" with the police minister, who Burr was certain would appreciate "the value of his views." Gaps in the journal make it impossible to trace this development with precision. Apparently, Otrante's reaction was not unfavorable, for on 30 May Burr transmitted to him a written memorial outlining some of his proposals to the emperor, a transaction which can be described as another example of the colonel's penchant for associating himself with the wrong people at the wrong time. Only a few days later, Napoleon learned with great anger that during the preceding spring his minister of police had conducted secret negotiations with the British enemy. On 3 June, Otrante was relieved of his post and fled the country, and when during the summer one of his aides was seized in France, the American minister to that country, John Armstrong, informed his government that the captured man had linked the name of Aaron Burr to Otrante's intrigues with the British.

Very likely, this charge damned the colonel "completely in the opinion of Napoleon and his court." Most certainly, it filled Paris with wild rumors, for on 11 December 1811—by which time Burr was no longer in France—an American, writing from there and signing himself "Citizen of the United States," sent President James Madison an amazing report on the colonel's relationship with the now fleeing Duc d'Otrante. To "the Duke," wrote Madison's anonymous informant, Burr "delivered a memorial of 63 folio pages . . . The object of this memorial was: to procure peace between France and England. France was to offer to secure England, with all her forces, even by the loan of 100,000 men, or more; the conquest of the Northern parts of the United States. With such a secret treaty or an understanding between the two nations, it was proposed that English fleets should carry, from time to time, to Canada and Nova Scotia as many troops, as would be judged necessary, and there wait under some pretence till the moment was favorable for the operation. That time was provisionally stated by B[urr] to be the next election of P. & V.P. He added: that he strongly relied on his consummate local knowledge of the various dispositions & inclinations of the inhabitants of the Eastern and Southern states, and of the local prejudices which he would, between this and that time, encite [sic] by means of his numerous friends, who were dispersed over every part of the Country." These individuals were to act in "concert with the Chief of an insurrection that was to be raised in New Mexico, the Province of Texas, W. Florida. This chief was to be himself with the appointment from his F.M. [French Majesty] of Generalissimo over the armies in the South, 1,500,000 francs was required for this part of the expedition." Very illegal, these proposals, and very treasonable—but wholly at odds with Burr's letters to Otrante, quoted above, in which he mentioned only "the independence of the Spanish American colonies" and related objectives, and asked for "neither men nor money."

If word of the rumors about him ever reached Burr's ears, they in no way deflected him from his purposes. Well into the summer of 1810, Burr continued his efforts to obtain a meeting with Napoleon. The early days of July found him preparing a new memorial of his proposals. On the ninth he asked Roux for an appointment to "peruse" this writing with him, and on the eleventh the young official invited him to breakfast, offered "some civil remarks," and suggested that the colonel seek another audience with Cadore, a step Burr decided not to take. Instead, he went to see his friend and mentor, Baron de Dalberg, only to be refused admission for two days running. "I did not much like the look of this," he wrote in the journal. "Considered myself as denied, and thus the last hope of communication [with the emperor] cut off." But Dalberg had not deserted him. On 20 July we find Burr showing his revised memorial to the baron, and on the twenty-third, having meanwhile had it "nicely" copied, he left it with Dalberg, along with a letter addressed to Hugo Bernard Maret, duc de Bassano —a cabinet-level minister with the title of Secretary of State— with the understanding that the baron would see that it got to Napoleon via that official. "*Voila fini*," Burr noted in his diary. "*S.M.* [Sa Majesté] will probably read it this day."

Perhaps he did; Burr would never know. On three occasions in late July he called again on Roux, to be treated with "cold civility" and informed that there was "no news." And on the twenty-ninth, Roux submitted to Cadore what was to be his last report on Burr's proposals. Obviously, the foreign minister was not impressed by the local gossip linking the colonel to the intrigues of the recently deposed minister of police. "In the account of these conversations given to me and enclosed . . ." he told Napoleon in the letter transmitting Roux's final report, "Your Majesty will see that Mr. Burr confined himself to repeating one portion of what he had previously said, and that he spoke only of Florida and Canada. Would this, then, quiet the rumor of the communications directed against his own [Burr's] country, which he was accused of having made to the duc d'Otrante?"

At this point, Burr's endeavors on behalf of X ended. Months before, while in London, he had pronounced his project dead, only to resurrect it. Now it was gone, never to be revived —at least not by Aaron Burr. Almost from the moment of his arrival in the French capital, he sensed an iciness in the air, an unspoken but palpable indifference to the potentialities of his plans. In May, calling in person at the prefecture of police, he demanded a passport to the United States, only to be told that such applications must be addressed to the minister of police. By July, when he got around to submitting his request to that functionary, Otrante was gone and his place taken by Anne Jean Marie René, duc de Rovigo. Rovigo's answer was prompt and clear. Burr could have a passport to any place within France he wished to go, but he could not have one for any place outside the empire. No explanation accompanied this pronouncement, but Burr was quick to attribute it to the "machinations of our worthy minister, General Armstrong, who has been, and still is, indefatigable in his exertions to my prejudice." Whatever the cause of the problem, it was one that he must tackle immediately. His funds were running low. With every passing week he came nearer to having none at all. He wrote letters—to Rovigo, to Cadore, to Bassano. He visited Rovigo on the day set aside by that minister to receive the public—and was grimly amused when Rovigo, passing down the reception line, inquired of a "very ill-looking" individual: "Êtes-vous le colonel Burr?" Nothing came of these and similar efforts. Everyone told him the same thing, that his request for a passport to the United States was being looked into by higher authority; and everyone, when later asked what was happening, muttered the same reply; namely, that he had "received no *answer*"—an expression that as Burr had long since recognized constituted the polite French way of saying "nothing doing." "*Me voila prisonier d'etat et presque sans sous*," he exclaimed in the journal—a "prisoner of the state and almost without a cent." Such was his condition in the last week of July 1810. Such it remained for the next nine months, for Burr's struggle to shake the soil of France from his feet proved almost as frustrating and even more time-consuming than his now abandoned campaign for X.

6

THE JOURNAL TELLS MOST, although not all, of the story of those nine months, and tells it vividly. It is the story of the human spirit transcending tribulations. In the fall of 1810, Burr was no longer living in a hotel. He was paying thirty francs a month for a room in the home of the Family Peloughs at 7, rue du Croissant. He described the Peloughs as "a very amiable Genevoise family," adding "of which I am a member"; and indeed it is clear that he was adoringly tended by one of the servant girls; "Ju," he called her, for Julie. His Paris home, approximately ten feet square, was no Richmond Hill. A "very high bed," an "immense table," and a single chair all but filled it. Still, as he told Theodosia, there was this advantage: "I can sit in my chair and reach every and anything that I possess."

As the cold months came on, life became a day-by-day scrabble for warmth and sustenance. "Winter approaches," he wrote. "No prospect of having leave to quit the empire, and still less of any means of living in it." When he went out, he informed his daughter, he wore "no surtout for a great many philosophic reasons; principally because I have not got one." His ovenlike fireplace was five feet wide and three deep, but it was built "on *French principles*—the principles of stupidity." The heat went up the chimney, the smoke into the room. He bethought himself of Benjamin Franklin, his idol among the American great. If Franklin could invent a fireplace capable of warming a room, so could Aaron Burr. He called in a "fumiste" and ragged the poor fellow to distraction, directing the laying of every brick. But, eureka! when the job was done and a fire laid, the temperature of the chamber shot up to 41 degrees Fahrenheit. He enjoyed the fullness of his triumph when, calling at the home of one of his few American friends in Paris, a wealthy widow, he found the thermometer in her luxuriant drawing room standing at thirty-five! But even his rectified fireplace was no proof against a prolonged January gale that blew "directly down" the chimney "with such force as to carry ashes and coals over the whole floor. I have been since 4 o'clock in purgatory . . . at length discovered I could exist by laying flat on the floor . . . laid a blanket; and reposing on my elbows with a candle at my side . . . have been reading 'L'espion Anglois' [*The English Spy*], translated from the English."

For weeks on end, he lived on rice and potatoes, or on the thick bouillon soups that Julie insisted on preparing for him. Often the meals were cold, the colonel having neither coal nor faggots to burn on his Franklinized hearth. All his life he had managed to cure minor ailments by fasting; now he discovered that fasting past a certain point could be detrimental to one's health. He suffered from an almost chronic diarrhea, a recurrent indigestion. How disgusting, he reflected. "A sick man," he observed, "is an object of contempt." But most of all he suffered from ennui, from the lack of something big to do. "[W]alked," he wrote of one winter night, "got to the Pantheon without thinking whither I was going. I then stood some minutes to discover who I was. In what country I was. What business I had there. For what I came abroad. And where I intended to go." The pain of this was very sharp to him. Much of his life was a struggle to escape it. Aaron Burr might have been a successful man had he been able to content himself with the practice of the law, at which he was unusually good. Or if he had been born with a creative talent to develop—but, as he himself more than once admitted, he had "great sensibility" to the arts but "no science" in any of them.

He survived the terrible months in Paris largely by borrowing where he could or by selling one by one the expensive presents he had collected to take home to his daughter and to "Gampilo," the grandson. Theodosia could send him nothing, desperately as she longed to do so; and it is not clear whether this was because her husband felt he had financed his impecunious father-in-law long enough or because Alston himself was short of cash as a result of the embargo. Burr borrowed sous from Julie—forty of them on one occasion, all she had at the time. He borrowed crowns from Vanderlyn and louis from his wealthier friends. Among the Americans in Paris willing to be seen with him was Edward Greswold, a onetime member of the New York bar, now residing in Europe and looking for speculative investments. The first time Burr asked Greswold for a modest sum, "one hundred and fifty guineas," the New Yorker refused; but later he lent the colonel "2000 francs, about 333 dollars." Within a month or so, however, this money was gone, much of it spent on gifts for Theodosia—gifts that by the time another month had passed the colonel had sold to keep himself alive. Once, limping on an injured and swollen foot, he walked miles out of his way to avoid passing a street vendor, an old woman to whom he owed a few sous. Once, in return for a hundred louis, he undertook "the translation from English into French of two octavo volumes," a labor enlivened by the presence in the book of "a quantity of abuse and libels on A. Burr." Privation brought with it a comprehension of things he never before had had reason to think about. "I now conceive," he wrote, "why the poor eat so much when they can get it." At intervals, as an economy, he tried to make do with cheap wines, only to decide that this was not wise. Though "a man may be a little the poorer for drinking good wine," he decided, "yet he is, under its influence, more able to bear poverty."

He entertained himself by entertaining Theodosia with word pictures of the Parisians and their city. "The people of this place are prone to detraction," he told her. He assumed that she would find it of interest to know that when the number of a Parisian house was "transparent, i.e. on a box where is a lamp, it is the signal of a gambling house." Stopping once to watch the people coming and going from one such emporium, he "contemplated with pity the anxious faces." He regaled her with a summary of the delights of walking in the French capital. "No sidewalks," he noted. "The carts, cabrioles, and carriages . . . run up to the very houses. You must save yourself by bracing flat against the wall . . . Most of the streets are paved as Albany and New York were before the revolution with an open gutter in the middle. Some arched in the middle, and [a] like gutter to each side . . . It is fine sport for the . . . hack driver to run a wheel in one of these gutters, always full of filth, and bespatter fifty pedestrians . . . braced against the wall." *Muse* was plentiful on these grimy promenades, but it was not always to his liking. The women of the city of love, he concluded, were cold and calculating. Such passion as they had was not in the heart, "only in the head." It is a fascinating man we accompany along the filthy streets of Paris: amazingly composed under stress, loyal to friends and tolerant toward enemies, self-defeating but undefeatable, sophisticated in many respects and naïve in many others. All this his daughter in South Carolina understood very well. "Believe me . . ." Theodosia wrote him, "you do not yet know the world."

Perhaps if he had known the French world better, he would have procured a passport sooner. Day after day, week after week, he lived in the anterooms of the bureaucracy, begging, cajoling, listening to the melancholy refrain, "no answer received." For a short time in the early fall he was given to understand that the coveted pass was about to be delivered, only to learn that such statements as he had heard to that effect were but empty talk. "I am just where I was four months ago," he lamented in late September, "only with less money."

Money! If he must remain in the empire, he must have money to live on. Then, in October, he was seized with a speculative possibility, a get-rich scheme of the sort he had entertained so often in the past. This one was connected with the Holland Land Company, a conglomeration of Dutch banks with economic interests on both sides of the Atlantic. Burr's link to this outfit went back to 1796 when, by a judicious distribution of bribes to the right individuals, he jammed through the New York legislature a law highly profitable to the Dutch entrepreneurs. By 1810, owing to developments generated by the war in Europe, the shares of the company had fallen to the merest fraction of their onetime value, and some speculators in Paris—Burr's friend Greswold among them—were quietly buying up the depressed stocks in the hope of profiting from an anticipated upswing. By mid-October 1810, Burr somehow had contrived to associate himself with this venture, and was looking forward to being the possessor of countless francs. When that happened, "Oh! what beautiful things I will send you," he exulted to Theodosia via the journal. "Gampillus, too, shall have a beautiful little watch, and at least fifty trumpets of different sorts and sizes . . . have been casting up my millions and spending it. Lord, how many people I have made happy." But there was a hitch. To realize his dream of wealth, he must get to Amsterdam, to the headquarters of the Holland Company; and to obtain a passport there he must first obtain one to the United States; and to do that he must find some way of getting around the representatives of his country in Paris, none of whom was even remotely interested in contributing to the prosperity of the arch-conspirator.

Burr initiated this ploy by asking for a *permis de séjour*, a certificate stating that its possessor was a citizen of the United States. The colonel's reasoning, nowhere explicitly expressed, seems to have been that once he had this paper in hand, no one could prevent him from going home. As Minister Armstrong was away, he directed his request to the chargé d'affaires, Jonathan Russell of Massachusetts, who replied that "the province of granting passports" belonged to the American consul in Paris and that Burr should apply to that official. Burr did, but with a sigh, for the consul was Alexander MacRae,* who as a member of the government's legal team at Richmond had made no secret of his conviction that the former Vice President was a proven traitor. "What a prospect!" the colonel exclaimed as he took pen and courage in hand and wrote to MacRae, whose prompt response was that "his knowledge of the circumstances under which Mr. Burr left the United States" rendered it his duty to decline giving him "either a passport" or a certificate of citizenship. "Although the business of granting" such documents was "generally confined to the consul," MacRae added, "the chargé des affaires unquestionably possesses full authority to grant protection in either of those forms to any person to whom it may be improperly denied by the consul." Again, and with another sigh, Burr wrote to Russell, who, of course, supported the action of the consul. "The man who evades the offended laws of his country," the chargé d'affaires informed the colonel, "abandons, for the time, the right to their protection. This fugitive from justice, during his voluntary exile, has a claim to no other passport than one which shall enable him to surrender himself for trial for the offences with which he stands charged. Such a passport Mr. Russell will furnish to Mr. Burr, but no other." Dated 4 November, this communication left Burr's battle to escape the empire exactly where it had been for months; which is to say, nowhere at all. And so it might have remained had not the

---

* Burr spelled the name M'Rae, as many people did.

closing weeks of the year brought a development that from the standpoint of the weary petitioner can be described as a happy accident.

7

WHEN ON 1 DECEMBER Burr called at the home of the Baron de Dalberg, it was to learn that the baron's wife had forgotten all about a promise she had given to obtain for the colonel a ticket to an exhibit at the Louvre. Conscience-stricken, Dalberg gave Burr a note of introduction to Dominique Vivant, baron de Denon, assuring him that Denon, as director general of the museums of France, could provide him with a ticket. An artist in his own right, Denon was also the author of a widely praised book on Egypt, and when later that day Burr arrived at his home he made a point of letting the museum director know that he had read and admired it. A case, it would appear, of following his own advice, for of "all races of animals," he once admonished his daughter, "authors are the vainest . . . No eulogies of their works can be too gross or too-often repeated." To attribute the subsequent upsurge in his fortunes to a piece of nicely turned flattery might be going a little far; but it helped, for Denon took an instant liking to his well-read visitor. It has been written of Napoleon's museum director that he "enjoyed, but never *used* the confidence of the emperor." At any rate, when on 28 December the colonel was invited to Denon's house for a breakfast of oysters and turkey, he found among the guests "le Duc de Bassano, secretary of state." The breakfast began at 3:30 in the afternoon, and when it ended at about five, Bassano asked Burr to accompany him into an adjoining room. There the secretary listened with care to the American's recital of his futile attempts to get out of France and responded with such encouraging remarks that when Burr got back to 7, rue du Croissant he was able to write in the diary that he had reason to believe that the long-sought passport would be in his hands in the near future.

It was. But precisely how it got there, we may never know; for suddenly, on 18 February 1811, the journal falls silent. There are no entries between that date and mid-May. It was during this interval that the arrangements were made for Burr to leave the empire, and for the relevant events of the period we must depend on some extant letters—two of them to Jonathan Russell, another two to Theodosia, and a letter received by Burr from a friend in Paris. The story which emerges from these somewhat confusing communications runs thus:

Early in April, Burr learned that he could have a passport to any place he wished to go, but by the end of the following month he had been notified that this precious document had been lost in the course of its passage through the bureaucratic maze, and that it would be at least another six weeks before a replacement could be issued to him. Eager to consummate the Holland Company deal, Burr decided to put the waiting period to good use by making a hurried trip to the Netherlands. Consequently, when the journal resumes on 14 May, we find him passing through the French town of Arras, en route to Amsterdam.

One of his first actions, after reaching that busy seaport four days later, was to seek out the local American community in the hopes of finding a ship that could carry him to the United States. He found one "of near 400 tons" called the *Vigilant*, but was disappointed to learn from its captain, a New Englander named Combes, that the vessel had been confiscated by the authorities and was under orders to remain where it was for the time being. On 23 May the colonel visited the offices of an Amsterdam business establishment and deposited "7000 francs" to be laid out "in Holland Company actions." Later he got some money for himself out of this transaction. How much is not known, though it was obviously considerably short of the millions he had dreamed of spending on Theodosia and Gampilo. Apparently, his financial situation had eased somewhat, for on the twenty-seventh he left the big Dutch city to spend the next two weeks enjoying a sightseeing tour of the low countries of Holland, Germany, and Belgium.

On his return to Amsterdam, he was delighted to hear that the *Vigilant* had been released from custody. Immediately he arranged with Captain Combes to book passage for the United States, provided he could obtain the requisite passport by the time the vessel was ready to sail; and on 22 June he was back in the capital of France, trying to bring this long endeavor to an end. Again the American diplomatic corps gave him trouble. "On my return to Paris," he informed the French minister of police, "I applied to Mr. Russell . . . to give another [passport], which he refused to do." Meanwhile, Burr had turned for help to his friends. Dalberg and Denon had good advice for him. The Duc de Bassano, recently appointed by the emperor to succeed Cadore as minister of foreign affairs, had something even more effective—information concerning Mr. Russell which that upright son of New England did not wish the world to know. On 17 July, Bassano sent a note to a lady temporarily out of the city, instructing her to return to Paris for the purpose of telling Mr. Russell that Aaron Burr was to have his passport. This was not the new foreign minister's only kindness to Burr. When on 20 July the colonel, passport in hand, began his return journey to Amsterdam, all his debts in Paris had been discharged—thanks to a generous loan from the Duc de Bassano.*

---

* One of the codicils of Burr's last will and testament reads in part: "I give to the Duke de Bassano [blank] Francs, for which he has my note, payable without interest, which sum he advanced me in the most liberal and delicate manner . . . which I very Much regret that it has not been sooner in my power to repay. And which I now beg him to receive with my thanks." (Original in the collections of the Henry E. Huntington Library and Art Gallery.) Born in 1763, Bassano was still living at the time of Burr's death in 1836.

He arrived in Amsterdam on 20 July, and was greatly relieved to discover that the *Vigilant*, scheduled to sail at an earlier date, was still standing by at the Dutch-owned island of Texel in the North Sea and would not be leaving for some weeks. Quickly, he looked up Captain Combes and paid his passage money, 480 guilders, a sum raised by selling more of the presents intended for the folks at home. He had exactly thirty French louis in his pockets when on 13 September he stepped aboard the boat which was to carry him and the other passengers to Texel. "I feel as if I were already on the way to you," he wrote Theodosia in the journal, "and my heart beats with joy." In truth, it would be another seven months before Aaron Burr laid eyes on his native land. Only a few hours after the *Vigilant* set sail, bound for Boston, it was seized by his Majesty's frigate *La Désirée* and carried to the British port of Yarmouth, to be placed on trial as a potential prize of war.

Now, through no fault of his own, Burr was within the jurisdiction of the country that two and a half years before had banished him from its shores. What was he to do? With only a few coins to his name, how was he to live while waiting to learn whether the *Vigilant* was to be sold as a prize or allowed to proceed to Boston? Could he join his friends in London, 114 miles away? If he did, would the authorities arrest him? He wrote to John Reeves in the Alien Office. Reeves responded promptly. Yes, he could come up to the British capital. No, the government would not bother him. In mid-October he was back at Yarmouth. Word had reached him that the trial of the *Vigilant* had been postponed. It was anybody's guess when that matter would be settled. Meanwhile, he must do something about his luggage, for notwithstanding the sale of many of his smaller possessions, his personal property still filled "thirteen trunks, boxes, and portmanteaus." Included were three hundred books purchased in Europe, some of them rare items of considerable value. At Yarmouth he arranged for everything to be carried to London on a coasting vessel, while he himself returned there by stage.

Already many of the old doors in the British metropolis had opened to him. Once more, he came and went from the house of the William Godwins as though he were a member of the family. Once more, Jeremy Bentham's Bird Cage was his second home in the city. Here he took Christmas dinner, and for its master he penned a letter about General Miranda, a letter (later forwarded to the general) which Bentham requested, stating that all advocates of independence for Spanish America should work together and respect one another. "[T]hat part of Miranda's character which constitutes his greatest eulogy," Burr wrote in this communication, "is the purity of his political creed, and the constancy and consistency with which he has persevered in it . . . With these sentiments, you may be assured of my disposition to contribute, if it should happen to be in my power, to the success of Miranda and his patriot countrymen. There is a possibility . . . that I may mingle personally in the affairs of Spanish America." X was not dead in the colonel's mind; it never would be. No sooner was he back in London than he was in touch with Mariano Castilla and with such other Latin American revolutionaries as were still in residence there.

In England as in France, he pursued a variety of get-rich schemes, in an effort to pass hours that otherwise would have been demoralizingly empty. With William Graves, a London broker, he canvassed the possibilities of an improved steamship, calculated to make both of them wealthy. He picked up a pamphlet describing a cheap way of extracting vinegar from trees, and at once there took form in his imagination a great and profitable vinegar-producing installation in the forests of America. He spent days laboring over this "chymical experiment" in a laboratory lent to him by one of Bentham's scientist friends. Dreaming of millions, he supported himself by small loans and by parting with more of his dwindling stock of presents, living in a dingy room in Clerkenwell Close (rent, eight shillings a week) and, when not invited out, dining as a rule on boiled rice and milk.

February 1812 brought first good and then bad news. The good news was that the *Vigilant* had been acquitted and could now continue its journey. The bad was that Captain Combes had altered his destination. Instead of heading for Boston, he now was planning to go to New Orleans. He trusted this change would be all right with Burr, but it was not all right. New Orleans, as far as he knew, was still "under a sort of military regime, and in the hands of my inexorable enemies." And while he was tussling with this difficulty, even worse news arrived, "A bad, bad day," he noted in the journal on the twenty-second. "My hopes of being soon in New Orleans, or elsewhere in the United States, have vanished. A letter this day . . . from the captain [Combes] says that he was been warned *at his peril* by the [American] consul at Yarmouth . . . not to take me on board, and that he is afraid, and must refuse me passage." Willy-nilly, Burr blamed this development on Jonathan Russell, who had been shifted from France to England and was now the American chargé d'affaires in London. But never mind the reason for the problem, he lectured himself; his job was to solve it by finding another vessel willing to take him across the Atlantic. He asked Combes to return his passage money, but the captain had been compelled to pay the costs connected with the trial of the *Vigilant* and said he couldn't do so. He offered Burr ten pounds, which the proud colonel disdainfully refused. He should have taken it, for when in mid-March he was put in touch with a Captain Potter, ready to carry him across on the ship *Aurora*, he was hard put to raise the thirty guineas demanded in advance for his passage. "It seems I must always move in a whirlwind," he wrote of his frantic effort to convert Theodosia's cambric handkerchiefs, Gampilo's medals, and some bottles of seltzer water into cash. When on Wednesday 24 March he learned that the *Aurora* would be sailing at noon the following day, from Gravesend, a dozen miles down the Thames from London, he was still twenty pounds short.

Months before, John Reeves had lent him some money. Perhaps Reeves would help again. At the Alien Office, Burr quickly explained the nature of his plight, whereupon, without uttering a word, the young official wrote out a draft on his banker, "and how I did gallop across the park to said banker's to get my twenty pounds," wrote Burr.

But the colonel's well of woe was not yet drained. At the stagehouse, reached early the next morning, he discovered that the schedule had been changed, that the morning diligence to Gravesend had already gone. It was 1 P.M. before he was able to board another, late afternoon before he arrived at Gravesend, to be told that the *Aurora* "had sailed with the first ebb at noon" and was moving down the Thames. The colonel did the only thing he could—pledged almost all his remaining guineas in return for the promise of the owner of a wherry and his crew to speed him downriver to the departing ship. Night came on, the southwest wind was piercing, and the colonel in the little open boat was without an outer coat. Twelve miles below Gravesend, he cajoled the boatmen into halting briefly at a dockside tavern—"so benumbed," he noted in the journal, that he could not leave the wherry on his own or "even walk without help." A "good drink and a dish of tea" at the inn thawed him out, ninepence worth of straw strewn on the bottom of the boat rendered the remaining fifteen miles of the chase endurable, and exactly at midnight Burr climbed the ladder of the vessel that was to carry him across the Atlantic. On his passport and on the ship's registry he was listed as "Adolphus Arnot." In his journal that very night, he penned his final salute to Albion. If he ever visited that country again, he vowed, it would be "at the head of fifty thousand men . . . adieu, John Bull. Insular inhospitabilis, as it was truly called eighteen hundred years ago." The *Aurora* proved to be a good sailor, for only thirty-nine days later he was home. But not quite at his destination. Boston, where the *Aurora* docked on 4 May 1812, was not New York, and Burr had long since decided that if ever he got back to the United States, he would settle in his old home town as the one place where he could make a living as a lawyer—provided that the government refrained from arresting him and that his New York friends and supporters could persuade importunate creditors to leave him alone.

Nor was his destination immediately reachable. When on 5 May a wigged and heavily whiskered Mr. Adolphus Arnot stepped onto the docks of Boston, he carried with him exactly thirty-two dollars—nowhere near enough to cover the transference of his luggage and the purchase of a ticket on one of the vessels plying the coastal waters to New York City. Once more, to get where he wished to go, he had to engage in a weary round of selling and borrowing. He took quarters in a boarding house run by the widow of a sea captain, purchased a copy of the city directory, and carefully examined its contents, looking for names of the people he might know. He found one, a Mr. Jonathan Mason. A "college-mate" at Princeton, Burr recalled, "and heretofore, through all changes in politics, my friend." Mason, inquiry developed, was but recently retired after a prosperous mercantile career. Burr sent him two letters by messenger. In the first of these, he expressed the hope that should Mason "recognize the handwriting," he would not give away the "*incog.*" under which the colonel was living for the time being. In the second, he reviewed the "circumstances" which had so long detained him against his will in Europe. "Thus my finances have become exhausted," he explained, adding that he was the owner of some "six to eight hundred dollars" worth of books, which "I would propose to sell to you, or to deposit with you [as security for a loan] as you may prefer." Mason's first responses, conveyed verbally by the messenger, were a case of hemming and hawing. At length, however, he came right out and said what was on his mind. The former Vice President was not in good odor in Boston. Assisting him would be detrimental to the retired merchant's social and commercial standing.

Burr wrote off the effort to experience. Such things had happened to him in the past; they would happen again, frequently, in the future. Then, through offices of a newly made friend, he succeeded in selling two of the most valuable of his books to Dr. John Kirkland, president of Harvard College—and, in the twilight hours of 7 June, Aaron Burr found himself treading the cobblestones of the New York City waterfront. Cheerfully "and rejoicing in my good fortune," he hastened to 66 Water Street, where Sam Swartwout was living. But the house was dark and repeated knockings produced no answers from within. He walked on, looking for lodging, finally, at midnight, finding a room—already occupied by five other men—in a "plain house" along a dark alley. Back to 66 Water Street the next morning. This time Sam was home, and Aaron Burr's long conversation on paper with his daughter closes with these words: "He led me immediately to the house of his brother Robert, and here I am, in possession of Sam.'s room in Stone-street, in the city of New-York, on this 8th day of June, anno dom. 1812. Just four years since we parted at this very place."

14

"A Green Old Age"

FOR ALMOST THREE WEEKS, Burr remained hidden in the house on Stone Street, New York, while his supporters bestirred themselves on his behalf. The indictment against him in Ohio, they learned, was no longer a problem. After months of diplomatic wrangling, the United States Congress had signaled its intention of breaking off relations with Great Britain. The Madison Administration, bracing for the hostilities later known as the War of 1812,* had neither the time nor the inclination to pursue charges against Burr and Blennerhassett. John Wickham, writing from Richmond in response to an inquiry from Sam Swartwout, reported that "Col. Burr's friend in Phila. (Mr. Pollock I think)" had reimbursed one of the signers of the bail forfeited by the nonappearance of the defendants at the Ohio court; no proceedings against Luther Martin, another signer of the bond, had been taken. Only the numerous judgments for debt against the colonel presented a difficulty, and on Sunday 5 July 1812 he was able to inform an old Revolutionary War comrade that for the moment this situation, too, was under control. "Having so far arranged for my Creditors here that I shall have time to turn about," Burr wrote "fellow soldier" George Gardner of Newburgh,

* The declaration of war was issued on 18 June 1812, just eleven days after Burr's arrival in New York City.

359

New York, "I have taken a house at no. 9 Nassau Street, shall tomorrow open my office, advertise it in the papers, and go to work." On the morrow he did. A small tin sign, brightly lacquered and inscribed "A. Burr," announced to the world that with ten borrowed dollars and a law library lent by his onetime intimate friend and longtime political foe, Robert Troup, the former Vice President had embarked on a second legal career and was available to clients. And the clients came, hundreds of them on the first day alone. However the inhabitants of New York viewed Aaron Burr the man, they had not forgotten the skills of Aaron Burr the advocate. By the end of business twelve days later, his receipts in fees and retainers totaled $2,000. It was a hopeful beginning of a new life—to be followed, with stunning speed, by two awful tragedies.

A single mail in late July or early August brought separate communications from South Carolina, one from his daughter and the other from her husband. "A few miserable days past my dear father & your late letters would have gladdenned [sic] my soul," Theodosia wrote, "& even now I rejoice at their contents as much as it is possible for me to rejoice at anything— but there is no more joy for me, the world is a blank, I have lost my boy, my child is gone forever—he expired on 30th June—My head is not now sufficiently collected to say any further. May Heaven by other blessings make you some amends for the noble grandson you have lost." But that there were no amends for such a loss certainly crossed Burr's mind as he unsealed her husband's letter. It confirmed hers. Little Gamp had died on the thirty-ninth day of his eleventh year.* "That boy on whom all rested," Alston wrote, ". . . he who was to have redeemed your glory, and shed new lustre upon our families—that boy is taken from us." Neither he nor the boy's mother had yet decided how to give shape to their lives from now on. "My present wish," Alston informed his father-

* Born 22 May 1802, according to *PJAB* (Davis), II, 169.

in-law, "is that Theodosia should join you with or without me, as soon as possible." Yes, Burr doubtlessly agreed, for almost at once he was seized with a troubling premonition. He sensed that unless his daughter came to him in New York in the near future she might never get there at all. On this point he unburdened himself in a letter to Jeremy Bentham. It was a typical Burr letter: no lamentations, no effort to verbalize his grief, simply two statements of fact. "Theodosias [sic] boy, her only child is dead," he reported to his London friend, "& I have much reason to apprehend that she will not long survive him."

One of his many relatives, the only one so far as we know, endeavored to console him. This was his niece by marriage, Mrs. Robert Wescott, nee Catherine DeVisme Browne. Catherine learned of Gamp's death from a friend and on 3 August wrote the stricken grandfather from Philadelphia, averring her "inexpressible sorrow" and imploring "my dear uncle" to apprise her of the details "by *return mail*." Burr did not limit himself to a written answer. A few months later, his niece was reminding him of his declaration, while visiting at her home, that he intended to bring his daughter North if he had to use "force" to do so: a provocative remark, coupled as it was with Mrs. Wescott's repetition of local gossip to the effect that Alston was mistreating his wife. "[F]or God's sake," she wrote Burr, "by *a single word* give me some assurance on this subject." The "word" came promptly. Shortly thereafter, Mrs. Wescott was writing to "rejoice" at her uncle's assurance that the "surmises respecting" Alston's conduct toward Theodosia were groundless. "What a calumniating World is this," she observed, "& how cautious ought one to be in listening to malicious whispers." Whatever the "whispers," the problems connected with bringing Theodosia North took time to unravel. Alston's duties as the recently elected governor of his state made it impossible for him to accompany her, and with or without him the long trip overland by coach would have been too much for her failing strength. "You must not be surprised to see her very low, feeble, and emaciated," Burr was warned in a letter from Charleston. Obviously, the sick woman must be moved by water, and as speedily as possible. By the end of November, her father's retired lawyer friend Timothy Green was in South Carolina, sent there by Burr to help with the travel preparations and to serve as his daughter's escort. On 22 December, Green was in a position to assure Burr that the requisite arrangements had been made. He, Mrs. Alston, and one or two of her maids would be coming North on "the privateer *Patriot*, a pilot-boat-built schooner, Commanded by Captain Overstocks." Out privateering until recently, the *Patriot* had put into the port of Georgetown, South Carolina, and was now storing its guns below decks and refitting for a run to New York. The boat was a fast one, capable, it was understood, of reaching its destination in five or six days at the most. Although Alston had chartered it and was planning to send along a cargo of rice to defray Theodosia's expenses, Green somehow got the impression that he was displeased with the *Patriot*, that he regarded the little schooner as an "undignified" "mode of conveyance" for a governor's wife. But Mrs. Alston was "fully bent on going," and at noon 31 December 1812,* at the bar of the Georgetown harbor, Alston bade his wife goodbye. As a British fleet was known to be standing off the capes, he provided the captain of the *Patriot* with a note requesting that the vessel carrying his wife and her companions be allowed through. Later—much later—it was noised about that a British warship did stop the pilot boat. The note was read, the

---

* "All of Burr's biographers have mistakenly given the date of Theodosia's departure . . . as December 30," writes Ray Swick in his article "Theodosia Burr Alston" in the autumn 1975 issue of *The South Atlantic Quarterly*. "This is based upon the statement of Joseph Alston in a letter to his father-in-law dated 19 Jan. 1813, that 'I wrote you on the 29th ult. [i.e. December], the day before Theo sailed.' Alston corrected himself in a later letter to Burr dated 31 Jan. 1813, when he wrote, 'I parted with our Theo . . . about noon on Thursday, the last of December' . . . 31 December 1812 fell on a Thursday."

story goes, and the *Patriot* permitted to proceed—after which it was never seen again.

Sunk by the gale reported to have struck the coastal waters off Cape Hatteras in the opening days of 1813—or seized and scuttled by pirates? Both stories have been advanced. To the end of his days Burr, quite understandably, preferred to believe that his daughter, not yet thirty at the time of her disappearance, perished in a storm; but the accounts of piracy and murder on the high seas, repeatedly appearing in the press over the next fifty years, are not unconvincing. Typical of these newspaper reports, and significantly consistent with most of the others, was this statement in the 23 June 1820 New York *Advertiser:*

A gentleman recently from New Orleans, has communicated to a friend of the family of the late Mr. Greene [sic] that two of the Pirates, lately sentenced to suffer death at New Orleans, confessed that they composed part of the crew of the Pilot Boat *Patriot!* that after being at sea 2 or 3 days they rose upon the captain and passengers, and confined them below—when they stood close in shore, and after plundering the passengers of a considerable sum of money and plate belonging mostly to Mrs. Allston [sic], they launched the boat and scuttled the vessel, which soon filled and went down with the unfortunate inmates confined below. The dreadful tragedy was performed in the dead of night. These wretches succeeded in reaching the shore with the boat, and had thus far escaped detection and punishment for this horrible crime.

2

THERE IS NO NEED to labor the effects of Theodosia's disappearance on the men she left behind. Alston never recovered. "You are the only person in the world with whom I can commune on this subject," he wrote Burr as it dawned on him that both his son and his wife were gone, "for you are the only person whose feelings can have any community with mine. You knew those we loved." It angered the bereaved rice planter that the members of his family in South Carolina had never fully appreciated his son's "talents" and that they seemed to view the death of Theodosia as though it were "the loss of an ordinary" person. "Alas!" he exclaimed, "they know nothing of my heart. They never have known any thing of it . . . the man who has been deemed worthy of the heart of *Theodosia Burr* . . . will never forget his elevation." For two years Alston went through the motions of his governorship, after which, although elected to the state senate, he spent most of his time in seclusion on his estates, seemingly waiting for death.

Burr kept going. Outwardly he remained as calm, as collected as ever. Perhaps a little more so. Only occasionally in some of his personal communications did the inner turmoil surface. In a note to a relative, outlining the circumstances of his daughter's death he referred to the *Patriot*, Captain Overstocks commanding, as "the Patriot, Capt. Soustocks," the intrusion of the French word for "under" providing a slip of the pen interesting to post-Freudian readers. To Alston he described himself as "severed from the human race." Certain it is that he was now walled about within. Nothing could ever hurt him again, nothing at all.

For a time after his return to America, he seems to have been the beneficiary of a slight shift in public sentiment, of a feeling on the part of many of his fellow citizens that he had suffered enough, had been properly and adequately punished. But this tolerant attitude quickly subsided. For the rest of his life, he lived in the penumbra of popular disapproval, almost universally regarded as "an ambitious, intriguing, thoroughly disreputable politician, as Hamilton's murderer, a monster of licentiousness, a reckless trifler with feminine hearts, a traitor to his country . . . Machiavelli, Don Juan and Benedict

Arnold rolled into one"—in short, "a festering mass of moral putrefaction." Nor did the opprobrium cease with his death. As late as 1918, a historical magazine, recalling the visit to Astoria, Oregon, a hundred years earlier, of the colonel's stepson Bartow Prevost, apologized to its readers for connecting "even in the spirit of romance or gossip the distasteful name of Aaron Burr with Oregon history."

During the almost twenty-four years of life that remained to Burr, he coped as he best could with this proscriptive consensus. As he came and went on the streets of New York, it was his practice to avert his gaze when he saw an old acquaintance approaching, thus making it easy for the other person, were he so inclined, to pass him without speaking. When spoken to, he spoke back, always courteous, always the Chesterfieldian gentleman, always noticeably—and to some observers no doubt amusingly—out of style in the long single-breasted jacket, standing collar, and black knee breeches and stockings of an earlier age; and always, when in the company of people willing to listen, delighted to regale them with stories from a richly furnished memory. He attempted no defense of his past actions, offered no apologies, uttered no complaints, and claimed no enemies; and all in all was so seemingly unperturbed by the contempt in which he was held as to suggest that he found in this negative distinction some little solace for the losses he had endured.

"Why, colonel," a lady is reported to have said to him, "if they were to accuse you of murder, I don't think you'd deny it." His reply: "Why should I? What good would it do? Every man likes his own opinion best. He may have not a hundred thousand dollars, but he has his opinion. A man's opinion is his pride, his wealth, himself. As far as I am concerned, they may indulge in any opinion they choose." He was not always so forgiving of his detractors. Once, when a lady wondered "if you ever *were* the gay Lothario they say you were," he rebuked her with a flash of his luminous eyes and an uplifted finger. "They say! *they say!* THEY SAY!" he taunted. "Ah, my child, how long are you going to continue to use those dreadful words? Those two little words have done more harm than all the others."

Burr's interest in political affairs continued strong, but now he was most discreet about expressing them. "I know . . . my word is not worth much with Madison," he said to Dr. Ebenezer Sage, a New York congressman, soon after the outbreak of the War of 1812, "but you may tell him from me that there is an unknown man in the West, named Andrew Jackson, who will do credit to a commission in the army if conferred on him." After the war and after Jackson's celebrated victory over the British at New Orleans, Burr tried to launch what amounted to a one-man drive to break the hold of the Virginia dynasty on the Presidency by electing the Tennessean to the White House. Realizing that to put himself at the fore of such a movement would be to doom it from the first, the colonel endeavored to work through his son-in-law. When in November 1815 it became known that an impending congressional caucus was to nominate Virginian James Monroe to succeed Madison, Burr wrote to Alston, exhorting him to do everything in his power to see that this did not happen. On Monroe the colonel heaped the most scathing denunciations he ever directed at any human being; indeed, almost the only such denunciations he is ever known to have made. He described the nominee-to-be as "Naturally dull and stupid; extremely illiterate; indecisive to a degree . . . ; pusillanimous, and, of course, hypocritical; has no opinion on any subject, and will be always under the government of the worst men." He was being touted as a soldier in the Revolutionary War, but Burr knew from personal experience that Monroe had "never commanded a platoon, or was ever fit to command one." He called himself a lawyer, but in that field "Monroe was far below mediocrity. He never rose to the honour of trying a cause of the value of a hundred pounds. This is a character exactly suited to the views of the Virginia junto." Let the junto be destroyed and let Jackson be nominated for the Presidency. "If this project should accord with your views," he wrote Alston, "I could wish to see *you* prominent in the execution of it. It must be known to be *your* work."

A vehement call to arms, but Burr was wasting his eloquence. Alston was in the throes of his last illness, an illness obviously more of the spirit than of the body. He wrote back that his "sentiment" coincided with that of his father-in-law, but that "the energy, the health necessary to give practical effect to sentiment are gone. I feel too much alone, too entirely unconnected with the world, to take much interest in anything." These words were written on 16 February 1816, and on the following 10 September the wealthy rice planter was dead at the age of thirty-seven. His last message to his father-in-law was in his will, stipulating that all of Burr's debts to him were to be forgiven. Burr's attempt to use his son-in-law as a stalking horse in a Presidential sweepstakes was his last political fling of consequence, but it was not his last effort to influence the course of his country's affairs. There was to be one more such effort; that astonishing and little-known episode came toward the very end of his own long life, where it will be described.

To say that during his declining days he held aloof from the political wars is not to say that he was indifferent to them. He kept a close watch on the Presidential election of 1824, the first such campaign in which Jackson participated as a candidate. "I well remember," a Quaker friend of the colonel wrote him in the fall of that year, "the first time I saw thee on thy return from Europe . . . thou observed that *Jackson was thy man* . . . I hope now that he will be elected and that he may prove as well disposed to thee, as thou was to him at that time." But it was to be another four years before Jackson went into the Presidency, and when he did, he offered nothing to Burr and Burr was too proud to ask for anything. Some of his friends, to be sure, benefited from the change of Administration. Sam Swartwout, for one; to Sam went the collectorship of the Port of New York, a trust he proceeded to betray by funneling over a million dollars of federal money into his own pockets. As late as 1832, in his seventy-fourth year, Burr was writing to Aaron Ward, a New York congressman, to wish him "fun and honor & profit" during Ward's forthcoming fight for reelection, a sentiment consonant with Burr's assumption, so annoying to Jefferson and other statesmen of his day, that "fun and honor & profit" were what politics was all about.

His concern with the affairs of Latin America never left him. One of his last actions before leaving Europe was to impress on his Argentinian friend Mariano Castilla how vital it was for the Ibero-American revolutionaries to rely on their own resources. "To prevent a dependance [sic] on foreign countries for arms," he advised Castilla, "you should establish manufactories at home . . . The machinery, and everything necessary for such an establishment, could be had from the United States." Once back in New York, Burr devoted a good deal of time and labor to furthering the independence movements rapidly emerging in all the colonies of Spain and Portugal in the New World. Agents of these developments were pouring into the United States. Sooner or later, practically all of them got in touch with the New York attorney. Burr did what he could to assist them in their search for funds, ships, and supplies; and his letters during these years show that their sources of financial aid in America included, among others, William Duane of the Philadelphia *Aurora* and members of the Rodney, Ogden, and Biddle families. From time to time, Burr acted as a legal representative for Latin American interests. In 1817, in the New York Supreme Court, he defended John Novion against charges arising from Novion's privateering activities under a "patente de corso" sold to him by Pedro Gual on behalf of the government of Cartagena and involving a boat captained by Luis Aury, ruler of Amelia, an island off the coast of Florida then being used as a shelter for privateers illegally fitted out in the United States to prey on Spanish vessels. In 1818, in the same forum, the colonel represented Francis Ribas, a brother-in-law of an aunt of Simón Bolívar, in a suit concerning a family estate.

Burr's contact with some of the Ibero-American revolutionary agents was frequent and intimate. With most of them, however, it was occasional and indirect, with two English-born merchants, John Alderson and Robert Cartmel, acting as intermediaries. In 1817, Alderson, a native of Chester, moved with his family to Philadelphia and soon became one of Burr's regular correspondents. When Antonio Gonçalves da Cruz arrived in New York to raise money for an expedition against the Portuguese crown in Rio de Janeiro, Alderson sent him to Burr. "I hope to God," Alderson wrote, "you may be of use to him . . . I'm afraid the services of these fine fellows will be comparatively lost without talents like yours to give them lustre." When in 1819 the mercantile enterprises of Robert Cartmel fell into disarray, Burr's skills were called on to free him from debtors' prison. The full picture of Burr's involvement in the Spanish-American independence struggles of the early nineteenth century cannot yet be presented, as many of the details remain buried in the archives of South America. Eleanor V. Shodell, after a search in some of these sources and others, concludes that Burr's motives were neither altogether patriotic nor altogether mercantile. "Rather," she writes, he "combined his belief in the patriots' cause with a shrewd sense of the economic opportunities awaiting him if independence were achieved. By seeking the good will of the patriots who came to the United States for help he proved the sincerity of his attachment to the cause of independence. By involving himself in the sometimes shady financial arrangements that accompanied and followed the wars of revolt, he also proved his devotion to the dollar."

On nonpolitical matters close to his heart—the superior qualities of Quakers, the war of the American Revolution, and the education of women, to list a few—Burr was always willing to speak his piece. "Your account . . . of your quaker connections . . . gratified me much," he notified one of his legal associates. "I advise you to adhere to them . . . They understand Social life better than the other denominations—they indemnify themselves in their domestic intercourse, for the privations to which their institutions subject them in those which we call public amusements—you will find in their Social circles . . . Ease, Vivacity & a decorous freedom which you will seek in Vain among the self-styled fashionables, the devotees of dissipation." Burr was getting on in years when in 1833 he received a visit from Judge Benjamin Silliman of Brooklyn, a grandson of one of the officers with whom the colonel had served in the Revolutionary War. The judge had heard that Burr had once planned to write a history of the conflict, and wondered why he had never done so. Burr listed three reasons. One was that he "no longer had a motive for" such an undertaking, since "he had outlived all for, or of, whom he would wish to write." Another was that the copious notes he had assembled for the book had been stored in tin boxes and left with his daughter, and these had disappeared when she did. And the third reason was that the account he had in mind would have been so unlike the "received history" of the war that no one would believe it, for the reason "that the world had always rather repose in a lie than in truth . . ." As for the schooling of women—a young foreigner, calling at the colonel's office one day, found the aging lawyer's observations on that subject worthy of preservation in his diary. Burr, the young man recalled, expressed "surprise that so little" was being done to advance "female education," that it was more important than the education of men. His reasoning was that, until the age of twelve, both sexes received "nearly all of their ideas and impressions" from their mothers. "Women," Burr added, were "the repositories of all the moral virtues," and it was from them that men drew whatever "excellence" they possessed. May we suppose that he was thinking of the mother he never knew and against whose "desertion" of him at an early age he at times did seem to be thrashing his mental fists? Did he perhaps suspect in himself a certain lack of the moral sensibility, of which, in his view, mothers were the natural carriers?

Once back in his native land, he made a point of getting in touch with some of his closer relatives. At least one of them (most likely there were others) spurned these overtures. This was his late sister's husband, Tapping Reeve, founder and head of the famous law school in Litchfield, Connecticut, and chief judge of the superior court of his state. What makes the aloofness of Burr's brother-in-law a little puzzling is that Federalist Reeve was no stranger to the risks involved in bucking the powers that be, having once tangled with President Jefferson under circumstances which came near to landing him in jail. More to the point, the two men had much in common. Reeve has been described as the "first eminent lawyer" in America to "arraign the common law of England, for its severity and refined cruelty, in cutting off the natural rights of married women and placing their property as well as their persons at the mercy of their husbands." Perhaps it was while Aaron was studying law in his brother-in-law's office that his own pronounced opinions on this point took form. Nonetheless, in 1813 feminist Reeve wished to have nothing to do with feminist Burr. During the latter's absence in Europe, his late sister's only child, Aaron Burr Reeve, had died, leaving behind a widow named Annabelle and a son named Tapping Burr. On 20 August 1813, Burr wrote his brother-in-law chiding him for not welcoming him home, and requesting information concerning Annabelle and her boy. There was no answer. On 11 September, Burr wrote a second letter, more or less repeating the contents of his previous one. Again no answer.

Other kinsmen were more considerate. Guardian Uncle Timothy Edwards, now in his mid-seventies and in failing health,* was as warm as ever. Shortly after Burr returned, Timothy wrote to express the hope that one of these days he and his wife—the Aunt Rhoda Ogden Edwards who brought Aaron up—would have the pleasure of seeing the colonel at their house in Stockbridge, Massachusetts. Later Timothy wrote again, this time to ask a loan of "$100 or at least 50." It is a safe guess he got it, and the autobiography of a blind minister of Stockbridge describes Burr's subsequent visit to the home of his foster parents. During Burr's stay in Europe, Timothy from time to time called on the members of his church to pray for his wandering nephew, and Aunt Rhoda had not yet given up on him. Sometime during Burr's visit she took him into "the north room" for a private conversation. "Colonel Burr," she is quoted as saying, "I have a thousand tender memories associated with you . . . and I feel the deepest concern over your erring steps. You have committed a great many sins against God, and you killed that great and good man, Colonel Hamilton. I beseech you to repent, and fly to the blood and righteousness of the Redeemer for pardon. I can not bear to think of you as lost . . ." Burr's answer, according to the blind minister: "Oh, Aunt, don't feel too badly. We shall both meet in heaven."

Not every American, of course, endorsed the conclusion of a widely read nineteenth-century magazine that there "never was a greater villain than Aaron Burr—never!" Burr was in his seventies when in the spring of 1832 he had a visit in his office from George W. Johnson, a lawyer from Buffalo, New York. Johnson had never seen the other attorney before, and

---

* He died 28 October 1813, in his seventy-fifth year.

afterwards he jotted down his impressions. *"Col. Burr,"* he wrote:

> Has a green old age. Dresses well. Manners refined to simplicity. Approachable and frank. Communicative. Witty, especially on doctors and lawyers. In a word, a cheerful, fine-looking gentlemanly old man. All greatness, physical and moral, at first disappointing from simplicity. Col. Burr impressed me favorably at first sight, almost: A great man, and perhaps as good as the average of our statesmen. A victim of circumstances. Had another vote made him president instead of Jefferson,* their destinies might have been exchanged. He was a brave man. If it is ever right to kill in duel, he was right to kill Hamilton. It was a fair fight between one duelist and another, and both military men. He was fond of women, but was always decent: worse offenses than that. Not by any means a model man—a good man; but not so bad as it is the fashion to paint him.

3

AT THE TIME of his return to the United States in 1812, Burr was in his fifty-seventh year. It was a rather advanced age at which to begin a new career, but on the whole his business prospered. It "affords me a decent support," he wrote Alston, and in 1813 a South Carolina newspaper estimated his law practice to be "worth $30,000 per year." Whatever his income, it was never remotely equal to his obligations. These constituted a bottomless pit that could never have been filled even had he harbored a burning desire to do so, and

---

* The statement that Burr missed the Presidency by only one vote has been endlessly repeated, probably because it has a satisfyingly dramatic ring. The actual mathematics were these. In the electoral college Burr and Jefferson tied, seventy-three votes apiece. On the thirty-sixth and decisive ballot of the election in the House of Representatives, where the vote was by states, ten of the then sixteen states gave their votes to Jefferson, four gave theirs to Burr, and the remaining two came in blank. See my earlier book, *Aaron Burr: From Princeton to Vice President,* 293–4.

there is no evidence that he did. All his life, where debt was concerned, Burr had ducked and feinted, and this was his practice to the end. Luther Martin sued him for $20,000 (ostensibly for legal services) and judgment was rendered and marked satisfied on the docket; but this was a friendly transaction, designed to stall off other creditors. Burr assured Alston that he had learned his lesson, that he was never going to borrow again; but this would appear to have been wishful thinking. So complicated and speculative were some of the larger actions he steered through the courts that at intervals he had to borrow to keep them going. For these short-term loans, since the extent of his financial embarrassment was known to all, he had no choice but to resort to usurers. Year in and year out his creditors pursued him, most of them getting little or nothing for their pains. In the fall of 1815, he informed Alston that during the preceding winter many of "his old creditors (principally the holders of the Mexican [expedition] debts) came upon me with vindictive fury. I was held to bail in large sums, and saw no probability of keeping out of prison . . . This danger is still menacing but not quite so imminent." And so he lived for the rest of his life—in the shadow of the jailhouse.

It did not keep him from working hard—or for that matter from playing hard, for the ability to ferret out entertainment never deserted him. Once more, he rode the judicial circuit, passing a portion of each year at the courts in Albany, in Utica, and in other parts of the state. "Arrived this evening [at Albany] . . . having been forty-five hours in the stage without intermission," he reported to one of his assistants in his seventy-eighth year. "Stages in very bad order . . . the curtains torn and flying all about, so that we had plenty of fresh air." Compelled to spend time in a quiet village, he asked the tavern-keeper if anything of interest was going on and was directed to a traveling exhibition of waxworks. There he came upon a crude tableau, showing him and Hamilton firing at one another on the dueling grounds of Weehawken. Attached to its base were these lines:

> O Burr, O Burr, what hast thou done?
> Thou hast shooted dead great Hamilton.
> You hid behind a bunch of thistle,
> And shooted him dead with a great hoss pistol.

We do not need the word of his fine biographer, James Parton, to know how Burr reacted: he laughed.

Indifferent though he was to his creditors, he was always vulnerable to a hard-luck story and seemingly incapable of denying a request for help from a friend or relative in need. He was a compulsive giver; the attribute would seem to be common to the gambling temperament, of which he was so conspicuous an example. "Oh God what is to become of me," Catherine Bolton wondered in a despairing note to him, "left without a friend in the fear of imprisonment in a house without a frock to put on but I shall trust to your kindness . . ." The trust was well put. "I stand security for Mrs. Boltons [sic] rent," Burr assured her landlord. "If you can let me have but $5 . . . it will be sufficient to relieve our present wants," Mrs. Hector Scott wrote him from New Jersey. "I beg you to accept our thanks for what you have already done for us." Young Samuel B. H. Judah, just out of prison, turned to Burr in his struggle to create a new life for himself. Samuel expressed a desire to read law in the colonel's office. The wish was promptly granted. From Samuel Bradstreet in Albany, elderly and impecunious member of an otherwise wealthy family, came a tale of woe. "I now find out when too late," Bradstreet lamented, that "it is an abominable crime to be poor . . ." The unfortunate man needed enough "to buy new clothes and to move to another town." Within a month after these wants were transmitted, Bradstreet was writing to tell Burr that it was "past my means of expression to thank you sufficiently." In 1819, Luther Martin, the famous Maryland attorney who had defended the colonel so ably at Richmond, suffered a paralytic stroke which left him unable to work for the remainder of his long life. About a year later, Burr moved the old lawyer into his New York home and cared for him there for the next three years.

As his practice grew, he took on assistants: students, clerks, office managers, and on occasion a partner. His surviving legal papers yield the names of some of them. They also yield some of his comments about them. Of Gurdon W. Lathrop, who joined the staff in 1813 and was still there at the time of his death of cholera in 1831: "a man of decided talents," said Burr. "His cases were prepared with great industry . . . But his habits were periodically very bad. For weeks, sometimes for months, he would confine himself to business, a model of regularity and sobriety. [Then he would go on a drunken spree] and come back months later, watch gone, clothes torn. I furnished him with means to renew his clothes as often as he returned destitute . . . In no respect, was Mr. Lathrop an ordinary man." Thomas H. Flandrau: "has talents & learning," Burr informed the mother of a woman to whom Flandrau appears to have proposed marriage. "But his habits are eccentric owing to the influence of pride & passion & possessing no great share of firmness of purpose his conduct seems generally the result of accident or chance." The streak of Puritanism in Burr lay close to the surface.

Running through what remains of his correspondence during his last twenty-four years are a handful of letters penned by some of his women friends. A series of chatty effusions, originating in Albany and seemingly the work of a very young admirer, contain a number of teasing references to the colonel's enduring reputation as a ladies' man. "You had better when you write to Mrs. De^n," Mary S. Chalmers warned him, "tell her to discharge the little girl she has named Betsey—as she goes Every where telling people that Col^n B— only comes to

her Mistress at *night*—and then he is muffled up &c &c . . .
and another terrible story I have heard about you and a French
Lady who has a young Child . . ." Mary addressed Burr as
her "Honored & Revered Friend," and in one of her outpour-
ings expressed the hope that he had had "a pleasant journey,"
wondered whether he had wasted "one thought on your poor
good for nothing Mary," and said she did not "have time for
a long letter," adding that she was sure he would say "thank
god for that," as she enjoyed writing him and sometimes did
so as much as three times a day. Melancholy wafted from a
communication from a Mrs. S. Clark in Philadelphia, who
reminded Burr that he had once "honored" her with his friendship, confessed that during the intervening years she had given
"herself up to the dreadful vice of intoxication," and begged
him to get and send to her a trunk she had left with a couple
in New York as security for an unpaid laundry bill. The
"Cloathes" in this "old white Hair-trunk," she explained, were
"not of much value," but it held "a number of family papers—
which it would be cruel to have exposed to the World." Much
different in manner were the literate and world-weary musings
of Catherine B. Thompson, a schoolmarm in Beaufort, South
Carolina. To her Burr sent copies of Bentham's works and with
him she shared her Goethean repinings at the crassness of life.
"I am well," she assured him, "but in that I do not rejoice, why
should I rejoice at a long continuance in a world where nothing
but Sorrows and vexations fall to the lot of the only beings in
it I love." She had come to think of the earth as a "paradise
of fools and of fools only." She hated crowds, she told him,
"because in crowds every body tried *to appear* happy & nobody
is so—I wonder how the 'great multitude whom no man can
number' continue to be so happy in heaven where there is
always sunshine & always a crowd." She undertook a translation for Burr, but it went slowly, owing to the constant inter-
ruptions by the "unfledged reptiles" on whose tuitions she
depended. Often she covered reams of paper with her thoughts,

only to decide not to send them on "because I can't bear to Annoy a Man of Sense with 'Such stuff as *letters* are made of.' "

The love letters, if such they may be called, vouchsafe a few romantic passages and a few echoes of long-ago intimacies, fondly remembered; but only those written by Mrs. Rebecca Smith Blodget, a Philadelphia widow, can be described as pointing to a relationship of some depth and significance. A surviving engraving shows Mrs. Blodget to have been a handsome and aristocratic-looking woman, and her letters to Burr bespeak a good mind and a strong character. It appears from her half of the correspondence—his half being lost—that their acquaintanceship went back to about 1787, when Rebecca, the daughter of a Reverend "Dr. Smith," was fifteen. For her it was love at first sight, but at that time Burr was happily married to the first Theodosia and in 1791 or 1792 Rebecca became the wife of Samuel Blodget, only to seek out Burr in an effort to resume their old friendship after her husband's death. The ostensible purpose of her earliest communication to the colonel, a note dated 10 June 1814, was to enlist his legal services in an effort to assert her equity in a tract of upstate New York land belonging to her late father's estate. Plainly, other property was involved in this matter, for shortly after Burr entered the case, we find him writing to Gurdon Lathrop that "I have [told] Mrs. Blodget that she may Convey to you her 1000 acres of land in Delaware in order to facilitate partition." Though references to this litigation recurred in several of Rebecca's subsequent letters, they were quickly overshadowed by themes of a more personal nature. In August 1814, she was scolding Burr for his delay in sending some promised instructions concerning her lawsuit, reminding him that their relationship was not exclusively legal, and imperiously demanding to know "how I have *deserved* to be so neglected by you?" By the summer of 1815, her words had assumed an even warmer tone. "If I did not love you more than all the rest of the world," she wrote him, "I shou'd be more inclined to give you a blow on the face than a kiss, to which both my daughter and myself are ready to welcome you *in September."* His visit, whenever it occurred, was not all that she had hoped it would be. "It was a bad thing to spend *a short* time with me," she lamented afterward. "I am restless & wish I had not seen you." Viewed as a whole, the picture conveyed by a correspondence which persisted off and on for almost a decade is that of an essentially amatory interlude, marked on her part by considerable ardor and by an obvious pride at being connected with an individual of Burr's background and fame; and on his part by a guarded response to her advances, followed by the growing alarm of a man confronted by problems beyond his ability to handle.

For it is quite clear that his legal labors on her behalf were unavailing, and the last of her letters to come down to us trace the melancholy ending of the affair. "I have been a whole week," she wrote him in early December 1823, "fighting for the courage to write this letter . . . requesting you for the first time in my life to send me a small sum . . . Singular in all my sentiments opinions & feelings—because a refusal from a stranger would not pain me—& because I ever wished to avoid laying myself under an obligation . . . which could . . . render my professions of friendship doubtful—When we parted on the Steam boat & I had no money 'to pay my way' you would have forced money upon me—I refused it, tho I fear I pained you in doing so—but I could do without [then] . . . but now I am facing life—ill—without flannel or money for my winters wood—I board at 3$ a week in a private family, where I am distracted by the noise of five small children which I am obliged to endure or sit without fire in my bedroom where I now write to you . . . rolled up in a blanket—If you can oblige me I know you will—if not, your silence on that subject will afflict on my heart the pang of knowing that *you* are *without the means."* A few weeks later, she was writing him again, this time in a happier vein. Word had reached her that Burr had won a big case, was now in possession of some funds. If so, she had another favor to ask—not for herself, however, but for her son, John Adams Blodget. She described John as a young lawyer struggling to get started in the "wilds of Pennsylvania." It occurred to her that now that Burr was rich, he might wish to retire. Actually he was not rich, but she could only go by what she had heard. If he now decided to give up his practice, she ventured, perhaps he would be good enough to turn over his current causes to son John. With the penning of this request in the closing days of 1823, the record falls silent—to be broken approximately one year later by what appears to have been Rebecca's last message to Aaron. "I read your short letter in reply to the one I wrote you by Captain Walsh," she told him, "but it was not calculated to soothe my feelings . . . Your reason for not writing to me was, that my letters were filled with details of distress which you had not the power to relieve. O, surely you could not suppose me capable of making [known] such details with a [hope] . . . of obtaining relief from you! Alas! I am no stranger to your feelings or your circumstances—I never descended to *indirect* measures[.] If you were rich I should directly and *unashamedly* ask you for *every thing* unless, which is highly probable, you prevented me by giving it before I could ask it—but not being rich, believe me, I have felt really as much for your difficulties as for my own and regard hearing from you but a continuation of that regard to which I think myself entitled . . . by the constancy of my friendship for nearly 35 years & when I tell you of my distresses, it is because it is a relief to my own heart."

Rarely in Burr's personal papers for this period do we encounter the names of any of the men who figured in the dazzling escapades of his earlier life. Consequently, we have no way of knowing the extent to which the colonel was aware of their diverse fates. Of the six persons indicted with him on charges of treason and misdemeanor, only Davis Floyd was convicted, and the circumstances surrounding his trial in Indiana Territory in August 1807 suggest that his fellow Hoosiers did not take his crimes very seriously. Shortly after fulfilling the terms of his sentence—a $20 fine and three hours in jail!—Floyd was elected clerk of the lower house of the territorial legislature. Later he was given a circuit judgeship. Still later, he was named to a federal commission and sent to West Florida, from whence he wrote Burr in February 1825 to remind him that some of the moneys Floyd had expended in the interests of the expedition had never been repaid and to ask the colonel to "procure for me a few Law Books," saying that "any Kind almost" would be acceptable. The minute the last of the charges against Jonathan Dayton was nolle prossed at Richmond, "old slyboots," as Harman Blennerhassett dubbed that enterprising gentleman, hastened West to pick up the bits and pieces of his land speculations in the Ohio Valley. His fortunes rebuilt in this manner, the former senator returned East, to pass the residue of his life in comfortable obscurity at his New Jersey home.

Two of the other indictees—Senator John Smith of Ohio and Blennerhassett—paid dearly for their association with Burr. After a move to expel Smith from the Senate failed by only one vote in 1808, he resigned from that body—only to discover on returning to his mercantile business in Cincinnati that the people there would no longer deal with him. By 1809 nothing was left of his once extensive estate, and in 1810 he left Ohio, never to return. His last years were spent in St. Francisville, Louisiana, where he died on 10 July 1824, a victim, according to a perceptive student of his life, of public misunderstanding and of the schemes of enemies, some of whom were at least as closely linked to the Burr "conspiracy" as was Smith himself. To Blennerhassett, the years following the collapse of the expedition were a long and losing struggle with poverty and ill health. Rejoining his wife and family in Mississippi Territory in 1808, the onetime master of the enchanted isle purchased in the vicinity of Port Gibson a 1,000-acre cotton plantation known as La Cache, "the hiding place." But dirt-farming was not the answer for Harman and Margaret Blennerhassett. By 1814, the Jefferson embargo and the War of 1812, coming on the heels of mounting debts, had forced them to put La Cache up for sale; and four years later, their funds practically gone, they left the Mississippi Valley. Disappointment awaited them at their next stopping place, Montreal, where a promised position for Harman in the Canadian court system fell through as a result of the sudden death of an influential friend. That they survived at all was owing to the kindness of one of Harman's sisters, a spinster, who took them into her home in England. There Harman died, at the age of sixty-six, in 1831.

At Richmond, James Wilkinson only narrowly escaped being added to the list of those indicted for treason, but from that point on he lived a charmed life—which is to say that the arm of Thomas Jefferson proved long enough to protect him for the rest of his days. From three congressional investigations and two court-martials the "monster of iniquity" emerged unscathed. In 1813 he was commissioned major general and sent to the St. Lawrence frontier, where his ineptitudes as a commander contributed spectacularly to the American losses on that front in the War of 1812. Withdrawn to Washington, he quarreled with the Secretary of War, was dropped from the service, and wrote his *Memoirs of My Own Times*, a bombastic and confusing miscellany of gingerly selected letters and self-serving reminiscences. For a while after the publication of the *Memoirs*, he resided on a plantation below New Orleans. Then he moved to Mexico, where he was awaiting the outcome of a Texas land claim when death came on 23 December 1825. Friends arranged for his interment in the

Church of the Archangel San Miguel, and there he lies with others in a common vault.

4

MUCH OF BURR's legal exertion during the decade following his return from Europe went into a series of court actions known collectively as the Medcef Eden Case. The history of this now famous proceeding can be said to have begun in 1775 when Medcef Eden the older, an English-born brewer in New York City, married Martha Whittier Pelletreau, the daughter of John Whittier of Fairfield, Connecticut, and the widow of Elias Pelletreau. Martha brought to her new home the three children of her first marriage, John Pelletreau and his two sisters, and later bore to her second husband two sons, Medcef Jr. and Joseph. When the older Medcef died in 1798, he provided generous bequests for his stepchildren but left the bulk of his estate—a large number of properties on Manhattan Island and in adjoining Westchester County—to his own sons. Under the terms of his will, Medcef Jr. and Joseph got approximately equal shares, and if either of them died childless, the survivor was to inherit the other's estate. Evidently, these young men were appreciative of the good things of this world; and just as evidently, they had little or no comprehension of its pitfalls. It took them only a couple of years to go from riches to rags. By 1800 they were broke and were borrowing at the bank of the Manhattan Company on the basis of three promissory notes endorsed by a couple of knowledgeable money-lenders then "in partnership under the name and firm of John and William Wood." When a year later the notes came due, neither of the brothers could pay; and by the end of 1801, Medcef had discharged his debts by assigning to one of the note-endorsing partners—John Wood, Jr.—all the lands and buildings devised to him by his father; and Wood, as trustee for Medcef's creditors, was arranging for the sheriff's sales that would convert them into money. Simultaneously, Joseph lost his portion of the patrimony as the result of foreclosures and public auctions instigated by creditors.

It is not known exactly when Aaron Burr learned of this financial debacle. It is abundantly clear that, when he did, the something in him which could not resist a thumping challenge was aroused; to say nothing of his acquisitive instincts, since, with every passing year, the real estate involved was increasing in value. Tradition has it that the Eden brothers went to Alexander Hamilton to ask if their possessions could be retrieved in the courts, and were told that they could not. The same tradition says that they also consulted with Burr, who said they could. All that can be stated with confidence is that shortly after the colonel reactivated his practice in New York —along about 1815, to be as precise as the record allows—he heard that Joseph Eden had died without issue, and at once set out in search of the remaining brother.

He found Medcef somewhere in Westchester County, again mired in debt and living in absolute destitution. The colonel was confident that some of the estate could be recovered, provided the surviving Eden was willing to put himself under Burr's control, becoming as it were a passive instrument in his lawyer's hand. Medcef accepted these terms and the colonel got busy. Only recently, Eden had married Rachel Wyatt Maltbie, widow of John Maltbie of Connecticut and mother by her earlier marriage of three small daughters, Sally Ann, Elizabeth, and Rebecca. Burr's initial step was to lodge Eden and his new family in the colonel's New York home. At the same time, or soon thereafter, he took into his law office John Pelletreau, Medcef's friend and half brother. Finally, Burr looked about for the funds that would be needed for the impending legal battle. Somehow, his own shaky finances notwithstanding, he acquired "upwards of eight thousand dollars." Then he went to court.

The most valuable pieces of the estate lay in New York City, but as most of these were held by the Bank of New York or other corporations capable of commanding first-rate legal counsel, Burr ignored them in the beginning. Instead, he concentrated on a farm in Westchester County occupied by one John Anderson. Privately, Anderson was given to understand that if he limited his resistance to token proportions he would be allowed to buy the place back at pretty much his own terms. Obviously, he acceded to this arrangement, for after the court action had ended, he continued living on the premises. Burr won this case, appealed it, and won again. Then, having established the precedents and principles on which he could proceed with some hope of success, he fell upon the properties in New York, deluging the courts with ejectment actions and with actions of trespass for mesne profits that kept several state and federal benches busy for the next ten years.

The case was too complicated for one attorney to handle, and the popular picture of Burr as shunned by the more distinguished members of his profession fades before the ease with which he obtained the assistance of some of the country's most celebrated lawyers. The list included Martin Van Buren, Daniel Webster, and Henry Wheaton, then reporter of the decisions of the United States Supreme Court. To be sure, there was talk to the effect that Van Buren lent his services out of a belated sense of filial obligation, gossip of the day insisting that the future President was one of the colonel's natural sons. But an extant court document shows that Van Buren, in return for a modest amount ($1,000), became the owner of twelve acres of the Eden estate. As this parcel of land lay within the boundaries of fast-growing New York City, perhaps "Little Van" regarded its conveyance to him as inducement enough. As one by one the elements of the estate reverted to Medcef Eden or his heirs, John Wood, Jr., came into court, seeking an injunction to halt the onslaught and claiming "the whole estate" as Medcef's assignee. The frightened moneylender admitted having executed a paper waiving his rights to some of the properties, but asserted that Burr had tricked him into this action. Wood's story was that Burr persuaded him to seek the advice of another lawyer, suggesting that he go to Edward Greswold, who had abandoned his residence in Paris and returned to the New York bar. Wood went to Greswold under the impression that he was talking to "an upright, impartial and disinterested counsellor at law," only to discover later that Greswold was associated with Burr in the litigation and had a "material interest" in its outcome. The judges rejected Wood's pleas, and early in 1824 the newspapers were crediting Burr with a gigantic triumph in the courts, and from many parts of the country individuals, under the mistaken impression that he was now rolling in wealth, were writing to remind him that he owed them money.

Medcef Eden was not around for the happy ending. He died on 24 July 1819, leaving a will that had the effect of making Burr the guardian of his three stepdaughters. It also gave the colonel the last word in the disposal by sale of the restored properties and stipulated that, should any of the daughters "marry without the consent of my friend Aaron Burr, she shall forfeit her share" in the inheritance.

The Medcef Eden Case enlivened Burr's later years in more ways than one. It gave him something big to do, something that drew heavily on his extraordinary, if not always prudently exercised, talents. It also gave him a family, or more exactly the beginnings of one, for the Eden girls* were only the first of the several children with whom he surrounded himself for many years, providing homes for them sometimes in Albany, sometimes in New York, and occasionally in other parts of the Empire State or in Philadelphia. Some idea of what life was like in these busy establishments can be gleaned

---

* By the time of the death of Medcef Eden the younger in 1819, the three girls had assumed their stepfather's surname and were known as Sally Ann, Elizabeth, and Rebecca Eden.

from a letter to Burr from one of his wards, written at a time when the child, a girl, was away from home temporarily. "How sorry I am you Cant find the keyes," she wrote. "The key to the Sideboard I laid over the fireplace in front of the looking glass. The key of the closet I left in the door. I have been here not quite two days and it appears a month; not but what I am perfectly satisfyed for they do every thing in their power to make me happy . . . but how can I be happy when I can't see you every day. I think all the time you want something I can get for you . . . What in the world is the matter with our old Black Cat? I think you had Better put her head in a poringer [sic] to keep her [in] . . . they have a delightful time here with bed Bugs as well as we had at home."

Inviting an old friend to visit him in 1823, Burr warned that "I am a housekeeper—with all my children about me." Some of the youngsters were relatives—Katherine and Phoebe Bartow, for example—members of his late wife's family, whose own homes had been diminished by the death of a parent. Some of them come down to us as nothing more than names in their guardian's correspondence—"Andrews," for one, who one winter day left the nest and went off to sea. At least two of the boys, Aaron Burr Columbus (who later changed his name to Aaron Columbus Burr) and Charles Burdett, were the colonel's sons by different women. Such at least was common report, for on this as on all private topics the colonel himself was noninformative. To a gentleman who chided him for accepting any boy or girl attributed to him by this or that woman, he is reported to have said that "when a lady does me the honor to name me the father of her child, I trust I shall always be too gallant to show myself ungrateful for the favor!" James Parton, in his fascinating study of Burr, dismissed out of hand the assumption that the little girls mentioned in his will—one of them six and the other only two at the time of Burr's death in his eightieth year—were his offspring. "[P]hysically impossible," argued Parton, who preferred to think that the colonel accepted the responsibility for these children in conformance with his chivalrous views on such matters. Burr, in the will, referred to them as "my Two Daughters" and made them his residuary legatees. Though at the time of his death the residue, about $10,000 worth of real and personal property, was unavailable owing to its devisor's indebtedness, the older daughter, Frances Ann Watson, subsequently received a small legacy as a result of Burr's ownership of a reversionary interest in a piece of real estate.

Aaron Columbus Burr, according to a knowledgeable student of the family, was the son of a Frenchwoman, "a member of the DeLisle family," who sent the boy to Burr along about 1813 or earlier. From Bergen, New Jersey, whence Aaron Columbus was sent to school, he wrote regularly to "Dear Godfather," exhibiting a way with the language that was the despair of his pedagogically fastidious mentor. In one letter, "In the morning in school," he told Burr, "I write, I read and say latin grammar and say epitome historique sacrée and in the afternoon I read and then cypher and spell and then I go home and drink tea at five o'clock and go to bead . . ." In another: "I will tride to spell better to please you. I was very sorry to here that you dit not like my letter . . . if I had a Dictionary I would look for avery woard." Perhaps Burr sent him a dictionary. At any rate, on coming to adulthood, Aaron Columbus learned the jewelry trade, became the owner of his own shop, prospered, married twice, sired a boy, and in his later years endeavored to interest President Lincoln in settling American blacks on a tract of land that Aaron Columbus and others had purchased in British Honduras.

Charles Burdett's mother was an American, and very much on the scene, her letters showing up with some frequency in Burr's correspondence. Her first name remains a mystery. As a rule, she signed herself "A. Burdett," sometimes "E.E.," and sometimes, when the whimsy was upon her, "A.B." Not that A. Burdett was all gaiety and froufrou. The impression that comes through is that of a woman of boundless complaints and unending demands. "It is a long time," she wrote Burr, "since the mother of [Charles] . . . made any request of a pecuniary nature but she is going this evening at a large party chez Mrs. ONeil, and would like a handsome *collar* to match with an elegant cape made by herself—what can the Col contribute toward the embellishment of said Mother—La belle niece will call for an answer at twelve."

Be it remembered that Voltaire, whom Burr read with such passionate approval in his younger days, was the father of several natural children, whom the great French liberal blithely abandoned to be raised in poorhouses and workhouses. Not Burr. He hovered over his chicks, natural or otherwise, as a hen over hers. As far as he was concerned, his creditors could go begging, but not his children. They must have the best of everything, and especially the best of the worlds of learning and the arts. He anguished over the problems incident to getting them educated. On this subject, as we know, his ideas were elevated and rigorous. Youth was not a time to be wasted on fun and games. All play and no work rendered one as dull as vice versa. Every hour, every minute must be devoted to sharpening the intellect, stocking the mind, strengthening the body, and improving the character. One must keep in view, Burr wrote the headmaster of a boys' school where one of his charges was enrolled, "the very great importance of forming at an early age, habits of industry, application to study." He saw to it that Charles Burdett ran the academic gamut as it existed at that time: from Hartwick Seminary near Cooperstown, New York, to be drilled by its director, Ernest L. Hazelius, in "French and German . . . Latin and Greek, writing and Arithmetic"; to a military academy in Middletown, Connecticut, to spend fifteen months acquiring self-discipline; and finally to Princeton, where Charles was graduated in August 1829, to the great delight of A. Burdett, who in one of her billets-doux to Burr identified herself as "the mother of the

Graduate of fifteen." Once Charles had put Princeton behind him, Burr launched him on an adult career by obtaining for him a midshipman's warrant in the navy. Though Charles seems to have been an apt enough student, he was also on occasion an unwilling and obstreperous one. From the Hartwick Seminary, Hazelius wrote to advise Burr to keep the boy away from "company . . . injurious to his morals," the youngster having "contracted the habit of using . . . low & improper language." Hazelius also requested the colonel to discourage A. Burdett, when her son was allowed to visit her, from keeping Charles away from school beyond the allotted time. From the military academy he played hookey once or twice, and at Princeton he proved to be a chip off the old block, acquiring a reputation there for addiction to what one disapproving observer described as "follies," and leaving behind some rather substantial debts, to be discharged by his unamused father.

In those days, schools open to women were few and far between, and for a short time the colonel, desperately seeking a good course in German, arranged to place one of his feminine charges in an institution ordinarily confined to boys. In 1828 we find him seeking to enroll another young lady at a place called Williams College, and in 1829 we find him making the necessary inquiries, preparatory to sending a fifteen-year-old to the well-known Bethlehem Seminary for Women in Bethlehem, Pennsylvania. His ideas about what women should be taught are generously illuminated in his letters. In 1823 he was instructing two of his girls "to work like tigresses at theme A—in—arithmetic to fit . . . thy comprehension for the Sublime Study of astronomy." By way of gently dissuading a suitor for the hand of one of his wards, Burr informed the lovesick gentleman that the young woman he had in mind had received the finest education available, in the course of which, however, she had acquired "no single one of those talents which are commonly called useful in a female—i.e. she can neither 'darn a stocking' nor make a pudding . . ."

Shortly after Medcef Eden the younger died in 1819, the oldest of his daughters, Sally Ann, married Benjamin Waldron of New York and went to live in a home of her own. Her younger sisters, Elizabeth and Rebecca Eden, remained with Burr, to become the "Liz" and "Becky" of his correspondence and the "comfort of my life," as he wrote his friend Robert Cartmel. In April 1825, when those affectionate words were penned, Becky was in her sixteenth year and Liz a year or so her senior. No human beings could replace Theodosia and Gamp in Burr's heart, but Liz and Becky came close to doing so. Their many letters to him brim with adoration for "Chere Papa" and present a pleasant picture of two lively-minded girls growing into charming and confident women under the tutelage of a devoted parental surrogate. Liz wrote poems in his honor and once congratulated him on the patience with which he endured the antics of his "little torments." Aware of the importance he attached to education, the sisters studied hard —too hard perhaps in the case of Becky, who tended to be sickly and whose mother, Rachel Eden, scolded at the colonel for asking too much of the child. For several months, Burr lodged both girls with his relatives in Philadelphia, where tutors in French and Spanish were available. Becky fell ill and Burr, after several visits to check her condition, finally took her back to New York, where her mother could help care for her. Liz lingered on, to regale Chere Papa with her impressions of life in the Quaker City. Went to "a Quaker Meeting where a Marriage was to be," she wrote him in the summer of 1824. "As I entered the gallery, I espied a Mrs. Davis, an acquaintance . . . by whom . . . I seated myself. It was full an hour before the Spirit moved any one of the members to say a word. In the meantime Mrs. D & myself were not without amusement. As we both happened to have large hats on we could smile now and then with impunity. We occupied ourselves with making sundry remarks to each other on the different things that we saw. The poor bride did not escape our critical observation. It was perhaps naughty of us to behave so, [for] . . . we were placed there to think, I suppose, of divine & holy things . . . About 11 o'clock a Mr. Moore spoke a little. Then the groom . . . rose & said I take Mary to be my wedded wife . . . She then also spoke but was so much agitated that she could scarcely utter a Syllable . . . When she was seated an old woman got up, *spouted* . . . a little . . . and then reseated herself. The certificate of marriage was then read, to which both the groom & Bride signed their names. After all which a prayer closed the meeting . . ." It was not, one gathers, a happy day for Burr when at length the right men came along and he consented to the ceremonies that in the second half of the 1820's made Becky the wife of John Lyde Wilson, an ex-governor of South Carolina, and Liz the wife of Isidore Guillet of Paris, an accomplished diplomat. Even then, the colonel did not at once step out of his adopted daughters' lives. In 1829 we find him rejoicing at Becky's second lying-in and negotiating for the services of a competent midwife.

Against this backdrop of Burr as a tireless paterfamilias, it is of interest to note the way in which many of his American contemporaries viewed him. A deep-seated longing to believe that retribution is not necessarily postponed to the hereafter is discernible in the widely held perception of the arch-conspirator as passing his last twenty-four years in wretched loneliness, spurned by all decent people and banished from those empyrean social circles wherein he once had roamed. True, Burr made it a point to avoid imposing himself on persons who didn't want him around; still, even among the elite, he had well-wishers. The Biddles of Philadelphia remained loyal. His clients and business associates included some of the most highly regarded individuals of his day: several of the New York Livingstons; Haym M. Salomon, son of the Haym Salomon of Revolutionary War fame; Captain Samuel Chester Reid, naval hero of the War of 1812; Aaron Ogden, a New Jersey governor; Benjamin Latrobe, famous architect; and Samuel M. Hopkins and Elisha Williams, prominent New York attorneys. Pertinent to this aspect of his waning years is a letter, dated 25 March 1818 and written by Ann (Mrs. Charles) Debost to her father, the Reverend David Schuyler Bogart, eminent New York divine. Just come from her first meeting with Burr, Ann wrote to share her impressions. She and her husband called at the colonel's home in the evening and found their host so fascinating that they stayed "till almost twelve oclock [sic]." Burr's manners, Mrs. Debost recalled, were "extremely interesting[,] his conversation singular, original[.] I was not only 'touch'd but wrapt not waken'd but inspir'd.' "* Mrs. Debost on her father's side was blood kin to the Schuyler and Hamilton families.

5

"Allow me," John Greenwood, one of Burr's law clerks, wrote his boss on 17 January 1824, "to express my pleasure at the prospect of the strong amendment of your Situation which the decision in the Eden causes affords, and the Sincere hope that you may hereafter be so fortified with comforts as to be beyond the reach of troubles of any species."

But Aaron Burr was a lightning rod for troubles. He always had been, always would be. The Medcef Eden Case was long and energy-consuming. So much money went into it—to say nothing of the sums expended in support of the Eden girls and their mother—that Burr's triumph in the

* I am indebted for a copy of this letter to a descendant of the Reverend Mr. Bogart, Clarissa Downing (Mrs. Bidwell) Moore of McLean, Virginia. The letter is preserved in a family scrapbook owned by Mrs. Moore's mother, Mrs. Paul H. Downing of Sykesville, Maryland, and was copied for me by Mrs. Moore's daughter, Clarissa Elizabeth Moore. A minister of the Protestant Reformed Dutch Church of North America, the Reverend Mr. Bogart officiated at Burr's second marriage (see p. 395). His mother was a sister of Alexander Hamilton's father-in-law, General Philip Schuyler.

courts left his financial situation pretty much what it had been since the start of his second career. Most of the largess he bestowed on his many charges came from his practice. In addition, he had a £50 annuity that he had purchased in England, a Revolutionary War pension of $500 a year, some properties in New York and Connecticut, and, toward the end of his life, another annuity of $500 as the result of his conveyance of a valuable farm to a son of one of the lawyers who had defended him at Richmond. On two different occasions, for varying lengths of time, he was given reason to hope for some reimbursement of the moneys he had spent out of his own pocket on members of his wartime regiment, but neither of these movements, one initiated on the state level by friends in the legislature and the other on the national level by Burr himself, came to anything.

In the fall of 1830 his pecuniary problems were the burden of a letter to his onetime ward, Katherine Bartow. "Pretty Kate," as Burr called her, had married Isaac Hawes and gone to live in Poughkeepsie, New York. Burr had promised to visit the Haweses and wrote to explain why he couldn't do so for the time being. He confessed that his reason for not coming was "very disagreeable to tell . . . ; yet Rather than lay under any suspicion of Want of appreciation or want of good faith towards you, it must come out—Know then, my dear friend, that it is the want of Money—I mean even Money to bear my expenses." Burr expressed the hope that "you & Mr. H. will read this letter to yourselves before you talk about it to the *Children*." Recently, he explained, efforts to mortgage some of his properties had fallen through. Worse yet, his law business had "been ruined by an artful, but dishonest, young man in whom I had placed entire confidence." As a result, "instead of being profitable," his practice was now costing him money. Only to someone as close to him as "Pretty Kate" could Burr have written such a letter; and at the end of it he was his sanguine self again. Relief was on its way, he assured her. "I

Hope . . . & believe that I shall, within a few months, Surmount these Entanglements . . ."

He did not specify the form he expected the relief to take, but a turning point in his life, occurring less than three years later, indicates the direction in which his mind was bending. Many years before, he had toyed with the idea of making things easier for himself and his creditors by marriage to a woman of fortune. The possibility, it appears, had remained with him, and when he at last decided to act upon it, he proceeded with characteristic thoroughness. On the evening of Monday 1 July 1833 he took as his second wife Eliza Bowen Jumel, commonly spoken of as Madame Jumel, widow of a French-born wine trader, and probably the wealthiest woman in the United States. The site of the wedding was her home on New York's fashionable Harlem Heights, a handsome structure known originally as the Roger Morris House and later, after 1810, as the Jumel Mansion.* The officiating minister was the Reverend Mr. Bogart, long a friend of the bridegroom, and a cousin of Mrs. Alexander Hamilton. Burr was seventy-seven, his bride fifty-eight; and in a letter acknowledging the congratulations extended by John P. Bigelow, a Boston attorney, Burr likened Bigelow's apparently flowery words to "a sort of Epithalamium," adding, however, that "really my friend you did not Consider that the parties who were the subject of congratulations were past their grand climacteric and it would therefore have been utterly impracticable either by invocation of muses, or even by beat of drum, to have Summoned the loves or graces to such a Celebration."

Much that has been written about Burr's second wife rests on the successful effort of relatives, after her death in 1865, to break a will in which she left the bulk of her huge estate to charity, by proving its maker to have been unstable. These

---

* Today this house at 160th Street and Edgecombe Avenue, known officially as the Morris-Jumel Mansion, is a museum. During the Revolution, it served as one of Washington's headquarters.

accounts turn Madame Jumel into a Hasenuah by picturing her as a whore in her youth, which she was, and as an ill-tempered and mentally incompetent harridan in her later years, which she was not. In truth, Eliza's life could be offered as a Horatio Alger saga, an exemplification of the cherished American notion that what counts about people is not their status at birth but the degree to which they better themselves by their own endeavors as they mature.

Madame's beginnings were notably unpromising. Born Betsey Bowen in Providence, Rhode Island, in 1775, she was the daughter of Phebe Kelly, a woman of the streets, and John Bowen, a sailor. In her twelfth year Betsey hired out as a servant, only to find this sort of work uncongenial and to begin following her mother's profession. At nineteen she gave birth to a boy, whom she called George Washington and who to the end of his ninety years as a character on the streets of Providence gloried in the repeated rumors that he had come honestly by his distinguished name. His mother resigned him to the care of friends and left Providence to try her luck in New York. There she lived under a variety of aliases. She had become Madame de la Croix when in 1797, in her twenty-second year, Saint-Mémin executed the miniature of her which shows us a blond beauty of markedly refined features.* Later she was known for a time as Eliza Brown, and apparently it was during this period that she worked as a supernumerary in one of the troupes managed by the theatrical impresario William Dunlap, whose uncomplimentary comments on her in his diary reflected the prevailing masculine conviction that once a strumpet, always a strumpet.

In 1800 Stephen Jumel, part owner of a successful wine business in New York, made Eliza his mistress; and four years later, on 9 April 1804, he made her his wife. Resurgent gossip had it that she tricked him to the altar, that he came back

---

* No. 715 in the Saint-Mémin collection in the print room of the New York Public Library.

from one of his buying trips to find her dying, that she intimated through the physician that she was fearful of going to hell unless Stephen made her an honest woman, and that then and there he did. No evidence whatsoever underlies this scenario; and the suspicion arises that Jumel married the lady in 1804 because by that time he had realized that she was a better businessman than he was. So events were to demonstrate. Along about 1826, while the Jumels were residing in Europe, the wine business came upon hard times. By way of sidestepping creditors, Stephen put his assets in his wife's name and gave her power of attorney. Returning to the United States by herself, Eliza, during the next three years, converted approximately one million dollars' worth of real estate and stocks into three million dollars' worth. She did this, biographer William Duncan asserts, by buying and selling pieces of property and batches of stocks one after another "with an almost infallible nose for the present conditions and probable future values."

Some idea of the labor and acumen that went into this accomplishment is evident in one of her letters in French to her absent husband. Writing to "Mon Cher Stephen" on 1 December 1826, she informed him that an illness which had confined her for four weeks had abated and that "my first outing will be to attend to our business matters." She began with a discussion of problems connected "with the quarterly dividends" on one of their investments. "You don't tell me anything about Mr. Lesparre," she scolded. "I repeat again to have an order sent to him to sell, or dispose of as you like, the Hartford bridge shares, otherwise you can be sure we'll lose them the same way we lost Mr. Nelson's house. You mustn't trust anyone because we need everything that's left for ourselves." She had good news for him. She had rented "the Broadway House to Mr. Workmaster, & he pays 2,100 gourdes [the Franco-American term for dollars], and if I had been here last year I would have gotten at least 2,500." She added that she had put the tenants out of the "Liberty Street house," as it was "really dirty (C'est en très mauvais état)" and in need of new paper. "For the vestibule," she told Stephen, "I would like 24 or 30 rolls of gray and 14 rolls of clear blue with clouds . . . I leave the other papers to your choice, since they are cheaper in Paris than New York."

Stephen returned from Europe to find his affairs in fine order. He had long since become the owner of the mansion on Harlem Heights, and he was happily playing the country gentleman there when he fell from a wagon carrying a load of hay and suffered the injuries from which he died on 22 May 1832. Again there was talk. This time the whispers were that Madame expedited his departure by loosening a bandage on one of his arms. "I utterly disbelieve this wretched gossip," wrote James Parton in his biography of Burr. Like the colonel, it would seem, the rich widow was a natural target for small minds with big tongues.

Burr appears to have come within the orbit of Madame Jumel when, shortly after the death of her husband, she called at the colonel's office to solicit his advice concerning a real-estate matter. Parton tells us that the two of them had known each other well "in other days," and that Burr was courteous and deferential, as he was to all clients—perhaps a little more so in this instance, since it wasn't every day that so much money walked into his place of business. Not only did he supply Madame with a written opinion on her problem, he also soon thereafter added to his staff a young lawyer named Nelson Chase, who only recently had become the husband of Mary Bowne (or Bownes), Eliza's niece and adopted daughter. Obviously, the colonel went out of his way to please a potentially profitable customer; and just as obviously, his tactics worked. As word of the wedding traversed New York, businessman Philip Hone took cognizance of it in his now famous diary. It was "benevolent" of the "celebrated Mrs. Jumel," he opined on 3 July 1833, "to keep the old man in his latter days."

But she was not to keep him long. Indeed, the seeds of the dissolution of their union were sown in its first days. During a honeymoon into New England, the newlyweds stopped at Hartford, Connecticut. Either the late Monsieur Jumel had not taken Madame's advice to dump his stocks in the toll bridge that spanned the Connecticut River at Hartford, or he or Eliza had procured others; for one of Madame's purposes in halting at Hartford was to examine the condition of the bridge company with the idea of purchasing additional shares. In the end, however, she not only bought no more stocks but sold those she had. Biographer Duncan intimates that Burr talked her into this action, and knowing the colonel, we can believe it. At any rate, Burr was permitted to sit in on the final conference with the company officials, and when a check for $6,000, covering the sale of the shares, was handed to Madame, she grandly waved it aside, pointed to Burr, and said, "Pay it to my husband."

Madame had made a mistake, for never again would she set eyes on that $6,000. It is impossible to say exactly what Burr did with this money or with whatever other portions of his second wife's fortune he succeeded in laying his hands on. Three letters in his extant papers, however, suggest that some of it may have gone into an effort by a young woman, Mrs. Jane McManus, to settle lands she owned in Texas with immigrants from Germany and elsewhere. Mrs. McManus, writing to Burr in what seems to have been the year 1832, outlined some difficulties her endeavor had encountered and told the colonel that her plans to sail from New York to Texas with some of her potential settlers would have to be canceled unless Burr could lend her $250. Apparently he did, for she and her associates sailed, and in the fall of what seems to have been the same year, Burr was writing to her at New Orleans, urging her not to allow the fact that she was a woman to deter her from completing her ambitious project. "[Y]our enterprize," he wrote, "has something of the air of Romance and Quioxtteism; but it is not without precedent: a young woman of twenty Five in the year 1785 led a Colony from Rhoade Island [sic] to the Western Shore of the Seneca Lake then more than one Hundred miles distant from any White inhabitant—the Colony flourished . . . and is now a monument to her intelligence her Courage and her discretion . . ." Enclosed with this letter was one that Mrs. McManus was to hand to James Workman, Burr's old friend and supporter in New Orleans, asking the former judge to help the young pioneer in any way he could. "Allow me the liberty," Burr wrote Workman, . . . to introduce . . . *A Lady!*—be not alarmed, for it is not intended that she should tax your Hospitalities nor, but very Slightly, your Gallantry: for she is a woman of business . . . eminently qualified for this enterprize . . . and she will be able to send out one or two hundred substantial settlers in less time and with better selection than any man of half a Dozen men whom I this day Know—she has always . . . adheared [sic] to the Catholic faith . . . and is much esteemed . . . by the Clergy of that denomination . . . her family and their Connexions in Ireland are extensive and respectable, she has in an eminent degree that peculiar discernment or tact in the character and disposition's [sic] of men—a talent peculiar to her sex but she has also (which is rare) courage Stability and perseverance."

As these developments appear to have occurred prior to the wedding in the Jumel Mansion, it is unlikely that Madame knew anything about them other than that Burr was interested in a young woman named Jane McManus. Eliza's own account of the colonel's way with her money was recorded by William Dunlap in his diary. "Today in the street," Dunlap wrote on 19 June 1834, "a woman accosted me by name who I immediately recognized as the Madam Jumel Aaron Burr married about a year back." Dunlap quoted Madame as saying, "You don't know me, Mr. Dunlap," and himself as saying, "Oh yes, Mrs. Burr. How does Coll. Burr do?" To which Madame answered, "O, I dont see him any more. He got 13,000 dollars of my property, and spent it all or gave it away & had money to buy him a dinner. I had a new Carriage & pair of horses cost me 1000 dollars he took them & sold them for 500." The import of this remark is clear. What annoyed Eliza was not so much that Burr grabbed some of her money as that he accomplished nothing with it. Her adopted daughter's husband, Nelson Chase, had assured her that the colonel was astute about such matters; but now it turned out that he was no such thing. Madame had worked too hard and too long for what she had to let it be frittered away by an improvident husband. Nothing more vividly shows "her business ability," historian Ray Swick has observed, than the dispatch with which she got rid of Aaron Burr. On 12 July 1834 she filed for absolute divorce, asking the court to enjoin Burr from coming in on her property and funds and accusing him of adultery with "one Jane McManus . . . and other females."

At first Burr fought back, charging "Madame of the Heights" (his name for her in private) with adultery and naming the gentlemen involved. Later, in December 1835, he withdrew this countersuit and agreed to permit his wife's bill of complaints to be "taken pro confesso" on two conditions. One was that the court costs be divided, with Madame paying her share. The other was that there be no alimony. As, under New York law, absolute divorce could be issued only on proofs of adultery, Madame presented two witnesses, both of whom asserted, in the words of one of them, that Burr's conduct with Jane McManus had been "indelicate and unchaste." From the standpoint of the plaintiff, the more satisfactory of these witnesses was Maria Johnson, a black woman servant, who said that she had worked for Burr for about two and a half years. Though the colonel's inadequately dated correspondence with Mrs. McManus renders it doubtful that she was in the New York area in August 1833, the testimony offered by Maria Johnson was that on two occasions that month, in a first-floor room at the rear of a house in Jersey City, she saw the colonel and Mrs. McManus engage in a "mean act." Small wonder that after the divorce took effect and after Burr had died, a grand jury for the city and county of New York, summoned to consider a suit brought by Mrs. McManus, indicted Maria Johnson for "Perjury against the state," the true bill alleging that "in fact, the said Aaron Burr did not at the said time and place commit adultery with the said Jane McManus."*

Maria's statements during the divorce action in the New York (State) Court of Chancery were taken in March 1836. They were graphic and circumstantial, as is shown by the following extract from the record of the cross-examination by Burr's counsel on the seventeenth of that month:

[Question to Maria Johnson by one of the lawyers] Where was you when you saw them for the first time? *A* I came up stairs to fetch a pitcher of hot water to Coln Burr . . . and saw Jane McManus on the settee and Coln Burr had his hand under her clothes . . . They were sitting . . . and Coln Burr had his trousers all down . . . *Q* When was it you saw them next together? *A* On Saturday afternoon. *Q* Where was you then? *A* I got up on the shed & turned the window blind and looked through it . . . I sat down on my hunkies and turned the blind & looked in . . . *Q* How close was they together? *A* About as close as they could set together . . . *Q* Had he [Burr] been struck with the Palsy at that time? *A* . . . Not that I know of—not until he had removed back [to New York] from Jersey City.†

On 14 July 1836 the decree of divorce was granted. Burr protested, calling the acts ascribed to him impossible at his age

* The records covering the further disposition of this matter, if any, do not seem to be available.

† Maria Johnson was as wrong about this as she was about everything else. Burr's correspondence shows a decided tremor in his hands as early as 1824. See AB to Thomas H. Flandrau, 13 Feb. 1824, MPAB.

("almost 80") and the testimony against him "inconsistent, variant and contradictory"; but on 14 September—the day of his death—the decretal order became final.

6

NATURALLY, THE MARRIAGE and divorce were much talked about, but an interesting mission undertaken by the colonel in his seventy-fifth year was not, for the reason that, except for the principals involved—Burr and the great abolitionist leader, William Lloyd Garrison—nobody knew anything about it at the time. The only information we have about this incident is contained in a biographical study entitled *William Lloyd Garrison 1805–1879. The Story of his life told by his children* and originally published in four volumes between 1885 and 1889.

The story, as the anti-slavery journalist conveyed it to his sons, is that Aaron Burr visited Boston shortly after Garrison, in 1831, began publication there of the *Liberator*, the newspaper destined to become the main mouthpiece of Americans battling for immediate emancipation of the slaves. After reaching the Massachusetts city, Burr dispatched a message asking the editor of the *Liberator* to give him "an interview . . . at the Marlboro' Hotel . . ."

Burr, Garrison recalled, "received me with . . . suavity and politeness . . . and . . . undertook to dissuade me from prosecuting the anti-slavery cause, and [from] continuing to publish the *Liberator*—skillfully setting forth the hopelessness of my object, the perils to which I should be subjected, the dangers of a general emancipation to the country, the powers and spirit of the slave oligarchy etc. etc. His manner was patronizing . . . He had a remarkable eye, more penetrating, more fascinating, than any I had ever seen, while his appearance was truly venerable . . . As he revealed himself to my moral sense, I saw he was destitute of any fixed principles, and that unyielding obedience to the higher law was regarded by him as credulity or fanaticism. Yet I do not remember that he undertook to argue the rightfulness of slavery . . .*

"We parted—he was courteous and plausible to the last, and I firm and uncompromising—and we never met again. What other object brought him to Boston, I could not learn: the next day he returned to New York."

It is strange how concerned the "traitor" was to his dying day about the welfare of his country.

7

AND SO, after Burr returned to the United States, the years passed for him. Pleasantly enough, it would seem. He had his children. One by one, to be sure, they grew up and went their separate ways; however, in the very year of the colonel's death we find eighteen-year-old Henry Oscar Taylor, while testifying for the defendant in the divorce trial, calling Burr his legal guardian and describing himself as under the colonel's care. Burr, as we know, suffered from a morbid fear of boredom, and almost to his last hour his practice kept that dread at bay. Not that he enjoyed the work all that much. Many years earlier, following his election to the United States Senate, he confessed that one of the reasons he looked forward to his new job was that it would release him from "office drugging"; and one senses the weariness wafting from his reference, in a letter written at the age of seventy-seven, to the

---

* Perhaps at this time Garrison, half a century younger than the colonel, was unaware that Burr, while in his state legislature decades before, had fought to achieve immediate freedom for the slaves of his state. It is interesting to find in the 8 January 1858 *Liberator* an editorial opening with these words: "It is certainly to his [Burr's] credit that while he was a member of the New York Legislature in 1784, a bill having been introduced for the gradual abolition of slavery in that state, 'he was in favor of a speedier extinction . . . and moved to amend the bill so as to totally abolish slavery after a certain day.' His amendment having been rejected, he voted for the original bill, which was lost."

"thraldom of business." Still, his practice provided him with an outlet for a profound need to help everybody and anybody except his creditors. His office correspondence yields numerous examples of actions to protect frightened wives from brutal husbands, and to get debtors out of jail and young men, needed at home, out of military service. That most of these endeavors were charity cases there can be no doubt. And from time to time during the final phase of his life, as in the past, he busied himself with get-rich-quick schemes: faster canal boats, more efficient steam engines, settlements in Texas, half a dozen other ideas that blazed like bonfires in his mind and in the minds of his cohorts in speculation, only as a rule to sputter out on exposure to the real world.

For many years he remained hale and hearty, but eventually the ills of age appeared. In 1830 a stroke in his right side disabled him temporarily, and in 1834, at which time he was living in Jersey City, there was a second stroke, from which he never recovered. Friends carried him to New York, to the old Jay Mansion on the Battery, now become a boarding house. Here, for two years, he enjoyed the affectionate ministrations of Mrs. Hannah Newton, the housekeeper, and the company of many visitors. Then came word that the Jay Mansion was to be demolished, and his friends and relatives assembled to determine what should be done about him. One of them, Judge Ogden Edwards of the circuit bench of the New York Supreme Court, lived on Staten Island. At his suggestion, the old man was removed to the Hotel St. James on the island at Port Richmond, close by the judge's house.

In this stylish hostelry, in a pleasant second-floor room overlooking the harbor of New York and the bay of Newark, Aaron Burr died on 14 September 1836. It was his wish to rest alongside the graves of his father and grandfather in the President's Plot of the college burial ground at Princeton, New Jersey. On 16 September, accordingly, there were ceremonies in the college chapel—prayers and an oration delivered by the

Reverend James Carnahan, the college president—and after that, a procession to what is now the Princeton Cemetery, at the corner of Witherspoon and Wiggins Streets. For twenty years, the grave went unmarked. Then a relative arranged for the installation of a simple marble slab bearing the appropriate dates and identifying Burr as "colonel in the army of the Revolution" and as "vice-president of the United States."

Sources and Notes

Sources and Notes

JW, *Memoirs*	James Wilkinson, *Memoirs of My Own Times*, 4 vols., 1816
LC	Library of Congress
MPAB	Microfilm Edition of the Papers of Aaron Burr, Mary-Jo Kline, ed.; Joanne Wood Ryan, asst. ed.; C. Susan Feuerwerger, Linda Raven, and Eleanor V. Shodell, assts. to the eds., 1978
NA	National Archives
PJAB (Bixby)	*The Private Journal of Aaron Burr*, William K. Bixby, ed., 1903
PJAB (Davis)	*The Private Journal of Aaron Burr*, Matthew L. Davis, ed., 1838
PRO	Public Records Office
RG 21, NA	Photostatic Copies of Documents in the Aaron Burr Treason Case at the United States District Court of the Eastern District of Virginia, Marion Johnson, compiler, NNGJ, 11 Aug. 1960, Record Group 21, NA
Robertson, *Trial*	David Robertson, *Reports of the Trials of Colonel Aaron Burr . . . in the Circuit Court of the United States . . . Richmond . . . Virginia*, 2 vols., 1808
Theo Jr.	Mrs. Theodosia Burr Alston
TJ	Thomas Jefferson
TJ, *Correspondence* (Bixby)	Thomas Jefferson, *Correspondence Printed from the Originals in the Collection of William K. Bixby*, 1916
TJ, *Works* (Ford)	Jefferson, *The Works of*, Paul L. Ford, ed., 12 vols., 1904–5.
TJ, *Writings* (Lipscomb–Bergh)	Jefferson, *The Writings of*, Andrew A. Lipscomb and Albert Bergh, eds., 20 vols., 1903

PREFACE

XIII   Treason "odious." See page 339.

XIII   "cipher letter" not written by AB. See pages 118–22.

XIII   "more important papers." Guide and Index to MPAB, 2.

XIV   vanished land-speculation letters. Davis, *Burr*, II, 375.

XIV   TJ's 27 Nov. 1806 proclamation. J. D. Richardson, *Messages of the Presidents*, I, 404.

XIV   "reported . . . rumors . . . as facts." Stuart Seely Sprague, "The Louisville Canal: Key to Aaron Burr's Western Trip of 1805," *The Register of the Kentucky Historical Society*, LXXI (Jan. 1973), 69.

XVI   "My idea of the devil." James Parton, *The Life and Times of Aaron Burr*, 1857 ed., 64. Cited hereafter as Parton, *Burr* (1857).

XVII   "I am a housekeeper." AB to Samuel C. Reid, 28 Dec. 1823, MPAB.

1. THE AMERICAN FRONTIER AND AGENT 13

3   "tale . . . a horrid one." Daniel Clark to JW, 17 Sept. 1805, Clark, *Proofs*, 141.

5   "would as soon have thought of taking . . . the moon." Davis, *Burr*, II, 378n.

5   "*First*, The Revolutionizing of Mexico." Ibid., 379.

5   "*La trahison*." Margaret Boveri, *Treason in the Twentieth Century*, 19.

5   "There! You see?" Parton, *Burr*, 1864 ed., II, 319. Cited hereafter as Parton, *Burr* (1864).

6   "Wilkinson was the projector." Charles Biddle, *Autobiography*, 411.

6   more than "any Christian in America." James Ripley Jacobs, *Tarnished Warrior: Major General James Wilkinson*, 63. Hereafter, Jacobs, *Wilkinson*.

6   AB's talks with Jay. Davis, *Burr*, II, 376.

7   Jay for AB in 1804. Peter Jay Munro to AB, Apr. 1804, MPAB.

7   Land carried Americans westward. Bernard De Voto, *The Course of Empire*, 407.

8   Americans hoped to add Canada. Julius W. Pratt, *Expansionists of 1812*, 11–14, 125–41, 274.

8   TJ for letting West go if it so wishes. To James Madison, 16 Dec. 1786, TJ, *Writings* (Lipscomb–Bergh); to same, 20 June 1787, Jefferson, *Papers*, Julian P. Boyd, ed.; and to John Breckinridge, 12 Aug. 1803, TJ, *Works* (Ford).

8   "nest from which all America . . . should be peopled." Irene Nicholson, *The Liberators*, 62.

8   Hamilton on annexing West. 29 Dec. 1802, John C. Hamilton, ed. *History of the Republic . . . as Traced in the Writings of Alexander Hamilton*, VI, 551–52.

9   Size of Spanish America. William Spence Robertson, *Rise of the Spanish-American Republics*, 1.

9   Spanish and French defiance of Treaty of Paris and reaction of American settlers. French E. Chadwick, *The Relations of the United States and Spain: Diplomacy*, 25–28; Frederick J. Turner, "The Significance of the Louisiana Purchase," *Review of Reviews*, XXVII, 160 (May 1903), passim.

13   Character and early career of JW. In the main, my coverage of these matters follows Jacobs, *Wilkinson*.

15   "gross irregularities." JW in *Dictionary of American Biography*.

16   "No friend . . . warmer . . . than James." Charles Biddle to AB, 13 Mar. 1802, MPAB.

17   JW as Agent 13. Clark, *Proofs*, 8–22 and passim; Max Savelle, *George Morgan: Colony Builder*, 215–17; letters relating to Wilkinson in AHN–ME and Henry Adams Transcripts.

19   "believe . . . France has acquired . . . Louisiana." Andrew Jackson to Robert Hays, 8 Jan. 1797, Jackson, *The Correspondence of*, John Spencer Bassett, ed., I, 24. Hereafter, Jackson, *Correspondence* (Bassett).

19   Blount Conspiracy. I. J. Cox, *The West Florida Controversy*, 38–55.

20   TJ "subject to Wilkinson's influence." Ibid., 38; and same

PAGE

author, "The Louisiana–Texas Frontier," pt. 1, *Quarterly of the Texas State Historical Association*, X, 55n.

21 "mischievous" Morales. Cox, *West Florida Controversy*, 146.

21 "day France takes . . . New Orleans." TJ, *Works* (Ford), VIII, 143–47.

21 Ceremonies in New Orleans. Charles L. Dufour, *Ten Flags in the Wind*, 133; Marquis James, *The Life of Andrew Jackson*, 314.

22 JW brought 170 men downriver. JW to Henry Dearborn, 20 Dec. 1803, Clarence Carter, ed., *The Territorial Papers of the United States*, IX, 138.

22 "hasty Scral." Ibid.

23 JW asks $20,000, gets $12,000. JW to Casa Calvo, 12 Mar. 1804, AHN–ME, Legajo 5545, expediente 15; Irving Brant, *James Madison: Secretary of State*, 203; "Reflections on Louisiana by Vincente Folch [actually by JW]," in James Alexander Robertson, ed., *Louisiana under the Rule of Spain, France, and the United States*, II, 325–47.

2. THE "MARCH TO THE CITY OF MEXICO" BEGINS

24 "bold enough." Hamilton to John Rutledge, 4 Jan. 1801, quoted in Philip McFarland, *Sojourners*, 65.

25 all "human quests." W. H. Auden, "Balaam and His Ass" in *The Dyer's Hand and Other Essays*, 47.

26 "To save time." 23 May 1804, MPAB.

26 "You are deceived." 24 May 1804, Ibid.

26 JW brought maps east. I. J. Cox, "Hispanic-American Phases of the Burr Conspiracy," *The Hispanic-American Historical Review*, XII (May 1932), 147.

26 Nolan planned invasion of Spanish America. Ibid, 146; same author, "Louisiana–Texas Frontier," pt. 1, 59.

26 "Call . . . see my maps." 26 May 1804, misdated 26 Mar., MPAB.

27 "Your affectionate . . . friend." 24 May 1804, Ibid.

27 "think of you always." 26 May 1804, Ibid.

27 Rumors JW Spanish pensioner around since Washington's day. Andrew Ellicott, deposition, JW, *Memoirs*, II, app. xxviii; Ellicott to Pickering, 5 June 1797, Ibid., 164.

27 never heard him "speak ill." Biddle, *Autobiography*, 303.

27 "hog latin." AB to?, post 13 Apr. 1804, MPAB.

28 "Thousands of . . . falsehoods." AB to Joseph Alston, 13 July 1804, Davis, *Burr*, II, 327.

28 AB trying to meet debt. AB to William P. Van Ness, 11, 12, and 13 July 1804, MPAB.

28 Biddle checks on AB. *Autobiography*, 269n, 303.

29 AB "seen walking." Thomas Robson Hay, "Charles Williamson and the Burr Conspiracy," *Journal of Southern History*, II (1936), 184.

29 Character and careers of Merry and wife. Coverage follows Malcolm Lester, *Anthony Merry Redivivus*, and Sir Augustus John Foster, *Jeffersonian America: Notes on the United States*.

31 Pell-mell dinner and Yrujo's remarks. Lester, *Merry*, chap. 3; TJ to William Short, 23 Jan. 1804, *American Historical Review*, XXXIII (1928), 832–33; Rufus W. Griswold, *The Republican Court*, 332; Dumas Malone, *Jefferson the President: First Term*, 379–80.

31 TJ breaks rule. Malone, *Jefferson the President: First Term*, 387; Philadelphia *Aurora*, 13 Feb. 1804.

32 Williamson's character and career. Coverage follows Helen I. Cowan, *Charles Williamson: Genesee Promoter;* Raymond A. Mohl, "Britain and the Aaron Burr Conspiracy," *History Today*, III (June 1971), 391–98; and Hay, "Charles Williamson and the Burr Conspiracy."

34 Merry's 6 Aug. 1804 report on Burr. FO 5/42, PRO.

35 Williamson calls Burr's project "March to the City of Mexico." Williamson to Lord Justice-Clerk, 3 and 6 Jan. 1806, and 12 July 1807, Lord Melville Papers, Newberry Library.

36 Miranda's character and career. Coverage follows Robertson, *The Life of Miranda*, and Joseph Francis Thorning, *Miranda: World Citizen*.

38 "certain circumstances." 6 Oct. 1804, Melville Papers.

38 Williamson under impression American West has seceded.

Williamson to Lord Justice-Clerk, 11 Dec. 1806, Melville Papers. Sees advantages to Britain: to Windham, 20 Dec. 1806, Ibid.

38 Williamson urges AB's project as "counterbalance" to Napoleon. 3 Jan 1806, Ibid.

39 "what does the United States require." Ibid.

39 Why Williamson's pleas unheeded. Mohl, "Britain and the Aaron Burr Conspiracy," 398; Thorning, *Miranda*, 191–93.

40 AB got permit to travel in Florida. AB to Gov. Enrique White, 22 Sept. 1804, East Florida Papers, LC.

40 "must be in New-York." AB to Theo Jr., 21 Aug. 1804, and to Alston, 11 Aug. 1804, Davis, *Burr*, II, 335, 332.

40 Storm strands AB. AB to Theo Jr., 12 Sept. 1804, Ibid., 339. Gets to Florida: to Theo Jr., 26 Sept. 1804, Ibid., 342.

41 "Cotton Lands . . . for *very little money.*" 17 Dec. 1803, MPAB.

41 White hates Americans. Lewis to AB, Ibid.; George R. Fairbanks, *History of Florida*, 251.

41 AB travels by canoe to visit Alstons. AB to Theo Jr., 2 Oct. 1804, Davis, *Burr*, II, 345.

41 "As to the boy." AB to Theo Jr., 10 Apr. 1805, Ibid., 367.

3. A WINTER'S TALE

43 "a crooked gun." TJ to William Branch Giles, 20 Apr. 1807, TJ, *Works* (Ford), X.

43 Truce in TJ–AB relationship. Vol. I, this book, 363–64.

45 "Wilkinson and Browne will suit." 10 Mar. 1804, Davis, *Burr*, II, 360.

45 "Mexico glitters." Cox, "Western Reaction to the Burr Conspiracy," *Transactions of the Illinois Historical Society, 1928*, 79.

46 "hourly expected." 10 Mar. 1805, misdated 1804, Davis, *Burr*, II, 360.

46 petitioned the Congress for 25,000 acres. Matthew Lyon, deposition, JW, *Memoirs*, II, app. lxxvii.

PAGE

47 "all the rights . . . of citizens." *Annals*, 8th Cong., 2d Sess., 1015.

47 "House . . . sold." AB to Theo Jr., 5 Nov. 1804, Davis, *Burr*, II, 349.

48 "has been intimated." AB to Truxton, 6 Jan. 1804, MPAB.

48 "famine and pestilence." AB to Charles Biddle, 31 Jan. 1805, Ibid.

48 "should be considered a farce." Charles Felton Pidgin, *Theodosia: The First Gentlewoman of Her Time*, 272.

48 "suffering a debility." 10 Mar. 1805, Davis, *Burr*, II, 358–59.

49 Duane spots AB at inauguration. Allan C. Clark, "William Duane," *Records of the Columbia Historical Society*, IX, 54.

49 AB calls on Mrs. Merry. AB to her, 4 Mar. 1805, MPAB.

49 Merry told of Mexican plan. Memo of 13 Dec. 1806 of John Poo Beresford in Beresford–Peirse Archive, North Riding Record Office, County Hall, Northallerton, England, quoted in Lester, *Merry*, 110–11.

49 Merry's 29 Mar. 1805 report to Harrowby. FO 5/45, PRO.

51 Louisiana deputies mystified. Abernethy, *Conspiracy*.

52 "No man is better fitted." *William Plumer: Memorandum of Proceedings in the U.S. Senate*, 213.

53 Yrujo warns officials. To Casa Calvo, 23 May 1805, encl. in letter to Cevallos, 24 May 1805; and to Cevallos, 5 Aug. 1805, Henry Adams Transcripts.

53 Attempt to bribe editor angers TJ. Yrujo to William Jackson, attached to letter from Jackson to TJ, 7 Sept. 1805, TJ Papers, LC; Irving Brant, *James Madison: Secretary of State*, 209–11.

54 AB lingers in Philadelphia. AB to JW, 10 Apr. 1805, Bacon Report, 196–97; to Joseph Wheaton, 22 Apr. 1805, MPAB; and to John Vanderlyn, same date, Ibid.

4. ON THE WESTERN WATERS

55 Nature of AB's travels. Joshua Gilpin, *Pleasure and Business in Western Pennsylvania*, I, 63; George W. Ranck,

History of Lexington, Kentucky, 115; Sprague, "The Louisville Canal," 77, 78, 78n; AB to Theo Jr., Davis, *Burr,* II, 369.

57 Movements dictated by canal company plans. Ibid., 309; AB to John Brown, 8 May 1805, MPAB: Cincinnati *Liberty Hall,* 14 May 1805; AB to "Dear Sir," 7 Oct. 1805, MPAB; Cox, "The Burr Conspiracy in Indiana," *Indiana Magazine of History,* XXV (Dec. 1929), 258, 267.

57 "Send . . . letters &c to Louisville." 30 Apr. 1805, misdated 1808, Bacon Report, 197.

58 "a floating house." AB to Theo Jr., 30 Apr. 1805, Davis, *Burr,* II, 368.

58 Meeting with Lyon, stay with Wallace. Lyon, deposition, 25 Feb. 1811, JW, *Memoirs,* II, app. lxxviii; Ray Swick, "Harman Blennerhassett: An Irish Aristocrat on the American Frontier," 179; AB to William Biddle, 4 May 1805, MPAB; Marietta *Register,* 19 Oct. 1808.

60 Character and early life of HB. Swick, "Blennerhassett," passim.

63 AB's first visit to island. Ibid., 217; undated ms. entitled "Blennerhassett" in HB Papers, LC.

65 On Senator Smith and conference at his home. Robert W. Wilhelmy, "Senator John Smith and the Aaron Burr Conspiracy," *The Cincinnati Historical Society Bulletin,* XXVIII (Spring 1970), 43.

65 Bank formed, AB gets loan. Thomas Perkins Abernethy, *The Burr Conspiracy,* 22–23.

66 On Jonathan Dayton. Dayton in *Dictionary of American Biography* and *National Cyclopedia of American Biography,* I, 306; HB, *Papers* (Safford), 35, 105.

66 Smith sounds out Spanish officials for TJ. Jacob Burnet, *Notes on the Early Settlement of the Northwest Territory,* 295.

67 "What a conspiracy!" *Rise of the West,* 340–41.

67 AB leaves letter for JW. 19 May 1805, JW, *Memoirs,* II, app. lxix.

67 "I was to have introduced." JW to John Adair, Clark, *Proofs,* 158.

68 "the intentions of Colonel Burr." Davis, *Burr,* II, 379–80.

68   On Jackson. Joe Gray Taylor, "Andrew Jackson and the Aaron Burr Conspiracy," *West Tennessee History Society Papers*, 1–2 (1947–48), 81–90; Robert V. Remini, *Andrew Jackson and the Course of American Empire*, chap. 10.

68   "Burr would have been proud." Ibid., 241.

69   AB–JW talks at Fort Massac. Davis, *Burr*, II, 370; Parton, *Burr* (1857), 391; deposition, Daniel Hughes, 20 Jan. 1811, JW, *Memoirs*, II, app. lxxx.

70   Background on Edward Livingston. Follows William B. Hatcher, *Edward Livingston*.

71   AB visits convent and finds supporters. Davis, *Burr*, II, 371, 382.

72   Clark to Vera Cruz. Clark, *Proofs*, 107.

72   Claiborne on AB's visit and establishment of cipher. Charles Gayarre, *History of Louisiana*, 4th ed., IV, 82.

72   AB sees Morales, ignores Casa Calvo. Claiborne to Madison, 6 Aug. 1805, Carter, *Territorial Papers*, IX, 489; JW to Casa Calvo, 14 Sept. 1805, MPAB.

73   AB calls on Clark. Clark, *Proofs*, 94.

73   AB outlines travel plans. Davis, *Burr*, II, 369–74.

5. YRUJO AND THE INVENTION OF A CONSPIRACY

76   AB "knew" Yrujo author of "Queries." Erich Bollman to TJ, 26 Jan. 1807, TJ Papers, LC; see also Cox, "Western Reaction to the Burr Conspiracy," 78; and Thomas D. Clark, *Frontier America: The Story of the Westward Movement*, 2d ed., 252–53.

76   Merry pleased and alarmed by "Queries." 4 Aug. 1805, FO 5/45, PRO.

77   *Kentucky Gazette* reprints "Queries." Cox, "Western Reaction," 78.

77   "ravings of a concealed traitor, or . . . some emissary of a foreign government." *Aurora*, 30 July 1805; and see on Yrujo's attempt to embarrass TJ, Brant, *Madison: Secretary of State*, 188–89.

PAGE

77   Burr at Liberty Hall. Davis, *Burr*, II, 374; John Brown in *Dictionary of American Biography*.

77   of "more talents and information." AB to ?, 7 Oct. 1805, MPAB.

78   Clark warns JW their names linked to AB's schemes. Clark, *Proofs*, 95.

78   Kentucky press on plots of JW and AB. ASP Misc. I, 572.

78   Bruff's background. Francis B. Heitman, ed., *Historical Register and Dictionary of the United States Army*, I, 256; Carter, *Territorial Papers*, XIII, 16–17.

78   Bruff "to watch the motions" of JW and AB. ASP, Misc. I, 571; Cox, "Opening the Santa Fe Trail," *Missouri Historical Review*, XXV (1930), 46.

79   "six or eight miles" downriver. JW to Bruff, 28 June 1805, Bacon Report, 228.

79   Bruff's account of conversations with JW. ASP Misc. I, 571–73; Bacon Report, 202–12, 223, 233, 236.

81   "The colonel strictured the situation." ASP Misc. I, 573; Bruff to Joseph Nicholson, misdated 22 Aug., probably 22 Sept. 1805, Bacon Report, 233.

81   AB's "consciousness of superiority." See, e.g., Washington *Federalist*, 13 Mar. 1805.

81   "Mr. Burr" spoke "of the imbecility of the Government." *Annals*, 1807–8, 611; Walter Flavius McCaleb, *The Aaron Burr Conspiracy*, 1966 ed. (hereafter, McCaleb, *Conspiracy*), 36–37.

82   AB learned West not for disunion. TJ to James Bowdoin, 2 Apr. 1807, TJ, *Writings* (Lipscomb–Bergh), XI, 183–86.

82   "settled the plan for an attack on Mexico." Abernethy, *Conspiracy*, 32.

82   JW advocates seizure of Mexico. To Dearborn, Jacobs, *Wilkinson*, 221.

83   JW reconnoiters routes to Mexico. Ibid., 220, 225–26; Cox, "Opening the Santa Fe Trail," 35, 45.

83   Bruff approached by Easton. ASP Misc. I, 573.

83   Kibbey approached by JW. Kibbey, deposition, 6 July 1807, Henshaw, *Documents*.

83   "Burr is about something." ASP Misc. I, 551.

84 Nature of exploratory expeditions ordered by JW. Jacobs, *Wilkinson*, 218–19; De Voto, *Course of Empire*, 265, 363, 612.

84 "having made fortunes for many." ASP Misc. I, 572.

85 JW suggested AB travel on general's boat. AB to JW, 10 Apr. 1805, Bacon Report, 197.

85 *"Before you touch the Kentucky shore."* JW, *Memoirs*, II, app. lxix.

85 "false claim of debt." Cox, "The Burr Conspiracy in Indiana," 263.

85 "never take . . . liberty with any man's secrets." 26 Sept. 1805, MPAB.

86 "It is necessary." *American Historical Review*, X, 837–40.

86 "Wilkinson . . . lieutenant to no man." ASP Misc. I, 494.

86 "wild reports." Clark, *Proofs*, 140–41.

87 On Minor. John Ray Skates, *Mississippi: A Bicentennial History*, 45, 51, 63; Albert Jeremiah Beveridge, *The Life of John Marshall*, III, 296.

87 Yrujo behind spread of rumors. Cox, *West Florida Controversy*, 189; Beveridge, *Marshall*, III, 296.

88 "love the society of that person." AB to JW, 6 Jan. 1806, JW, *Memoirs*, II, app. lxxxvi.

88 "a tub of Burr." JW to Daniel Clark, 8 Mar. 1806, Clark, *Proofs*, 141.

88 "from your friendship a boon." JW, *Memoirs*, II, 303; Bacon Report, 199.

6. SETBACKS, CHANGED PLANS, AND THE CIPHER LETTER

90 "replete with resources." Yrujo to Cevallos, 5 Aug. 1805, Henry Adams Transcripts.

90 AB borrows twenty dollars. Van Ness, memo, 20 Apr. 1806, MPAB.

90 Dayton and AB call on Merry. Lester, *Merry*, 104.

92 Louisiana boundary questions. Chadwick, *The Relations of the United States and Spain*, chap. 4 and passim; Malone, *Jefferson the President: Second Term*, chap. 4; Bemis, *Diplomatic History*, 180–81; TJ, "The Limits and Bounds of Louisiana."

PAGE

93   Duane on Yrujo's "insolence." G. F. Rowe, *Thomas Mc-Kean: The Shaping of an American Republicanism*, 367–68.

93   Yrujo sues Duane. Ibid.

93   "the expedition of *Burr*, having been frustrated." *Aurora*, 24 Dec. 1806.

94   Advice to TJ from Monroe and Armstrong. Malone, *Jefferson . . . Second Term*, 55.

94   Cabinet decisions reached. Cabinet memo of 12 Nov. 1805, TJ, *Works* (Ford), I, 308–9.

95   "Mr. Burr . . . still" knows "Secrets of this Government." Merry to Lord Mulgrave, 25 Nov. 1805, FO 5/45, PRO.

95   TJ "determined to have West Florida." Bemis, *Diplomatic History*, 183.

96   Richmond *Enquirer* reprints "Queries." Malone, *Jefferson . . . Second Term*, 232.

96   "seceded from the Idea." Merry to Lord Mulgrave, 25 Nov. 1805, FO 5/45, PRO.

96   "no war with Spain." Davis, *Burr*, II, 375.

96   "views . . . explained to . . . Govt." AB to Henry Clay, 1 Dec. 1806, MPAB.

96   "discontent with the . . . policy of the English ministers." William Spence Robertson, *Miranda*, 293.

97   King urges Miranda to sound out government. Rufus King to G. Gore, 9 Mar. 1806, Charles R. King, ed., *The Life and Correspondence of Rufus King*, IV, 529.

97   Miranda—AB meeting. AB to Jeremy Bentham, 16 Oct. 1811, *PJAB* (Davis), II, 254.

97   AB "detestable." Robertson, *Miranda*, I, 294.

98   Miranda guest of President. Ibid., 294; Thorning, *Miranda*, 173–75.

98   TJ and Madison deny condoning Miranda's project. TJ to Duane, 26 Mar. 1806, TJ, *Works* (Ford), X, 242; Madison to Armstrong, 15 Mar. 1806, Madison, *Writings*, Gaillard Hunt, ed., VII, 202–4.

99   Yrujo's report on talk with Dayton. To Cevallos, Henry Adams, *History of the United States of America*, III, 237. Hereafter, Henry Adams, *History*.

99   Yrujo warns Vasconcelos after Miranda sails. Robertson, *Miranda*, I, 300.

100   Smith and Ogden acquitted. Thomas Lloyd, *The Trials of William S. Smith and Samuel G. Ogden . . .* , 242, 287.

100   Adams, Hamilton, and Harper on Bollman. Griswold, *The Republican Court*, 333; Harper to AB, 29 May 1804, MPAB.

101   AB bids HB join him. HB, *Papers* (Safford), 115–21.

102   AB consults with Bollman and Dayton on scheme to get money from Spain. Bollman to TJ, 26 Jan. 1807, TJ Papers, LC.

103   Yrujo reports first talk with Dayton. To Cevallos, 5 Dec. 1805, No. 590, Henry Adams Transcripts.

103   Motive of Dayton's call on Yrujo. Erich Bollman to TJ, 26 Jan. 1807, TJ Papers, LC.

103   Yrujo reports second talk with Dayton. To Cevallos, 1 Jan. 1806, AHN–ME.

105   Yrujo told to handle AB with caution. Cevallos to Yrujo, 26 Mar. and 12 July 1806, Henry Adams, *History*, III, 249; Nathan Schachner, *Aaron Burr: A Biography*, 312.

105   Border incident and TJ's messages. Abernethy, *Conspiracy*, 35, 47–48; *Annals*, 9th Cong., 1st Sess., 30 Dec. 1805; Cox, *West Florida Controversy*, 182.

106   "You will know." JW, *Memoirs*, app. lxxvi.

106   Burr shows Dearborn's letter to Davis. Cox, "Burr Conspiracy in Indiana," 263.

106   "would have given up." Charles Biddle, *Autobiography*, 313.

106   AB seeks judgeship. Rowe, *Thomas McKean*, 386.

106   TJ's memo on talk with AB. TJ, *The Complete Anas of*, Franklin B. Sawvel, ed., 237–41.

107   "I had never seen Colo. Burr." TJ, *Works* (Ford), I, 301–4.

109   Gold medal for Truxton. Eugene S. Ferguson, *Commodore Thomas Truxton . . . A Description of the Truxton–Biddle Letters in the collections of the Library Company of Philadelphia*, 13. Hereafter, Ferguson, *Truxton–Biddle*.

109   AB's talks with Truxton. ASP Misc. I, 496.

109   AB's talks with Eaton. Ibid., 493, 537. For a view of these talks wholly at odds with mine, see Louis B. Wright and

Julia H. MacLeod, "William Eaton's Relations with Aaron Burr," *Mississippi Valley Historical Review*, XXXI (Mar. 1945), 523–36.

110 Plumer on Eaton. His *Memorandum*, 473, 479–80, 516; and on JW, Truxton and Eaton, Ibid., 542.

111 "any enterprise." HB, *Papers* (Safford), 118; and "a speculation," Ibid., 120.

111 AB's contract with Lynch. AB: bills of exchange on G. M. Ogden, 14 Nov. and 11 Dec. 1806, MPAB; ASP Misc. I, 598–600.

112 Clay believes transaction legal. Plumer, *Memorandum*, 549.

112 Three amazing maps. AB: Maps of Gulf Coast region left with Dr. James Cummins, [July 1806?], MPAB.

112 "Had Burr's project gone forward." McCaleb, *Conspiracy*, 78.

113 AB's movements in spring and summer 1806. AB to HB, 15 Apr., 17 May, and 24 July 1806, HB, *Papers* (Safford), 119–23; Charles Biddle to A. Gilchrist, 28 Mar., to Joseph Alston, 2 Aug., to John P. Van Ness, 11 Aug. 1806, and to A. Gilchrist, 22 Jan. 1807, Charles Biddle Papers, Historical Society of Pennsylvania; AB to Robert Goodloe Harper, 7 May, and to William P. Van Ness, 15 May 1806, MPAB; Leslie Henshaw, "The Aaron Burr Conspiracy in the Ohio Valley," *Ohio Archaeological and Historical Quarterly* XXIV (1915), 135.

113 "with his accustomed frequency." Yrujo to Cevallos, 9 June 1806, Henry Adams Transcripts.

114 "Respected Sir." William Duane to TJ, 8 Dec. 1806, TJ Papers, LC.

115 "execution of our project is postponed." JW, *Memoirs*, II, app. lxxxiii.

115 "I . . . put the letter out of my hands." Robertson, *Trial*, I, 329.

116 Copy of cipher letter and of the cipher material in Dayton's hand. In McGregor Collection, box 1, folder 5725, U. of Va. Lib.

118 Swartwout's deposition. Henshaw, *Documents*, 53–54.

118 Tazewell on Swartwout. ASP Misc. I, 588.

119 code based on a miscellany of elements. ASP Misc. I, 587;

Kline, editorial note for 22–29 July 1806 entries, MPAB; cipher material in Dayton's hand, McGregor Collection, U. of Va. Lib.

120 "For some time after your departure." Theo Jr. to F. Prevost, 18 Aug. 1806, MPAB.

121 Dayton's character. See Dayton in *Dictionary of American Biography; National Cyclopedia of American Biography*, I, 306; HB, *Papers* (Safford), 358, 458.

7. PREPARING THE EXPEDITION

123 "first characters in Pittsburgh." McCaleb, *Conspiracy*, 74.

124 *Commonwealth* on AB. ASP Misc. I, 502.

124 Morgans' testimony untrue. AB to Jonathan Rhea, 25 July 1807, MPAB.

125 Morgan linked to Spanish Conspiracy. Savelle, *Morgan*, chap. IX and 232–35; Jacobs, *Wilkinson*, 94.

125 Burr's remarks reported to President. Neville and Roberts to Madison, 7 Oct. 1806, MPAB; Morgan to Neville, 2 Sept. 1806, McGregor Collection, box 1, folder 3639, U. of Va. Lib.; TJ to Morgan, 19 Sept. 1806, TJ Papers, LC.

125 "mad project." TJ to Katherine Duane Morgan, 26 Jan. 1822, TJ, *Correspondence* (Bixby).

126 Theme of Daveiss's letters to TJ. Daveiss, *View*, passim.

127 Malone on TJ's handling of Daveiss's reports. *Jefferson . . . Second Term*, 225.

127 AB's talk with Blennerhassetts on isle. ASP Misc. I, 500–1.

128 HB to spend, Alston to underwrite. HB to Joseph S. Lewis & Co., 18 Oct. 1806, HB, *Papers* (Safford), 142–43; Alston to HB, 22 June 1807, HB Papers, LC.

129 Contract for bateaux. HB, *Papers* (Safford), 131; Swick, "Blennerhassett," 339.

130 Talk of West's leaving union not uncommon. See, e.g., Duane to TJ, 16 Oct. 1807, TJ Papers, LC.

130 HB talks with Hendersons. ASP Misc. I, 507, 526, 433.

131 Hendersons and Blennerhassetts long-time foes. Swick, "Yankees and Tuckahoes," Ms. of article in progress.

131 Background on Theodosia. Swick, "Theodosia Burr Al-

ston," *The South Atlantic Quarterly*, LXXIV (Autumn 1975), 459–506.

134 "Burr is with me." Remini, *Jackson and the Course of American Empire*, 147.

134 "have seen from the late paper." Ibid., 149.

135 Jackson "an accomplice." Ibid., 148.

135 "to divide the Union." Jackson to George W. Campbell, 15 Jan. 1807, Jackson, *Correspondence* (Bassett), I, 169.

136 Jackson warns Claiborne. 12 Nov. 1806, ASP Misc. I, 563.

136 Warns Jefferson. Jackson to Campbell, 15 Jan. 1807, *Correspondence* (Bassett), I, 169.

136 Writes AB and gets answer. Ibid.

137 De Pestre calls on Yrujo. HB, *Papers* (Safford), 416–17; Yrujo to Cevallos, 10 Nov. and 4 Dec. 1806, Henry Adams, *History*, III, 261–65.

137 Vidal starts trip. Henshaw, "The Aaron Burr Conspiracy in the Ohio Valley," 135.

137 Davis Floyd at Falls, visited by AB. AB to Henry Clay, 1 Nov. and 27 Nov. 1806, MPAB; to William Henry Harrison, 25 Nov. 1806, Ibid.; Cox, "Burr Conspiracy in Indiana," 269–80.

137 "ready before you are." Clark, *Proofs*, 122.

138 Daveiss, Marshall, and *Western World*. Daveiss, *View*, 94; Humphrey Marshall, *The History of Kentucky*, II, 386–92.

138 Daveiss on another junket. Cox, "Burr Conspiracy in Indiana," 269–80; Daveiss to Madison, 16 Oct. 1806, Daveiss, *View*, 98.

139 Daveiss piqued at AB. HB, *Papers* (Safford), 373.

139 "mysterious movements." Marshall, *Kentucky*, II, 386–87.

140 Taylor's travels. ASP Misc. I, 499.

140 "beg leave to inform you." John Smith to AB, 23 Oct. 1806, Wilhelmy, "Smith and the Aaron Burr Conspiracy," 47.

141 "may be an unnecessary caution." *Annals*, 9th Cong., 1st Sess., 291–92.

141 Henry Adams on AB's denial to Smith. *History*, III, 276.

141 Smith's "fears" removed. Wilhelmy, "Smith and the Aaron Burr Conspiracy," 49.

142 Grand jury hearings in Frankfort. U.S. v. Aaron Burr, Federal Court Case No. 5, United States District Court,

Kentucky, under date of 8 Nov. 1806, MPAB; Daveiss, *View*, 99; McCaleb, *Conspiracy*, 153; Willard Rouse Jillson, "Aaron Burr: A sketch of his life and 'Trial' at Frankfort, Kentucky, in 1806," 22–23; Frankfort *Palladium*, 27 Nov. and 11 Dec. 1806; John Wood, *A full Statement of the Trial and Acquittal of Aaron Burr . . . before the Federal Court at Frankfort, Ky.*, 34–35; Schachner, *Burr*, 351.

8. THE BETRAYAL

150 crisis on the frontier: American and Spanish views. TJ, "The Limits and Bounds of Louisiana," 27; Cox, "The Louisiana–Texas Frontier," pt. 1, 1, pt. 2, 4–23; McCaleb, *Conspiracy*, 94; *Annals*, 9th Cong., 2d Sess., 913.

151 Spanish soldiers retreat, Cordero defiant. Ibid., 515, 914–15.

152 Spanish officials believe government behind AB. McCaleb, *Conspiracy*, 95.

152 Spanish soldiers mass, American settlers alarmed. Cox, "Louisiana–Texas Frontier," p. 2, 37; W. C. C. Claiborne to Henry Dearborn, 28 Aug. 1806, Claiborne, *Letter Books*, III, 386–90.

152 "existing circumstances." JW, *Memoirs*, II, app. lxxxvii.

152 Dearborn amends orders. Ibid.

153 "From recent information." Ibid, app. xc.

154 JW countermands secretary's orders. Claiborne to Cowles Mead, 28 Aug. 1806, *Letter Books*, III, 391.

154 "want of water in Ohio." See pages 115, 121, and 154, this book.

155 "I shall obey the military mandate." McCaleb, *Conspiracy*, 106–7.

155 "I shall . . . push them over the Sabine." Ibid., 113–14.

155 "The time looked for by many." Schachner, *Burr*, 334.

156 Herrera crosses Sabine. Col. Cushing to Herrera, 5 Aug. 1806, *Annals*, 9th Cong., 1st Sess., 915–16; Herrera to Cushing, 6 Aug. 1806, Ibid., 916–17.

156 Claiborne and Mead issue proclamation. Turner to Clai-

borne, 8 Aug. 1806; and the proclamation, Claiborne, *Letter Books*, III, 379–82.

156 "My present impression." 9 Sept. 1806, McCaleb, *Conspiracy*, 104.

157 "Let the President be assured." 8 Sept. 1806, JW, *Memoirs*, II, app. lx; ASP Misc. I, 562; *Annals*, 1807–8, app., 568.

158 JW takes two weeks to get to Natchitoches. McCaleb, *Conspiracy*, 109.

159 "patrols are daily pushed forward." Abernethy, *Conspiracy*, 140.

159 JW's demand on Cordero. *American State Papers—Foreign Relations*, II, 803.

160 Cordero says decision up to Salcedo. JW to Dearborn, 21 Oct. 1806, *Annals*, 9th Cong., 2d Sess., 924.

161 Bradford a Burrite. Abernethy, *Conspiracy*, 29.

163 "the ground from whence we had driven them." *Annals*, 1807–8, 570.

164 "in a disguised hand." ASP Misc. I, 558.

164 Dayton's letter. Ibid., 553.

164 "materially influenced." Ibid., 540.

164 JW aware of attacks on him. McCaleb, *Conspiracy*, 154.

165 JW doctors cipher letter. ASP Misc. I, 540–42.

165 "I have looked for it." Ibid., 543.

165 "I have not." Ibid.

165 JW confides plans to Cushing. Ibid., 557–58.

166 JW's recollection of talk with Swartwout. Ibid., 472, 540.

166 Swartwout's recollection. Henshaw, *Documents*, 53–54.

167 "numerous and powerful association." JW to TJ, 20 Oct. 1806, Burr Papers, LC; JW, *Memoirs*, II, app. lcv.

167 "I have never . . . found myself under such . . . perplexity." JW to TJ, 21 Oct. 1806, Ibid., app. xcv.

168 "soles of a slipper." Smith deposition, JW, *Memoirs*, II, app. xclv.

168 no "hostile intentions." JW to Cordero, 4 Oct. 1806, *Annals*, 9th Cong., 2d Sess., 921–22.

168 Burling delivers JW's proposal. Burling, deposition, JW, *Memoirs*, II, app. xcvii.

PAGE

169 Cabinet had favored neutral area. Cox, "Louisiana–Texas Frontier," pt. 2, 14–15.

169 JW ordered to avoid fight with the Spanish. TJ: Cabinet Memorandum, 8 Nov. 1806, TJ Papers, LC.

170 Salcedo pleased. Abernethy, *Conspiracy*, 155.

170 "a small Frenchman." ASP Misc. I, 541.

170 "Every thing and even heaven itself." 16 July 1806, McGregor Collection, folder 5726, U. of Va. Lib.

170 Donaldson's warning. ASP Misc. I, 559.

171 "We must repair the old defences." 7 Nov. 1806, JW, *Memoirs*, II, app. xcix.

171 "the plot thickens." Ibid.

172 "a deep, dark and wide-spread conspiracy." JW, *Memoirs*, app. c.

173 JW read cipher letter to Briggs. Briggs 2d deposition, Ibid., app. lix.

174 effort to bilk Spanish viceroy fails. McCaleb, *Conspiracy*, 141–45; Davis, *Burr*, II, 400–4.

9. STIRRINGS IN WASHINGTON, OPERATICS IN NEW ORLEANS

176 "gunboats" being built. James Taylor to Madison, 13 Oct. 1806, McCaleb, *Conspiracy*, 89.

176 "Several Gentlemen." Nicholson to TJ, TJ, *Correspondence* (Bixby), 134–36.

177 Memos covering cabinet meetings on AB. TJ, *Works* (Ford), I, 400–3.

180 "mammoth of iniquity." Henry Adams, *John Randolph*, 83.

180 TJ's proclamation. Richardson, *Messages of the Presidents*, I, 404.

181 "amusing to see" men turn on AB. Burnet, *Notes*, 294–95.

181 Some feel Jackson, too, should be burned in effigy. Remini, *Jackson and the Course of American Empire*, 153.

182 *Kentucky Gazette* deserts AB. McCaleb, *Conspiracy*, 169.

182 JW's efforts to protect city, nab AB. Gayarre, *Louisiana*, IV, 159–69; ASP Misc. I, 601.

183 "the flagitious enterprise of one of the badest men." Gayarre, *Louisiana*, IV, 168.

184 Ogden and Swartwout charged with "misprision of treason." *Annals*, 10th Cong., 1st Sess., 1008–16.

10. THE "BURR WAR"

186 "to inquire into Burr's movements." TJ, *Works* (Ford), I, 403.

186 Graham meets with Wood Count citizens' committee. Abernethy, *Conspiracy*, 104–6.

187 "We trust that public rumor." Ohio lawmakers to TJ, U. of Va. mss.—2595, Ohio Documents for 1806, Supplement 24.

187 militiamen assemble along Ohio River. Washington *National Intelligencer*, 23 Jan. 1807.

187 Cincinnati alarmed and conduct of soldiers. Cincinnati *Western Spy*, 23 Dec. 1806; Schachner, *Burr*, 360; McCaleb, *Conspiracy*, 248; HB, *Papers* (Safford), 664.

188 the "Semi-Savages." 12 Jan. 1807, Fuller mss., IV, A, 28, Princeton U. Lib.

188 "take forcible possession." Edward W. Tupper, deposition, Henshaw, *Documents*, 13–27; Dudley Woodbridge, testimony, Robertson, *Trial*, I, 518–26.

188 Tupper's poem. HB, *Papers* (Safford), 661–65.

189 Types of boats built. Robertson, *Trial*, I, 519, 521; Archer Butler Hulbert, *The Ohio River*, 300.

189 "the beginning of the end of Burr's conspiracy." Abernethy, *Conspiracy*, 107.

189 only four vessels and thirty-five men. Tupper, deposition, Henshaw, *Documents*, 26.

190 could have taken 1,200 downriver. Abernethy, *Conspiracy*, 113.

190 all members of expedition men. Marshall, *Kentucky*, II, 431.

190 "a few women and children." W. H. Wooldridge to Cowles Mead, 14 Jan. 1807, Mississippi, *Third Annual Report of the Department of Archives and History*, app. II, 54–55. Hereafter, Mississippi Archives, *Third Annual Report*.

PAGE

190 "hub-bub and confusion" on island. Tupper, deposition, Henshaw, *Documents*, and copy filed with same in RG 21, NA.

192 "On our arrival at the house." Hulbert, *Ohio River*, 304–5.

193 Wages and bonuses for recruits. *National Intelligencer*, 9 Jan. 1807.

193 Jackson satisfied AB's intentions legal. To George S. Campbell, 15 Jan. 1807, Jackson, *Correspondence* (Bassett), I, 169.

193 Jackson returns $1,725.62. Schachner, *Burr*, 361.

194 AB at Hermitage. To Robert Hays, between 13 and 22 Dec. 1806, MPAB.

194 Donelson with AB. Remini, *Jackson and the Course of American Empire*, 152–53.

195 "about ten boats." *Annals*, 9th Cong., 1st Sess., 1017.

195 Dunbaugh joins expedition. ASP Misc. I, 514–15, 524–25, 590–91.

196 "warlike posture continued." Robertson, *Trial*, II, 449.

196 "some men" picked up. HB, *Papers* (Safford), 187.

196 AB at Chickasaw Bluffs. ASP Misc. I, 610–11.

196 JW orders Jackson arrested. Hughes, deposition, 20 Jan. 1811, Bacon Report, 303–18.

197 "penetrated to the bottom." *Aurora*, 1 Dec. 1806.

198 "unquestionably . . . engaged" in scheme to sever union. 3 Nov. 1806, quoted in Malone, *Jefferson . . . Second Term*, 245.

198 Is "Wilkinson sound in this business?" Briggs, deposition, JW, *Memoirs*, II, app. lix.

199 "any information." *Annals*, 9th Cong., 2d Sess., 334–59.

199 TJ calls AB's guilt "beyond question." ASP Misc. I, 472.

200 "this lying spirit." 2 Feb. 1807, John A. Schutz and Douglas Adair, eds., *The Spur of Fame*, 76.

200 "may be a hoax." *Columbian Sentinel*, 31 Jan. 1807.

201 TJ to Lafayette. 14 July 1807, TJ, *Writings* (Lipscomb–Bergh), XI, 279; and to Bowdoin, 2 Apr. 1807, Ibid., 183–86.

201 TJ knows expedition minuscule. TJ to JW, 3 Feb. 1807, JW, *Memoirs*, II, app. xxx.

201   Plumer concludes AB's object "not seperation." *Memorandum*, 534–53, 619.

202   Alston's letter. To Gov. Charles Pinckney, Feb. 1807, HB, *Papers* (Safford), 227–30.

202   "night and day." Schachner, *Burr*, 393.

203   Senate votes to lift writ, House refuses. *Annals*, 9th Cong., 2d Sess., 402–25.

207   "You are calumniated." JW, *Memoirs*, II, app. lxxvi.

207   "You have . . . seen a good deal of malicious insinuation." 3 Feb. 1807, Ibid., app. xxx.

208   Pension office denies pursuit of AB a "war." Papers in Burr's Expedition, entry 54, box 14, Record Group 94, NA.

208   a "wily" man. Gayarre, *Louisiana*, IV, 168.

209   "suspend the elegance of debate." Mead–AB agreement, 20 Jan. 1807, Natchez *Mississippi Messenger*, 20 Jan. 1807.

209   "perfidious!" "vile falsifications." AB to Mead, 12 Jan. 1807, MPAB.

209   Davis Floyd and Ralston visit Dr. Carmichael. Carmichael, deposition, JW, *Memoirs*, II, app. lxxxv.

210   Carmichael blabs to JW. Abernethy, *Conspiracy*, 205.

210   Adair seized, sent East, released. Ibid., 180–82.

211   Expedition encamps at Thompson's Bayou. Ibid., 205.

211   Munitions on boats. ASP Misc. I, 514, 524, 602; HB, *Papers* (Safford), 188.

212   "Reports . . . utterly false." Letter left on table by AB, 12 Jan. 1807, MPAB.

212   "in good order but Darn hungry." 14 Jan. 1807, Mississippi Archives, *Third Annual Report*, app. II, 49–51.

213   AB ready to submit to civil authorities. AB to Fitzpatrick, 13 Jan. 1807, MPAB.

213   Mead orders Claiborne to Cole's Creek. Mississippi Archives, *Third Annual Report*, app. II, 62–63.

213   "We are all bustle." 13 Jan. 1807, ASP Misc. I, 477.

213   Mead bids AB to meeting on Cole's Creek. 15 Jan. 1807, MPAB.

213   AB surrenders. Mead to Dearborn, 19 Jan. 1807, *Annals*, 9th Cong., 2d Sess., 1019; Mead–AB agreement, *Missis-*

sippi Messenger, 20 Jan. 1807; same under date of 16 Jan. 1807, MPAB.

214 "this mighty alarm." Mead to Dearborn, 19 Jan. 1807, *Annals*, 9th Cong., 2d Sess., 1019.

214 Rodney ready to "put on 'old '76.'" HB, *Papers* (Safford), 191.

215 JW offers Dinsmoor $5,000 to get AB. JW to Dinsmoor, 4 Dec. 1806, Burr Papers, LC.

215 "a special order." Ibid.; Robertson, *Trial*, I, 114.

215 AB's drafts refused, followers restive. HB, *Papers* (Safford), 191–92.

215 AB–Graham conversation. ASP Misc. I, 520–30.

216 Grand jury hearing in Mississippi. Extracts from the Minute Books, Supreme Court of Mississippi Territory, 2 Feb. 1807, MPAB; Rodney's charge to jury, U.S. *v.* AB., treason and misdemeanor, 3 Feb. 1807, Ibid.; Mississippi Archives, *Third Annual Report*, app. III, 101.

219 "We are all in a flurry here." Dinsmoor to Col. McKee, Schachner, *Burr*, 377.

219 Carmichael dissuaded. Ibid., 380.

219 "armed with Dirks and Pistolls." ASP Misc. I, 566, 593; Henshaw, *Documents*, 35–38.

219 Williams's proclamation. Williams to Madison. 23 Feb. 1807, MPAB. AB's protest, 12 Feb. 1807, and Williams's reply, 13 Feb. 1807, Ibid.

221 dispersing "themselves through the territory." J. F. H. Claiborne, *Mississippi as a Province Territory and State*, I, 282.

11. THE TRIAL AT RICHMOND BEGINS

222 AB's flight, arrest, and trip to Richmond. Albert J. Pickett, "Arrest of Aaron Burr," *Flag and Advertiser—Extra*, Montgomery, Ala., *ca.* 1850; Robertson, *Trial*, I, 2–3, 109–10.

223 Gaines ordered to send AB East. Williams to Gaines, 1 Mar. 1807, Miss. Dept. Archives and History, RG 2–28.

PAGE

227 "near to telling the truth." Schachner, *Thomas Jefferson: A Biography*, 606.

227 Hearing in "retired room." Robertson, *Trial*, I, 1–3.

228 Courtroom then and now. W. Asbury Christian, *Richmond: Her Past and Present;* interviews with Mrs. Charlotte Troxwell and other hostesses at Virginia State Capitol.

229 Hay presents case. Robertson, *Trial*, I, 3–4.

230 "abounding in crudities." Ibid., 6–8.

230 Rodney's speech. Malone, *Jefferson . . . Second Term*, 299.

231 *"Exclude this letter."* Robertson, *Trial*, I, 12.

232 "Hitherto . . . believed our law to be." 2 Apr. 1807, TJ, *Writings* (Lipscomb–Bergh), XI, 185–86.

233 140 government witnesses. Robertson, *Trial*, I, 532.

233 "Was there in Greece." 26 Apr. 1807, Davis, *Burr*, II, 405.

234 Hay writes over fifty letters to TJ, etc. Paul S. Clarkson and R. Samuel Jett, *Luther Martin of Maryland*, 246n.

235 "Who is Blennerhassett" speech. Robertson, *Trial*, II, 96–97.

236 Richmond fills up. Beveridge, *Marshall*, III, 400; McFarland, *Sojourners*, 75; Christian, *Richmond*, 54, 68.

237 "not a lady." Samuel H. Wandell, *Aaron Burr in Literature*, 130.

237 "population being Negro." To Lord Justice-Clerk, 5 June 1807, Melrose Papers, Newberry Library.

238 "There he stood." Winfield Scott, *Memoirs*, I, 13.

238 at least $100,000. A conservative figure. TJ devoted $11,000 of a contingency fund to employ the lawyers who assisted Hay. In addition, the government had to transport some 140 witnesses and maintain them for varying lengths of time in Richmond. See Malone, *Jefferson . . . Second Term*, 303; *Annals*, 10th Cong., 1st Sess., 78, and 2d Sess., 321.

240 "surprised and afflicted." 25 May 1807, TJ Papers, LC.

240 Toast at Elkton. Clarkson and Jett, *Martin*, 363.

240 Argument over Hay's motion to commit on treason. Robertson, *Trial*, I, 51–52, 55–59, 67, 71, 76–81, 91, 96.

PAGE

242   AB's bail raised. Ibid., 104–8.

243   "Still waiting for Wilkinson." 3 June 1807, Davis, *Burr*, II, 406.

243   "flog their negroes." Clarkson and Jett, *Martin*, 248.

244   Argument over AB's motion for subpoena *duces tecum*. Robertson, *Trial*, I, 113 ff.

245   "This is a peculiar case." Ibid., 128.

245   AB on Martin's tactics. HB, *Papers* (Safford), 487.

246   Marshall scolds both sides. Robertson, *Trial*, 143; rules on motion to call President, Ibid., 177–89.

248   "not indifferent on the subject." Ibid., 189.

248   Chapin on Jefferson's response. *The American Law of Treason*, 104.

248   "The receipt of these papers." Robertson, *Trial*, I, 254–55.

249   AB says no need for TJ to appear. TJ, *Correspondence* (Bixby), 144.

249   "federal bull-dog." 19 June 1807, TJ, *Works* (Ford), X, 402–3.

250   Hay gets affidavit from Graybell. Document 32, RG 21, NA.

250   "tremendous hat." HB, *Papers* (Safford), 316.

250   Jackson harangues crowd. Beveridge, *Marshall*, III, 404.

251   Bollman–Hay exchange. Robertson, *Trial*, I, 180–96.

251   JW arrives. Ibid., 196; AB to Theo Jr., 18 June 1806, MPAB.

251   Irving on JW's entrance. To James K. Paulding, 22 June 1807, Irving, *Letters*, I, 239.

252   Wilkinson on it. 17 June 1807, Burr Papers, LC.

253   cipher never introduced in testimony. Mary-Jo Kline, "The Road to Exile," editorial note.

253   Randolph on JW before grand jury. 25 and 28 June 1807, Burr Papers, LC.

253   Indictments presented. Robertson, *Trial*, I, 305–6, 330–50.

253   "Col de Pestre." HB, *Papers* (Safford), 328–29.

254   Indictment against AB. Document 3, RG 21, NA.

255   "founded on the following allegations." 24 June 1807, MPAB.

255   "many . . . intrinsic difficulties." Marshall to Cushing, 29

June 1807, R. T. Paine Papers, Mass. Historical Society.

256 AB's jailmates. Francis F. Beirne, *Shout Treason*, 127.

257 "airy and healthy," etc. AB to Theo Jr., 30 June, 3 and 6 July 1807, Davis, *Burr*, II, 409–10.

257 "great difficulty in gaining admission." Beirne, *Shout Treason*, 138–39.

257 "If absent" and "I am informed." 24 and 30 July 1807, Davis, *Burr*, I, 410–11.

258 Alstons stay till treason trial ends. HB, *Papers* (Safford), 390, says they left Richmond on 6 or 7 Sept. 1807.

12. ACQUITTED: "NOT PROVED"

260 "I have little doubt." 29 June 1807, HB, *Papers* (Safford), 245.

260 "I was not half an hour here." 4 Aug. 1807, Ibid., 274–75.

261 "Ex-Vice President Turned Traitor." Clarkson and Jett, *Martin*, 256.

261 "Have you said . . . Burr . . . guilty?" Robertson, *Trial*, I, 370.

261 "guilty of something." Ibid., 376.

262 "the traitor." Ibid., 377–78.

262 "first name is *Hamilton*." Ibid., 383.

262 Hay's opener. Ibid., 433–51.

264 "Would you begin . . . a tale at the end?" Ibid., 454.

264 "better informed." HB, *Papers* (Safford), 343.

265 "O by God." Robertson, *Trial*, I, 495.

265 "contained high Treason." Ibid.

265 "some . . . went a-shooting." Ibid., 496.

265 "What kind of guns?" Ibid.

265 "saw some powder." Ibid.

266 "Gracious God!" HB, *Papers* (Safford), 283.

267 "seven or eight muskets" pointed. Robertson, *Trial*, I, 509.

267 AB cross-examines Allbright. Ibid., 510.

267 Tupper denies Allbright's story. Henshaw, *Documents*, 23.

267 "have some considerations to offer the court." Robertson, *Trial*, I, 514.

268 AB cross-examines Love. Ibid., 516–18.

269 "court must hear the objections." Ibid., 530.

270 "greatest forensic effort." Schachner, *Burr*, 432.

270 "no person can be convicted." Robertson, *Trial*, I, 533.

270 "there are no accessories." Ibid., 534.

271 "principals" and "accessories" distinguished in U.S. law. Ibid., 550.

271 "no common law of the United States as such." Ibid., 549.

271 Marshall interrupts Wickham. Ibid., 584.

272 resistance to process not treason. Ibid., 594.

273 AB has some forty witnesses. Documents 12 and 13, RG 21, NA.

273 "I wish, sincerely wish." Robertson, *Trial*, II, 28.

274 "if a body of men be assembled." Ibid., 62.

274 "*it is not extrajudicial.*" Ibid., 63–64.

275 "I cannot promise . . . tropes." Ibid., 123.

276 No official orders for militia to invade island. Ibid., 136.

276 Flu epidemic in Richmond. HB, *Papers* (Safford), 376.

277 "Hay . . . [insinuated] an impeachment." Ibid., 370.

277 Marshall understands very well. Robertson, *Trial*, II, 238.

277 "rear-guard." HB, *Papers* (Safford), 377.

277 "Will o' the wisp treason." Robertson, *Trial*, II, 337.

277 "I have . . . heard it said." Ibid., 377–78.

278 "no proof that treason had been committed." Ibid., 333–34.

278 "a confession of the misdemeanor?" HB, *Papers* (Safford), 379.

279 "I should rather suppose." Robertson, *Trial*, II, 319.

280 Bollman–Swartwout opinion "incomplete." Chapin's book, 102.

280 "difficulty of proving a fact will not justify conviction without proof." Robertson, *Trial*, II, 437.

281 "overt act . . . *not proved by a single witness.*" Ibid., 443.

282 Parker "Jeffersonian partisan." HB, *Papers* (Safford), 339.

283 "event has been . . . to prevent the evidence." TJ, *Writings* (Lipscomb–Bergh), XI, 360–61.

285 "exhibited himself." HB, *Papers* (Safford), 390.

285 Island sold by county. Swick, "Blennerhassett," 352.

285 "quite unaccountable." HB, *Papers* (Safford), 466–67.

285 Suits against AB total $36,000. Ibid., 466.

286 "at a Mr. Walton's." Ibid. 394–95.

286 "as gay as usual." Ibid., 402.

287 "In six months." Ibid.

288 Why expedition members signed up. See in ASP Misc. I, testimony of Thomas Hartley (503), William Love (507–8), James McDowell (513–14), Stephen S. Welch (518–19), and others.

288 or "send him to Carter's mountain." ASP Misc. I, 537–39.

288 "Did you promise?" Ibid., 514–18.

289 Hay washes hands of JW. To TJ, 15 Oct. 1807, TJ Papers, LC.

289 *"desist from further prosecution."* MPAB.

290 Depositions gathered for Ohio point to no crime. See Henshaw, *Documents.*

290 AB planning to go to England. HB, *Papers* (Safford), 443. HB's comments, 415–17.

291 De Pestre says Yrujo saw through AB. Ibid., 417.

291 "I have had more of his confidence." Ibid., 415.

291 "I will hint to him." Ibid., 451–52.

292 regiment plays "Rogue's March." Ibid., 475.

292 HB watches rioters from garret. Ibid., 478–81.

292 "to disguise his very hints." Ibid., 442.

293 "I feel myself released." Ibid., 517; and "have broken with Aaron Burr on a writ," Ibid., 517–18.

293 Blackmail threat. Theo Jr. to AB, 10 May 1811, *PJAB* (Davis), II, 160–61.

293 HB gets sum from Alston. HB to Alston, 2 Mar. 1811, HB, *Papers* (Safford), 534.

293 "pale and dejected." Biddle, *Autobiography*, 323.

294 Phineas Bond warns England. 30 Dec. 1807, FO 5/531, PRO; quoted in Mary-Jo Kline, "Road to Exile."

295 AB writes Williamson. 19 June and 19 July 1808, *PJAB* (Davis), I, 23.

295 Death of Williamson. Hay, "Charles Williamson and the Burr Conspiracy," *Journal of Southern History*, II, 207.

296 "a bearer of dispatches." Pinkney to Madison, 2 Apr. 1808, Schachner, *Burr*, 450.

296 "on his own business which is mercantile." AB to Robert Goodloe Harper, 27 Nov. 1807, MPAB.

296 "the article of *cotton bagging*." 26 Aug. 1808, Parton, *Burr* (1857), 524n.

297 "grand Hegira." AB to Theo Jr., no date, *PJAB* (Davis), I, 21.

297 "immediately to present himself." Davis, *Burr*, II, 21.

297 "G. H. Edwards" reaches London. *PJAB* (Bixby), I, 2.

298 "some Enterprize against Spanish America." Schachner, *Burr*, 450.

13. EXILE: WANDERINGS IN EUROPE

300 "a sort of non-existence." *PJAB* (Bixby), I, 21. As most of this chapter rests on this source, references are given, as a rule, only in the case of material taken from other sources.

304 "Col. Williamson's letters." *PJAB* (Davis), I, 26–27.

304 "a contingency." Ibid., 23.

304 "could not see Mr. Canning." 6 Nov. 1808, Davis, *Burr*, II, 413–14.

304 AB considers going home. To Hosack, 10 Nov. 1808, *PJAB* (Davis), I, 80–31; to Green, 9 Sept. 1808, Fuller collection, I, A, 29, Princeton U. Lib.

305 "world begins to cool." 30 Sept. 1808, *PJAB* (Davis), I, 58.

306 "Tell me." 31 Oct. 1808, Ibid., 72–73.

306 "plan for opening Spanish America." Ibid., 20; Eleanor V. Shodell, "Narrative report on AB's Ibero-American connections," 3.

306 AB forges links to Latin American revolutionaries. *PJAB* (Bixby), I, 11, 15; II, 387; Shodell, "Narrative report," 4, 9.

307 Effort to interest Cortes in Bentham's "Tactics." Ibid., 4, 5, 11; *PJAB* (Bixby), I, 4.

308 "more than hospitality." AB to Mrs. Augustine Prevost, 27 Aug. 1808, *PJAB* (Davis), I, 35.

309 "second to no one." AB to Theo Jr., 9 Sept. 1809, Ibid., 47.

309   "pregnant with interesting facts." Parton, *Burr* (1857), 521–22.

310   Theo Jr. works on translation. *PJAB* (Davis), I, 46–47, 50–51, 67–68, 147, 176, 237.

310   "unaccountable folly." 22 Apr. 1809, Ibid., 210–11.

312   "Driving out every day." 13 Jan. 1809, Ibid., 135.

312   "trifling affair." 1 Mar. 1809, Ibid., 176.

313   Deportation asked by Apodaca. William W. Kaufmann, *British Policy and the Independence of Latin America*, 43, 47.

314   "London (Limbo)." *PJAB* (Davis), I, 193–94.

315   "should leave town." AB to L. J. Mallet, 13 Apr. 1809, Ibid., 195.

316   "Mr. Burr's respectful compliments." 20 Apr. 1809, Ibid., 203–4.

317   "I presume." Albert Gallatin, *The Writings of*, Henry Adams, ed., I, 375–76.

318   "Honesty" of the Swedes. 13 Oct. 1809, *PJAB* (Davis), I, 315–18.

319   "Be careful what you write." 26 Sept. 1809, Ibid., 310–11.

320   "more than twelve hundred English miles." AB to Henry Gahn, 12 Oct. 1809, Ibid., 312.

321   "love of intrigues." Foster, *Jeffersonian America*, 282–83.

321   "two American savages." To Mr. Gram, 12 and 17 Sept. 1809, *PJAB* (Davis), I, 305.

322   "stupefied . . . by the blow." Ibid., 285.

322   "pass the night without closing my eyes." 31 May 1809, Ibid., 239.

323   "the gentleman who promised . . . funds." 1 Aug. 1809, Ibid., 284–85.

323   "Why . . . is my Father banished?" Schachner, *Burr*, 479.

323   Plea to Gallatin. 9 Mar. 1811, *PJAB* (Davis), II, 155–56.

327   Bourrienne on AB. Quoted in Davis, *Burr*, II, 417–18.

336   None "signed or initialed by" AB. Samuel Engle Burr, Jr., *Napoleon's Dossier on Aaron Burr*, 9.

340   AB writes Otrante. *PJAB* (Davis), I, 441–42.

341   Charge probably damned the colonel "completely in the

     opinion of Napoleon." Kline, "Aaron Burr and Napoleon's Court."

341 "Citizen of the United States" to Madison. Quoted in Schachner, *Burr*, 472–73.

342 "Your Majesty will see." Quoted in Kline, "Aaron Burr and Napoleon's Court."

343 "machinations of our worthy minister." AB to Edward Greswold, 3 Aug. 1810, *PJAB* (Davis), II, 29–30.

347 "Believe me." 31 May 1809, Ibid., I, 240.

349 AB's correspondence with Russell and MacRae. Ibid., II, 70–2.

350 "authors are the vainest." AB to Theo Jr., n.d., Ibid., I, 20.

350 "enjoyed but never *used*." Parton, *Burr* (1857), 570.

351 Letters we must depend on. AB to Russell, 9 Mar. and 23 Apr. 1811, *PJAB* (Davis), II, 154–55, 158; to Theo Jr., 1 Apr. and 11 July 1811, Ibid., 157–58, 235–36; B. Lane to AB, 25 Mar. 1811, Ibid., 156–57.

352 "On my return to Paris." AB to Duc de Rovigo, 18 July 1811, Ibid., 236–37.

352 Lady told to return to Paris. Bassano to Denon, 18 July 1811, Ibid., 238–39.

354 "That part of Miranda's character." 16 Oct. 1811, Ibid., 254–55.

14. "A GREEN OLD AGE"

359 Wickham's letter. 4 July 1812, Schachner, *Burr*, 496.

359 AB to Gardner. MPAB.

360 "A few miserable days past." 12 July 1812, Ibid.

360 "That boy on whom all rested." 26 July 1812, Davis, *Burr*, II, 426–27.

361 AB to Bentham. 27 Aug. 1812, MPAB.

361 "inexpressible sorrow." Ibid.

361 "For God's sake." 8 Dec. 1812, Ibid.

361 "What a calumniating World." 30 Dec. 1812, Ibid.

362 "You must not be surprised." Timothy Green to AB, 22 Dec. 1812, Davis, *Burr*, II, 429.

364 "will never forget his elevation." 26 Feb. 1813, Ibid., 430–32.

PAGE

364 "Capt. Soustocks." AB to Kate Bartow, 7 Feb. 1813, MPAB.

364 "severed from the human race." Parton, *Burr* (1857), 599.

364 "an ambitious, intriguing," etc. *New York Review* of Jan. 1838, quoted in Merrill D. Peterson, *The Jefferson Image in the American Mind*, 144.

365 "distasteful name" of AB. T. C. Elliott, "The Surrender at Astoria in 1818," *Oregon Historical Society Quarterly*, XIX (Dec. 1918), 271.

365 "Why should I?" and "THEY SAY!" Parton, *Burr* (1857), 626, 637.

366 "an unknown man . . . named . . . Jackson." Schachner, Burr, 509.

366 AB on Monroe. 29 Nov. 1815, Davis, *Burr*, II, 433–36.

367 *"Jackson was thy man."* Levi McKeen to AB, 15 Nov. 1824, MPAB.

368 "fun and honor & profit." 14 Jan. 1832, MPAB.

368 "To prevent a dependance." 2 Mar. 1812, Ibid.

368 AB represents Novion and kin of Bolívar. Abraham S. Hallett *v.* John B. Novion, N.Y. Supreme Court (Albany), Aug. term 1817, MPAB; Francis Ribas . . . *v.* Manuel Camacho, N.Y. Supreme Court (Albany), Jan. term 1818, Ibid.

369 "I hope to God." 16 Oct. 1817, Ibid.

370 "devotion to the dollar." "Narrative report," 9.

370 "quaker connections . . . gratified me." To Thomas H. Flandrau, 28 Oct. 1823, MPAB.

370 "rather repose in a lie than in truth." Parton, *Burr* (1864), II, 399–400; Thomas Jones, *History of New York During the Revolutionary War*, I, 608–10.

370 AB on "female education." Ms. diary of John Hough James, King Library, Miami U., Oxford, Ohio.

371 "first eminent lawyer." Charles Burr Todd, *A General History of the Burr Family in America*, 154.

372 Talk in "the north room." William Henry Edwards, compiler, *Timothy and Rhoda Ogden Edwards*, 21.

372 "never was a greater villain." *Harper*, 1857, quoted in Parton, *Burr* (1857), 641.

373 "Has a green old age." 8 May 1813, MPAB.

373 "affords me a decent support." 16 Oct. 1815, Davis, *Burr*, II, 433.

373 "worth $30,000 per year." *The Carolina Gazette*, 9 Jan. 1813.

374 "old creditors . . . came upon me." 16 Oct. 1815, Davis, *Burr*, II, 433.

374 "Stages in very bad order." Mar. 1834, Ibid., 25.

375 "O Burr, O Burr." Parton, *Burr* (1857), 616.

375 "Oh God what is to become of me." 1829, MPAB.

375 "let me have but $5." 1833, Ibid.

375 AB helps Samuel B. H. Judah, Samuel Bradstreet, Luther Martin. S. Judah to AB, 10 Nov. 1823, MPAB; AB to S. Judah, 17 Nov. 1823, Ibid.; B. B. Judah to AB, 20 Nov. 1823, Ibid.; Samuel to AB, 26 July 1824, Ibid.; Bradstreet to Oliver Lathrop, forwarded to AB, 17 Feb. 1824, Ibid.; Bradstreet to AB, 27 Feb. and 29 Mar. 1824, Ibid.; Clarkson and Jett, *Martin*, 303; Thomas H. Flandrau to AB, 9 Sept. 1824, MPAB.

376 "man of decided talents." George W. Johnson: account of visit with AB, 8 May 1832, MPAB.

376 "habits are eccentric." AB to Mrs. Mc—, 27 Jan. 1825, Ibid.

376 Some letters from women. MPAB: Mary Chalmers, early Jan 1815; Mrs. S. Clark, 23 Apr. 1820; Catherine Thompson, 17 Sept. 1813, 27 July and 19 Dec. 1814.

378 Mrs. Blodget's earliest letter. MPAB.

378 "I have [told] Mrs. Blodget." Aug. 1814, Ibid.

378 "how I have *deserved*." 18 Aug. 1814, Ibid.

378 "If I did not love you." 21 July 1815, Ibid.

379 "It was a bad thing." 21 Nov. 1815, Ibid.

379 "I have been a whole week." 3 Dec. 1823, Ibid.

380 Mrs. Blodget asks help for son. 28 Dec. 1823, Ibid.

380 "I read your short letter." 3 Dec. 1824, Ibid.

381 Floyd's trial in Indiana and aftermath. Cox, "Burr Conspiracy in Indiana," 277.

381 "procure for me a few Law Books." 22 Feb. 1825, MPAB.

381 "old slyboots." HB, *Papers* (Safford), 397.

381 Last years of Senator Smith. Wilhelmy, "Smith and the Aaron Burr Conspiracy," 58 and passim.

382 Last years of HB. Swick, "Blennerhassett," 352–54.

382 Last years of JW. *Dictionary of American Biography.*

383 Medcef Eden Case. In the main, my coverage rests on John Wood: Bill of Complaints, filed 21 July 1825, NYCH Case No. 270, MPAB.

385 Wood claims "whole estate" as assignee. AB to Daniel Webster, 8 June 1828, Ibid.

386 Judges reject Wood's pleas. Eden Case, NYCH No. 270, 10 July 1828, Ibid.

386 AB's creditors dun him. MPAB: letters from Thomas Taylor, 9 Feb. 1824; James Cummins, 2 Jan. 1824; Joseph Ficklin, 19 Feb. 1824; Davis Floyd, 22 Feb. 1825.

386 "without the consent of my friend Aaron Burr." Wood: Bill of Complaints, 16, 17, MPAB.

387 "How sorry I am." Katherine Bartow to AB, 25 July 1813, Ibid.

387 "when a lady does me the honor." Parton, *Burr* (1857), 653.

387 "Physically impossible." Ibid.

388 $10,000 worth of property. *Chronicle of the Aaron Burr Association*, XIII, 14 Oct. 1960.

388 Ann got legacy. Guide and Index, MPAB, 27.

388 "member of the DeLisle family." Stilwell, *Burr Portraits*, 65.

388 "In the morning in school." 30 Nov. 1818, MPAB.

388 "will tride." 16 Mar. 1819, Ibid.

388 Aaron Columbus's career. Marie B. Hecht and Herbert S. Parmet, "New Light on Burr's Later Life," *The New-York Historical Society Quarterly*, XXIV (1915), 408.

389 "It is a long time." 4 Feb. 1830, MPAB.

389 "habits of industry, application." AB to Ernest L. Hazelius, 22 Nov. 1824, Ibid.

389 "French and German." Hazelius to AB, 14 Jan. 1825, Ibid.

389 Burdett graduates Princeton. AB to Gen. Porter Buel, 18 Feb. 1829, Ibid.

389 "mother of the Graduate of fifteen." A. Burdett to AB, 4 Feb. 1830, Ibid.

390 "injurious to his morals." 18 Apr. 1824, Ibid.

390 "follies" and debts. T. W. Scott to AB, 21 Apr. 1830, and

AB to John MacLean, 17 July 1829, MPAB.

390 AB seeks schools for his girls. To Hazelius, 20 Jan. and 30 Jan. 1825; to Rev. E. D. Griffith, 1828; to Rev. Charles Seidel, 6 Aug. 1829, Ibid.

390 "work like tigresses." AB to Liz and Becky Eden, 20 Oct. 1823, Ibid.

390 "no single one of those talents." AB to Alden Partridge, 22 Feb. 1828, quoted in Schachner, *Burr*, 503.

391 "comfort of my life." 16 Apr. 1825, MPAB.

391 ages of Eden girls. AB to Hazelius, 20 Jan. 1825, Ibid.

391 "to a Quaker Meeting." 1–3 June 1824, Ibid.

394 "disagreeable to tell." 11 Oct. 1830, Ibid.

395 Toyed with idea of marriage for money. *PJAB* (Davis), II, 415–16.

395 "a sort of Epithalamium." 9 Sept. 1833, MPAB.

395 Madame's life. In the main, my coverage follows William Henry Shelton, *The Jumel Mansion*.

397 "Mon Cher Stephen." Fuller collection III, A, 17, Princeton U. Lib.

399 "Pay it to my husband." William Cary Duncan, *The Amazing Madame Jumel*, 263.

399 McManus asks $250. Letter undated, but filed under 1832 in MPAB.

400 AB's letters to and about McManus. AB to Workman, 16 Nov. [1832], enclosed in AB to Jane McManus, 17 Nov. [1832], Ibid.

401 Divorce proceedings. Jumel *v.* AB, NYCH Case No. 291, 11 July 1834, Ibid.

402 Perjury indictment. Ibid.; also in Jumel Box, Burr Papers, New-York Historical Society.

404 "office drugging." AB to Theodore Sedgwick, 3 Feb. 1791, Sedgwick Papers, Mass. Historical Society.

405 "thraldom of business." To John P. Bigelow, 9 Sept. 1833, MPAB.

Bibliography

Bibliography

I. MANUSCRIPTS

GEORGETOWN UNIVERSITY LIBRARY
Microfilm Edition of the Papers of Aaron Burr

HENRY E. HUNTINGTON LIBRARY
Burr File and Burr–LeGuen Correspondence

HISTORICAL SOCIETY OF PENNSYLVANIA
Charles Biddle Papers
Dreer Collection
Simon Gratz Collection

LIBRARY OF CONGRESS
Papers of Harman Blennerhassett, Aaron Burr, Thomas Jefferson, Joseph H. Nicholson, and William Plumer
East Florida Papers
Facsimiles from the *Archivo Histórico Nacional—Madrid, Estado*
Henry Adams Transcripts from the *Spanish State Papers: Casa Yrujo, 1801–1807*
Microfilm Edition of the Papers of Aaron Burr

MASSACHUSETTS HISTORICAL SOCIETY
Theodore Sedgwick and R. T. Paine Papers

MISSISSIPPI DEPARTMENT OF ARCHIVES AND HISTORY, Jackson, Miss.
Silas Dinsmoor papers, Record Group 2–28

NATIONAL ARCHIVES
James Wilkinson's Order Book and Papers in Burr's Expedition, Record Group 94
Photostatic Copies of Documents in the Aaron Burr Treason Case at the United States District Court of the Eastern Dis-

trict of Virginia, Marion Johnson, compiler, NNGJ, 11 Aug. 1960, Record Group 21. These documents are also available on the Microfilm Edition of the Papers of Aaron Burr

NEWBERRY LIBRARY
Charles Williamson's letters in the Lord Melville Papers

NEW-YORK HISTORICAL SOCIETY
Papers of Albert Gallatin and James Parton
Jumel Folder in the Aaron Burr Papers

PRINCETON UNIVERSITY LIBRARY
Manuscripts from the C. P. G. Fuller Collection

PUBLIC RECORDS OFFICE, KEW, ENGLAND
Anthony Merry's Letters to the Foreign Office

UNIVERSITY OF VIRGINIA LIBRARY
McGregor Collection
University of Virginia Manuscripts—2595, Ohio Documents for 1806

YALE UNIVERSITY LIBRARY
Papers of the Burr Family and Timothy Edwards

II. PRINTED SOURCES

ADAMS, Henry. *History of the United States of America*, 9 vols., 1898.
———. *John Randolph*, 1882.
ALSTON, J. Motte. *The Recollections of*, Arney R. Childs, ed., 1953.
American State Papers: Miscellaneous, Vol. I, 1834.
Annals of the Congress of the United States, 1849.
BACON, Ezekiel, chairman. *Report of the Committee Appointed to Inquire into the Conduct of General Wilkinson*, 26 Feb. 1811.
BIDDLE, Charles. *Autobiography*, 1883.
BLACKSTONE, William. *Commentaries on the Laws of England . . . with notes and references to American decisions by George Chase*, 1873.
BOWRING, John. *The Works of Jeremy Bentham*, 10 vols., 1843.
BURDETT, Charles. *Margaret Moncrieffe, the First Love of Aaron Burr*, 1860.

BURNET, Jacob. *Notes on the Early Settlement of the Northwest Territory*, 1847.

BURR, Aaron. *The Private Journal of*, William K. Bixby, ed., 1903.

———. *The Private Journal of*, Matthew L. Davis, ed., 1838.

BURR, Samuel Engle, Jr. *Napoleon's Dossier on Aaron Burr*, 1969.

CARTER, Clarence Edwin, ed. *The Territorial Papers of the United States*, Vols. III, V, VI, IX, 1935–40.

CHESTERFIELD, Philip Dormer Stanhope, Fourth Earl of. *Lord Chesterfield's Letter to His Son and Others*. Everyman's Library edition, 1929, 1963.

CHRISTIAN, W. Asbury. *Richmond: Her Past and Present*, 1912.

CLAIBORNE, W. C. C. *Official Letter Books*, Dunbar Rowland, ed., 5 vols., 1917.

CLARK, Daniel. *Proofs of the Corruption of Gen. James Wilkinson*, 1809.

DAVEISS, Joseph Hamilton. *A View of the President's Conduct Concerning the Conspiracy of 1806*, 1807.

DAVIS, Matthew L. *Memoirs of Aaron Burr*, 2 vols., 1836–37.

DUNLAP, William. *Diary of*, 1969.

EDWARDS, William Henry, compiler. *Timothy and Rhoda Ogden Edwards*, 1903.

FERGUSON, Eugene S. *Commodore Thomas Truxton 1775–1822: A Description of the Truxton–Biddle Letters in the Collections of the Library Company of Philadelphia*, 1947.

FOSTER, Sir Augustus John. *Jeffersonian America: Notes on the United States . . . in the Years 1805–6–7 and 11–12*, Richard Beale Davis, ed., 1954.

GALLATIN, Albert. *Writings*, Henry Adams, ed., 1879.

GARRISON, William Lloyd. *. . . The Story of his life told by his children*, 1894.

GILPIN, Joshua. *Pleasure and Business in Western Pennsylvania [in 1809]: The Journal of*, 1975.

HAMILTON, John C., ed. *History of the Republic . . . as Traced in the Writings of Alexander Hamilton*, 7 vols., 1852–64.

HEITMAN, Francis B., ed. *Historical Register and Dictionary of the United States Army*, 1909.

HENSHAW, Leslie, ed. "Burr–Blennerhassett Documents," *Quarterly Publication of the Historical and Philosophical Society of Ohio*, IX, Jan. and Apr. 1914.

IRVING, Washington. *Letters*, Ralph M. Aderman and others, eds., 2 vols., 1978.

JACKSON, Andrew. *The Correspondence of*, John Spencer Bassett, ed., 6 vols., 1926–33.

JEFFERSON, Thomas. *The Complete Anas of*, Franklin B. Sawvel, ed.

————. *Correspondence Printed from the Originals in the Collections of William K. Bixby*, 1916.

————. "The Limits and Bounds of Louisiana," in *Documents Relating to the Purchase and Exploration of Louisiana*, 1804.

————. *The Papers of*, Julian P. Boyd, ed., 19 vols., 1950–.

————. *Works of*, Paul L. Ford, ed., 12 vols., 1904–5.

————. *Writings of*, Andrew A. Lipscomb and Albert Bergh, eds., 20 vols., 1903.

KING, Charles R., ed. *The Life and Correspondence of Rufus King*, 6 vols., 1894–1900.

KINNAIRD, Lawrence, ed. *Spain in the Mississippi Valley, 1765–1794*, translations of Materials from the Spanish Archives in the Bancroft Library. Part II: Post War Decade, 1782–1791, *Annual Report of the American Historical Association*, 1945.

LLOYD, Thomas. *The Trials of William S. Smith and Samuel G. Ogden for misdemeanors, had in the Circuit Court of the United States for the New-York district in July 1806*, 1807

McCALEB, Walter Flavius. *The Aaron Burr Conspiracy*, 1903.

————. *A New Light on Aaron Burr*, 1936.

MADISON, James. *Writings*, Gaillard Hunt, ed., 9 vols., 1900–10.

MAYO, Bernard, ed. *Instructions to the British Ministers to the United States, 1791–1812*, 1971.

MISSISSIPPI. *Third Annual Report of the Director of the Department of Archives and History*, Dunbar Rowland, ed., 1903–4.

MONROE, James. *The Writings of*, Stanislous M. Hamilton, ed., 7 vols., 1900.

PARTON, James. *The Life and Times of Aaron Burr*, 1857.

————. *The Life and Times of Aaron Burr*, enlarged ed., in two vols., 1864.

PICKETT, Albert J. "Arrest of Aaron Burr," *Flag and Advertiser —Extra*, Montgomery, Ala., *ca.* 1850.

PIDGIN, Charles Felton. *Theodosia: The First Gentlewoman of Her Time*, 1907.

PLUMER, William. *Memorandum of Proceedings in the U.S. Senate, 1803–07*, E. S. Brown, ed., 1923.

ROBERTSON, David. *Reports of the Trials of Colonel Aaron Burr . . . in the Circuit Court of the United States . . . Richmond . . . Virginia*, 2 vols., 1808.

SAFFORD, William H. *The Blennerhassett Papers*, 1864.

SCHUTZ, John A., and Douglas Adair, eds. *The Spur of Fame: Dialogues of John Adams and Benjamin Rush, 1805–13*, 1966.

SCOTT, Winfield. *Memoirs*, 2 vols., 1864.

SHELTON, William Henry. *The Jumel Mansion*, 1916.

STILLWELL, John E. *The History of the Burr Portraits*, 1928.

TODD, Charles Burr. *A General History of the Burr Family in America*, 1878.

WANDELL, Samuel H. *Aaron Burr in Literature*, 1936.

WEBSTER, Sir Charles K., ed. *Britain and the Independence of Latin America, 1812–1830. Select Documents from the Foreign Archives*, 2 vols., 1938.

WILKINSON, James. *Memoirs of My Own Times*, 4 vols., 1816.

WILLIAMS, William Appleman, ed. *The Shaping of American Diplomacy: Readings and Documents in American Foreign Relations, 1750–1955*, 1956.

WOOD, John. *A full Statement of the Trial and Acquittal of Aaron Burr . . . before the Federal Court at Frankfort, Ky.*, 1807.

III. NEWSPAPERS

Boston Columbian Centinel, 1807
Charleston, S.C., The Carolina Gazette, 1813
Cincinnati, Ohio, Liberty Hall, 1805
Frankfort, Ky., Palladium, 1805–6
Frankfort, Ky., Western World, 1806
Lexington, Ky., Kentucky Gazette, 1806
Marietta, Ohio, Register, 1888
Nashville, Tenn., Impartial Review, 1806–7
New Orleans Orleans Gazette, 1807
New Orleans Moniteur de la Louisiane, 1806
New York Commercial Advertiser, 1833
New York Evening Post, 1833
Philadelphia Aurora, 1806–8
Philadelphia, Reif's Philadelphia Gazette, 1804–18
Philadelphia United States Gazette, 1804–18

Bibliography

Philadelphia United States Gazette for the Country, 1806–7
Pittsburgh Commonwealth, 1806
Richmond Enquirer, 1807
Washington Federalist, 1805
Washington National Intelligencer, 1805–7

IV. OTHER RELATED WORKS

ABERNETHY, Thomas Perkins. "Aaron Burr in Mississippi," *Journal of Southern History*, IV (1949), 9–21.
————. *The Burr Conspiracy*, 1968.
ALEXANDER, Holmes Moss. *Aaron Burr: The Proud Pretender*, 1937.
AMBLER, Charles Henry. *Thomas Ritchie: A Study in Virginia Politics*, 1913.
AMMON, Harry. *James Monroe: The Quest for National Identity*, 1971.
ANDREWS, Martin R., ed. *History of Marietta, Ohio*, 1902.
ATKINSON, Charles Milner. *Jeremy Bentham: His Life and Work*, 1905.
BEARD, W. E. "Colonel Burr's First Brush with the Law: An Account of the Proceedings Against Him in Kentucky," *Tennessee History Magazine*, I (1915), 3–20.
BEIRNE, Francis F. *Shout Treason: The Trial of Aaron Burr*, 1959.
BEMIS, Samuel Flagg. *A Diplomatic History of the United States*, 5th ed., 1965.
BENSON, Adolph B. "Aaron Burr in Sweden," in American Swedish Historical Foundation *Yearbook*, 1952.
BEVERIDGE, Albert Jeremiah. *The Life of John Marshall*, 4 vols., 1919.
BOVERI, Margaret. *Treason in the Twentieth Century*, Jonathan Steinberg, trans., 1963.
BRADLEY, Jared W. "W. C. C. Claiborne and Spain; Foreign affairs under Jefferson and Madison, 1801–1811," *Louisiana History*, XII (1971), 297–314, and XIII (1972), 5–28.
BRANT, Irving. *James Madison: Secretary of State, 1800–1809*, 1953.
CARTER, Hodding (with Betty Carter). *Doomed Road of Empire: The Spanish Trail of Conquest*, 1963.

CARUSO, John Anthony. *The Mississippi Valley Frontier: The Age of French Exploration and Settlement,* 1966.

CHADWICK, French E. *The Relations of the United States and Spain: Diplomacy,* 1909.

CHANNING, Edward. *A History of the United States,* Vols. IV and V, 1917, 1921.

CHAPIN, Bradley. *The American Law of Treason: Revolutionary and Early National Origins,* 1964.

CLAIBORNE, J. F. H. *Mississippi as a Province Territory and State,* Vol. I, 1880.

CLARK, Allan C. "William Duane," *Records of the Columbia Historical Society,* IX (1905), 14–62.

CLARK, Thomas D. *Frontier America: The Story of the Westward Movement,* 2d ed., 1969.

CLARKSON, Paul S., and R. Samuel JETT. *Luther Martin of Maryland,* 1970.

COMBS, Jerald A. *The Jay Treaty: Political Battleground of the Founding Fathers,* 1970.

CORWIN, Edward S. *John Marshall and the Constitution: A Chronicle of the Supreme Court,* 1919.

COUES, Ellicott, ed. *The Expeditions of Zebulon Montgomery Pike,* 3 vols., 1895.

COWAN, Helen I. *Charles Williamson: Genesee Promoter,* 1941.

COX, Isaac Joslin. "The Burr Conspiracy in Indiana, *Indiana Magazine of History,* XXV (Dec. 1929), 257–80.

———. "General Wilkinson and His Later Intrigues with the Spaniards," *American Historical Review,* XIX (1913–14).

———. "Hispanic-American Phases of the Burr Conspiracy," *The Hispanic-American Historical Review,* XII (May 1932), 145–75.

———. "The Louisiana–Texas Frontier," *Quarterly of the Texas State Historical Association,* X (July 1906); XVI (July and Oct. 1913).

———. "Opening the Santa Fe Trail," *Missouri Historical Review,* XXV (1930), 30–66.

———. "The Pan-American Policy of Jefferson and Wilkinson," *Mississippi Valley Historical Review,* I (Sept. 1914), 212–239.

———. *The West Florida Controversy, 1798–1813,* 1918.

————. "Western Reaction to the Burr Conspiracy," *Transactions of the Illinois Historical Society, 1928*, 73–87.

CRAWLEY, C. W. "French and English Influences in the Cortes of Cadiz, 1810–1814," *Cambridge Historical Journal*, VI (1938–40), 176–208.

DANGERFIELD, George. *The Awakening of American Nationalism, 1815–1828,* 1965.

DANIELS, Jonathan. *The Devil's Backbone: The Story of the Natchez Trace,* 1962.

————. *Ordeal of Ambition: Jefferson, Hamilton, Burr,* 1970.

————. *They Will Be Heard: America's Crusading Newspaper Editors,* 1965.

DARLING, Arthur Burr. *Our Rising Empire, 1763–1803,* 1940.

DE VOTO, Bernard. *The Course of Empire,* 1952.

DUFOUR, Charles L. *Ten Flags in the Wind: The Story of Louisiana,* 1967.

DUNCAN, William Cary. *The Amazing Madame Jumel,* 1935.

ELLIOTT, T. C. "The Surrender at Astoria in 1818," *Oregon Historical Society Quarterly*, XIX (Dec. 1918), 271–82.

FAIRBANKS, George R. *History of Florida,* 1871.

FAULKNER, Robert K. "John Marshall and the Burr Trial," *Journal of American History* (June–Sept. 1966), 247–58.

FICKLEN, John R. "Was Texas Included in the Louisiana Purchase?" *Publications of the Southern History Association*, V (Sept. 1901).

FORTIER, Alcée. *A History of Louisiana,* 4 vols., 1904.

GAYARRE, Charles. *History of Louisiana,* 4 vols., 4th ed., 1903.

GIBSON, Charles. *Spain in America,* 1966.

GREEN, Thomas Marshall. *The Spanish Conspiracy,* 1891.

GRISWOLD, Rufus Wilmot. *The Republican Court . . . in the Days of Washington,* 1854.

GUDDE, Edwin G. "Aaron Burr in Weimar," *South Atlantic Quarterly*, XL (1941), 360–67.

HATCHER, William B. *Edward Livingston,* 1940.

HAY, Thomas Robson. "Charles Williamson and the Burr Conspiracy," *Journal of Southern History*, II (1936), 175–210.

HECHT, Marie B., and Herbert S. PARMET, "New Light on Burr's Later Life," *The New-York Historical Society Quarterly*, XXIV (1915).

HULBERT, Archer Butler. *The Ohio River,* 1906.

HUMPHREYS, R. A., and John LYNCH. *The Origins of the Latin-American Revolutions, 1808–26*, 1965.

HURST, James Willard. *The Law of Treason in the United States*, 1971.

JACOBS, James Ripley. *Tarnished Warrior: Major-General James Wilkinson*, 1938.

JAMES, Marquis. *The Life of Andrew Jackson*, 1938.

JILLSON, Willard Rouse. "Aaron Burr: A sketch of His Life and 'Trial' at Frankfort, Kentucky, in 1806," 1944.

JONES, Thomas. *History of New York During the Revolutionary War*, Vol. I, 1879.

KAUFMANN, William W. *British Policy and the Independence of Latin America, 1804–1828*, 1951.

KERR, Charles, ed. *History of Kentucky*, 5 vols., 1922.

KLINE, Mary-Jo. "Aaron Burr as a Symbol of Corruption in the New Republic," in *Before Watergate: Problems of Corruption in American Society*," Abraham Eisenstadt and others, ed., 1978.

LESTER, Malcolm. *Anthony Merry Redivivus: A Reappraisal of the British Minister to the United States, 1803–6*, 1978.

LYNCH, John. "British Policy and Spanish America," *Journal of Latin American Studies*, I (1969), 1–30.

McFARLAND, Philip. *Sojourners*, 1979.

McLAUGHLIN, J. Fairfax. *Matthew Lyon: the Hampden of Congress*, 1900.

MALONE, Dumas. *Jefferson and the Ordeal of Liberty*, 1962.

———. *Jefferson the President: First Term 1801–1805*, 1970.

———. *Jefferson the President: Second Term 1805–1809*, 1974.

MARSHALL, Humphrey. *The History of Kentucky*, 2 vols., 1824.

MOHL, Raymond A. "Britain and the Aaron Burr Conspiracy," *History Today*, III (June 1971), 391–98.

NICHOLSON, Irene. *The Liberators*, 1969.

NOLAN, Charles Joseph, Jr. *Aaron Burr and the American Literary Imagination*, 1980.

PARMET, Herbert S., and Marie B. HECHT. *Aaron Burr: Portrait of an Ambitious Man*, 1967.

PETERSON, Merrill D. *The Jefferson Image in the American Mind*, 1962.

PHILBRICK, Francis S. *The Rise of the West, 1754–1830*, 1965.

PITCHER, M. Avis. "John Smith, First Senator from Ohio, and

His Connections with Aaron Burr," *Ohio State Archaeological and Historical Quarterly*, LXIV (1936), 66–80.

PRATT, Julius W. *Expansionists of 1812*, 1925.

RANCK, George W. *History of Lexington, Kentucky*, 1872.

RANCK, James B. "Andrew Jackson and the Burr Conspiracy," *Tennessee History Magazine*, 2d series, I (1930–31), 17–28.

REMINI, Robert V. *Andrew Jackson and the Course of American Empire, 1767–1821*, 1977.

ROBERTSON, James Alexander, ed. *Louisiana under the Rule of Spain, France, and the United States . . . as portrayed in . . . accounts of Dr. Paul Alliot [and others] . . .* , Vol. I, 1910.

ROBERTSON, William Spence. "The Beginnings of Spanish-American Diplomacy," in *Essays in American History, Dedicated to Frederick Jackson Turner*, Guy Stanton Ford, ed., 1910.

———. *France and Latin-American Independence*, 1939.

———. "The Juntas of 1808 and the Spanish Colonies," *English Historical Review*, XXI (1916), 573–85.

———. *The Life of Miranda*, 2 vols., 1929.

———. *Rise of the Spanish-American Republics*, 1918.

ROWE, G. F. *Thomas McKean: The Shaping of an American Republicanism*, 1978.

ROWLAND, Dunbar. *History of Mississippi*, Vol. I, 1925.

RYDJORD, John. *Foreign Interest in the Independence of New Spain*, 1935.

SAVELLE, Max. *George Morgan: Colony Builder*, 1932.

SCHACHNER, Nathan. *Aaron Burr: A Biography*, 1937.

———. *Thomas Jefferson: A Biography*, 1951.

SHREVE, Royal Ornan. *The Finished Scoundrel: General James Wilkinson*, 1933.

SKATES, John Ray. *Mississippi: A Bicentennial History*, 1979.

SKINNER, Constance Lindsay. *Pioneers of the Old Southwest*, 1919.

SMELSER, Marshall. *The Democratic Republic, 1801–1815*, 1968.

SPRAGUE, Stuart Seely. "The Louisville Canal: Key to Aaron Burr's Western Trip of 1805," *The Register of the Kentucky Historical Society*, LXXI (Jan. 1973).

STAPLES, Charles R. *The History of Pioneer Lexington (Kentucky) 1779–1806*, 1939.

SWICK, Ronald Ray. "Harman Blennerhassett: An Irish Aristocrat on the American Frontier," unpublished doctoral thesis, Miami U., 1979.

————. "Theodosia Burr Alston," *The South Atlantic Quarterly*, LXXIV (Autumn 1975), 459–506.

TAYLOR, Joe Gray. "Andrew Jackson and the Aaron Burr Conspiracy," West Tennessee Historical Society *Papers*, 1–2, 147–48.

THORNING, Joseph Francis. *Miranda: World Citizen*, 1952.

TURNER, Frederick J. *The Significance of the Frontier in American History*, 1894.

————. "The Significance of the Louisiana Purchase," *Review of Reviews*, XXVII, No. 160 (May 1903), 578–84.

WANDELL, Samuel H., and Meade MINNIGERODE. *Aaron Burr*, 2 vols., 1927.

WEST, Rebecca. *The New Meaning of Treason*, 1964.

WEYL, Nathaniel. *Treason: The Story of Disloyalty and Betrayal in American History*, 1950.

WILHELMY, Robert W. "Senator John Smith and the Aaron Burr Conspiracy," *The Cincinnati Historical Society Bulletin*, XXVIII (Spring 1970), 39–60.

WILLIAMS, Samuel C. "Nashville as Seen by Travellers," *Tennessee History Magazine*, 2d series, I (1930–31).

WORTH, Gorham A. "Recollections of Cincinnati, from a Residence of Five Years, 1817 to 1821," *Quarterly Publications of the Historical and Philosophical Society of Ohio*, XI (1916), Nos. 2 & 3, April–July.

WRIGHT, Louis B., and Julia H. MACLEOD. "William Eaton's Relations with Aaron Burr," *Mississippi Valley Historical Review*, XXXI (March 1945), 523–36.

V.   WORKS IN PROGRESS

KLINE, Mary-Jo. "Aaron Burr and Napoleon's Court," editorial note for use in the published version of the Papers of Aaron Burr.

————. "The Road to Exile," editorial note for use in the published version of the Papers of Aaron Burr, covering the transition from the close of Burr's trials in Richmond to his departure for England.

Bibliography

SHODELL, Eleanor V. "Narrative report on AB's Ibero-American connections, with three appendices: A, Location of Papers of Burr Correspondents; B, Manuscript Catalogues and Printed Collections; and C, Libraries in Latin America and Spain."

SWICK, Ray. "Yankees and Tuckahoes," manuscript of an article in progress, dealing with the political tensions along the upper Ohio River frontier in the days of Harman Blennerhassett.

Index

Index